D1522304

From Communion to Cannibalism

From Communion to Cannibalism

AN ANATOMY OF METAPHORS OF INCORPORATION

Maggie Kilgour

PRINCETON UNIVERSITY PRESS

PRINCETON, NEW JERSEY

Library of Congress Cataloging-in-Publication Data

Kilgour, Maggie, 1957–
    From communion to cannibalism : an anatomy of metaphors of
incorporation / Maggie Kilgour.
        p. cm.
    Includes bibliographical references.
    ISBN 0-691-06792-9 (alk. paper)
    1. Literature—History and criticism. 2. Metaphor. I. Title.
II. Title: Incorporation.
PN523.K5 1990
809'.915–dc20   89-36342
                                                                      CIP

This book has been composed in Linotron Galliard

Princeton University Press books are printed
on acid-free paper, and meet the guidelines for
permanence and durability of the Committee on
Production Guidelines for Book Longevity of
the Council on Library Resources

Printed in the United States of America by Princeton University Press,
Princeton, New Jersey

10 9 8 7 6 5 4 3 2 1

In memory of Betty Kilgour
my mother, who was a voracious reader

quoniam itaque deserebar tam magno eius solacio, sauciabatur anima et quasi dilaniabatur vita, quae una facta erat ex mea et illius.
   —Augustine, *Confessions*, 9.12

Contents

Acknowledgments

I MIGHT TRACE the ostensible source of this book to my second year as an undergraduate at the University of Toronto. I happened to read Ovid, Dante, and Melville at the same time and began wondering why there were so many cannibals running around literature, and, even more, why no one else had seemed to notice. Sensing a glaring omission in tradition here, I boldly set out to do for cannibalism what Freud had done for incest. I took heart as I uncovered more and more cannibalism in the canon, and so much more critical interest than I had expected that I now find myself part of a veritable cannibalism renaissance. As time went on, however, my subject swallowed more and more material, expanding until my master metaphor of "cannibalism" metamorphosed into the even more subsuming term "incorporation." Exploring the relation between these two terms and their more benign counterpart, "communion," will be my task here.

Over the past few years, I have been fortunate to have had time and encouragement to figure out why I developed such an unsavory obsession. In 1984–85, The Mrs. Giles Whiting Foundation enabled me to concentrate for a year on refining some of my ideas in their early stages. From 1986 to 1988, the Social Sciences and Humanities Research Council of Canada provided me with the time it took to shape a truly grotesque anatomy into something a bit more streamlined (I put the manuscript on a strict diet until it lost forty pages). During this period, McGill University generously first afforded me time and then greatly appreciated financial support that was necessary to get me through the final throes. Special thanks are due to the English department and to McGill's Humanities Research Grants Subcommittee for final and crucial funding.

Thanks, too, are due to the various institutions that allowed me to incorporate their property. Quotations from *The Odyssey*, trans. Richard Lattimore, copyright © 1965, 1967 Richard Lattimore, appear by permission of Harper and Row, Publishers, Inc. Quotations from Ovid's *Metamorphoses* are reprinted by permission of the publishers and the Loeb Classical Library and are taken from *Metamorphoses*, 2 vols., trans. Frank Justus Miller, revised by G. P. Goold (1916; reprint Cambridge, Mass.: Harvard University Press, 1976–1977), copyright ©1984 by the President and Fellows of Harvard University. The English translations of the *Confessions* are from the *Confessions* by Saint Augustine, trans. R. S. Pine-Coffin (Harmondsworth: Penguin Classics, 1961), copyright © R.S. Pine-Coffin, 1961, and those from *The Histories of Gargantua and Pantagruel* by François Rabelais, trans. J. M. Cohen (Harmondsworth: Penguin Classics, 1955), copyright © J. M. Cohen, 1955, are all used by permission of Penguin Books Ltd. Selections afrom Dante's *Commedia* are from *Dante Alighieri, The Divine Comedy*, trans. with commentary by Charles Singleton, Bollingen Series 80: vol. 1: *Inferno*, copyright © 1970 by Princeton University Press; vol. 2: *Purgatorio*, copyright © 1973 by Princeton University Press; vol. 3: *Paradiso*, copyright © 1975 by Princeton University Press.

My savory quotation from Stephen Sondheim's "The Little Priest" is included through the courtesy of Revelation Music Publishing Corporation and Rilting Music, Inc., copyright © 1979.

Permission to reproduce George Wither's emblem is by courtesy of the Librarian, Special Collections, Glasgow University Library; while permission to use Jan van Hemessen's *Virgin and Child in a Landscape* was granted by the National Museum, Stockholm.

There are many people, too, who, whether they like it or not, are in some sense inside this text. I don't even know how to begin describing my debt to Northrop Frye, in whose class I discovered Ovid and pretty well everything else. What I have written here is partially my own attempt to escape being subsumed by his encyclopedic vision. Among my other teachers, Patricia Parker, Magdalene Redekop, and Amilcare Iannucci at Toronto, and Margaret Ferguson, Harold Bloom, John Hollander, and Thomas M. Greene at Yale fed my early interests. Thanks, too, to Bob Brown at Princeton University Press, whose good humor (tried by some of my more disgusting jokes) was much appreciated, as was his brilliant and flattering choice of Angus Fletcher and Geoffrey Galt Harpham as readers. Their thoughtful and suggestive readings provided me with some very helpful food for thought.

Among my many friends who might find little tidbits of themselves in here, I should give particular credit to Barbara Folsom, whose enthusiastic personal and professional help has been gargantuan, Ian Duncan, Paul Morrison (who always hoped it would turn into a cookbook), and David Hensley. Hugh Roberts and Rachel Gamby deserve a special and very large reward for all kinds of endless support, from the sublime to the really ridiculous: they helped with the final frantic corrections, kept me company throughout, fed me, *read* me, generally spoiled me rotten, and, not least of all, put up with my metaphors in the last stages of revision when I felt like the proverbial dog returning to its vomit. Caroline Greenwood gets a prize for being Caroline Greenwood (and for not—*most* of the time—asking embarrassing questions). Nutritional counseling was courtesy of Chris Heppner. The entire faculty and student body at McGill deserves thanks for stomaching the cannibalistic totems on my office door. Finally, Kit, my budgie, was a constant source of inspiration as a vivid daily representation of life arrested in the oral phase; I suppose it was only just, too, that portions of this manuscript should have been eaten.

Last, but never least: many, many thanks as always to the delectable, "incomparable et sans parragon," Lisa Darrach, whose cooking and companionship have nourished me for some time now. As for the dedication, it is only appropriate, as my mother brought me up on cannibal jokes.

From Communion to Cannibalism

Metaphors and Incorporation

> For what is outside is also inside; and what is not outside man is
> not inside.
> — Paracelsus

> He killed the noble Mudjokovis.
> Of the skin he made him mittens,
> Made them with the fur side inside,
> Made them with the skin side outside.
> He, to get the warm side inside,
> Put the inside skin side outside;
> He, to get the cold side outside,
> Put the warm side fur side inside,
> That's why he put the skin side outside,
> Why he turned them inside outside.
> — George A. Strong, "The Modern Hiawatha"

MUCH OF THE literary criticism of the past few decades, under the influence of structuralism and its descendants, has been concerned with the role
of binary oppositions in the production of meaning. Structuralism revealed
that without differences there can be no meaning; poststructuralism, that
any meaning constructed by differences defined as absolute antitheses
needs constant questioning. Where structuralism isolated oppositions, deconstruction, Marxism, and feminism make different attempts to dismantle
them. Over the past years a wide variety of binary pairs have been studied
from different critical positions, pairs such as cooked/raw, center/periph-
ery, voice/writing, spirit/flesh, art (culture)/nature, male/female, content/
form, proper/improper, literal/metaphorical, public/private, work/home,
production/consumption, author/reader, host/guest, familiar/foreign, clas-
sic/grotesque, high/low, autonomy/relatedness.[1] Although I do not think
these pairs can be reduced to a single, original, and therefore explanatory
opposition, they are similarly structured, each constituting a divided, hi-
erarchically ordered, and yet apparently coherent system, in which order is
guaranteed by the authoritative and superior term's control of the inferior.
Such couples represent experience as a *concordia discors* where extremes
meet, although not in an equal relation but in an identity achieved through
the subordination, even annihilation, of one of the terms.

In order to suggest some of the problems resulting from these representations of experience, I would like to examine the relation that I believe plays an important role in the conceptualization of all antitheses, that of inside and outside, which Derrida also sees as the foundation of all binary oppositions.[2] As a spatial metaphor, this opposition has the illusion of stability and substance,[3] but it is in fact totally relative, as it depends on where one is standing. The model for the antithesis is based in bodily experience and the sense that what is "inside" one's own body is a coherent structure that can be defined against what lies "outside" of it.[4] It is the most basic of oppositions, and perhaps also the most infantile; according to Freud, it originates in the primary oral phase and is the ground on which all future decisions are based:

> Expressed in the language of the oldest, that is, of the oral, instinctual impulses, the alternative runs thus: "I should like to eat that, or I should like to spit it out"; or, carried a stage further: "I should like to take this into me and keep that out of me." That is to say: it is to be either *inside* me or *outside* me. . . . The original pleasure-ego tries to introject into itself everything that is good and to reject everything that is bad. From its point of view what is bad, what is alien to the ego, and what is external are, to begin with, identical.[5]

In other words, it is also the foundation of a crude system of values in which what is "outside" the territory of the self is bad, and what is "inside" is good, a schematization that underlies many more sophisticated notions of individual and corporate bodies. So Montaigne notes that "each man calls barbarism whatever is not his own practice,"[6] and body politics, whose coherence and unity can be asserted through the analogy with the body corporeal, tend to view what exists beyond themselves as evil, for "the most mortal of sins is to be an outsider," to be different, separate, and unassimilated by a system which maintains that "nothing at all may remain outside, because the mere idea of outsideness is the very source of fear."[7]

To consider other oppositions by means of this one is one way of showing how they are constructed not by essential differences but by position, suggesting in turn that they, like Hiawatha's mittens, are infinitely reversible. But the apparent firmness of this opposition is deceptive. The relation between an inside and an outside involves a delicate balance of simultaneous identification and separation that is typified by the act of incorporation, in which an external object is taken inside another. The idea of incorporation, upon which I will be focusing, depends upon and enforces an absolute division between inside and outside; but in the act itself that opposition disappears, dissolving the structure it appears to produce.

In terms of this opposition it is usually, as Freud suggests (with important exceptions I will consider), the inside that appears as the superior, as the literally central term. The outside is considered secondary, extraneous—and yet ultimately threatening. As it is obvious at the most basic level that the circumference contains the center, in order to maintain a situation of centripetal control, what is outside must be subsumed and drawn into the center until there is no category of alien outsideness left to threaten the inner stability. This process often appears in the form of an attempt to invert actual relations by projecting a desire for assimilation from a center to a periphery, a tactic that has been shown to be at work in psychic defenses, misogyny, racism, and imperialism. According to Melanie Klein, whose studies focus on the oral phase of development, the infant's fear of being devoured by the parent is a reaction against its own desire to assimilate and possess what is external to the self, while recent studies of imperialism and "colonial discourse" have indicated how a society's desire to appropriate other cultures can be disguised through the projection of that impulse onto the other.[8] To accuse a minority that resists assimilation into the body politic of that body's own desire for total incorporation is a recurring tactic: during the Middle Ages the Jews were accused of cannibalism, after the Reformation the Catholics were, and Christ has continually been accused of being the head of a Jewish cannibal sect.[9]

The attempt to eliminate any remaining external remnant, to turn, like Hiawatha, the outside inside, suggests that at the basis of the dualism is a nostalgia for total unity and oneness. Current discussions of binary oppositions usually lead into critiques of idealist notions of identity, authorship, and conventional Western definitions of individual and textual autonomy. I hope to explore the ways in which antitheses support totalizing systems by showing how the inside/outside division presupposes a lost state of total inwardness, a Golden Age before individuation that is represented by myths which I call, stealing a title from Northrop Frye, "fables of identity." Fictions such as those of the classical Golden Age, of the paradise of Genesis and Milton, of Coleridge's dream of a "Self, that no alien knows" ("Religious Musings," 154), of Ahab's Moby-Dick, and of Freud's oral phase, are bound to a nostalgia for a state of total incorporation that underlies many of the major trends of Western thought: idealism, scientific rationalism, traditional psychoanalysis, as well as imperialism, and theories in general which try to construct a transcendental system or imagine a single body that could contain all meaning.[10] A similar kind of nostalgia may also be at work in the modern definition of the individual and in tendencies to view personal, authorial, and textual identity in terms of autonomy—an autonomy achieved, however, through a resolution of differences that really means their assimilation and subsumption.

As my title should suggest, there are different methods of incorporation available, ranging from the most metaphorical and sublime, to the most literal and, if not always ridiculous, frequently gothic and grotesque. The root of the word *incorporation* is in the body; it is a process concerned with embodiment and the bringing of bodies together.[11] The body itself can be imagined (though it does not have to be) as a corporation of its members, which together form a unified and clearly defined structure whose boundaries separate the self from others and so mark off individual identity. But bodily needs also indicate that the appearance of autonomy is an illusion, for the body must incorporate elements from outside itself in order to survive. The need for food exposes the vulnerability of individual identity, enacted at a wider social level in the need for exchanges, communion, and commerce with others, through which the individual is absorbed into a larger corporate body. Eating is the most basic of all these needs, which it can also stand for, and in most cultures it is regulated by strict social practices that determine what can and what cannot be eaten.[12] As "you are what you eat," eating is a means of asserting and controlling individual and also cultural identity; one nation will refer pejoratively to another in terms of a habit of eating that it itself is repelled by (as, for example, the English call the French "Frogs" because they eat frogs' legs). The most basic model for all forms of incorporation is the physical act of eating, and food is the most important symbol for other external substances that are absorbed.

The most obvious way for me to approach my subject, then, is by looking at the ways in which, in different texts, images of eating provide a model for the encounters between individuals or individual texts and the world that exists outside them. Most of the texts I will be considering are concerned with eating and its analogues, none more so than the works of Rabelais, whose preoccupation with food has been analyzed at length by Mikhail Bakhtin. Contrasting the modern, shrunken, closed body with the medieval grotesque body, Bakhtin notes that it is in the act of eating that the latter most reveals its own openness:

> the body transgresses here its own limits: it swallows, devours, rends the world apart, is enriched and grows at the world's expense. The encounter of man with the world, which takes place inside the open, biting, rending, chewing mouth, is one of the most ancient, and most important objects of human thought and imagery. Here man tastes the world, introduces it into his own body, makes it part of himself. . . . Man's encounter with the world in the act of eating is joyful, triumphant; he triumphs over the world, devours it without being devoured himself. The limits between man and the world are erased, to man's advantage.[13]

Despite Bakhtin's insistence that this is a joyful communion, such an exchange sounds less like his own "dialogic" ideal than a monologic bloodbath—it requires the rending, the breaking of one term by another. "Man" is fed "at the world's expense"; the relation between the two terms is not one of reciprocity but one of total opposition, as the eater is not himself in turn eaten but secures his own identity by absorbing the world outside himself. "Man" defined in this way slides uneasily into the isolated and alienated modern individual withdrawn from the world whom Bakhtin contrasts with the medieval member of the body politic.

I shall return in chapter 4 to Bakhtin's version of the discovery of the individual and use his distinction between medieval and modern concepts of the body to suggest how attitudes toward incorporation change depending on our relations to our own bodies and self-definitions. At present, I would merely play the part of Ovid's Pythagoras and point out that even the most apparently benign acts of eating involve aggression, even cannibalism. As Bakhtin himself notes, one of the most important characteristics of eating is its ambivalence: it is the most material need yet is invested with a great deal of significance, an act that involves both desire and aggression, as it creates a total identity between eater and eaten while insisting on the total control—the literal consumption—of the latter by the former. Like all acts of incorporation, it assumes an absolute distinction between inside and outside, eater and eaten, which, however, breaks down, as the law "you are what you eat" obscures identity and makes it impossible to say for certain who's who. Paradoxically, the roles are completely unreciprocal and yet ultimately indistinguishable. Ambiguity, however, is difficult to bear for prolonged periods of time; the history of Western tradition, at least, is marked by a recurrent desire to resolve uncertainty; and in the struggle between desire and aggression, between identification and the division that creates power over another, a struggle which is finally that between communion and cannibalism, cannibalism has usually won. As I hope to show, one product of that victory is the identity of the modern subject or individual who desires to eat without in turn being eaten.

To continue a rough classification of methods of incorporation: a less totalizing but still bodily image for incorporation is that of sexual intercourse, which is often represented as a kind of eating. In French, to consume and to consummate are the same word.[14] The Patristic Fathers warned against the intimate relationship between gluttony and lust,[15] and countless metaphors ally eating and intercourse; as Theodor Reik notes, "A lover can well say to his sweetheart that he would like to eat her up and thus express his tender desire for incorporation."[16] Like eating, intercourse makes two bodies one, though in a union that is fortunately less absolute and permanent.

According to Aquinas, sexual incorporation is a substitute for a total identification that is the real object of desire: "Lovers would wish for two to become one; but since this would result in the physical destruction of one or both they seek the union that befits them."[17] However, Aquinas may be unrealistically optimistic about the human ability to bear dissatisfaction; Freud, too, will claim that sexual intercourse is always disappointing in its failure to recapture the perfect symbiotic union of the oral stage and argue that unsatisfied energy must be directed elsewhere—ideally, by being sublimated into culture and civilization.[18] But the fact that sex is an incomplete act of incorporation may be seen as intensifying desire to the point where it becomes transformed into not art but aggression. In his commentary on the metamorphosis of Ovid's hermaphrodite, George Sandys notes that "the reason why lovers so strictly imbrace; is to incorporate with the beloved, which sith they cannot, can never be satisfied." In Sandys's reading of the story, however, dissatisfaction leads not to the acceptance of limitations but to a longing that becomes cannibalistic and ends in the total union of the two bodies. Describing the embrace of lovers, he emphasizes the relation between the two forms of incorporation, translating Lucretius's description of lovers who kiss "with ravenous teeth" as:

> They greedily imbrace, joyne mouthes, inspire
> Their soules, and bite through ardor of desire:
> In vaine; since nothing they can thence translate,
> Nor wholly enter and incorporate.[19]

The desire to become one with another slides easily into an act of aggression. So in his *Philosophical Dictionary*, in the entry on "Antropofages," which comes shortly after that on "Amour," Voltaire writes dryly: "I have spoken of love. It is hard to move from people who kiss one another to people who eat one another"[20]—knowing full well that in civilized society the two are often uneasily alike. Kissing and eating are obviously both oral activities, and at an extreme level of intensity the erotic and aggressive sides of incorporation cannot be differentiated, so that it becomes difficult to tell at what point the desire for consummation turns into the desire for consumption.

Another oral activity that is similar to eating but offers a less physical model for exchange is verbal communication, rooted in the body and yet detached from it. If cultures are defined by what they eat, they are also stereotyped by how they speak, as "barbarian" referred originally to those who could not speak Greek.[21] Food is the matter that goes in the mouth, words the more refined substance that afterward comes out: the two are differentiated and yet somehow analogous, media exchanged among men, whose mediating presence may prevent more hostile and predatory relations. From Plato's *Symposium* on, feasting and speaking have gone together, and there is a long tradition of seeing literature as food, which Jonson refers to in *Neptune's Triumph*: "There is a palate of the understanding, as well as of the senses. The taste is taken with good relishes, the sight with fair objects, the hearing with delicate sounds, the smelling with pure scents, the feeling with soft and plump bodies, but the understanding with all these, for all which you must begin at the kitchen. There the art of poetry was learned and found out, or nowhere, and the same day with the art of cookery."[22]

Reading is therefore eating, an act of consumption. But in part this is simply because it belongs to a tradition which, as Genesis most dramatically represents, sees knowledge as the food with which we feed our egos. Not only do we, like Saint John, devour books, but we also swallow food for thought, then ruminate or chew it over until it is well digested. For *homo sapiens*, to think is to taste, as in the act of knowledge we imagine that we draw the outer world into our minds and possess it.[23] All of our senses make contact with the world outside of our own bodies and so may be imagined as introducing it into ourselves. We "take things in" with our eyes and absorb sounds through our ears; both seeing and hearing are therefore often considered to be more refined versions of taste. However, as a model for knowing, taste is not only the most basic and bodily way of making contact with the world outside of the individual but also the most intimate and intense way, resulting in a strict identity between eater and eaten.

To imagine knowledge as tasting or eating is to set up an epistemology in which subject and object are strictly differentiated and yet finally totally identified. As it seems that most people would prefer to be a subject rather than an object—which means to eat rather than be eaten—such total identification is seen with a great deal of ambivalence. While taste is the sense that identifies and the tongue is an image for union and communication, the ideal of aesthetic taste focuses upon discrimination and division, so that the tongue can also be a symbol which, like Lacan's phallus, represents not fertile union but separation.[24] Intellectual taste is associated with choice and control, the mastery of what is eaten by the eater. As Walter Ong describes physical tasting, it is also an assertion of will over an object: "The sense of taste is basically a discriminatory sense, as the other senses are not. . . . Taste is a yes-or-no sense, a take-it-or-don't sense, letting us know what is good for us and what is bad in the most crucial physical way, for taste concerns what we are inclined to take into ourselves by eating, what will by intussusception either actually become ourselves or refuse to be assimilated and perhaps kill us."[25] The sense of control may be necessary as a way of combating the danger Ong indirectly suggests: one can be poisoned by what one takes in. As our most basic need, eating, physical tasting, reveals the fallaciousness of the illusion of self-sufficiency and autonomy that the inside/outside opposition tries to uphold by constructing firm boundary lines between ourselves and the world. The inside depends upon, is nourished or harmed by, substances that come from outside. The identification of aesthetic taste, taste in a "higher" form purified of its bodily origins, with choice is one tactic of guarding against the vulnerability involved in receiving nourishment and gifts from outside the private property of the individual body. The emphasis on choice and discrimination creates the effect that the body, though admittedly vulnerable in the act of reception, is a solid and stable structure that controls its exchanges with the world beyond itself and monitors strictly what it admits into itself.

Such monitoring is possible when dealing with real food—though diets are hard to stick to, most of us can exercise enough willpower to keep from making ourselves sick if not fat—but becomes more difficult in relation to mental food that is incorporated by more abstract methods. At the opposite end of the spectrum from cannibalism are the mental acts of identification by which the self knows, not things, but other humans, and takes them into itself to create its identity. Cannibalism is relatively easy to determine and control (as Ong says, it's a matter of taste, you either do or you don't, and there isn't really any *tertium quid* in the matter), but the mental absorption of others—central to Renaissance ideals of self-fashioning and poetic *imitatio*, and to their modern descendants, such as Freudian defenses of internalization and introjection, and the transumption of poetic precursors that helps assuage the anxiety of influence—is much more difficult to determine and regulate. While bodily existence gives us the sense of living inside a coherent and unified structure whose boundary lines are carefully marked out, the mind's territory is less clearly defined—which perhaps might be read as justification for policing the territory more closely for fear it be infiltrated. In its metaphorical senses, the phrase "you are what you eat" very disturbingly calls our basic concepts of personal identity into question.

As I have already suggested, the inside/outside distinction depends upon a nostalgia for total insideness, for a fable of identity involving the total identification of opposites. There are many myths, both within Western tradition and outside of it, that trace an existing state of dualistic conflict to a fall from a state of oneness. In its most basic bodily form, this myth appears as the story of the breaking of the originally cosmic body of one man who incorporated all humanity as members of himself.[26] When this body was broken—in some versions eaten—and its limbs scattered, the separated members found themselves in a relation of complete opposition and even cannibalistic antagonism. Northrop Frye describes Blake's version of the primal man, Albion, and the consequences of his dismemberment: "The eternal world is one of mutual co-operation in which all forms of life are nourished and supported by all other forms, as in the economy of the individual human body. In this world the reverse is true, and getting food in nature usually involves killing or maiming life. As all living things are part of the mangled body of Albion, all living things are nourished in a mutual cannibalism."[27] Redemption from this fallen world, whose inhabitants are divided into the roles of eater and eaten, is imagined as the re-membering or reincorporation of that primal symbiotic body, as through the restoration of original bodily wholeness the cosmic "Intestine War" (*Paradise Lost*, 6.259) can be ended.

The sexual version of this myth appears in the story in the *Symposium* of the division of the hermaphrodite into two sexes, and the figure of the hermaphrodite appears throughout the neoplatonic tradition as an image for the reincorporation of the primal duality of male and female.[28] Such myths feed the assumption predominant within the Platonic and Judeo-Christian tradition that duality itself, the very existence of "otherness," is an evil and unity a good, ultimately identifiable with a transcendent deity behind or above (and therefore in fact *outside*) the multiplicitous world of appearances, from which humanity came and to which it should strive to return. In the *Timaeus* a similar narrative is represented as the emanation of the Many from the One, to which the good ultimately return, while the bad remain in exile.[29] Incorporation becomes identified with a return to home and proper identity from a state of alienation; its opposite is eternal homelessness and a continual metamorphosis into alien forms, a state recalled by Ovid in the *Metamorphoses* and by Dante in the *Inferno*. While this abstract version of the myth, which provides the basic pattern for quest-romance as a journey from and back to a point of origin, might seem remote from the graphic and even primitive story of the rending of the primal body, in neoplatonism the desired return is frequently represented by the most violent of bodily images. In Plutarch, the reunion with the One is envisioned as a supreme conflagration in which the god "sets fire to nature and reduces all things to one likeness"; even more significantly for the present discussion, "by the same logic the myth of Saturn eating his children was greeted as a promise of redemption: the Many returning to the One, a reversal of primeval 'dismemberment.' "[30]

Cannibalism might seem a somewhat suspicious figure for transcendence, appearing less as a reversal of a fall than as its perpetuation. The use of the image reflects the fact that the return to a Golden Age is actually treated with a great deal of ambivalence that reflects both desire and aggression, nostalgia and horror. While traditionally the time is represented as one of such harmony between man and nature that the former is fed spontaneously by the latter, it is also ruled by Saturn, who is the god of the most ambivalent of feelings, nostalgia's intimate relation, melancholy, and who preys upon his own children.[31] As a result, the idea of return is both idealized as a return to communion with an originary source and a primal identification, and demonized as regression through the loss of human and individual identity: one returns to the father by being eaten by him; one reenters the garden by becoming a vegetable.

The terror that return to an earlier form of existence is regression is predominant also in Freud's description of the oral phase, the Golden Age of human sexual development, which according to Freud must, however, be left behind in the quest for mature genital sexuality. Like the classical Golden Age, Freud's first stage of sexual development contains dangerous elements of cannibalism. According to him, the child is originally unaware of anything outside of itself; it is aware only of the mother's breast, which it does not see as a separate object at all but, as it can be taken into itself, as a part of itself. In this primary state of identification the eater *is* the eaten—or at least imagines it is. The discovery of the difference between the two provides the infant with the concept of self and other; this occurs also during what Freud calls the oral or cannibalistic stage of development. For Freud, therefore, cannibalism appears to be at the very basis of the concept of self and other, which occurs when the symbiotic relationship between mother and child of eater and eaten becomes divided. The child discovers that what it had previously experienced as a part of itself is in fact separate; what was once inside becomes detached and outside, the familiar becomes strange, the canny uncanny. Furthermore, when the child discovers that the breast is actually outside of itself, an independent object which it cannot completely control, it attempts to get it back inside and restore the primal relationship. But the infant's attitude is now ambivalent, motivated by a mixture of love and aggression toward the once familiar object that has suddenly become unfamiliar and external, and so "the very source of fear."

The estrangement of the familiar is also one function that post-Wordsworthian readers have expected literature to perform but which has always been implicitly enacted by metaphor, in which a word is transferred from its original meaning and made identical to something alien to itself. Metaphor is a trope of "translation," which is frequently described in such terms as "a trespass across boundary lines, a usurpation of the 'proper' by the 'alien' term, an imposter or 'guest' who displaces the 'host.' "[32] When the canny becomes completely uncanny the result is the gothic, but even in less extreme cases a metaphoric meaning is an alien meaning and, like all aliens, potentially threatens the system it infiltrates. There is a long tradition of suspecting metaphor and of identifying it with deceit and duplicity. It is a basically dualistic trope that depends upon a difference between its inside and outside, its literal and figurative meanings; "antimetaphorical" positions dream of abolishing this duality in order to return to a proper and literal meaning.[33] A distrust of metaphor is implicit in stances that privilege unity over diversity—especially when it is reduced to duality—and that describe the relation between thought and language as essentially one of essence and appearance, in which appearances are read as misleading cloaks that hide an inside truth. It seems appropriate that, as I will discuss further in chapter 3, the debate over the relation between the substance and accidents in the Eucharist, which itself ultimately turned into a debate over the constitution of individual identity, was in fact an argument about the nature of metaphor, particularly as a means of articulating the relation between spiritual and bodily functions.

However, as it brings opposites together, metaphor itself can be read antithetically, as a source of both alienation and identification, which enacts either the estrangement of the familiar or the familiarization of the strange.[34] Traditionally these two aims have been viewed as opposites, the first associated with forms of romanticism and revolutionary art that enable us to imagine the world anew, and the second with "colonial discourse" and bourgeois art that work to create an idealized and homogenized norm.[35] But both involve a combination of opposition and identification that may be difficult to control and determine absolutely. Metaphor, the trope by which opposites—guest and host, body and mind, food and words—meet, is a means of incorporation that subverts normal definitions of identity. It is the revolutionary trope Northrop Frye sees as embodying his fable of identity, as he tries to imagine "a world of total metaphor, in which everything is potentially identical with everything else, as though it were all inside a single infinite body."[36] While from one perspective metaphor alienates, from another it unites and brings about an apocalyptic ending of alienation and the re-membering of an original unity. For Derrida, therefore, descriptions of metaphor themselves are based also on a pattern of fall and return that involves an original alienation of a proper meaning followed by its reappropriation and restoration to self-identity.[37] What Derrida suggests is that the traditional reading of metaphor as a form of linguistic transgression is in fact a reassuring version of a *felix culpa*. Estrangement is seen as a carefully controlled and ordered preliminary stage, a necessary detour of meaning, that leads to and even guarantees a total recovery of loss through an ascent to a higher level of meaning.

In his later work, Freud attempted to find a model for the oral phase and the fall from communion into cannibalism in actual history. In *Totem and Taboo* and *Moses and Monotheism*, he imagined a fall in which the primal sons ate the original father to incorporate his power and so essentially become him, a fall that is perpetuated as it is internalized and repeated in each individual. The sons discovered, however, that they had only internalized the father's power against them, just as the individual ego fulfills its desire to be its own father only through the internalization of authority in the form of the superego which oppresses it mercilessly from within. To incorporate the alien in these instances is to admit poison into the body: the dualism of eater/eaten is not transcended or sublimated through internalization, but perpetuated. In such instances, to eat the father is the same as to be eaten by him: the complement of Freud's myth is that of Saturn devouring his children.

In Greek mythology, father/son antagonism is essentially that of eater and eaten,[38] and when it is not transcended it becomes instead, once more like Hiawatha's mittens, infinitely reversible. The genealogy of the Greek gods is a succession of devouring fathers and castrating sons that ends only with Zeus, who takes rather drastic precautions against filial rebellion. In Hesiod's version, he swallows his mate, Metis, to assimilate her potentially subversive female energy and appropriate the act of procreation for himself alone; in Homer's, he gains power through abortion, or rather abstinence, when, forewarned of the consequences, he refuses to mate with Thetis and father a son greater than himself.

However, according to Homer, Thetis marries Peleus instead, and their wedding is the genesis of the Trojan War, which also involves a foreign guest invading the home—and wife—of his host. The struggle is displaced from heaven to earth, finding its first home in the unhappy house of Atreus. The cannibalistic conflict between parent and child cannot be repressed, but becomes a central image in the formulation of an antagonistic relation between past and present that emerges with the interest in the revival of the past in the Renaissance. The embodiment of the new progressive scientific thinking, Bacon, warns: "it seemeth the children of time to take after the nature and malice of the father. For as he devoureth his children, so one of them seeketh to devour and suppress the other; while antiquity envieth there should be new additions, and novelty cannot be content to add but it must deface."[39] Freud will internalize this set of hostile relations within each individual by using it to define the intestine war between the ego and its own past, and so ensure even further its perpetuation.

In his bizarrely earnest and literal *Myth and Guilt*, Theodor Reik revises Genesis, the Bible's explanatory myth of fall and loss, to make it fit Freud's scenario. He turns the two trees into a primary totem that is a later displacement of the father. When Adam and Eve eat the fruit of knowledge to be "as gods" they are really devouring the father to become him. However, the terms of Christianity with great care revise the relation between father and son in order to prevent cannibalistic antagonism. Between the two potentially conflicting extremes, orthodox Christianity interposes the mediating third term of the Trinity: the Word. According to traditional formulations, the Word is produced through an act of love and reflection between Father and Son, a mutual mirroring or breathing forth of the spirit, in which both of their identities are revealed in relation as both are defined against the other. In the act the two are identified but—perhaps fortunately when we consider what happens when Saturn gets together with his offspring—also kept apart. In the Christian doctrine, the nominal division between the divine *nature* that is single and *persons* that is three-fold—a distinction echoed in that drawn between the *substance* and *accidents* of the Host—permits the identification between Father and Son that is not absolute, or cannibalistic.

As we shall see later, however, there is a potential for cannibalism in the sacrament of the Eucharist. Freud claimed that what the church recognized as penance was actually the perpetuation of the crime: the repetition of the eating of the father by his sons. However, communion sets up a more complicated system of relation in which it becomes difficult to say precisely *who* is eating *whom*. It is a ritual to restore a primal unity, in which man and God are returned to an original identity, ideally not through absolute identification but through the obfuscation of identity and rigid role-playing. Both God and man play "host," a metaphor that itself has a variety of meanings which permit both identification and differentiation. Man is a host in that he literally takes God, in the form of the Host, into himself. But the Host is the kind of food that converts the feeder into himself; as Augustine's God explains, "cibus sum grandium; cresce et manducabis me. nec tu me in te mutabis sicut carnis tuae, sed tu mutaberis in me" ("I am the food of full-grown men. Grow and you shall feed on me. But you shall not change me into your own substance, as you do with the food of your body. Instead you shall be changed into me").[40] The act is one of reciprocal incorporation, as both are identified by the single word and substance, the Host, so that the absolute boundary between inside and outside, eater and eaten, itself appears to disappear.

Such a flexible definition of communion would appear to provide the beginnings of a model for relations that go beyond the binarisms which lead to cannibalism. It is a relationship which is mutually constructed so that the identities of the two terms are not fixed and determined absolutely but emerge through an exchange involving a balance between identity and differentiation. As reading is imagined as a form of communion, the partaking of an incarnated meaning, it could prove suggestive for interpretation and the devouring of texts.

Yet the history of the interpretation of the Host, to which I shall return later, shows a tendency to destroy that balance. The fate of the word *host* itself may be seen as a linguistic version of the dismemberment of a primal unity. Originally, it appears to have been one of what Freud, following Karl Abel, describes as primal words that unite antithetical meanings. Freud points out that in the early stages of language extremes of meaning meet: *sacer* means both blessed and cursed, or, to take another famous example from his writings, "canny" refers to what is both familiar and unfamiliar.[41] In ancient Greek, *xenos* meant " 'stranger', 'foreigner' and sometimes 'host', a semantic range symbolic of the ambivalence which characterized all dealings with the stranger in that archaic world,"[42] while in Latin *hospes* originally meant both host and guest.[43] In both cultures, opposites meet in a relation of complementarity—exchanging substances, food, and gifts—and are therefore nominally identified. Those who share food together are particularly felt to be united through participation in a common substance.[44] But when in Latin *hospes* is divided into two distinct meanings, the relation becomes defined not as one of complementarity but of antagonism between a *hostis*, enemy, and *hostia*, victim. The third term, the shared substance that perhaps prevented conflict, drops out, so that one of the opposing terms feeds upon the other.

For J. Hillis Miller, who imagines "The Critic as Host," the way to avoid critical cannibalism is to read the text as the lost third term, "that ambiguous gift, food, host in the sense of victim, sacrifice," which is "broken, divided, passed around, consumed by the critics."[45] Readers can come back to a *Symposium*, not to be incorporated literally together, but to partake of a verbal feast they mutually enjoy. Reading becomes a new form of communion, involving a triple reciprocity, for not only do the readers share the text among them, but, as it informs them individually and unites them as a group, so each transforms it.

In this study I shall be looking more closely at these different concepts of incorporation, from the literal to the metaphorical. At the more elevated end are acts of mental internalization, such as that imagined by Miller, by which people and texts are imagined as taking outside material into themselves in order to construct themselves. At the lower end of the stratum are images of eating and ultimately of cannibalism that insist on total physical identification. Replacing more orthodox though indirect means of communication, the image of cannibalism is frequently connected with the failure of words as a medium, suggesting that people who cannot *talk* to each other *bite* each other. According to Nicholas Abraham and Maria Torok, cannibalism is the ultimate "antimetaphor": whereas metaphors put the mouth into words, antimetaphors put words (in the form of textual figures) into mouths.[46] It is obviously the most demonic image for the impulse to incorporate external reality and get everything inside a single body, be it physical, textual, or social.

But the opposition between cannibalism and antimetaphor on the one hand and communion and metaphor on the other may not be as simple as one might wish. Metaphor itself is a suspiciously dualistic trope that yet collapses opposition. The distinction between communion and cannibalism—which Northrop Frye would treat as the apocalyptic and demonic forms of a single image—itself appears as a dualism, which I have just referred to as "higher" and "lower" forms of incorporation. My own schema would suggest that the relation between the two is one of "sublimation," in which the higher is a superior, more refined because mental or internalized version of the lower, which is more basic and materialistic because still rooted in the external body. I seem to have set up a hierarchy in my anatomy, based on a privileging of spirit and interiority over body and exteriority, in which eating is at the bottom, sex in the middle, and talking at the top; this might suggest that I too would like to turn the lower forms into their more lofty counterparts.

A desire to "sublimate" seems dominant within the other dualisms with which I began: as alchemists try to turn matter into spirit, so the humanist turns nature into art, the anthropologist sees the raw becoming the cooked, Freud dreams of the id's appropriation by the timid yet imperialist ego, the body politic as well as the glutton fantasizes about absorbing what's outside into itself, and so on. For Derrida, sublimation, in the form of Hegel's *aufhebung*, is a leap to a higher level of thought by which apparent contradictions are resolved, as "the spirit, elevating itself above the nature in which it was submerged, at once suppresses and retains nature, sublimating nature into itself, accomplishing itself as internal freedom, and thereby presenting itself to itself, *as such*," a complicated move in which opposition is simultaneously denied, resolved, and raised up to create an illusion of unity which is, however, essentially an affirmation of the identity of the dominant term.[47] Sublimation is therefore a central tactic of logocentric thinking, in which differences are set up in order to be synthesized. Furthermore, Peggy Reeves Sanday, an anthropologist who has written recently on literal cannibalism, draws an interesting if unsettling analogy between alchemical sublimation and cannibalism, noting that both are symbolic systems which attempt to make matter significant.[48] Sublimation aims at transforming a material base on the premise of a division between a lower, outside, bodily and material form and a higher, inside, mental or spiritual content. Like cannibalism, it is a means of subsuming what is outside the self, another kind of colonial discourse that makes the strange familiar, and so it is, as Peter Stallybrass and Allon White note, "the main mechanism whereby a group or class or individual bids for symbolic superiority over others: sublimation is inseparable from strategies of cultural domination."[49] It has the great advantage over cannibalism, moreover, in that it, like certain other strategies of domination, can claim to subsume the other for the other's own good.

As the neoplatonists said, extremes meet, and it seems difficult to keep communion from collapsing back into cannibalism. Like Bakhtin's description of man eating the world, Miller's picture of devouring texts sounds at times like the release of repressed carnivoracity. As Swift suggests in his portrayal, in *The Battel of the Books*, of the goddess who, herself incorporating medieval descriptions of Envy, feeds on books as well as her own spleen, criticism itself can be not only invidious but frankly cannibalistic. One problem with images of eating, which is also a source of their power, is that they seem to have a tendency to consume the mediating power of figures, subverting the possibility of a free communion between individuals, by drawing extremes into a catastrophic meeting that is less "face to face" than mouth to mouth. As I have been suggesting, most acts of incorporation are extremely ambivalent, taking place between two extremes whose meeting seems very dangerous: a desire for the most intimate possible identification with another and a desire for total autonomy and control over others who are treated therefore as food, so that all exchanges are reduced to the alternatives of "eat or be eaten."

Before really beginning, I should say something in defense of the shape of my own anatomy. To many readers, a work set up like this might seem the epitome of what it sets out to disrupt: the impulse to homogenize by reducing complexities to a single theme. I have always referred to this project as *The Text That Ate the World*, imagining it as a B-movie (written by Stephen King and directed by George Romero) about the "encyclopedic impulse" to incorporate everything. I admit that I am parodying my own appetite, as well as all theories or works that set out to swallow reality in a single gulp. If I have chosen a figure that can subsume all other figures (*my* metaphor's bigger than *your* metaphor), it is with the serious reminder that totalizing ideals are essentially cannibalism in its most sterile form. I began with two quotations, one mystical, one nonsensical, to demonstrate the proximity between discourses that attempt to include and explain everything and utter nonsense.

Furthermore, having worked on this for some time now, I am somewhat conscious of what is inside me and what outside—though also of how tenuous those boundaries can really be. What I have chosen to take into my text has been dictated partially by my "taste"—what I have wanted to take into me. After the seventeenth century, I have concentrated on English texts because, as I hope to make clear later, this has seemed to me the point at which a focusing on a particular national identity is important, in a way in which earlier it had been less so. For the most part I have chosen "canonical" texts, works "inside" the Western literary tradition; this has also helped determine my choice of personal pronouns: the orthodox concept of individual identity I am exploring has been defined traditionally in masculine terms, and so I use "he" and "man" quite specifically throughout the text.

Finally, I am by no means deluded enough to think this is an exhaustive survey, that I've got *everything* inside. Everyone I've talked to about this has offered me another tidbit for my rumination, and there's always another cannibal joke/story that eludes me. I'm not omnivorous. I've omitted analysis of some authors who would seem obligatory, especially Shakespeare and Conrad, because (1) I think I would use them to say what I say by other means, and (2) there is an enormous amount of excellent writing on these authors that I would rather supplement than regurgitate. There has been much recent work on colonial discourse, gender issues, and the representation of the body that I consider essentially related to what I am doing, and to which I will be referring without feeling compelled to try to subsume it all. I am assuming that my reader is aware of some of the issues, and I have used notes to point outside of myself to what I can't include but have found relevant and exciting. As I tried to illustrate in my first citation, notes are a wonderful means of incorporation. Perhaps they are our most useful model for a benign way of including without consuming. At any rate, I've chosen authors I know reasonably well, who illustrate different aspects of my concerns and who together tell a story I see about the increasing foregrounding of dualisms and their relation to a deeply melancholy longing for the recuperation of an imagined lost unity. That means, of course, that my readings are highly selective, as the works are treated only in terms of my own master metaphor. Perhaps it would have made more sense to concentrate on one dish and do it well rather than try to cook up so many. But the advantage to working this way may be that of the smorgasbord, which offers enough variety to suit different tastes through serving up some interesting combinations; as there's not a lot of one single substance I hope that the reader won't get fed up too soon.

CHAPTER I

Classical Incremental Visions

HOMER

In his discussion of the nostalgia for a lost pastoral ideal that underlies the antithesis between the rural and the urban in *The Country and the City*, Raymond Williams notes how such an ideal is infinitely regressive, projected backward in time by each generation to an immediately preceding time, which it glimpsed briefly in childhood.[1] The Golden Age of harmony between man and nature, the "good old days," has always just turned into an Iron Age with the present generation's passage into adulthood. As Williams notes, although each "fall" involves the perception of some real change—the most significant of which being the industrial revolution that totally metamorphosed the relations between man and nature—it is obvious that the Golden Age is to a certain extent the projection of an adult's fantasy of an idealized childhood.[2] Such Golden Ages typically appear as worlds of plenitude, in which all appetites are satisfied by a generous nature that voluntarily offers itself to man, and in which there is no private property or sense of divisions at all. These are states of total identity and harmony between subject and object, man and nature, microcosm and macrocosm, inside and outside, comparable also to Freud's oral phase and Lacan's Imaginary. It is the discovery that such a world *is* imaginary, that there are boundary lines around private property and around the even more private territory of the individual, lines that divide him from the world outside and introduce the possibility for an antagonistic relation with this external surrounding environment, that constitutes the fall.

Attempts, whether religious, anthropological, or psychoanalytical, to locate a stage of unfallen existence assume that if one could go back in time far enough one would come at last to a truly unfallen world.[3] Traditionally, early Greek culture has been described in terms that recall the depictions of the Golden Age: "In Greek classical society man is at home in the universe, moving within a rounded, complete world of immanent meaning which is adequate to his soul's demand."[4] The early Greek is represented as inhabiting a world dominated by mythic thinking, in which life "is felt as an unbroken continuous whole which does not admit of any clean-cut and trenchant distinctions. The limits between the different spheres are not insurmountable barriers; they are fluent and fluctuating. There is no specific difference between the various realms of life. Nothing has a definite, invariable, static shape. By a sudden metamorphosis everything may be turned into everything."[5] Reconstructions of the Homeric universe, in particular, imagine it as this world of correspondence between inside microcosm and outside macrocosm, a harmony between man, nature, and the gods.[6] It is described as a world in which the individual is not divided, as body and mind are not yet seen as distinct.[7] But neither is the individual individuated, for the self is seen merely as an aggregate of faculties, and there is no sense of it constituting a unified structure separated from the world outside of itself.[8] The identity of Homer is undeterminable and ultimately irrelevant because he has no identity in the way we conceive it.[9] As Eric A. Havelock has shown, Homer is a product of an oral culture, in which the individual is entirely submerged in a tradition from which he is unable to separate himself.[10] It is a culture that can be described as oral in a number of senses, based as it is on a kinship model that has at its center the sharing of food around a hearth that unites host and guest.[11] It is furthermore described as a gift culture, in which the primary form of exchange is seen as the voluntary bestowing and receiving of gifts.[12]

As both Marcel Mauss and Lewis Hyde have suggested, gift-giving may provide a model for relations that can offer an alternative to the economic, market-oriented paradigm that later becomes the standard in the Western world. But in terms of early Greek social arrangements, the notion of the gift in fact covered a variety of relations that we would consider as precisely trade, and even bribery. Gift-giving could be read as a benign cover for real hostility, just as the ancient emphasis upon hospitality can be seen as a way of controlling an intense ambivalence toward the stranger or outsider who enters a host's home.[13]

Moreover, out of this background emerges the figure of Odysseus, who from the very beginning appears as a problematic hero. Within a tradition that values consistency and "the elimination of contradictions"[14] appears a totally contradictory hero, grandson of the shape-shifting Autolykos, himself a thief and a liar, who "knew how to say many false things that were like true sayings" (19.203).[15] Odysseus's use of lies and disguises depends on a division between an outward sign and its internal referent, and between his own outer metamorphosing appearance and a stable inner identity.[16] As a brilliant storyteller, he will become, as he does in Ovid, a figure for the poet; but by Virgil and Dante he will be mistrusted for some of the same reasons that Plato and his followers mistrust all arts in which appearance and essence are not identical. Within the mythic harmony usually associated with the Homeric universe, Odysseus suggests the presence already of a difference, a gap between inside and outside, which anticipates the writings of Plato.

The story of Odysseus is one of return and constitutes "the fundamental quest romance"[17] that retells the story of loss and the restoration of unity with which I began.[18] To return is to come home, to be no longer a foreigner, a guest eating at another's hearth, but to be the true host once more. For Odysseus, to quest is to be not only an outsider but literally to be hungry. The *Odyssey* shows one form of appetite, the hunger for home, that is often threatened by its more literal model, as the hero's return is delayed by a series of banquets. As Fielding pointed out, it is a great "eating poem," whose hero "seems to have the best stomach of all the heroes."[19] Reflecting the significance of feasting and gift-giving in ancient Greek culture, the primary relation in the poem is that of host and guest. But it is already an ambivalent relation. As Peisistratos explains, "a guest remembers all his days the man who received him / as a host receives a guest, and gave him the gifts of friendship" (15.54–55).[20] Zeus is "the guest god" who, repairing the sins of his father, is associated with law and order and taboos against cannibalism. His law is hospitality and he avenges wrongs against guests (9.270–71). But because this is a world where gods can still consort with men there is a further pressing need to be kind to strangers:

> For the gods do take on all sorts of transformations, appearing
> as strangers from elsewhere, and thus they range at large through the cities,
> watching to see which men keep the laws, and which are violent.
>
> (17.485–87)

One needs to be careful, for one doesn't always know who one's guest is until it's too late.

Furthermore, behind the story of Odysseus's return lurks that of Agamemnon, who found his home and wife invaded by a treacherous guest. The feast in celebration of his return is the scene of his murder. As eating is the time when the body is most vulnerable to influences from abroad, so banquets can be suspicious occasions, especially for the members of the house of Atreus, who can never be totally sure what—or who—is for dinner. Agamemnon's murder is the perpetuation of the intestine war within his family. His death is avenged by his son, Orestes, who is presented as a possible model for Odysseus's son, Telemachos, to follow. For while Odysseus has been away, his home has been invaded by tricky guests who, though not feeding on him literally, are, as Homer repeatedly puts it, eating up his "substance."[21] The aim of his quest is not only to come home, but to come home properly: to remove the guests who have appropriated his place and recover his property that marks his true identity as host.

Penelope claims that Odysseus was the best and most generous of hosts (19.314–16); she also tells the disguised Odysseus that he is the best and most thoughtful of guests (19.350–53). While he incorporates and so potentially reconciles both terms of relation, it is as a guest, an alien and outsider, that we see both him and Telemachos most frequently throughout the poem. Telemachos leaves home to seek his father and is received with elaborate hospitality and gift-giving by Nestor and Menelaos. Odysseus encounters a benign host in Alkinoös, but his account of his travels is of a series of dangerous and potentially fatal receptions. He appears first in the narrative as the captive of the infatuated Calypso. As Menelaos remarks (15.69–71), excessive friendship can be as dangerous as intense hatred in a host, and love as much as hate creates the obstacles blocking Odysseus's return. Hospitable alien territory is still alien, and therefore threatening. Circe turns men into pigs, "to make them forgetful of their own country" (10.236), and those who succumb to the temptations of the lotus-eaters "forget the way home" (9.97). In foreign lands it appears to be extremely dangerous to eat indigenous substances: the men who eat the oxen of Helios are appropriately punished when "the god took away their homecoming" (12.419).

This is the worst fate imaginable to a Greek of Homer's time: to be an alien, a *barbaros* in exile forever.[22] To eat in a country is potentially to be eaten by it, to enter into a false identification by being absorbed by a foreign culture—what we call "going native"—and so be prevented from returning to a place of origin in which one is truly at home. The opposite of returning to one's own hearth is ultimately to be subsumed totally by a hostile host. The episodes of the lotus-eaters and Circe, hosts who offer dangerous substances that once taken in take over, serve as frames for the two encounters with the most threatening hosts of all: the Laistrygonians and the Cyclops Polyphemos.

Homer's description of the land of the Cyclops reveals the ambivalence inherent in Greek descriptions of the Golden Age that I have already mentioned. Like the Golden Age in its typical depictions, the world of the Cyclops is without labor, law, or any social organization, for, "each one is the law / for his own wives and children, and cares nothing about the others" (9.114–15). Like Hobbes's state of nature, this presocial order consists of isolated individuals who relate to others outside their private kinship system by cannibalism. According to Aristotle, a man who lives outside of society, and so who appears to be totally self-sufficient, must be either a god or a beast.[23] The Cyclops suggest the ambivalence toward both extremes, which are identified as "outside" the order of the body politic. Polyphemos appears primarily as subhuman, "a monster of a man," and even as nature incarnate, for he is "not like a man, an eater of bread, but more like a wooded / peak of the high mountains seen standing away from the others" (9.190–91). But the figure of the "man-mountain," to which I shall return in relation to Ben Jonson, is also a version of the primal man whose body contained the whole world, suggesting that from a human perspective the superhuman is difficult to distinguish from the subhuman.

Furthermore, Polyphemos is also a grotesque literalization of Odysseus's own appetite, his hunger for home, which has been inflated into a monstrous form that is almost entirely all mouth and eye: a huge gaping hole eager to take everything into itself.[24] In order to resist absorption, which would result in total identification with this image of appetite incarnate, Odysseus has to negate himself temporarily, reducing himself to "Nobody." This capacity for nominal self-annihilation ensures the perpetuation of "Odysseus," and it is dependent on his ability to divide himself, to separate essence from appearances, a true identity from the various embodiments it undergoes, in order to keep the inside true self intact and uncontaminated by external influences. Throughout his travels Odysseus is able to play the part of a shapeshifter because of his assumption that underneath the different personae is a true, unchanging, proper, or literal identity to which he will be restored on his return home.

Part of this division involves the separation of his quest from its material bodily base, appetite, which begins with the encounter with Polyphemos. Furthermore, before revealing his true identity, Odysseus appears in Ithaka in a parodic form of himself, as a beggar seeking food. In this shape, he appears to reduce his own quest to its lowest level, turning it into a form of human appetite that becomes the essential motive for all human action. He tells Eumaios:

> there is no suppressing the ravenous belly,
> a cursed thing, which bestows many evils on men, seeing
> that even for its sake the strong-built ships are handled
> across the barren great sea, bringing misfortune to enemies.

(17.286–89)

As Odysseus is ironically demonstrating, the voyager is no different from the beggar because all motives are ultimately appetitive.[25] According to Eumaios, hunger is the source of lies (14.123–25), as the belly is the origin of both deceit and poetic fictions.[26] To quest is simply and literally to be hungry and to beg food from hosts, often through the telling of stories.

In order to regain his proper identity, however, Odysseus has to separate himself from this materialistic definition. The fake beggar fights a real beggar, Iros, who is described as all appetite, an empty hulk who is the humanized form of Polyphemos and so also Odysseus's projected double and rival. Odysseus pretends to fight solely because "my villainous / belly drives me to do it" (18.53–54). By winning he detaches himself from his lower appetitive form. The loser is eaten, thrown to a cannibal king, for by the laws of poetic justice the punishment for greed fits the crime.[27]

There remain still Odysseus's rivals for his wife as well as substance to dispose of. For the suitors too the final feast, which should mark the end of Odysseus's quest, involves an unexpected sacrifice, when the alien in their midst suddenly reveals himself to be their host and presents them with the guest-gift of death. The host comes home, exterminates the parasites, repossesses his wife and property, and regains his true identity.

However, as a means of resolution and restoration of original identity, the narrative of return is incomplete, for the code of revenge necessitates retaliation on the part of the suitors' families.[28] While Athene intervenes and persuades Zeus to make peace, we know from Tiresias's prophecy that Odysseus will have to make a second voyage to expiate his crime (11.121–25). Even if you get home and the coast is clear, you may not be able to stay there. No one is ever just a host; no one, not even the man who is "Nobody," can avoid being, most of the time, a hungry guest dependent on others.

The tradition after Homer raises further questions concerning Odysseus's independence and capacity for total self-division. The possibility of a return to original identity, especially that of the host, seems undermined by certain parts of Odysseus's character that make him open to conflicting interpretations. On the one hand, his story was read by the neoplatonists as an allegory of the soul's purification and return to its source.[29] On the other, he comes to be seen as a liar inseparable from his own fictions, who lacks a stable, unified self to return to, and whose real desire, especially in Dante's revision, is not for home but for endless wandering.[30] In this century, moreover, his quest has been read as a type for the bourgeois individual: the self-affirming wanderer who, like later merchants and explorers, constructs a unified self against an external diversified landscape—which includes the diversity of his own forms and disguises.[31] In his study of *The Conquest of America*, Tzvetan Todorov has shown how the oral orientation of the New World natives, who were heavily embedded in the tradition, ceremony, and ritual that identify meaning and expression, made them vulnerable to exploitation by the Old World conquerors, who knew how to improvise and play roles, which separate them.[32] Centuries before this colonial encounter, the expert improviser, Odysseus, emerges out of an oral culture to prophesy its end through the discovery of the separation of the individual and tradition, essence and appearances, that an oral culture identifies. The hero in fact embodies the attributes that the Western tradition will associate with the opposite of the speech that is idealized as self-authenticating: its derivative and debased as self-divided form, writing.[33] Moreover, he is the model for later explorers and shipwrecked men, such as Robinson Crusoe, who epitomize *homo oeconomicus*, "the principle of capitalist economy," as their "very isolation forces them recklessly to pursue an atomistic interest."[34] Odysseus and Crusoe struggle not only against cannibals but also against the temptation to go native, to return to a past that seen from an enlightened perspective is a primitive state from which man has just managed to emerge.[35] They struggle to preserve their substance against forces that threaten to waste and consume it.

The words Homer uses for the substance of Odysseus that the suitors waste typically identify life and livelihood, suggesting a close connection between man and nature as well as a belief that one is what one has.[36] The identification of man and property is usually seen as typical of feudal relations, read as the class analogue of the oral phase of sexual development. In capitalism, considered as essentially anal (partially through the association of money and excrement), the relation is one not of identification but possession.[37] This later stage requires a sense of difference, in which nature becomes a separate thing that can be known and owned because of its alienation. This difference, however, is certainly available to Homer's near contemporary, Hesiod, for whom the landscape is an object to be worked upon in order to make money.[38] But it is present also in the *Odyssey* in the concept of an essential self that can be abstracted from its "properties," in the philosophical sense, from its accidents or various embodiments that exist prior to and so unaffected by expression.

Such a definition of the self will be expressed more forcefully by Socrates, who is described by Alcibiades as himself a figure in whom appearance and reality are opposed, a *silenus*: "you know the ones I mean—they're modeled with pipes or flutes in their hands, and when you open them down the middle there are little figures of the gods inside."[39] Socrates' own body in fact epitomizes a relation that will become increasingly significant, not least of all for models of interpretation, in which the outside is seen as a nonessential and grotesque shell, which must be cracked open to reveal the beautiful inner truth it contains. Socrates articulates ideas already available to Greek culture, defining the self as an autonomous, unified structure whose very unity is guaranteed by its division into higher and lower faculties, with the latter controlled by the former.[40] Ironically, he makes possible the separation of the individual from tradition, the subject from the object, the knower from the known, the abstract ideal from its particular incarnations, at the same time as he tries to bring them back into an ideal relation. However, for Socrates such a relation is based on a kind of divide-and-conquer method in which first two terms are separated and then one is put in control over the other. The need to maintain a proper order between the two terms leads to a mistrust of identification, especially that brought about by mimesis, as a potential regression in which the properly subordinate term "swallows" the other.[41]

Adorno and Horkheimer read the *Odyssey* as a myth of enlightenment, in which return represents a potential threat to the achievements won with difficulty. To go back is potentially to devolve into barbarism, a metamorphosis that might be represented as either becoming or being eaten by (and ultimately, of course there can be no difference between these alternatives) a Cyclops, or as being metamorphosed by Circe into a pig.

The ambivalence toward an original world of harmony imagined as a world of metamorphosis seems even greater when one leaps from Homer to Ovid's *Metamorphoses*. To take such a leap means to ignore many differences (such as the passage of a mere eight centuries or so) in order to try to draw a few connections useful for my argument. A central theme of Augustan literature is the working out of identity, both national and individual,[42] a process simultaneously occurring through the development of the Roman legal system, which was one of Rome's lasting contributions to the Western tradition. Socrates' discovery of the individual as a divided yet integrated unit makes possible the Latin concept of the *persona*. This was originally a definition of a person in terms of his social and legal roles, which, though it does not necessitate a division between a presocial and a social self, certainly facilitates it. Essentially, it is a definition of the self based on the concept of ownership: a persona owns his own body and actions.[43] One's identity is one's private property, a definition that may reflect the Roman view of private property as sacred, a view they inherited from the Greeks (including Plato) and reinforced.[44] So, in the *Fasti*, Book 2.7, Ovid celebrates the God of twoness, division, *Terminus*, whose statues were placed to mark boundaries around property. For Ovid, the arch role-player, who, Odysseus-like, exploits and manipulates his own personae, the separation of *meus* and *tuus* is a guarantee of harmony:

> conveniunt celebrantque dapes vicinia simplex
>   et cantant laudes, Termine sancte, tuas:
> tu populos urbesque et regna ingentia finis:
>   omnis erit sine te litigiosus ager.

> ("The simple neighbours meet and hold a feast, and sing thy praises, holy Terminus: thou dost set bounds to peoples and cities and vast kingdoms; without thee every field would be a root of wrangling.")[45]

As one who fatally transgressed the bounds of Augustan propriety, Ovid, in his later works certainly, seems concerned with marking the limits that define and regulate relations. Law, especially Roman law, is based on forms of *termini*, distinctions between *meum* and *tuum*, the mine and thine absent from the Golden Age, as it is concerned largely with defining the rights of property.[46] But property has a wide definition, as it can refer not only to land and to the self, but to others, to women (and Ovid was married three times) and to children, who were literally owned by the *paterfamilias*.[47] Ovidian metamorphosis, like incorporation with which it is ultimately identified, depends on such laws, divisions of territory and forms of life, which it simultaneously breaks down. At the time when the relations less formally defined by Homer become codified as a means of controlling them, Ovid represents the blurring of boundaries as a terrifying regression to a world of mythic harmony which, from an Augustan perspective, looks extremely sinister.

OVID

The world of Ovid's text is summed up by its title, *Metamorphoses*. The term describes Ovid's method of absorbing the poetic property of other authors into his text, as Homer, Hesiod, Horace, Lucretius, Virgil, and early mythographers are subsumed and transformed. But metamorphosis is also the literalized version of metaphor, the incarnation of meaning in words, represented in the text as the transformation of figures into new alien forms that conceal their original identity and meaning. Ovid's figures are metaphors in which inside and outside are simultaneously opposed and indistinguishable: one cannot judge a thing by its appearance—in fact, to know it at all, one must violate its outward form. In this world of paradoxically constant change metamorphosis identifies rather than distinguishes elements. Although everything changes, the new form is still identifiable with the old, creating a world full of dangerous identity and continuity, mapped out by invisible boundary lines that are not known until crossed. Identities are obscured, and because a tree may turn out to be not just a tree but also the woodsman's grandfather, all action is not only meaningful but also potentially guilty.

The book begins before creation, in a world consisting of chaos:

> rudis indigestaque moles
> nec quicquam nisi pondus iners congestaque eodem
> non bene iunctarum discordia semina rerum.

("a rough, unordered mass of things, nothing at all save lifeless bulk and warring seeds of ill-matched elements heaped in one.")[48]

Law and order are established by an unknown originator, "quisquis fuit ille deorum" ("whoever of the gods it was," 1.32), who sets about setting up boundaries to divide this mess into manageable parts. For Ovid, such division is essential, and yet formulas such as "quisquis fuit ille" ("whoever it was") or "nesquio quis" ("I don't know who") are used repeatedly to refer to sources. The obscuring of origins creates the impression that the poem can imagine no real creator or *auctor*, not even Ovid himself, who can make real divisions and shape a discrete beginning or end.[49] The body of the text is not organized by a linear progressive sequence that can be traced back to a point of origin, but by a metaphor, the transcendental term *metamorphosis*, which identifies figures across stretches of narrative time. The result is a paradoxically chaotic unity, in which it often appears that all transformations are happening, if not actually at the same time, then in such close sequence that a later story cannot revise the error of the earlier one but is forced to repeat it. The text struggles to emerge from chaos, but the relations between the tales become too intimate, and finally a world in which anything can turn into anything else is revealed to be a world in which everything is eating everything else.

With the divison and separation of conflicting elements, out of chaos emerges a Golden Age of peace and plenitude maintained without necessity of law or any of the arts of civilization (1.89–112). In Ovid's chronology, this time simply ends with the banishing of Saturn and the succession of his son Jove. Although Jove is traditionally associated with law and order and seen as the guarantor of justice, his reign marks the end of the earlier and ideal natural harmony. The establishment of law assumes the existence of potential conflicts that need reconciliation and of unruly elements to be controlled and mastered. To bring in Jove means to begin a Silver Age and, soon after, an Iron Age characterized by the totally hostile relations among its members:

> non hospes ab hospite tutus,
> non socer a genero, fratrum quoque gratia rara est;
> imminet exitio vir coniugis, illa mariti,
> lurida terribiles miscent aconita novercae,
> filius ante diem patrios inquirit in annos:
> victa iacet pietas, et virgo caede madentis
> ultima caelestum terras Astraea reliquit.

("Guest was not safe from host, nor father-in-law from son-in-law; even among brothers 'twas rare to find affection. The husband longed for the death of his wife, she of her husband; murderous stepmothers brewed deadly poisons, and sons inquired into their fathers' years before the time. Piety lay vanquished, and the maiden Astraea, last of the immortals, abandoned the blood-soaked earth." 1.144–48)

This complex kinship system of simultaneous identification and antagonism violates the Augustan ideals of justice and *pietas* with which Jove is associated, yet is the predominant characteristic of the world he rules.

Significantly, the first distinct metamorphosis in the poem is that of Lycaon, a host with nasty designs upon his divine guest. Lycaon wants proof of Jove's divinity and, with a logic worthy of the Salem judges, decides that murder is a relatively reliable test. He further violates the laws of hospitality that are as essential to Ovid as to Homer for the guarantee of order, by slaying a hostage and trying to feed him to the god. This travesty of human sacrifice outrages Jupiter, Homer's guest god, who not only turns Lycaon into a wolf, but plans to destroy all mankind lest the thirst for human blood spread further.[50] Jove, like René Girard, sees sacrificial violence as contagious and thinks he had better simply annihilate mankind and begin again. At the last moment, however, he changes his mind and preserves a remnant of humanity from the flood. Human life continues, but so does the crime of Lycaon. The first story of metamorphosis, incarnating the ethos of the Iron Age, sets a bad precedent and seems to leave behind it an inevitable legacy of violence inherited by the tales that follow.

Furthermore, after the first metamorphosis takes place, nothing in the world seems capable of keeping its shape. Change becomes contagious, and in a fluctuating world even such opposing figures as victor and victim may be more intimate than they at first appear. In Book 2, Lycaon's daughter, Callisto, turned into a bear by the proverbial (though changed and redirected so that even it is no longer predictable) wrath of Juno, meets her son, who assumes that what looks like a bear *is* a bear, and therefore, to him as a hunter, a creature to be hunted and killed. Innocently, he assumes that he is in a world of stable, as antithetical, definitions and identities. Jove prevents what would otherwise be matricide by suspending their confrontation, when he turns both mother and child into stars.

The destruction of a disguised human is not prevented, however, in the case of Actaeon, one of the unfortunate members of the house of Thebes, that infamous center of incest and cannibalism. In Book 3, his cousin Pentheus is also dismembered by his mother who, under the influence of Bacchus, believes her son to be a wild beast. Actaeon actually is turned into a beast for violating a taboo of which he was completely ignorant, transgressing one of the many strict but invisible boundary lines in the text.[51] In a world in metamorphosis there can be no such thing as innocence, for every action means more than the actor consciously intends and so incriminates him. Sheer accident effects a complete change in Actaeon's identity. In his new form, his companions and hounds cannot recognize him; the gruesome irony of the scene of the hunter hunted is heightened by the juxtaposition of his frustrated attempts to name and identify himself with the calling out of his name by his friends, who think him far away as they run him to ground. He has been torn from the name that designates his human identity; in his new bestial form he is quite literally torn apart.

The story of Actaeon plays upon the inversion by which the hunter becomes the hunted, the victor the victim. The story of Narcissus, which follows shortly after in the concatenation of the tales, also involves the collapsing of apparently rigidly separated categories, as the boy becomes both subject and object of his own affection.[52] Whereas Actaeon is torn in two, Narcissus is frustrated because he is not; the identification of lover and beloved within the same body prevents the possibility of erotic satisfaction, and the boy realizes

quod cupio mecum est: inopem me copia fecit.
o utinam a nostro secedere corpore possem!
votum in amante novum, vellem, quod amamus, abesset.

("What I desire, I have; the very abundance of my riches beggars me [my plenty makes me poor]. Oh, that I might be parted from my own body! and, strange prayer for a lover, I would that what I love were absent from me!" 3.466–68)

He is in the awkward position of experiencing desire with no lack, which does not make him self-sufficient like the hermaphrodites of the *Symposium*, but rather turns out to be the greatest kind of lack. Total presence, the complete identification between lover and beloved, frustrates desire: he cannot *have* himself for he *is* himself. Self-identity and self-possession are incompatible. The destructive self-knowledge prophesied by Tiresias includes the discovery that he cannot know himself completely and carnally; that, because he cannot literally divide himself in order to possess himself, he remains internally self-divided. As the later stories of incest will also show, it is proximity and not distance that causes frustration, for proximity is never quite close enough. It both stirs a longing for and stands in the way of total identification, as there is always some medium preventing direct contact. When Narcissus bends toward his own reflection, calling out to a mere image, in a self-conscious reflection upon his own desire toward and distance from his created image, Ovid breaks into direct address (3.432–36). But the figure he calls out to is itself only a "simulacra fugacia" ("a fleeting image," 432), reflected through words instead of water but kept apart from its source by the very medium that permits its existence.

However, water and words are both unstable boundary lines, and for a significant moment the author is drawn inside his own text. In the story of Hermaphroditus in Book 4, Ovid's ironic *Symposium*, water enables the breakdown of individual identity. Whereas in Plato the figure of the hermaphrodite is used as an image of man's original unfallen identity, in Ovid it appears in a tale showing the loss of the sexual differentiation that for Ovid seems to be fundamental to the human condition. The loss of this distinction through erotic union (though one that seems also an act of appropriation and aggression) involves the dissolution, not transcendence, of separate selves. Salmacis prays to be made one flesh with the boy, and the gods take her at her word. Their union produces the hermaphrodite (the male's name is retained at the expense of the female's), a suspiciously formless corporate body whose duality makes it a kind of walking contradiction, which, "nec duo sunt et forma duplex, nec femina dici / nec puer ut possit, neutrumque et utrumque videntur" ("they were no longer two, nor such as to be called, one, woman, and one, man. They seemed neither, and yet both," 378–79). This negatively imagined tertium quid borders on chaos, as to be both is also to be neither, and ultimately nothing at all.

From the story of the first flood (1.253–312) water has been a source of continuous dissolution. Flowing through the poem, the recurring image is both a means of thematic continuity and a source of contagion. It is difficult to tell one river from another, and the various waters are finally swallowed up by Pythagoras's river of time "edax rerum," in Book 15.

Similarly, one story flows into and feeds—perhaps poisons—another. As the poem continues, a tension develops between the proliferation of characters and the singleness of Ovid's subject. As G. Karl Galinsky has pointed out, Ovid's model for his own method is that of the great liar and storyteller, Ulysses, whom in the *Artis amatoriae* he described as being forced to repeat his story to Calypso: "Haec Troiae casus iterumque iterumque rogabat / Ille referre aliter saepe solebat idem" ("Again and again did she ask to hear the fate of Troy; often would he tell the same tale in other words," 2.127–28).[53] Like Ulysses, Ovid tries to tell the same story differently, but the differences among the episodes, though superficially great, seem undermined as the relations among stories become increasingly involved. A verbal echo of the paradox of Narcissus, "inopem me copia fecit" ("my plenty makes me poor," 3.466), is heard in the boast of Niobe in Book 6: "tutam me copia fecit" ("My very abundance has made me safe," or better perhaps, "my plenty makes me secure," 194). As a result of the parallelism, two antithetical adjectives become identified: to believe that one is secure is really to be poor and, as *inops* also signifies, helpless.[54] To be rich is to be vulnerable, particularly in a world in which abundance means danger: nature is full, but full of people and gods, so that no action or speech is really safe.

Furthermore, the stories are full of other stories. Niobe identifies herself: "mihi Tantalus auctor, / cui licuit soli superorum tangere mensas" ("I have Tantalus to my father, the only mortal ever allowed to touch the table of the gods," 6.172–73). Considering Tantalus's unsavoury eating habits, the allusion seems in rather poor taste. Ovid does not tell us the story of Niobe's father directly; instead he relates the fate of her unfortunate children, her *copia*, plenty and possessions, who are sacrificed to her pride. But the past crime is invoked and involved in the present scene, suggesting that Niobe has identified herself too fully with her *auctor*, father and creator, and imitates the past at the expense of the future. The omission of the feast of Tantalus is not reassuring; the most horrible, unspoken part of the story haunts the periphery of Niobe's tale, surfacing in the description of the dismemberment of Marsyas and in the reference to Pelops, who once suffered a similar *sparagmos*. As one who is torn apart and then re-membered, Pelops would seem to be a version of the figure of the primal corporate body. Yet his resurrection is not an end to but the renewal of the cannibalism of his father that is, in turn, passed on to his son, Atreus, and his family. Ovid suppresses the story of the father eating his son, but it does not stay down for long, erupting with even greater force in the tale of Philomela that follows.

Ovid's tale of Philomela has been read as a myth of the origin of poetry. The account he gives us is a violent and extremely nasty one, in which poetry is produced by the disorder of relations and confusions of identity represented as incest and cannibalism. The familiar is made terrifying indeed, as both cannibalism and incest (which are related—incestuously—as Lévi-Strauss suggests when he calls cannibalism "an alimentary form of incest")[55] threaten the normal distinctions and boundaries that define individual identity. The elaborate and gory description of the severing of Philomela's tongue (6.555–60), which takes on a life of its own as a mangled, twitching snake, draws attention to the theme of communication.[56] The means of verbal intercourse, which is also the organ of taste, is destroyed by the violence of the unmediated contact between victor and victim in the act of rape, the aggressive penetration and possession of the female body by a male.[57] The familiar or "proper" method of communication is replaced by a poetry that can only represent its own origin in incest and cannibalism.

Perverted intercourse leads to the confusion and distortion of relations; as Philomela warns Tereus, "omnia turbasti; paelex ego facta sororis, / tu geminus coniunx, hostis mihi debita Procne" ("You have confused all natural relations: I have become a concubine, my sister's rival; you, a husband to both. Now Procne must be my enemy," 6.537–38). Although Philomela is the center of attention in the story, in terms of an important pattern in the poem, Procne is a crucial figure. At the center of the *Metamorphoses* are the stories of Procne, Medea (bk. 7), Scylla, Ariadne, and Meleager's mother (all bk. 8), women who must choose between two men, usually a father and a lover or husband. A similar choice in fact determined female identity according to Roman laws of the time, which, upholding the total authority of the *paterfamilias* as both father and husband, saw women as a kind of property defined by one of two kinds of marriage.[58] In the first and oldest, a woman and her property were given over to her husband, who adopted her completely into his family. In the second, the woman gave only her person in marriage, while her father maintained his right to her inheritance. By Ovid's time, this latter form had become by far the most common, and though it facilitated divorce, it put women in a complicated situation in which their freedom was restricted by being bound by two conflicting ties. Ovid's women are kinds of hermaphrodites: two people collapsed into one, torn between loyalties that tie them to the past—their parents—and to the future—their husbands and children. Choice is necessary but tragic: to choose the past is regressive (in Ovid's terms incestuous and cannibalistic), while to choose the future borders on miscegenation: marriage with a foreigner, an alien and outsider, who may not be totally trustworthy.

Procne marries a foreigner, and when she discovers her husband's crimes the memory of her father moves her to take her ghastly revenge. Reminding herself of her origin, that she is "Pandione nata" ("daughter of Pandion," 6.634), she plans the destruction of her descendant; loyalty to the past is maintained at the expense and finally literal consumption of the future. In Roman society, the child was identified with its father, the *paterfamilias* who owned it, and Procne sees her son Itylus as the possession of her husband, Tereus, made in his image : "a! quam / es similis patri!" ("Ah, how like your father you are!" 621–22). Through revenge she turns similitude into absolute identity. She invites Tereus to what appears to be a traditional sacred feast, "mensis / et patrii moris sacrum mentita" ("a sacred feast after their ancestral fashion," 647), but whose real tradition lies in the house of Atreus. The feast becomes a demonic meal in which the father unwittingly eats his own substance in the form of his son: "ipse sedens solio Tereus sublimis avito / vescitur inque suam sua viscera congerit alvum" ("So Tereus, sitting alone in his high ancestral banquet-chair, begins the feast and gorges himself with flesh of his own flesh," 650–51). As in the story of Actaeon, the calling of names is used ironically to create a distance that is actually disappearing. Tereus calls for Itylus, and Procne replies, "intus habes, quem poscis" ("You have, within, him whom you want," 655); Tereus is now in a grotesque version of the position of Narcissus, and when he comprehends his situation he attempts to tear himself apart:

> et modo, si posset, reserato pectore diras
> egerere inde dapes semesaque viscera gestit,
> flet modo seque vocat bustum miserabile nati.

> ("Now, if he could, he would gladly lay open his breast and take thence the horrid feast and half-consumed flesh of his son; now he weeps bitterly and calls himself his son's most wretched tomb." 664–65)

In the masculine version of the traditional womb/tomb identification appropriate to a culture that invests all authority and power of origination in the *paterfamilias*, the father's stomach becomes the son's tomb, as the "natus" returns to the body that produced it and still owns it. Itylus's life comes full circle, but by following a cycle that aborts future progression, a return to origins in which—in a perverse form of communion—birth and death, father and son, are completely identified, as all differences dissolve in the belly of Tereus.

When, in the quarrel at Calydon, Meleager slays his uncle, his mother finds herself to be the battleground for conflicting identities, as "pugnat materque sororque, / et diversa trahunt unum duo nomina pectus" ("Mother and sister strove in her, and the two names tore one heart this way and that," 8.463–64). Like the dismembered satyr Marsyas, she is torn apart ("traho" is used to describe both experiences), not by divine forces, but rather by the two roles or "nomina" that are conflicting within her. Although nominally she can be both sister and mother, Meleager's act of violence demands that she take one side. Like Procne, she upholds the past, the family she came from, and the way of revenge. Ovid allows her no "nomina" of her own; a woman in a strictly patriarchal society, she is defined only in terms of her relations to the male members of her family, and at the point at which her maternal feelings are conquered she is named as "Thestias," daughter of Thestius:

> Thestias haud aliter dubiis affectibus errat
> inque vices ponit positamque resuscitat iram.
> incipit esse tamen melior germana parente
> et consanguineas ut sanguine leniat umbras,
> inpietate pia est.

("Thestius's daughter wavered betwixt opposing passions; now quenched her wrath and now fanned it again. At last the sister in her overcomes the mother, and, that she may appease the shades of her blood-kin, she is pious in impiety." 8.473–77)

The internal conflict is conveyed through the language itself, as pairs of related words with similar sounds ("consanguineas" / "sanguine," "impietate" / "pia") but antithetical meanings are brought into close proximity. The effect is one of simultaneous circularity and contradiction, as language circles back on itself to destroy itself.[59] As in the case of Tereus, the parent consumes its own substance, as she feeds the fire with "mea viscera" ("my own flesh," 478).

Book 8 concludes with a figure who literally consumes himself, first wasting the substance that is his property and finally wasting away from insatiable hunger. Erysicthon offends the gods by failing to offer sacrifices to them and furthermore profanes the grove of Ceres.[60] The punishment for a crime against the goddess of plenty is to be visited by the personification of want or lack—the gods having their own system of representation by reversal in cases where they need to exercise poetic justice. Fames comes to Erysicthon in his sleep and fills him with her emptiness. He dreams of "cibo delusum" ("fancied food," 826) and tries to devour the air around him. "Aura," air, suggests also "aurum," gold, anticipating the mercenary greed that will frustrate Midas's physical hunger in Book 9. But in Erysicthon the hunger for food and for money are not mutually exclusive but rather merge into a single appetite; he becomes a parodic embodiment of Virgil's "auri sacra fames" ("accursed hunger for gold," *Aeneid* 3.57), who consumes his wealth in order to feed his belly, until his literal appetite engulfs his entire substance. His is an appetite that grows with what it feeds on: "plusque cupit, quo plura suam demittit in alvum" ("The more he sends down into his maw the more he wants," 834), so that hunger becomes a self-perpetuating vicious circle: "cibus omnis in illo / causa cibi est, semperque locus fit inanis edendo" ("All food is in him but the cause of food, and ever does he become empty by eating," 841–42). In order to fill himself, he first exhausts his property, his inheritance from the past; when this is consumed, he turns on his legacy to the future and sells his other property—his daughter. When the gods grant her the power to change shape and so escape her new owners, he exploits the gift in order to recycle his merchandise. Finally, however, the exhaustion of all external sources of nourishment causes his appetite to turn inward and feed upon its source:

> vis tamen illa mali postquam consumpserat omnem
> materiam derantque gravi nova pabula morbo,
> ipse suos artus lacerans divellere morsu
> coepit et infelix minuendo corpus alebat.

("At last, when the strength of the plague had consumed all these provisions, and his grievous malady needed more food, the wretched man began to tear his limbs and rend them apart with his teeth and, by consuming his own body, fed himself." 875–78)

Tereus's devouring of his "natus," Meleager's mother's sacrifice of her "viscera" to the consuming flames, in Erysicthon become completely internalized and reflexive. At the very center of the *Metamorphoses* is this figure of the totally self-involved isolated self, subject and object of its own appetite, turning back on itself and so preying on itself.

The figure of Erysicthon looks back to that of Aglauros who, consumed by Envy,

> occulto mordetur et anxia nocte
> anxia luce gemit lentaque miserrima tabe
> liquitur, et glacies incerto saucia sole,
> felicisque bonis non lenius uritur Herses.

("eats her heart out in secret misery; careworn by day, careworn by night, she groans and wastes away most wretchedly with slow decay, like ice touched by the fitful sunshine. She is consumed by envy of Herse's happiness." 2.806–09)[61]

Erysichthon is also a version of Narcissus, as he knows himself by literally consuming himself. Subject and object become identified as eater and eaten, a relation that fulfills Narcissus's desire by eliminating differences altogether. The second half of the text contains a number of stories of incest which also revise that of Narcissus. In these tales, sexual desire threatens to involve a kinship system too closely, complicating family relations by trespassing across the boundary lines established through both law and language in order to ensure order. The stories in Books 7 and 8 of women torn apart by conflicting loyalties turn into the tales in Books 9 and 10 of Byblis and Myrrha, women who do not want to choose, and attempt to combine relationships, to be both sister or daughter and lover of the same man.

The nominal confusion created by incest was already suggested by Ovid in the story of Philomela. Byblis, therefore, hates the name of brother, as if it were the word itself that stood in the way of her desire. At the same time, however, she realizes that it is a good cover: they can get away with more intimate relations "dulci fraterno sub nomine" ("beneath the sweet name of brother and sister," 9.558). Still she fears that, as in the case of Narcissus, the very closeness of the connection between lover and beloved will prevent further intimacy. Similarly, Myrrha is frustrated by having in one way what she desires in another: "nunc, quia iam meus est, non est meus" ("But as it is, because he is mine, he is not mine," 10.339). Her paradoxical position strains language, but she recognizes that the fulfillment of her desires would cause even greater legal and linguistic confusion:

> et quot confundas et iura et nomina, sentis!
> tune eris et matris paelex et adultera patris?
> tune soror nati genetrixque vocabere fratris?

("Think how many ties [also duties, justice], how many names you are confusing! Will you be the rival of your mother, the mistress of your father? Will you be called the sister of your son, the mother of your brother?" 346–48)

She can suppress her worries about the consequences of her violation of moral law ("moris," 355), but her very speech enacts the confusion created by incest, which transgresses the normal bounds of relations with which we mark distinct identities. If Myrrha were to be called the sister of her son and the mother of her brother it would be very difficult to determine who she was.

Within the verbal universe of the poem, incest is seen primarily as a crime against identities produced by language, as it threatens to break down the verbal boundary lines between characters, resulting in total confusion. Incest is therefore also an image for both the author's and the reader's impulse to relate the stories so closely that there are ultimately no differences between them. As the poem struggles to assert its own order through the establishment of boundary lines and differences, acts of union become increasingly represented as confusion and the dissolution of identity that recalls the nebulous hermaphrodite. Ovid's weddings tend to turn into lugubrious occasions, and the happy ending usually becomes the beginning of antagonism. The motif of the wedding that turns into a funeral appears in the tales of Tereus and Orpheus, while the marriages of Perseus and Pirithoüs in Books 5 and 12 turn into full-scale battles. In these episodes, a rival or rivals for the bride, seen as somehow inferior to the proper bridegroom (in the case of the centaurs, subhuman), interrupts the ceremony, and jealousy expands into a contagious fray that draws in everyone in the vicinity. Those who try to keep out of the fight are brutally killed, propelling their avenging friends into the center. Finally everyone is forced to take sides, as later all countries will be forced to choose between Greece and Troy, and, finally, between Turnus and Aeneas.

The crucial wedding that Ovid does not describe is that of Peleus and Thetis, which is the origin of the Trojan War. But Ovid's omissions are always ominous: what is repressed will return in an even more uncanny and grotesque form. Furthermore, by entering the Trojan War indirectly, he once more rejects a comforting myth of origins and prevents the possibility of tracing violence to an identifiable and unique source. The only cause of the war is analogy: it does not emerge out of an originating event but from foreshadowing, and it has begun long before we get to it. Because all stories are related, the weddings that are described can stand in for the omitted one. The weddings that turn into wars not only summarize the events leading up to the Trojan War but, by their collapsing of two traditionally antithetical kinds of action, suggest the increasing simultaneity of the poem, as all events, especially opposites, become entangled. Everything is related and can become anything else. In the monstrous storm that overwhelms Ceyx's ship in Book 11 a second flood occurs; sea and sky collapse together, striving to meet in a descending and ascending rhythm that turns into a violent alteration between extremes that finally tears the ship apart. In the midst of the description (524–36), the ship becomes a citadel resisting the battering-ram of invaders attacking from outside. Through a mere metaphor we have slipped into the world of the Trojan War.[62]

For a poet of Ovid's time the authoritative version of the Trojan War was that of Virgil, not Homer, and Ovid's relationship to Virgil has been the subject of much critical speculation.[63] Ovid subsumes the *Aeneid*, compressing the main plot into a mere thirteen lines, in order to focus not upon the war itself but the events that guarantee its perpetuation. His interest is in the metamorphosis of Troy into Rome, the translation of the old world into the new by the hero Aeneas. Following a tradition that is not used by Virgil,[64] Ovid says that the gods allowed Aeneas to choose the possessions he wanted to take with him on his quest, and from all his property, "opibus" (13.626), he chose his father and his son. The past is carried away,

literally on Aeneas's back: "sacra et, sacra altera, patrem / fert umeris, ve-
nerabile onus, Cythereius heros" ("The heroic son of Cytherea bore away
upon his shoulders her [Troy's] sacred images and, another sacred thing,
his father, a venerable burden," 13.624–25). Beyond Virgil, Ovid finds a
perfect image for the continuation of tradition, one that truly embodies
the "burden of the past."

The last two books of the *Metamorphoses* describe the formation of the
identity of the new Rome from the ashes of the old Troy and could be read
as an upward movement reversing the previously downward direction of
metamorphosis.[65] In the Orphic tradition, this inversion is precisely what
happens through catharsis. But what makes such a reading difficult is the
presence of a figure associated with such beliefs. The philosopher Pythagoras, whose theories of metempsychosis and catharsis are closely connected
to the Orphic tradition,[66] appears suddenly to make a speech that subverts
the movement of the text toward transcendence and brings the poem full
circle back to the chaos in which it began.

Pythagoras's speech begins as a warning against the eating of flesh as a
crime against natural law:

> heu quantum scelus est in viscera viscera condi
> congestoque avidum pinguescere corpore corpus
> alteriusque animantem animantis vivere leto!
>
> ("Oh, how criminal it is for flesh to be stored away in flesh, for one greedy body
> to grow fat with food gained from another, for one live creature to go on living
> through the destruction of another living thing!" 15.88–90)

The language here returns to the reflexive rhetoric of incest and self-cannibalism. The conjunction of words that sound identical but refer to opposites bring eater and eaten into an uneasy identification. Pythagoras is
usually associated with ideas of the kinship of nature, and of the correspondence between microcosmic and macrocosmic bodies. Ovid's Pythagoras
claims that all things are equally the children of "optima matrum" ("the
best of mothers," 91), the earth, who feeds us so bountifully that there is
no need to revive the table manners of the Cyclops (93). But Pythagoras
seems to have forgotten that the age of the Cyclops was the Golden Age,
which he, in his revision of Ovid's stages of man in Book 1, has characterized as a time *free* of bloodshed. Within his own descriptions, the age of
Saturn is represented ambiguously. Origins are always unclear and so ambivalent; what is not remembered exactly might be either pure symbiosis
or mere cannibalism. One is never totally sure how or when anything begins: so also flesh-eating starts with another unknown originator, "quisquis fuit ille" ("whoever he was," 15.104), who "fecit iter sceleri" ("opened
the way for crime," 106).

Once the way is open and the first example set, it is continuously followed, for the world of Pythagoras is based on ceaseless repetition and imitation. Man does not need to fear death because there is none; our bodies decay, but "morte carent animae" ("our souls are deathless," 15.158), and so the world perpetuates itself:

> omnia mutantur, nihil interit: errat et illinc
> huc venit, hinc illuc, et quoslibet occupat artus
> spiritus eque feris humana in corpora transit
> inque feras noster, nec tempore deperit ullo,
> utque novis facilis signatur cera figuris
> nec manet ut fuerat nec formas servat easdem,
> sed tamen ipsa eadem est, animam sic semper eandem
> esse, sed in varias doceo migrare figuras.

("All things are changing; nothing dies. The spirit wanders, comes now here, now there, and occupies whatever frame it pleases. From beasts it passes into human bodies, and from human bodies into beasts, but never perishes. And, as the pliant wax is stamped with new designs, does not remain as it was before nor keep the same form long, but is still the selfsame wax, so do I teach that the soul is ever the same, though it passes into ever-changing bodies." 15.165–72)

Pythagoras's world is that of Ovid's poem, always different and yet still the same old thing over and over. If it frees us from the fear of death, it does so by metamorphosing us into figures of wax whose inner unchanging essence, the mind, becomes, as Harold Skulsky notes, "a palimpsest of embodiments."[67] Although our essences are freed from their embodiments, we are never able to forget completely our past incarnations, but carry them with us: Pythagorean recollection is not, as in the case of its Platonic counterpart, of a transcendental source, but merely of a series of receding previous existences, and, significantly, Pythagoras can trace his own lives back to the Trojan War. We are thus trapped in a world in which we are bound by memory to the past at the same time as we are swept along by the current of time. And as Pythagoras cries,

> tempus edax rerum, tuque, invidiosa vetustas,
> omnia destruitis vitiataque dentibus aevi
> paulatim lenta consumitis omnia morte!

("O Time, thou great devourer, and thou, envious Age, together you destroy all things; and, slowly gnawing with your teeth, you finally consume all things in lingering death!" 15.234–36)

Time is the greatest cannibal of all, who envies and so preys upon all human achievements: it is hardly surprising that there is an ancient confusion between *Chronos*, Time, and the *Kronos*, Saturn, who devours his children.

Metamorphosis becomes a continual creation and consumption of identity that prevents any return to and consummation with a transcendent source. The world described by Pythagoras epitomizes that of Ovid's poem, in which one story swallows and turns into another. There is no safe territory and no "sense of an ending"; even annihilation is never complete when there is some remnant of the past like the "pius Aeneas" to carry on tradition. While continuity may have the advantage of keeping things going, it may also become a curse, assimilating the future to the determined pattern of the past. Like metaphor, metamorphosis is translation (15.258); but in Ovid's world there is ultimately nothing beyond the process of metamorphosis, no literal or proper sense that is the origin and goal of meaning. All life is a translation of something else, "Haec tamen ex aliis generis primordia ducunt" ("Now all these things get their life's beginning from some other creature," 15.391), creating a chain of infinitely regressive reference that never can arrive at an original source.

Pythagoras's one exception to this bleak rule appears to be the phoenix, which is its own originator and source. But the son who literally is his own father, thus achieving what Freud will claim all men desire, appears less as a figure for liberating triumph, the assertion of originality, than of bondage in the most narrow and redundantly unoriginal of circles. Like the model Aeneas, the son bears the burden of the past on his back, "fertque pius cunasque suas patriumque sepulchrum" ("he piously bears his own cradle and his father's tomb," 15.405). In this case, however, there is no difference between father and son at all; furthermore, the son who is his father's tomb recalls Tereus, the father who becomes his son's tomb by literally consuming him.

Although the phoenix appears as an ideal, it is one that conceals more sinister possibilities. Moreover, the relation between father and son epitomized by the phoenix involves a belief in the total identification of past and present, which was a central part of Augustan ideology. Augustus's central claim, which served also to disguise the nature of his despotic rule, was that he was returning Rome to its original and ideal republican state through the revival also of lost values and traditions.[68] The desire to identify past and present, and the assumption that they can be identified, is expressed also in contemporary laws concerning succession and inheritance. According to Roman law, centering around the authority of the *paterfamilias*, the son was considered to be his father, and thus able to take his place and property; he was "heres suus," "heres sui ipsius" ("his own heir"), and "Between his father and him there is neither donation, nor legacy, nor change of property. There is simply a continuation—*morte parentis continuatur dominium.*"[69] At the end of the *Satyricon*, Petronius grotesquely literalizes the legal fiction: the dying benefactor asks his heirs to eat his dead body and so more completely absorb his substance and become him.[70]

For Ovid as well, the rigid identity between past and present disguised when idealized in the figure of the phoenix becomes connected with cannibalism. As souls pass from body to body, complicating the kinship system of his mythic universe, all flesh-eating is potentially the consumption of our ancestors, and so Pythagoras pleads:

> corpora, quae possint animas habuisse parentum
> aut fratrum aut aliquo iunctorum foedere nobis
> aut hominum certe, tuta esse et honesta sinamus
> neve Thyesteis cumulemus viscera mensis!

> ("We should permit bodies which may possibly have sheltered the souls of our parents or brothers or those joined to us by some other bond, or of men at least, to be uninjured and respected, and not load our stomachs as with a Thystean banquet!" 459–62)

The only way to make sure that one is not eating a relative is to take his advice, "ora vacent epulis alimentaque mitia carpant!" ("Make not their flesh your food, but seek a more harmless nourishment!" 15.478).

This is Pythagoras's last word, but the reader who has made it through the previous fourteen books may want to extend the warning even further. In Book 9 the nymph Dryope plucks a flower that turns out to be the metamorphosed form of another nymph. For this unconscious crime, Dryope is also turned into a tree, and, as she changes, she sends a warning to her son, urging him to be careful, "stagna tamen timeat, nec carpat ab arbore flores, / et fructices omnes corpus putet esse dearum" ("Still let him fear the pool, pluck no blossoms from the trees, and think all flowers are goddesses in disguise!" 9.380–81). The Homeric custom of treating guests well as they might be gods in disguise now has to be taken even further: not only may a goddess be masked as a beggar, but a close relative may be hidden inside a leaf. To make things more difficult, there is no logical method to metamorphosis that would allow us to decode natural forms and discover what lies inside them. The incarnation of figures in others leads to a simultaneous opposition and identification of inside and outside. Form and content are both completely different and yet too closely related to be told apart, so that all movement, even interpretation itself, becomes an act of aggression. Every action is significant and no one is innocent, for nature itself is not safe but inhabited, full of significance which is yet totally concealed by the natural form that contains it. As long as we cannot tell what or who is inside any part of nature, nothing is safe to eat, as even eating a carrot may turn out to be cannibalism. That a vegetable might be one's father is a distressing thought that could spoil anyone's appetite, but if one finally cannot eat anything in the object world, one may be reduced to the self-cannibalism of Erysichthon. Unfortunately, one is only completely safe if one doesn't eat anything at all.[71]

According to Pythagoras, cities, like everything else, move in cycles, growing out of ones that have come before. He notes the passing of Troy, Sparta, Thebes, and Athens, and sees Rome on the horizon, fulfilling the old prophecy that in it Troy would be reborn. As Aesculapius slides into Rome and the book slides into the present, we still seem to be looking backward, to the old city which the new one recreates. Ovid appears, however, to be claiming that the second city is a superior version of the first. Though Caesar is deified, Augustus is said to surpass his father as, Ovid insists, all men do. As examples he lists Agamemnon's superiority to Atreus, Theseus's to Aegeus, Achilles' to Peleus, and "denique, ut exemplis ipsos aequantibus utar, / sic et Saturnus minor est Iove" ("finally, to quote an instance worthy of them both, is Saturn less than Jove," 15.857–58). This last example, however, seems completely unexpected. From the very beginning of the poem Saturn has been associated with the Golden Age and Jove with an inferior one. The son's rule of law and order is constantly threatened by the nature of the world, and his insecurity about his power and fear that he in turn may be surpassed by his own child was illustrated in his rejection of Thetis, who, it was prophesied, would bear a son greater than his father (Book 11.224–28). This is power consolidated by abortion, by a cutting off of inheritance. The possibility of genuine progress and the success of Augustus's reign as the climax and fulfillment of Roman history seem highly questionable. Moreover, the presence of Saturn as well as Atreus suggests that if we should be careful lest we eat our fathers, we should also watch out in case they try to eat us. In a world in which the past is never completely forgotten, it may become a kind of vampire preying on the present, possessing it and turning it into an imitation of itself.

According to Northrop Frye, metamorphosis is a perfect symbol for the tenacious power of the past, representing, "the chain of authority and subordination that has persisted all through history. In its most concentrated form it is a closed circle, all efforts to break with it, like revolutions, ending in real revolution, that is, the wheel turning again."[72] This is the closed circle of exact repetition represented by the phoenix, the son who is his own father. Metamorphosis would then be an apt image for the Augustan Rome celebrated by Virgil, with its intense veneration of the past, its emphasis on *pietas, auctoritas*, and nostalgia for a return of the good old days.[73] But, as Brooks Otis says, "Virgil stood for a whole way of life that Ovid could not accept. Ovid wanted no revival of Roman heroism and morality, no return to the good old days of rustic virtue and morality."[74] In defiance of the Augustan nostalgia for *rusticitas*, Ovid is completely *cultus*, a forerunner of Oscar Wilde who, in the *Artis amatoriae*, represents life as imitating art. Tradition, pietas, and auctoritas depend upon a belief in a genuine, original way of life that can be perpetuated or recaptured. For Ovid, such a belief is an illusion, a trap of Augustan ideology, and a sinister form of the ideal that "ars est celare artem," which he celebrates in his early works but suspects in his later. Ovid deviates from the contemporary ideal by writing poetry not of originality, but of unoriginality, which draws attention to how it differs from and feeds on other sources. He writes poetry that is best represented by the macabre story of Philomela, poetry that "begins" with the transgression of already established boundary lines and laws.

Transgression may be an accessible model for creation for a poet who was sent into exile. It may be telling that no one knows what law Ovid broke that made his expulsion from the Augustan body politic seem necessary. Perhaps, like Actaeon, he simply went too far, stepping across a boundary line of propriety that was both absolute and unforeseeable. The paradox he sees is that the lines, termini, are drawn only through violation. So metamorphosis is both the epitome of tradition and the dissolution of tradition, as Ovid uses it at the end to subvert all authority. Augustan Rome, with all its myths of its unique authority and origin, becomes simply another example of the metamorphoses that occur in a world without beginning or end.[75] In its representation of the world, Ovid's text swerves from that of Virgil into that of Lucretius, whose *De rerum naturam* is one of the many other models Ovid's poem subsumes. Ovid extends Lucretius's claims that nothing comes from nothing, and that nothing dies, but only becomes something different, and makes his materialism even more material, by turning the endless stream of atoms into the figures who change as they meet one another. For Lucretius, the fall and *clinamen* of atoms preserves the continuity of the universe, which any difference or gap could totally destroy. Ovid's response to Lucretius complements his commentary on Virgilian tradition. He creates a world without beginning or end, which is full of material bodies—so full, in fact, that one cannot move without stumbling over one.

Defined by laws they already transgress, Ovid's relations with both past and future are themselves cannibalistic. Having subsumed past myths and works, his text takes in the present and looks toward the introjection of the future as well, as the author imagines his own survival. When he dies, like Hercules "parte tamen meliore mei super alta perennis / astar ferar, nomenque erit indelebile nostrum" ("Still in my better part I shall be borne immortal far beyond the lofty stars and I shall have an undying name," 15.875–76). His immortal part is not his soul but his "nomen," name, which can live on like the spirits that pass from body to body. He concludes,

quaque patet domitis Romana potentia terris,
ore legar populi, perque omnia saecula fama,
siquid habent veri vatum praesagia, vivam.

("Whatever Rome's power extends over the conquered world, I shall have mention on men's lips, and, if the prophecies of bards have any truth, through all the ages I shall live in fame." 15.877–79)

This is Ovid's last word, "I will live," and it is totally unoriginal, echoing Ennius and Horace *Odes* 3.30.[76] Ovid sees that, like all things, his self-perpetuation is guaranteed by metamorphosis and, in his case, the *Metamorphoses*. He will live in words, though they are not his property alone but are taken through the transgression of the termini of others; for finally the poet himself exists only in his poem, which has opened up to include its own author. His physical body disappears, subsumed by and turned into the textual body of his work.

This conclusion could be read, too, as a form of sublimation and transcendence, in which poetry is freed from its material base and origin in the individual author.[77] But what the poem suggests is that it is impossible to polarize these opposites because they too are finally identified in a world where all differences collapse. Ovid tells a dark, even gothic, version of what Barthes will call "The Death of the Author":[78] the loss of an originating principle, transcendental source, or goal beyond the poem, as even the author and the authority of Rome, upon which Ovid's immortality is made to depend, are subsumed. For Ovid, differences are necessary to uphold textual and social law and order, but differences defined as absolute termini always break down in a world where plenitude makes cannibalism inevitable. Within the fable of identity described by the transcendental term *metamorphosis* there can be finally no possibility for individual identity, not even that of the author himself, who is absorbed into a world of total incorporation in which all principles of differentiation, including those which produce meaning itself, are subsumed, and ultimately consumed.

CHAPTER II

The Word and Flesh

> The words of a wise man's mouth are gracious; but the lips of a
> fool will swallow up himself.
>
> —Ecclesiastes 10:12

UNDERNEATH the mythic unity and harmony of the classical world, there lies in fact an already uneasy relation between inside and outside that is potentially not only antithetical but also cannibalistic. For the Augustan Ovid, a world of total immanence is already extremely suspicious; for Christian writers (whose crucial event, that of the incarnation, significantly occurred also at the time of Augustus), it is even more so. Christianity, a model logocentric system, depends on the existence of a transcendental deity outside the world who guarantees meaning. One of its central problems is getting that deity inside the world without identifying Him totally with it. The Christian image for the reconciliation of opposites—God / man, host / guest, father / son—is the incarnation, which for Augustine and Dante provides a central paradigm for the union of spirit and flesh that informs their methods of representation and interpretation. In different ways, both writers are on quests whose success depends upon establishing a proper relation between inside and outside, especially when seen in terms of spiritual and bodily appetites.

AUGUSTINE

> All the labour of man is for his mouth, and yet the appetite is not
> filled.
>
> —Ecclesiastes 6:7

Like the *Odyssey*, Augustine's *Confessions* is a quest based on an analogy with appetite. It tells the story of a return home from a period of exile, and of a loss of unity and its recovery that involves a re-membering of the self through both the process of conversion and the narrative itself. Conversion is the Christian alternative to metamorphosis, in which change is defined not as endless cycles but as a definitive break.[1] In *The Varieties of Religious Experience*, William James describes conversion as a heightened form of a normal process of maturation undergone by every individual. While the self begins as divided, it develops toward greater self-unity through self-control and mastery: "the normal evolution of character chiefly consists in the straightening out and unifying of the inner self. The higher and the lower feelings, the useful and the erring impulses, begin by being a comparative chaos within us—they must end by forming a stable system of functions in right subordination."[2] James sees Augustine's experience as a classic example of the resolution of self-division.[3] Conversion itself is simply a more radical form of this "normal" process, in which "a self hitherto divided, and consciously wrong inferior and unhappy, becomes unified and consciously right superior and happy, in consequence of its firmer hold upon religious realities."[4] For James, the absolute distinction between the two states and the preferability of the latter is self-evident, as is the equation of "divided," "wrong," "inferior," and "unhappy," on the one hand, and "unified," "right," "superior," and "happy," on the other.[5]

For Augustine himself division is a sign of sin, the turning away from the indivisible God. His conversion involves a reunion both with himself and with God, through which he discovers his true identity. However, the actual effect of his conversion is not to resolve oppositions but to reinforce them at a higher level.[6] If the body of Socrates gives us a useful spatial model for an individual whose unity is based upon a fundamental self-contradiction, the conversion narrative of Augustine gives us a crucial temporal paradigm for the formation of such a self.[7] At the point of conversion, the body of the text itself breaks into two parts, as the story of Augustine's life turns into a meditation upon God. The final chapters are concerned with the construction of divisions, as God's creation of the world, which begins with the separation of opposites, becomes not only the subject but also the model for the creation of the entire text and of Augustine the author himself.

According to John Freccero, "the conversion marks the transformation of autobiography into biblical allegory."[8] Conversion is a form of sublimation, as it involves turning one thing viewed as inferior into its superior form. Like sublimation, too, it is ambiguous because it implies both radical change and continuity, as the first form inheres in the second. Kenneth Burke and Geoffrey Galt Harpham have discussed the way in which the principle of conversion operates in the text in relation to certain crucial concepts and images. Burke notes how the word *pondus*, meaning weight or heaviness, is gradually redefined to mean lightness, as Augustine learns that he gravitates not toward the flesh, but upward toward heaven.[9] For Harpham, a similar conversion of images is at work throughout the text. So, for example, Book 8, which opens with Augustine still held back from God by the bonds of bodily love, ends with the replacement of that love by a similar but higher one that does not impede conversion but helps lead to it. Torn between spiritual and carnal desires, he is beckoned to by the figure of Continence, "nequaquam sterilis, sed fecunda mater filiorum, gaudiorum de marito te, domine" ("not barren but a fruitful mother of children, of joys born of you, O Lord, her Spouse," 8.11; 176). According to Harpham, "The sexuality of *Continentia* has been purged of its weight through figurality, leaving only an essential lightness. Within the allegory, sexuality has been liberated from its literalness, its roots in the world. . . ."[10] A similar crucial sublimation or conversion occurs also in regard to food and words, especially speech, as it is through what and how he eats and speaks that he transforms himself, Augustine the object of the text, into his new identity, Augustine the subject and author.

Images of eating play a central role in Augustine's narrative, and food is his most common image for both the material objects that tempt man and for God himself. As the tradition from Genesis suggests, food is the quintessential temptation that offers instant gratification and easy physical satisfaction as a substitute for more difficult spiritual fulfillment.[11] For Augustine it becomes a symbol for all earthly substances that prevent man from reaching God. Chastising himself for greed, Augustine fears that he will be like Esau, the son who sold his inheritance for food, or like the Israelites in the desert, who longed to return to the relative comforts of exile and foreign food rather than endure the suspense of endless wandering in a less certain kind of exile. In Homer, to eat the food of others is to become one with them, and so to be alienated from one's true home and identity; so, too, according to Augustine, the Israelites lost their identity with God when they

> inmutatam gloriam incorruptionis tuae in idola et varia simulacra, in similitudinem imaginis corruptibilis hominis et volucrum et quadrupedum et serpentium, videlicet Aegyptium cibum, quo Esau perdidit primogenita sua.

> ("*had exchanged the glory of the imperishable God* for idols and all kinds of make-believe, *for representations of perishable man, and of bird and beast and reptile,* in fact, for that Egyptian food for which Esau lost his birthright." 7.9; 146)

Improper eating is a form of idolatry that prevents the end to exile that is achieved through the return to one's proper home. It is thus analogous to improper reading which, in *De doctrina christiana* 3, where Augustine formulates his theory of interpretation, is described as idolatrous when it rests in the visible sign, the letter, as a source of immediate gratification. The unhealthy eater is in fact also an unhealthy reader who mistakes matter for spirit, the sign for the signified. For Augustine, spiritual desire is analogous to bodily hunger yet also threatened by it. Odysseus's quest was a form of appetite that tried to detach itself from its bodily origin; for Augustine, too, literal eating provides a model for his quest that may also become a dangerous substitute for it.

As one cannot refuse food entirely, what becomes important is the way one eats; Augustine quotes Paul "omnia munda mundis" ("unto the pure all things *are* pure," Titus 1 : 15, King James Version), and recognizes, "non ego inmunditiam obsonii timeo, sed inmunditiam cupiditatis" ("It is the uncleanness of gluttony that I fear, not unclean meat," 10.31; 237). The rhythm of hunger and satiation is for Augustine an image of the pattern of loss and return. Meditating on the path to his conversion, he wonders why man enjoys the process of loss and restoration, "Quid ergo agitur in anima, cum amplius delectatur inventis aut redditis rebus, quas diligit, quam si eas semper habuisset?" ("What is it, then, that makes the soul rejoice more over things that it finds or regains than it would if it had always had them?" 8.3; 161). The answer is found by means of an analogy with appetite, "edendi et bibendi voluptas nulla est, nisi praecedat esuriendi et sitiendi molestia" ("There is no pleasure in eating and drinking, unless it is preceded by the discomfort of hunger and thirst," 162). Sexual pleasure is also increased through the deferral of gratification, and in *De doctrina* 2.6 Augustine will extend this pattern in order to account for the pleasure found in the process of interpreting symbols that whet the readers' appetites by not offering immediate satisfaction. In daily life the cycle of fall and redemption is enacted, especially in the constant creation and satisfaction of hunger. But eating is also the model for endless temptation. Man has to eat to stay alive, "reficimus enim cotidianas ruinas corporis edendo et bibendo, priusquam escas et ventrem destruas, cum occideris indigentiam satietate mirifica, et corruptibile hoc indueris incorruptione sempiterna" ("For we repair the daily wastage of our bodies by eating and drinking, until the time comes when you *will bring both food and our animal nature to an end*," 10.31; 234). In the daily satisfaction of desire lurks a danger: "sed dum ad quietem satietatis ex indigentiae molestia transeo, in ipso transitu mihi insidiatur laqueus concupiscentiae" ("But the snare of concupiscence awaits me in the very process of passing from the discomfort of hunger to the contentment which comes when it is satisfied," 235), as the pleasure found in eating exceeds necessity. Food is a temptation that must be constantly encountered, even after conversion:

> In his ergo temptationibus positus, certo cotidie adversus concupiscentiam manducandi et bibendi: non enim est quod semel praecidere et ulterius non attingere decernam, sicut de concubitu potui. itaque freni gutturis temperata relaxatione et constrictione tenendi sunt.

> ("In the midst of these temptations I struggle daily against greed for food and drink. This is not an evil which I can decide once and for all to repudiate and never to embrace again, as I was able to do in the case of fornication. I must therefore hold back my appetite with neither too firm nor too slack a rein," 237)

Eating involves the constant mastery of Augustine's own body, as self-control is one of the rewards, and burdens, of conversion.

Significantly, the obstacles that impeded Augustine's conversion are associated with improper eating, related also to an inability to imagine a temperate relationship between body and spirit. Augustine's primary difficulty with the Christian doctrine lay in his inability to conceive of a Word that could be made flesh, a God who was in any way substantial. At first he believed that an incarnate deity would be degraded and contaminated by the flesh that contained it (cf. 5.11 and 7.19). His distaste for a physical God led to his involvement with the Manichees, whose dualism offered him one solution to his problem. By repudiating the flesh, the elect believed that both God and their own inner beings remained pure and uncontaminated by sin or guilt.[12] By believing in a totally dualistic world, the Manichee elect were able to identify themselves solely with the spirit and the good and deny all connection with matter and evil.

In practice, however, the Manichean opposition of good (inside) spirit versus bad (outside) flesh led to a somewhat lurid fascination with material things. This may be the fate of all dualisms that attempt to transcend their material base; Claude Rawson notes the combination of disgust and fascination with the lower bodily functions, such as eating and excretion, which seems to accompany attempts to disassociate the spirit from the flesh.[13] Despite their pretensions to refinement, the Manichees believed in a grotesquely literal form of the sublimation or transubstantiation of matter. As a member of their group, Augustine came to believe

> ficum plorare, cum decerpitur, et matrem eius arborem lacrimis lacteis. quam tamen ficum si comedisset aliquis sanctus, alieno sane, non suo scelere decerptam, misceret visceribus, et anhelaret de illa angelos, immo vero particulas dei, gemendo in oratione atque ructando: quae particulae summi et veri dei ligatae fuissent in illo pomo, nisi electi sancti dente ac ventre solverentur.

> ("that a fig wept when it was plucked, and the tree which bore it shed tears of mother's milk. But if some sanctified member of the sect were to eat the fig—someone else, of course, would have committed the sin of plucking it—he would digest it and breathe it out again in the form of angels or even as particles of God, retching them up as he groaned in prayer." 3.10; 67)

Physical eating and excretion become completely identified with sublimation and transubstantiation. The opposition of body and spirit that the sect affirmed in fact is broken down in the strong stomachs of the elect, which can convert completely the base matter they take in.

After a while, Augustine decided that this dualism led only to materialism through confusion of different appetites, the desire for food and the desire for God. In reaction against the Manichees, whose doctrines he describes finally as food which "nec nutriebar eis, sed exhauriebar magis" ("did not nourish me, but starved me all the more," 3.6; 61), he turned to the platonic ideal of a completely spiritual and transcendent deity. In retrospect, however, he describes this interlude as the period of most extreme alienation from God. It is at this point, too, that the God he was attempting to imagine as pure spirit, calls out and identifies Himself as the most basic type for matter—food:

> et inveni longe me esse a te in regione dissimilitudinis, tamquam audirem vocem tuam de excelso: "cibus sum grandium: cresce et manducabis me. nec tu me in te mutabis sicut cibum carnis tuae, ed tu mutaberis in me."

> ("It was as though I were in a land where all is different from your own and I heard your voice calling from on high, saying 'I am the food of full-grown men. Grow and you shall feed on me. But you shall not change me into your own substance, as you do with the food of your body. Instead you shall be changed into me.'" 7.10; 147)

God is imagined as a food different from those Augustine has already encountered: the food of grown men, not infants, who eats as He is eaten. As I suggested earlier, both to eat and to be eaten simultaneously in communion provides a possible model for the transcendence of the opposition between guest and host, which Augustine will discover also in the combination of Christ's role in the incarnation. Christ is not only God and man, spirit and flesh, but also, "pro nobis tibi victor et victima, et ideo victor, quia victima, pro nobis tibi sacerdos et sacrificium, et ideo sacerdos, quia sacrificium" ("was for us both Victor and Victim in your sight, and it was because he was the Victim that he was also the Victor. In your sight he was for us both Priest and Sacrifice, and it was because he was the Sacrifice that he was also the Priest," 10.43; 251). By incorporating antithetical terms, Christ appears to become the one transcendental substance that can feed man; in him spirit and flesh meet, when: "verbum caro factum est, ut infantiae nostrae lactesceret sapientia tua, per quam creasti omnia" ("*the Word was made flesh* so that your Wisdom, by which you created all things, might be milk to suckle us in infancy," 7.18; 152).

However, while God and Christ appear as food that reconciles opposites, they are also associated with the separation of spiritual and bodily appetites. The climax of Augustine's protracted and oddly indefinite conversion occurs when he reads Romans 13 : 13:

> non in comissationibus et ebrietatibus, non in cubilibus et inpudicitiis, non in contentione et aemulatione, sed induite dominum Iesum Christum, et carnis providentiam ne feceritis in concupiscentiis.

("Not in reveling and drunkenness, not in lust and wantonness, not in quarrels and rivalries. Rather, arm yourself with the Lord Jesus Christ; spend no more thought on nature and nature's appetites." 8.12; 178)

Christ and the belly are directly opposed: "Pascuntur autem his escis qui laetantur eis, nec illi laetantur eis, quorum deus venter" ("This food nourishes only those who take joy in it, and there is no joy in it for those whose *own hungry bellies are the god they worship*," 13.26; 338). Augustine's new identity is based on a belief in the necessity of differentiating between spiritual and bodily appetites and of establishing James's "right subordination" of faculties through the control of the second by the first. The superiority of the first is demonstrated by the fact that whereas the body is divisible the soul is unified (10.7); moreover, while bodily hunger is temporal and therefore has no end in time, its spiritual counterpart is defined by the promise of ultimate and complete satisfaction in eternity:

> Cum enim cibo et potu id appetant homines, ut non esuriant, neque sitiant, hoc ueracitur non praestat nisi iste cibus et potu, qui eos a quibus sumitur, immortales et incorruptibiles facit, id est, societas ipsa sanctorum, ubi pax erit et unitas plena atque perfecta.

> ("For surely men seek food and drink that they may not hunger and thirst; this truly will not happen unless this food and drink which they take in makes them immortal and incorruptible, which is to be found only in the community of the saints, where there will be peace and unity that is full and perfect.")[14]

This separation of spiritual and bodily appetites involves, furthermore, a sublimation of food into words. Augustine's conversion is precipitated by the reading of a text, in which, however, it appears that the voice of God is speaking directly to him as it did in the platonic wilderness. As has been noted often, conversion is contagious, an act of imitation of others whose stories are related or read.[15] Conversion depends upon words, as Augustine's orality, his obsession with food, is bound up with another kind of orality: his obsession with language.[16] The self-accused glutton began his career as a rhetorician who taught the art of speaking. Rhetoric was the career chosen for him by his worldly father, who, "non satageret . . . qualis crescerem tibi aut quam castus essem, dummodo essem disertus vel desertus potuis a cultura tua, deus, qui es unus verus et bonus dominus agri tui, cordis mei" ("took no trouble at all to see how I was growing in your sight or whether I was chaste or not. He cared only that I should have a fertile tongue, leaving my heart to bear none of your fruits, my God, though you are the only Master, true and good, of its husbandry," 2.3; 45). The earthly father who urges the son toward what in retrospect will appear as the wrong kind of orality and fertility (as, in the next paragraph, also Patricius encourages his son's awakening sexuality) will be replaced by a heavenly father associated, like Continence, with a different form of fruitfulness.[17] The tongue itself as an instrument of speech will become an instrument of fertilization and feeding when used properly.

The transition from the earthly to the divine father is mediated through the figure of Augustine's spiritual father, Ambrose, whose "eloquia strenue ministrabant adipem frumenti tui, et laetitiam olei, et sobriam vini ebrietatem, populo tuo" ("gifted tongue never tired of dispensing the richness of your corn, the joy of your soil, and the sober intoxication of your wine," 5.13; 107). Ambrose's speech is itself a kind of spiritual food that he dispenses to his listeners. But one of the things that most interests Augustine about Ambrose is his mysterious and inexplicable habit of reading silently so that he becomes totally absorbed in private communication with God (6.3). Ambrose provides Augustine with a model that suggests the superiority of privacy and individuality over community, and reading over speech. Moreover, Ambrose's role in Augustine's lengthy conversion is to teach him to read silently and privately in another sense—to read figuratively. Before Ambrose, Augustine had been trapped in his own literality and his material imagining of God and the scriptures; Ambrose freed him from this, through his frequent quotation of 2 Corinthians 3 : 6: "the letter killeth, but the spirit giveth life" (6.4). Ambrose operates as a principle of division who leads into a further conversion in which speech and rhetoric, identified with the letter, will be replaced by writing, seen as more closely tied to the spirit.[18] Renouncing his old profession as purely materialistic and essentially mercenary, and his old self as a "venditorem verborum" ("vendor of words," 9.5; 189), Augustine retires, thanking the God who "eruisti linguam meam," ("rescued my tongue," 9.4; 185) from the improper fertility and orality associated not only with lust and gluttony but also speech, and begins writing.

Augustine's conversion in fact is an antithetical version of Ovid's story of Philomela, as it too tells the replacement of speech by writing. In Augustine's, the tongue, grotesquely dismembered in Ovid, is recreated as a symbol of union, and especially of the unity of the converted individual reborn as an autonomous whole. But it also creates divisions, and so operates as a phallus that is the very source of separation even as it appears to bring oppositions together through the process of conversion. Augustine's replacement of speech, associated with publicity, literality, and the body, by writing, privileged as more private, figurative, and therefore spiritual, also inverts the traditional Western view of the relationship, discussed by Derrida.[19] This conversion is never complete, however, and the relation between the two becomes in fact more complicated. The final conversion in the garden is the product of both a voice and a text, as it is through hearing a voice that Augustine is directed to go and read. In the platonic wilderness God calls out to him, and in the final chapters God and the Bible are continually represented as speaking directly to him. The converted man who is a writer is also a preacher, who now uses his orality to serve God. The last book of *De doctrina* is therefore a treatise on rhetoric, in which Augustine converts spoken words to the Word, by treating them not as the mere verbal equivalents of property, and thus as objects that can be sold and consumed, but as signs which point beyond their own apparent boundary lines. The ex-rhetorician is still able to use speech, but now it is a model for things other than itself, as the spoken word is kept in its place by an emphasis upon its referentiality. Eternity is the speech of God, in which all words occur simultaneously (*Confessions* 11.7; 259), while time is imagined as words spread out in a sentence (4.10; 80). The incarnation itself can be imagined as the verbal expression of thought which "apud se manens integra, formam uocis qua se insinuet auribus, sine aliqua labe suae mutationis adsumit" ("remains entire in itself and assumes the form of words by means of which it may reach the ear without suffering any deterioration in itself," *De doctrina* 1.13).[20] The spoken word (which at the same time appears here in print) provides a model for the incarnation of the Word, in which spirit, or meaning, is not degraded by the flesh, or form. Speech suggests a simultaneous dismembering and recollection, for even as meaning is broken down to be communicated it remains essentially whole.

The relation between the spoken and the written word is connected to that between the two senses of hearing and seeing. For Augustine, as for Homer, seeing is the most essential of the senses, as the principle means through which knowledge is acquired. However, this makes it also potentially the most dangerous; for seeing, like eating, is a continual process. Sights are always before him: "tangunt me vigilantem totis diebus, nec requies ab eis datur mihi, sicut datur a vocibus canoris, aliquando ab omnibus, in silentio" ("All day and every day, while I am awake, they are there before my eyes. They allow me no respite such as I am granted in moments of silence when there is no singing and sometimes no sound at all to be heard," 10.34; 239). Through the eyes he is constantly being sensually bombarded and tempted. Moreover, as sight is the chief means of knowledge, curiosity, the desire to know too much, becomes a kind of refined visual error and is therefore called "concupiscentia oculorum" ("*gratification of the eye*," 10.35; 241). Both sight and the desire to know are, like eating, forms of incorporation that are difficult to control but must be directed toward a proper object, the God of whom, according to 1 Corinthians 13:12, man will have direct vision in eternity. For Augustine, anticipating Dante in *Paradiso* 33, such vision itself is modeled on the act of reading, seen as a more refined and spiritual form of sight, as the angels,

> vident enim faciem tuam semper, et ibi legunt sine syllabis temporum, quid velit aeterna voluntas tua. . . . semper legunt et numquam praeterit quod legunt. . . . non clauditur codex eorum nec plicatur liber eorum, quia tu ipse illis hoc es et es in aeternum.

> ("ever gaze upon your face and there, without the aid of syllables inscribed in time, they read what your eternal will decrees. . . . They read it without cease and what they read never passes away. . . . The book they read shall not be closed. For them the scroll shall not be furled. For you yourself are their book and you for ever are." 13.15; 322–23)

According to Augustine, however, what the human mind perversely wants is to see without being seen:

> etiam sic caecus et languidus, turpis atque indecens latere vult, se autem ut lateat aliquid non vult. contra illi redditur, ut ipse non lateat veritatem, ipsum autem veritas lateat.

> ("In its blind inertia, in its abject shame, it [the mind] loves to lie concealed, yet it wishes that nothing should be concealed from it. Its reward is just the opposite of its desire, for it cannot conceal itself from the truth, but truth remains hidden from it." 10.23; 230)

As it is only God who can see everything without being seen (5.2), such a desire is another example of man's perverse imitation of God, and, in particular, his mimicking of divine autonomy. While a reciprocal seeing and knowing is prophesied in 1 Corinthians 13:12—where Paul claims that "now we see through a glass, darkly; but then face to face: now I know in part; but then shall I know even as also I am known"—in time, man is an object of vision and not a subject, despite his desire to know and take things in without in turn being known, taken in, and contained by anything outside himself.

If sight is the means by which we shall know God in eternity, hearing, however, is a means of communication more appropriate to a fallen world. It is necessary for God to speak to man out loud: "quibus omnibus vocibus corporaliter enuntiandis causa est abyssus saeculi et caecitas carnis, qua cogitata non possunt videri, ut opus sit instrepere in auribus" ("If the words he utters have to be spoken aloud so that the ear can hear, this is because the world is a deep sea and the flesh is blind: men cannot see thoughts and therefore the truth must be dinned in their ears," (13.23; 334). The blindness of men, their lack of spiritual or inner vision, necessitates a fall into an inferior because more material means of communication through words. Speech itself is a sign of our fallen nature. In Augustine's retracing of his own development he notes the different stages of maturation which in fact recapitulate his conversion of food into spoken and then written words. The infant begins sucking at the mother's breast, but soon that orality is converted into the making of signs and ultimately into speech, as it struggles to make its more complicated desires known (1.6–7). In turn, speech is succeeded by reading (1.9), although all of these stages persist incrementally and are carried across into the ones that follow (1.19).

Augustine's conversion is described both in terms of such continuity of development and of the discontinuity associated with conversion. As the narrator of his own life, Augustine is both a subject and an object, seer and seen, and through the interjection of later comments upon his narrative, the past and present man are constantly identified and differentiated. At the moments when Augustine stresses the difference between what he knew *then* and what he knows *now*, the two times in fact meet. Past and present are brought together by the faculty of memory, which he discusses at the end of his re-membering of his own career. A re-collection of himself is necessary as a result of the sin that divided him from both God and himself. As he re-members his past self, he discovers God's meaning and narrative: what had appeared to be a random series of events is revealed as having had all along a teleological order. Moreover, with his discovery of God's purpose, Augustine himself becomes a godlike creator or author, imposing order where previously there had been mere chaos. Through both the process of conversion and the narrative, he puts the pieces of himself back together into a coherent whole: "colligens me a dispersione, in qua frustatim discissus sum, dum ab uno te aversus in multa evanui" ("I shall retrieve myself from the havoc of disruption which tore me to pieces when I turned away from you, whom alone I should have sought, and lost myself instead on many a different quest," 2.1; 43).[21]

For Augustine, who even in his period of early intellectual error associated the good with unity and evil with division (4.15), sin itself is a self-contradiction. His conversion involves a meeting face to face not with God but with himself, one that is, however, brought about by God: "retorquebas me ad ipsum, auferens me a dorso meo, ubi me posueram, dum nollem me adtendere; et constituebas me ante faciem meam" ("you were turning me around to look at myself. For I had placed myself behind my own back, refusing to see myself. You were setting me before my own eyes . . . ," 8.7; 169). Seeing his own reflection has for him an effect antithetical to the response of Narcissus, with whom Augustine implicitly contrasts himself when he describes his discovery that the food he sought was already inside of himself:

nec iam bona mea foris erant, nec oculis carneis in isto sole quaerebantur. vo-
lentes enim gaudere forinsecus facile vanescunt, et effunduntur in ea, quae videntur et temporalia sunt, et imagines eorum famelica cogitatione lambiunt.

("The good which I now sought was not outside myself. I did not look for it in
things which are seen with the eye of the flesh by the light of the sun. For those
who try to find joy in things outside themselves easily vanish away into emptiness. They waste themselves on the temporal pleasures of the visible world. Their
minds are starved and they nibble at empty shadows." 9.4; 188)

While he was chasing after external idols and phantoms, God was always
present within him. As in the case of Narcissus, what was thought to be
outside turns out to be inside after all. But for Augustine, as also for Narcissus, self-knowledge involves the awareness of the self-division necessary
for one to be both subject and object of either one's own affections or
narrative. What is inside the self is what is most mysterious and unknow-
able, as the final chapters and the meditation on the mystery of memory
reveal. The blindness of our minds is such that we cannot know ourselves,
let alone anything else.

Augustine's self-confrontation in the garden in fact marks the beginning
of a new emphasis upon divisions. As autobiography is superseded by biblical commentary, Augustine moves toward a meditation on the creation
that begins with the separation of opposites. At the same time, the new
Augustine is ideally identified as a pure narrating subject who is purged of
the old object self that the text tries to distance itself from as it leaves his
life behind. However, investigating this new self, Augustine sees it as essentially divided between a body and a spirit. To define himself as "homo"
means that he is a compound of two parts:

corpus et anima in me mihi praesto sunt, unum exterius et alterum interius. . . .
sed melius quod interius. ei quippe renuntiabant omnes nuntii corporales prae-
sidenti et iudicanti de responsionibus caeli et terrae et omnium.

("I have both body and soul, the one the outer, the other the inner part of
me. . . . But my inner self is the better of the two, for it was to the inner part of
me that my bodily senses brought their messages." 10.6; 212)

The divisible and therefore inferior body is only the instrument of the indivisible mind, which receives its messages and restrains its desires.

The division of mind over matter that defines the self-contradictory human being is reenacted at a number of different levels in the final chapters.
Man is elevated over nature by virtue of his "superior" powers: his ability
to use language, and, even more particularly, to use the symbolism of the
sacraments, which for Augustine are epitomized by the Eucharist (13.23).

Moreover, surveying creation Augustine sees it as a basically hierarchical and dualistic system:

> videmus terrenis animalibus faciem terrar decorari, hominemque ad imaginem et similitudinem tuam, cunctis inrationabilibus animantibus ipsa tua imagine ac similitudine, hoc est rationis et intelligentiae virtute, praeponi; et quemadmodum in eius anima aliud est, quod consulendo dominatur, aliud, quod subditur ut obtemperet, sic viro factam esse etiam corporaliter feminam, quae haberet quidem in mente rationabilis intelligentiae parem naturam, sexu tamen corporis ita masculino sexui subiceretur, quemadmodum subicitur appetitus actionis ad concipiendam de ratione mentis recte agendi sollertiam videmus haec et singula bona et omnia bona valde.

> ("We see the face of the earth graced by the animals that live upon it. And finally we see man, made in your own image and likeness, ruling over all the irrational animals for the very reason that he was made in your image and resembles you, that is, because he has the power of reason and understanding. And just as in man's soul there are two forces, one which is dominant because it deliberates and one which obeys because it is subject to such guidance, in the same way, in the physical sense, woman has been made for man. In her mind and her rational intelligence she has a nature the equal of man's, but in sex she is physically subject to him in the same way as our natural impulses need to be subjected to the reasoning power of the mind, in order that the actions to which they lead may be inspired by the principles of good conduct. All this we see. Taken singly, each thing is good; but collectively they are very good." 13.32; 343–44)

The world is divided so that man rules over nature, reason over irrationality, male over female—a series of analogous hierarchies and systems of "right subordination" whose assumed equivalence serves to reinforce the justice of the control of the second term by the first.

In these chapters, then, division is not ended but rather converted into God's fundamental creative principle by which distinctions and hierarchies are established within an ultimately unified whole that is, however, as a result of these oppositions, "very good." Furthermore, Augustine the narrator himself becomes a model logocentric system whose internal unification of opposites depends upon an external source: God. Augustine's self-control, his imposition of his mind over his own matter that brings order out of chaos, is only possible with the help of God, who enables his self-containment or continence through which, as noted earlier, sexual desire becomes converted into a figure of self-restraint. Human beings in general are also signs that only have reality when they refer to something greater than themselves, a transcendental meaning they need to cling to:

> quoniam abs te sunt, non esse autem, quoniam id quod es non sunt. id enim vere est, quod incommutabiliter manet. mihi autem inhaerere deo bonum est, quia,

si non manebo in illo, nec in me potero. ille autem in se manens innovat omnia; et dominus meus es, quoniam bonorum meorum non eges.

("they have not absolute being in themselves, nor are they entirely without being. They are real in so far as they have their being from you, but unreal in the sense that they are not what you are. For it is only that which remains in being without change that truly is. As for me, *I know no other content but clinging to God*, because unless my being remains in him, it cannot remain in me. But *himself ever unchanged, he makes all things new. I own him as my God; he has no need of ought that is mine*." 7.11; 147)

Burke points out how the conversion of the word *pondus* is related to the discovery of dependency (*pendens*), which begins when "Augustine is speculating on the way he had come to learn language while depending (*pendens*) on the authority of his parents and the nods of adults."[22] Burke also notes the frequency and importance of the word *inhaerere*, to cling, which Augustine uses to express his dependence upon God, but also to describe a child's relation to its mother.[23] The helpless baby feeding at the mother's breast is for Augustine an image of the silent communion with God in eternity; the complete satisfaction of desire is represented in oral terms as the symbiotic union prior to the conversion of eating into speaking, a conversion which, from this perspective, appears as a fall.

Shortly before the death of Augustine's mother, Monica, mother and child have a foretaste of eternity and of the communion that is beyond human speech (9.10). Together they imagine a silencing of the world that would allow God's voice to be heard directly. Monica, who was a Christian, was the most significant influence in Augustine's life, but one from which he had to detach himself before converting to Christianity and establishing a new identity with the paternal deity. As John Freccero notes, the center of the conversion narrative is the separation of the child from its parents, "the separation of a nondifferentiated self from the self that thereby gains an irreducible identity."[24] In the case of Augustine, separation from the mother, the dominant figure in the pre-oedipal oral phase, appears particularly essential for the emergence of the individual.

From the very beginning, the elimination of both parents and their replacement by God has been prepared for, as they are introduced as merely the instruments through which God constructed his plot (1.6). But the death of Patricius, the earthly father who had led Augustine toward the wrong kind of verbal and sexual fertility, is striking in its understatement. In Book 3.4 it is mentioned in passing as something that had already happened: it does not enter and disrupt the narrative sequence but appears as something peripheral to the main story, an event which does not even occupy its own proper place in time. In some way, the structure of the narrative is definitely non-oedipal, which may account for the often noted nebulousness of Augustine's protracted conversion. It is hard to locate a single moment where a radical break occurs. If there is one, however, it is the death of Monica, which appears as the real crisis of the text. With her loss, Augustine experiences a new form of dismemberment: "quoniam itaque deserebar tam magno eius solacio, sauciabatur anima et quasi dilaniabatur vita, quae una facta erat ex mea et illius" ("because I was now bereft of all the comfort I had had from her, my soul was wounded and my life seemed shattered, for her life and mine had been as one," 9.12; 201). It is with Monica's death that the narrative breaks in half, as the story of Augustine's life turns into a more introspective meditation. Monica herself suggests that with Augustine's conversion her life has ended: as her function was to guide him to God, once that is accomplished she is effectively superfluous. A dream she had long before appears to have been fulfilled. In Book 3.11, Monica, worrying about the state of Augustine's soul, dreamt of an angel who told her not to worry, for, "ubi esset illa, ibi esse et me" ("where she was, there also was I"; 68)—a formulation that oddly anticipates Freud's description of the ideal relation between the id and the ego.[25] With the conversion, Augustine and Monica stand in the same place, as is illustrated by their final scene together of silent, symbiotic communion.

In an odd way, therefore, it appears as if the mother has been converted, sublimated into the son. His text, he claims, will fulfill Monica's last wish, which was to be remembered (9.13), and as she disappears physically from the text he gives a brief story of her life. For Freccero, the detachment of the individual from his parents that occurs at the center of the conversion narrative is analogous to the classical oedipal pattern by which the son achieves his identity by replacing his father.[26] But, as Peter Brown notes, in contrast to Pelagius, who defines man as a "son" in order to emphasize the separateness and autonomy necessary for free will (and who found the Confessions unsuccessful in their lack of a radical moment of conversion), Augustine again returns to the image of the baby at the mother's breast as a means of emphasizing man's failure to achieve true autonomy and independence.[27] Furthermore, even as he turns to a masculine deity, God the Father, Augustine clings to maternal images for both God and himself.[28] His identity is achieved not by replacing his father, but by replacing his mother, primarily in the role of food giver and nourisher. As Brown notes, for Augustine his basic role as minister was "to distribute food. The Scriptural idea of 'breaking bread,' of 'feeding the multitude,' by expounding the Bible, an idea already rich with complex associations, is central to Augustine's view of himself as preacher."[29] The replacement is achieved by taking the food his mother gave him as an infant and making it significant, which involves a conversion of an oral self, associated with food and the mother, into an oral self, associated with words and a masculine deity.

The end of Augustine's quest for wholeness is associated with a return to a female, maternal body which is not that of God but of his bride, the city of Jerusalem :

> recordans Hierusalem extento in eam sursum corde, Hierusalem patriam meam, Hierusalem matrem meam, teque super eam regnatorem, inlustratorem, patrem, tutorem, maritum, castas et fortes delicias et solidum gaudium et omnia bona ineffabilia, simul omnia, quia unum summum et verum bonum: et non avertar, donec in eius pacem, matris carissimae, ubi sunt primitiae spiritus mei, unde ista mihi certa sunt, colligas totum quod sum a dispersione et deformitate hac, et conformes atque confirmes in aeternum, deus meus, misericordia mea.
>
> ("I shall remember the heavenly Jerusalem my country, my mother. And I shall remember you her Ruler, you who give her light, you her Father, her Guardian, and her Spouse, you who are her pure, her deep Delight, you who are her constant Joy, you who alone are Goodness itself, the sovereign Good, the true Good. I shall not turn aside until I come to that abode of peace, Jerusalem my beloved mother, where *my spiritual harvest* is laid, the fountainhead of all that I know for certain on this earth. My God, my Mercy, I shall not turn aside until you gather all that I am unto that holy place of peace, rescuing me from this world where I am dismembered and disformed, and giving me new form and new strength for eternity." 12.16; 293)

The lost mother is further sublimated into other spiritual mothers, Jerusalem, Continence, the Church, with whom Augustine hopes to achieve a future symbiosis.[30] However, while it is the body of the mother that is longed for, it is God the father and her husband who Augustine must cling to as He guarantees that desire will be satisfied.

The end of the *Confessions* suggests a tension between these sexual partners, and between all oppositions in its simultaneous creation and complication of distinctions. The final chapters emphasize divisions, but they are also full of images of fertility and fullness that ultimately overpower and blur simple antitheses. For Augustine, the Bible that he is interpreting is itself a model for unification by division, as it is through it that:

> iustificasti impios et distinxisti eos ab iniquis, et solidasti auctoritatem libri tui inter superiores, qui tibi dociles essent, et inferiores, qui eis subderentur, et congregasti societatem infidelium in unam conspirationem.
>
> ("You [God] made just men of sinners and set them apart from the wicked; you established the authority of your Book between those above, who would be obedient to you, and those beneath, who would be made subject to them; and you gathered all the faithless together into one body." 13.34; 345)

God's written word unifies some by the fact that it divides superior men from their inferiors; it defines Christians, and the one body of the Church, against all others who are outside that body. But the role of the Bible in the last books is also more complicated, as after the initial creation through division, creation becomes increasingly described as the proliferation and multiplication of differences, an act of endless, but fruitful, dismemberment.[31] The creation of different life forms in Genesis becomes the model for the genesis of many meanings from a single textual source, which is seen as a higher form of generation that yet is designed to accommodate and please our senses (13.30 and 25).

Perhaps this is a result of the fact that the last books shift our focus from the act of writing to that of reading, from textual production to its consumption. Interpretation itself becomes the converted version of eating, as the text offers us a purely verbal feast. The one meaning of God's word gives birth to a number of equally true interpretations, and Augustine himself claims that as an author he would prefer to invite expansive rather than reductive readings (12.32). Elsewhere, the breaking of the bread in the form of the multiplication of the five loaves in the New Testament is read as an allegory of the scattering of the meaning of the pentateuch into different interpretations that can feed many.[32] The fertility of meaning cannot be contained and ordered by simple oppositions. But these dilations of a single source are ultimately dependent upon the existence of a unified God who is ultimately an unicarnated word, who is: "principium, quia, nisi maneret, cum erraremus, non esset quo rediremus. cum autem redimus ab errore, cognoscendo utique redimus" ("the Beginning, the abiding Principle, for unless he remained when we wandered in error, there would be none to whom we could return and restore ourselves," 11.8; 260). God is what remains outside our vision, knowledge, texts, and it is for this reason that He can be returned to. In this sense, He is the ultimate Father, whose identity, unlike that of the mother, cannot be appropriated except by perverse imitation, but whose detachment is seen as the guarantee of meaning and promise of an ultimate end to alienation.

DANTE

> The fool foldeth his hands together, and eateth his own flesh.
> —Ecclesiastes 4 : 5

In turning food into words or symbols, Augustine used a method similar to the typology of the Church Fathers, by which the material world as well as the letter of the Bible were read as texts that were both historically true and also significant.[33] Typology is the hermeneutic complement of the doctrine of the incarnation, as it insists on the simultaneous truth of literal and figurative meanings. For Dante, it is the allegory of the theologians that he claims to have appropriated for his *Commedia*, which operates on different levels of meaning: "istius operis non est simplex sensus, ymo dici potest polisemos, hoc est plurium sensuum; nam primus sensus est qui habetur per litteram, alius est qui habetur per significata per litteram" ("this work has not a single meaning, in reality it could be called polysemous, that is to say, of many senses; for the first sense is that possessed by the letter, the other that which is signified by the letter").[34] The significance of the letter can be further divided into three levels of meaning—the allegorical, moral, and anagogical—all of which can be called generally allegorical for the reason that "allegoria dicitur ab 'alleon' grece, quod in latinum dicitur 'alienum' sive 'diversum' " ("allegory is said to come from the Greek 'alleon,' which in Latin means alien or dissimilar," 344).[35] Figurative meaning is rooted in the letter and history, but it is still somehow other and alien. Sign and signified are both analogous and contiguous but are not completely identical, as there is always some sense that cannot be assimilated to or subsumed by the letter.

This typological or incarnational model not only informs Dante's poetics but also is behind the structure of the *Inferno*, which, as critics have noticed, is based on an analogy with the human body and its appetites.[36] Robert Durling, for example, sees Dante's descent as a movement down the anatomy from the head (the sins of incontinence), past the breast (the sins of violence), to the belly (the sins of fraud). The progress of the *Inferno* is, then, a prefiguration of the final literal descent of Lucifer's body, during which the figures who represent the various appetites become increasingly substantial. This is a descent into sheer materiality and literalism, the reduction of all appetite into grotesque modes of incorporation in the monstrous body of Lucifer, who is a demonic host, a body politic, a transcendent deity who absorbs the Many into his hairy Oneness by devouring them, and a perverted symposium that subsumes all knowledge. His sin even includes all others, and, as it essentially consisted of trying to contain too much, his punishment is to spend eternity stuffing himself.

This materiality is not, however, apparent in the opening cantos of the poem. As a number of critics have pointed out, the mode of representation of *Inferno* 1 and 2 looks back to Dante's previous unfinished work, the *Convivio*.[37] Like Augustine, Dante flirted with neoplatonism. In *Purgatorio* 30 and 31 the interlude will be described precisely as infidelity that occurred after the death of Beatrice, which involved also an idolatrous desire for visible material satisfaction when Beatrice became hidden. The product of this adultery was a kind of philosophical prototype of the *Commedia*, to which the later work refers but from which it finally detaches itself. The relation between the two texts is significant in terms of the development of Dante's poetics. As Erich Auerbach notes, "Both were planned as universal encyclopedias, as the sum of their creator's lifework,"[38] but it is the difference in their representations of the incorporation of knowledge that is significant and deserves to be looked at briefly.

The *Convivio* is set up as a *Symposium* in which the desire for knowledge is represented as a hunger for the bread of philosophy.[39] However, the structure of the text, its division between text and interpretation, reveals a basic opposition between bodily and spiritual modes of experience at work. The model for this text is what Dante calls the allegory of the poets, as an example of which he gives a neoplatonic reading of Ovid's tale of Orpheus. In such readings, poetic figures are only an outer cloak, "manto," hiding an inner meaning, "una veritade ascosa sotta bella menzogna" ("a truth hidden under a beautiful lie").[40] As the dualistic image of stripping implies, the senses are separated and ultimately opposed; the explications of his own texts become increasingly abstract and elaborate until they subsume the literal level entirely. The appropriate figure for the entire text is the totally disembodied Lady Philosophy, who appears to appropriate attributes she cannot incarnate. Though Dante tries to pass her off as the Word made flesh, she is a more appropriate model for speculation that cannot imagine the concept of the incarnation and for "pan de li angeli" that is finally too insubstantial to be at all satisfying.[41]

The *Commedia* tries to rematerialize the impulse behind the *Convivio*, to incorporate it in the sense of giving it a bodily form in narrative at the same time as it explores the connection between abstract idealism and a materialism that is ultimately identified with cannibalism. In *Convivio* 3.10, Dante had praised a rhetorical device he called "dissimulazione" ("dissimulation") and defined as "quando le parole sono a una persona e la'ntenzione è a un altra" ("when the words refer to one person and the intention to another," 153). As mentioned earlier, the fact that poetic figures conceal meaning has often made them a source of suspicion; words that mean other than they say are potentially duplicitous and deceitful, the concealment of a dreadful truth under a "bella menzogna." So when, in speaking to the envious in *Purgatorio* 14, Dante uses a periphrasis, one of the souls objects:

> Perché nascose
> questi il vocabol di quella riviera
> pur com' om fa de l'orribili cose? (25–27)

("Why did he conceal that river's name, even as one does some horrible thing?")[42]

It is typical of envy (itself a divisive vice) to suspect the worst, but when inner and outer are not only different but opposed, the result is fraud, which not only hides truth but doesn't want it found.

Dante encounters the fraudulent in the belly of Hell, one of the places where, as Robert Durling has noted, he is concerned with problems of representation.[43] In the *Odyssey*, Odysseus presented the belly as the source of lies and fraud; for Dante, drawing also on the antithesis between Christ the Word and the lying belly in Romans 16:17–19 and Philippians 3:18–21, the belly is associated with false and falsifying poetics. As John Freccero has shown at length, the story of Ugolino connects misinterpretation and literalism with cannibalism, as the father who cannot recognize the eucharistic symbols in his son's words takes them literally.[44] His punishment in Hell is to be a parody of communion, containing in himself the roles of both host and guest, victim and victor. In the case of Fra Alberigo, a host who murdered his guests at a banquet, flesh and spirit, outside and inside, have separated so completely that one is on earth and the other in Hell. There is in fact no body here, only a spirit, but a spirit that has been literalized in order to give the appearance of bodily presence. In Hell representation becomes what Freccero has called "infernal irony," or a "poetics of death," in which "dead souls are ironically represented as though they were living bodies."[45] The apparent substantiality of forms is due to the abuse of the relation between the letter and spirit on which typology is based. In Hell, especially in the belly, the spirit is abstracted from the letter and then substituted for it by a kind of infernal reification in which the polarized opposites collapse by consuming each other.

Dante's descent into the belly of Hell appears to involve a fall into the competely literal, as the passage through the *Inferno* calls attention to the increasing reduction of spirits to mere flesh. After the preliminary cantos, the souls become more substantial until they are reduced to the basic type for material substance: food. In Hell words, figures, are made flesh in order to be eaten, beginning in the circle of the gluttons when Dante and Virgil set their feet "sovra lor vanità che par persona" ("upon their emptiness, which seems real bodies," 6.36). The sudden earthiness of these spirits, following the flightiness of the lustful, seems appropriate: these are the souls of those who reduced desire to its most basic material form, hungering not after God, or even others, but mere food. But literal food represents for Dante, as it did for Augustine, all sources of immediate gratification that are chosen instead of the deferred satisfaction promised by God. The glutton Ciacco denounces the Florentines for their "superbia, invidia e avarizia" ("Pride, envy, and avarice," 6.74), and in the course of the *Commedia* all three will be described as related to unnatural forms of hunger, as the sins become (incestuously) related.

Even lust, which Dante represents less as literal than literary concupiscence, a desire to turn life into art by incarnating stories in real life,[46] in retrospect may be read as a form of greed, when Francesca's trembling "bocca" ("mouth," 5.136) becomes grotesquely triplicated in the three "bocche" of Cerberus, which Dante stuffs with mud (6.22). Paolo and Francesca, forever united in "una morte" ("one death," 5.106) in which they whirl with desire with no possibility of peace or satisfaction, set the pattern for an infernal fable of identity, as Hell is represented through a series of less romantic couples, as well as grotesque images of two figures incorporated as one. As in the *Metamorphoses*, union is seen as a form of regression. The desire for identification with another turns into a *coincidentia oppositorum* that creates monstrous hybrids: the centaurs (12), the harpies and suicidal vegetable men (13), Geryon (17), the metamorphosing thieves (24–25); or results in parodies of communion and marriage: Paolo and Francesca (5), Farinata and Cavalcanti (10), Ulysses and Diomedes (26), Master Adam and Sinon (30), the two brothers "D'un corpo usciro" ("issued from one body," 32.58) who in their hatred have returned to an infernal womb, Ugolino and Ruggiero (32–33), and finally the epitome of them all, the three-headed Lucifer whose three mouths are stuffed with the figures of the traitors.

Aside from the grotesque figure of Lucifer devouring his subjects, the most dramatic representation of the process of incorporation is in the cantos of the thieves. Here the world of the *Metamorphoses* is revealed, from Dante's perspective, to be the epitome of infernal identification and exchange.[47] In the *Inferno*, metamorphosis is related to perverted relations to property, both that of the self and of others. In canto 13 it is identified with profligacy and suicide, which both involve the wasting of one's substance. In cantos 24 and 25, it is associated with theft, the illegal appropriation of another's property, which Aquinas had defined as the antithesis of love or charity: "Now charity consists first in the love of God, but second in a love of one's neighbour to which it pertains that we wish and work our neighbour's good. By theft, however, one inflicts damage on one's neighbour in his effects, and if people made a general practice of stealing from each other, human society would perish."[48] For the writer of the encyclopedic *Summa*, a work that tries to contain and order all human knowledge of others and God, the opposite of love for the other (ultimately the love for God) is not merely love of the self (or all love not directed outside the material world) but aggression against the other. Because Aquinas is concerned with the establishing of religious and social coherence in a rather incoherent world by defining the proper relations among its members, such aggression is epitomized by the attack upon property that could cause the breakdown of the boundaries that uphold the body politic.

In *Inferno* 24 and 25 three quite different kinds of metamorphoses are described. The first (24.97–118) is that of Vanni Fucci, which takes for its central figure the destruction and reformation of the phoenix in *Metamorphoses*, Book 15. Within the Christian tradition, the phoenix became allegorized as Christ, whose death and resurrection were also behind the concept of conversion as the death of the old man and birth of the new. Here it is taken for the figure said to be the proudest soul in Hell (25.13–15), whose obduracy leads to an assertion of self-sufficiency that is the parody of conversion.[49] His change is the endless recycling of himself into himself, and the image most appropriate for this process is that of Ovid's phoenix which, as it epitomizes the entire world of the *Metamorphoses*, incorporates it into Dante's text. Dante isn't converting Ovid's figure, he's lifting it whole, as if it were a piece of poetic property that could simply be stolen and inserted into a new text. The figure is not allegorized as Christ but taken as what it was in Ovid: the epitome of redundancy. As Ovid's figure has not been transformed, its very appropriation is redundant, and it dramatizes the futility of exchanges within a literary tradition which merely repeat the same thing over and over.

The second metamorphosis appears in canto 25.49–78, and appropriates the transformation of Salmacis and Hermaphroditus in *Metamorphoses*, Book 4. As in the previous scene, the passage follows its source closely, representing the identification through Eros as a dissolution of identity. Ovid's response to the *Symposium* becomes for Dante a response also to himself, to his version of the *Symposium*, the *Convivio*, in which he upheld the Platonic ideal that:

> Amore, secondo la concordevole sentenza de li savi di lui ragionanti, e secondo quello che per esperienza continuamente vedemo, è che coniunge e unisce l'amante con la persona amata: onde Pittagora dice: "Ne l'amistà si fa uno di più." E però che le cose congiunte communicano naturalmente intra sé le loro qualitadi, in tanto che tavolta è che l'una torna del tutto ne la natura de l'altra, incontra che le passioni de la persona amata entrano ne la persona amante, sì che l'amore de l'una si communica ne l'altra, e così l'odio e lo desiderio e ogni altra passione.

> ("Love, according to the unanimous opinion of the wise who speak of it, and as we see by constant experience, is that which joins and unites the lover with the person loved: so Pythagoras says "friendship makes one of many." And because the united things naturally communicate their properties to each other, so much so that at times the one is turned entirely into the nature of other, it happens that the desires of the beloved enter into the lover, so that the love of one is communicated to the other, and similarily the hatred and desire and all the other passions." 4.1.162)

In the *Inferno*, this ideal of Eros is turned into infernal intercourse between two forms, which produces an ambiguous *tertium quid*, expressed negatively as something that "né l'un né l'altro già parea quel ch'era" ("neither the one nor the other now seemed what it was at first," 25.63) that becomes "non se' né due né uno" ("Neither two nor one," 25.69). As the two figures merge,

> Già eran li due capi un divenuti,
>   quando n'apparver due figure miste
>   in una faccia, ov' eran due perduti.

("Now the two heads had become one, when we saw the two shapes mixed in one face, where both were lost." 25.70–72)

The attempt to represent the unimaginable, "membra che non fuor mai viste" ("members that were never seen before," 75), turns into a description of a confused and grotesque mixing of limbs that produces only an "imagine perverse" ("perverse image," 77), the hermaphrodite. In Hell, as in Ovid, Eros leads not to the transcendence of identities or images but to their breakdown, as language fails as a means of representation.

Dante's reading of the phoenix and hermaphrodite follows Ovid's words closely; even more significantly, it is true to the spirit of Ovidian metamorphosis. The images enable Dante to incorporate his predecessor, but through an act of incorporation itself defined in terms of the sin of the canto—theft. At this point, his relation to Ovid is defined not by charity but by rivalry and aggression, as he steals his poetic property. The relation to his source is complicated even further in the last metamorphosis in 25.79–138, which not only has no obvious Ovidian precedent but in which Dante boasts that he surpasses both Ovid and Lucan:

> ché due nature mai a fronte a fronte
>   non trasmutò sì che'amendue le forme
>   a cambiar lor matera fosser pronte.

("for two natures front to front he never so transmuted that both forms were prompt to exchange their substance." 25.100–102)

Ovid described men who turned into snakes, and Lucan, men transformed when bitten by snakes; in both cases, a form is changed into another that did not previously exist. But Dante claims to have discovered a form of metamorphosis that his predecessors did not imagine, in which two already existing figures switch identities. His originality gives him the right to silence his sources.

The tone of that boast has been disputed, as readers have questioned the degree of self-consciousness in Dante's own lapse into pride.[50] Lawrence Baldassaro has shown how Vanni Fucci's prophecy at the end of canto 24 reverses his previous relation to Dante, as "the persecuted becomes the persecutor and vice versa," a reversal also enacted at a syntactical level.[51] But that reversal could be seen as going even further. At the very moment Dante asserts his own self-sufficiency and originality, he may be having his identity stolen, for he becomes the mirror image of the proud soul. Significantly, the basis of his claim for total originality is his description of two figures whose identities are interchangeable. Their exchange is a kind of sterile mirroring that results in an inversion of positions. In traditional descriptions of the relations among the members of the Trinity, the love of the Father for the Son is seen as a mutual breathing forth or mirroring that produces the Holy Ghost. But the relation here is totally dualistic rather than triadic, and it produces no new third term, not even the ambiguous hermaphrodite. Instead the opposition is simply reversed. Theft, not love, is the motive in this canto, the desire to take another's property, in which exchange involves antagonistic trespass and violation. While Harold Skulsky argues that by the appropriation of sources in these cantos Dante shows "one way of taking another's goods that leaves no one impoverished and many enriched,"[52] the metamorphosis Dante chooses as his original contribution to the theme illustrates the ease with which imitation, the copying or mirroring of a poetic past, can turn into theft, which produces only the futile exchange of rival identities.

Ultimately, these three metamorphoses, themselves presenting an infernal trinity in which the different forms or persons cannot be distinguished, are essentially different versions of a single phenomenon: the dissolution of individual identity that takes place when all souls are seen as members of the body of Lucifer that contains all Hell.[53] Throughout the *Inferno* the difference between the individual body and the social body seems tenuous, and at the belly of Hell the analogy between microcosm and macrocosm, inside and outside, collapses. So suicide is represented as a sin against the body politic, Master Adam's inflation of the economy is internalized, and Bertran de Born's dismemberment stands for the separation of the head of state from its body. The result of this confusion between inside and outside is the antagonistic identification of opposites represented as cannibalism. The climax of cantos 21 and 22 is the scene in which the devils, described as butchers and cooks spearing souls for their suppers, fall into the boiling pitch so that, as Singleton nicely puts it, "the cooks themselves are finally cooked."[54] In the opening of canto 23 this scene reminds Dante of the fable of the frog and the mouse, in which both eater and eaten are eaten. So, although Lucifer eats sinners, Hell itself is described as a gullet which "divora / Lucifero con Giuda" ("swallows Lucifer with Judas," 31.142–43). In such an intimately related body politic, all cannibalism must ultimately be self-cannibalism, as Dante dramatizes in figures such as Filippo Argenti (8.63), the Minotaur (12.14–15), Minos (27.124–26), who bite themselves in rage and frustration, and Ugolino who says that, while watching his children starve, "ambo le man per lo dolor mi morsi" ("I bit both my hands for grief," 32.58)—a gesture that prompts his son's eucharistic offering which he will reject only to later literalize. Through the laws of the *contrapasso* evil rebounds upon itself, so that in Hell all relations are ultimately redundant. This is a world very much like Ovid's, a totally enclosed body in which everything turns into everything else, for there is no difference between self and other, inside and outside, and so to eat is therefore also to be totally consumed.

This loss of differences is figured also in the flame of the thief and false counselor, Ulysses, which is, as Mazzotta points out, "the locus where distinctions between the inside and the outside are confused."[55] Dante's Ulysses is a projection of Dante the philosopher, seen also as a fraudulent poet, who misleadingly separated the inner meaning from the outer form that are in Ulysses's flame reunited.[56] For Dante, as for Augustine, Ulysses, whose voyage the neoplatonists allegorized as the soul's return to its source, came to represent "the presumptuous philosopher who would reach the truth unaided"[57] and the fallaciousness of imagining a return in terms of the transcendence of the body. Vanni Fucci, who is linked with one image of transcendence, the phoenix, identifies himself by the nickname of beast, "bestia" (24.126). The similarly self-sufficient and proud Ulysses urges his men to transcend the limits of their humanity,

> Considerate la vostra semenza;
>> fatti non foste a viver come bruti,
>> ma per seguir virtute e canoscenza.

("Consider your origin: you were not made to live as brutes, but to pursue virtue and knowledge." 26.118–20)

But as Ulysses goes beyond established boundary lines, which "l'uom più oltre non si metta" ("men should not pass beyond," 26.109), he becomes like his counterpart of *Paradiso* 26, Adam, who fell for "il trapassar del segno" ("the overpassing of the bound," *Paradiso* 26.117), as well as the literalist Ugolino. He believes that he can go beyond signs and rend the veil of allegory to gaze at the naked truth.

In this Ulysses repeats the error of the Dante of the *Convivio*, who had assumed that sign and significance were separable, and fiction a beautiful cloak over truth. This model, the inverse of that of Socrates, presumes two things: one, that the cloak can be removed, and the other, that the truth must be extremely ugly, or otherwise it would not remain hidden. The model of duality encourages one to think, like the envious, in terms of deceit, and to assume that what is hidden must be horrible—an assumption encouraged by Ugolino's infamous evasiveness. In *Purgatorio* 19 Dante turns Lady Philosophy into the Siren, associated with Ulysses, and reenacts his hermeneutics from the *Convivio* as the stripping of a beautiful woman, which reveals that the naked truth is rotten to the core.

As has been noted, Dante recalls and revises the *Convivio* in *Purgatorio* 2.[58] The hunger for knowledge is incorporated into the ascent to Paradise, as throughout the *Purgatorio* Dante represents his curiosity as a form of appetite that grows with what it feeds on. In *Purgatorio* 15.58–60, for example, he tells Virgil that his answers to Dante's questions leave him hungrier than ever, while when feasting his eyes upon the griffin of *Purgatorio* 31, "ch'è sola una persona in due nature" ("that is one person in two natures," 81), he experiences a paradoxical sensation: "l'anima mia gustava di quel cibo / che, saziando di sé, di sé asseta" ("my soul . . . was tasting of that food which, sating for itself, causes hunger for itself," 128–29). The "eating" of knowledge is both the satisfaction and the stimulation of appetite by a paradox analogous to that of the "doppia fiera" ("twofold animal," 122). As the griffin revises the hybrid corporate bodies of the *Inferno*, the appetite that grows as it is fed becomes a medium for representing a desire that may not be infernal. Both suggest the way in which Dante attempts to represent, as an alternative to the insubstantial forms of the *Convivio* and the reified ones of the *Inferno*, opposites that ultimately meet—signs that are substantial but not in themselves satisfying.

Through the ascent of *Purgatorio* figures are in some sense sublimated; as Dante reminds them, they "per salire ti dome" ("subdue yourself in order to ascend," 13.103). The forms here are not fixed to one place but are capable of change both internal and external, a metamorphosis very different from that possible in Hell. At the opening of the second *cantica*, Dante discovers that the form of Casella has no substance, but is only one of the "ombre vane, fuor che ne l'aspetto" ("empty shades except in aspect," 2.79), as his attempt to embrace him is frustrated. In Hell, figures could be touched, which in Hell meant basically to be beaten or eaten. But the status of figures in *Purgatorio* is less certain; these are souls whose identities are in progress and whose lack of definition makes physical contact, either affectionate or aggressive, impossible. In this threshold state the souls are not clear about their own status. They are both prospective, looking forward to Paradise, and retrospective, looking back to their families and friends on earth, and still experiencing an identification with their mortal bodies. They feel still the attractions of the flesh and, though shadows, are surprised at times by their own incorporality: Virgil and Statius forget that they have no bodies and try to embrace, "trattando l'ombre come cosa salda" ("treating shades as solid things," 21.136—adapted from Singleton). Dante himself is unsure how to read this realm, taking the emaciated figures of the gluttons literally until Virgil explains the formation of purgatorial shadows by the impression of the soul upon the air (25.79–108). Such images he compares to those reflected in a mirror, and Guinizelli refers to them as "corpo fittizio" ("shadowy body," 26.12—but "fittizio" also means imaginary and fictitious). In these passages, the concept of mirroring and the relation of original to reflection represented in the canto of the thieves undergoes its own metamorphosis, in which roles are not inverted but are seen as difficult to define.[59] While the souls in Paradise whom Dante first mistakes for mirror reflections turn out to be "vere sustanze" ("real substances," *Paradiso* 3.29), the figures here are only reflections of the reality they will become when they reach Paradise. Between old and new lives, these figures of mediation and metamorphosis suggest a transitional phase in which Dante redefines and refines his own poetics.

One central place for this process is in the purgatorial parallel to the cantos of the thieves and false counselors of *Inferno* 24–26. The inhabitants of *Purgatorio* 24–26, however, are not thieves or false counselors but the gluttonous and lustful; the boundary lines between sins become complicated, and different categories identified. One major means of identification is through a relation to poetry; as the fraudulent are dangerous poets, the gluttonous and lustful are erring poets, some of whom are Dante's friends, others his poetic sources. The poetics of thievery and fraud turns into the poetics of greed and desire at the point at which it begins to be redeemed.

If there are poets among the gluttons, one might expect they cared more for stuffing their mouths with food than opening them with words. In Purgatory, the gluttons are taught not to reject bodily impulses but rather to restrain them, "quanto è giusto" (24.154), both to hunger after what is just, and to hunger as much as is just. The ambiguity is important because it tempers two meanings, meanings which are, however, complementary rather than antithetical, and by so doing finds a means between the extremes of the self-destroyed Pier delle Vigne whose "giusto," justness, made him "ingiusto," unjust (*Inferno* 13.72). The examples of temperance Dante gives are of those who chose spiritual over physical food, who open their mouths not to take in food but to praise God. So, also, the gluttons are refined with the verse referred to in *Purgatorio* 23.10–12, "Domine, labia mea aperies; et os meos annuntiabit laudem tuam" ("O Lord, open thou my lips; and my mouth shall shew forth thy praise," Psalm 51 : 17 [15, in King James Version]). The opposite of the greedy, self-centered mouth that simply takes food in is the mouth that also opens to let words out and, specifically, to praise others.[60] So further on, in part of the paradisal counterpart to these cantos, Peter and James will appear to Dante as doves, "laudando il cibo che là sù li prande" ("praising the food which feeds them thereabove," *Paradiso* 25.24):[61] God is food that is both eaten and praised, that goes in but causes words to come out as well.

But as these cantos look back to the thieves, gluttony and lust are defined as more than mere desire for material satisfaction. To see them in terms of their infernal precedent would imply that they must be related to theft, and particularly, as the cantos are concerned with poets, the theft of poetic property. Of the poetic gluttons Dante meets, the Bonagiunta usually identified as Dante's character was apparently a more dedicated drinker than poet, and, in his earlier poetry, Dante had accused Forese Donati of gluttony. But Forese also exchanged poems with Dante, an exchange motivated by neither charity nor theft in its literal sense, but by mutual abuse, in which vituperation seems to indicate both affection and intense rivalry.

The relation between the poets produced an exchange of vicious and rather puerile verse that Dante later appeared to regret. As Barolini has noticed also, Dante's Bonagiunta seems greatly concerned with questions of personal authorship and influence.[62] Greed seems defined subtly in poetic terms as an impulse to appropriate authority from another, which involves the perception of the other as a rival whose power must be aggressively stolen and incorporated. Its motive is the desire to claim total originality that Dante manifested in his own boast in *Inferno* 25, and its product is not praise but an endless and fruitless exchange of abuse.

In *Purgatorio* 24, Dante replies indirectly to Bonagiunta's inquiries, turning the question into a discussion of tradition that focuses upon a source beyond the individual vessels of poetic inspiration.[63] Asked if he were the author of "*Donne che'avete intelleto d'amore*" ("Ladies that have understanding of love," 24.51), a canzone from *La vita nuova*, Dante redefines the question, identifying himself as,

> I' mi son un che, quando
> Amor mi spira, noto, e a quel modo
> ch'e' ditta dentro vo significando.

("I am one who, when Love inspires me, takes note, and goes setting it forth after the fashion which he dictates within me." 52–54)

As Durling has noted, Dante's description relies upon a subtle analogy with nutrition, as the poet says he takes in something from outside of himself.[64] Though he does, as Bonagiunta phrases it, bring forth rhymes, he positions himself in such a way that he does not appear as their ultimate source. His own work has an origin outside the self to which he can refer back, here "Amor," just as earlier he had represented Virgil as his source, a fountain flowing into him whom he called "mio maestro e'l mio autore" ("my master and my author," *Inferno* 1.85). In the *Inferno*, Vanni Fucci and the phoenix stood as models for a self that is its own source and so produces nothing but the same thing over and over, and for a self-sufficiency which, as it will admit nothing from outside of itself, ends in self-cannibalism. These are images for a possible poetics that Dante is detaching himself from in Purgatory, as he positions himself as part of a chain of consumption and production that tries not to be self-consuming.

The end of this chain is not that of literal ingestion, but rather words that are "significando"; as Durling puts it, "Hell is the belly that produces shit; Purgatory, the belly that produces new life."[65] Purgatory is a threshold space of sublimation where matter is turned into spirit and excrement into words. But the lack of absolute definition between the opposites here allows a possibility of both differentiation and identification not possible in Hell, where terms defined rigidly as antitheses collapsed into infernal identity. In Purgatory, inner and outer are analogous though separate, as Dante's expression is faithful to, though distinguished from, Love's inspiration. The flame of Ulysses, in which inside and outside disappeared, turns into the flame that refines the lustful—poets who charitably defer to each other—but which also points ahead to the flame of *Paradiso* 26, the canto in which Dante meets Ulysses's redeemed counterpart, Adam, and is tested on charity.

The goal of Dante's pilgrimage and poem is the place where he will experience an unmediated vision, seeing figures "con imagine scoverta" ("in your uncovered shape," *Paradiso* 22.60), when the cloak of fiction has been stripped away. Benedict promises him,

> Frate, il tuo alto disio
> s'adempierà in su l'ultima spera,
> ove s'adempion tutti li altri e 'l mio.
>
> Ivi è perfetta, matura e intera
> ciascuna disïanza; in quella sola
> è ogne parte là ove sempr' era,
> perché non è in loco e non s'impola.

("Brother, your high desire shall be fulfilled up in the last sphere, where are fulfilled all others and my own. There every desire is perfect, mature, and whole. In that alone is every part there where it always was, for it is not in space, nor has it poles." 22.61–67)

The end of Dante's quest, like that of Augustine, is a place of unity beyond oppositions where all desires are fed. The obvious poetic problem Dante faces is that of representing total satisfaction and the transcendence of differentiation through language that testifies to difference and dissatisfaction. To represent Paradise requires a redefinition of what figures can do. In *Paradiso* 24–25 Dante is examined on faith and hope. He defines the former by quoting, though translating, the Bible: "fede è sustanza di cose sperate / e argomento de le non parventi" ("Faith is the substance of things hoped for and the evidence of things not seen," 24.64–65). As these cantos look back to the Purgatory of the gluttons and lustful, they define poetic temperance as the acceptance of figures, verbal substances, as guarantees of an absent source of satisfaction to which they refer. Meaning is not fully incarnated in words; the danger of taking the incarnational model too literally is again suggested by Dante's comparison of the gluttons to "la gente che perdé Ierusalemme, / quando Maria nel figlio diè di becco" ("the people who lost Jerusalem, when Mary struck her beak into her son," *Purgatorio* 23.29–30). The allusion to Josephus's story of the siege and famine in which a mother named Mary ate her only son, suggests a grotesque parody in which the Word is made flesh in order to be eaten, and links gluttony with the literalism of Ugolino. For Dante, as for Augustine, improper reading is also improper eating; to pin down meaning, to fix it and make it certain, is to consume it.

The *Purgatorio* establishes a poetics of temperance in which the relation between inside and outside is kept open and fluid, in which, further, the process of sublimation does not lead to final consumption. In the *Paradiso*, which plays a part similar to that of the last books of the *Confessions*, opposites are not resolved, but their relation becomes a rhythm of alteration, suggested by the oscillation between images of emptiness and plenitude—as, for example, in the final canto where images of gathering together and spilling out, of memory and oblivion, alternate. As, according to Benedict, Paradise is beyond space, it is created through time, the movement between extremes, which prevents the formation of rigid binary poles while maintaining a difference among its parts. Here opposites can meet, not in space as did the hybrid monsters of the *Inferno*, but through a method that allows Dante to recreate these earlier figures in a different manner.

This movement is anticipated at the end of the *Purgatorio* with the appearance of the hybrid griffin. Both natures of the animal cannot be seen at once, for it appears, "or con altri, or con altri reggimenti" ("now with the one, now with the other bearing," 31.123). When Dante tries to fix it with his gaze and take in both its aspects at once, it eludes him, as he sees it "in sé star queta, / e ne l'idolo suo si trasmutava" ("stand still in itself, and in its image changing," 125–26). Unlike the thieves who exchange their matter, "matera," the griffin does not change substantially, although his "idolo," image or appearance, does. In an inversion of the Ovidian procedure, metamorphosis has become metaphor, and the violent conjunction of opposites found in Hell has been converted into the language of religious paradox that recalls descriptions of the Trinity and incarnation, in which opposites—nature and persons, substance and attributes, father and son, spirit and flesh—are redefined in terms of a simultaneous identification and differentiation which tempers opposition.

The use of such language increases throughout the *Paradiso* (see, for example, 13.26–28; 24.139–41; 33.1–6), as infernal hybrids are metamorphosed from visual to rhetorical figures in a conversion of language that recalls that of Augustine. Instead of figures presenting an ultimately illusory sense of presence and substance, Dante meets figures who emphasize their own status as signs, for they appear "per far segno" ("to offer a sign," 4.38—my translation). The rhetoric in the *Paradiso* deliberately calls attention to itself.[66] In *Paradiso* 26.49–66, for example, Dante piles the images upon each other as he describes himself being gripped by God's teeth (a daring image in the light of *Inferno* 34) and drawn by cords from the sea of perverse love. Although metaphors work to identify opposites, relating words across time, here the figures do not really mix or collapse into a hermaphroditic discourse; the sequentiality of the language keeps them apart, and their very excess further emphasizes their function as mere images. Infernal figures become verbal figures, which are created in time, not space, and so, as Benedict says, do not collapse the poles. Even the epitome of the redundancy of infernal identity, the metamorphosis of Vanni Fucci, is revised on an aural model, in the troping of "Cristo" with itself (12.71–75; 14.104–8; 19.104–8; 32.83–87) that suggests the incommensurateness of God.

This last example suggests that, as, according to Augustine, all sin is perverse imitation of God, self-sufficiency is an attribute appropriate to the Creator but not to the creature, in whom it becomes infernal. The values typically applied to the Renaissance individual and his heirs—autonomy and originality—Dante grants to God or sends to Hell. Since Burckhardt, it has been traditional to see the individual as a construction of the Renaissance and view medieval man as a social being defined by his role and place as member of a group, a limb of the body politic, from which he could not be isolated and dissected.[67] Leo Spitzer extended this view when he argued that the poetic identity as well as social identity of medieval man was defined in terms of relation.[68] As the boundary lines around the self are not yet tightly drawn, cutting off the members from each other, a more fluid self-definition is possible. According to Spitzer, what this prevented was precisely the concept of plagiarism: the theft of poetry was impossible, as literature was defined as communal rather than private property.[69]

The boundary lines around the Renaissance and the discovery of the individual seem less definite now than they did to Burckhardt.[70] For Dante the possibility of aspiring to personal and poetic autonomy is already imaginable, even if it is consigned to Hell. By separating Hell from Paradise, Dante attempts to circumscribe the contexts in which exchanges become thievery and cannibalism, and to disassociate his own poetry from it. Infernal exchanges occur in an Ovidian world where boundaries are so rigidly defined in terms of opposition that they can be crossed only by violation—by stealing another's property, and ultimately by cannibalism. Purgatorial and paradisal relations, on the other hand, occur where territorial definitions are not rigid or static, allowing interplay that never freezes into absolute opposition.

This difference in imagining relations is related to a difference in defining poetics. In the *Inferno*, letter and spirit, outside and inside, are defined as opposites which then collapse. In *Inferno* 32.11–13, Dante invokes the aid of the muse who helped to build Thebes, in order to ensure that his "verso" "dal fatto il dir non sia diverso" ("verses" "will not deviate from the facts they tell"—my translation). But for Dante, Thebes is the infernal body politic that abolishes differences among its members through incest and cannibalism. It is, in fact, a temperate diversity between "verso" and "fatto" that keeps the two from collapsing into each other and consuming each other. In the *Purgatorio*, the relation between the two is kept in flux, preventing their formulation as antitheses that might be identical. In the *Paradiso*, however, they once more emerge as potential opposites, but as terms whose potential antagonistic identification is prevented by constant alteration, the fluctuation between the two, which, like the mirroring between the Father and the Son, turns potential cannibalism into mutual love.

This is obviously a delicate balance, and one that emphasizes its temporality because it depends on continuation through time. But at the same time, its ultimate referent, which lies outside the poem's powers of representation, is beyond time. Dante's Hell is, like that of Ovid's *Metamorphoses*, a world of total incorporation, in which everything is included and ultimately identified completely through cannibalism. Like the *Convivio*, it is a dead end—except for the author himself who continues his quest. The descent into Hell leads to the body of Lucifer, who incorporates his members by consuming them. The ascent into Paradise leads to a transformed vision of incorporation based on a textual model—the volume of *Paradiso* 33 that gathers together the scattered elements of the universe, "sustanze e accidenti e lor costume" ("substances and accidents and their relations," 88). For Dante, as for Augustine, vision is associated with reading. The *Paradiso* ends with a vision of the paradox of the Trinity, both three persons and one nature, in which Dante, whose movement beyond language can only be imagined, as it was also in Augustine, through the image of the infant at its mother's breast whose "lingua," "tongue," is used only for sucking and not speaking (33.108), is absorbed into the centripetal force of his poetic source, "Amor." But time doesn't stop even at this epiphanic moment; in the definitive alteration between opposites, the end is converted into a new beginning, marking the centrifugal movement away from experience into representation. As soon as the poem reaches its place of origin it becomes itself.

Dante, like Odysseus, arrives home at the end of his quest only to find that he has to leave again. For Dante, like Ovid, this meant the experience of a very real exile. In the Middle Ages, the concept of the *peregrinus* or *alienus*, the pilgrim or exile, had ambiguous meanings.[71] Through the Fall, man was estranged from God and, in order to return to God, must estrange himself from the world, being alienated from human societies until he returns to the one society where, according to the Bible, "Ergo iam non estis hospites, et advenae; sed estis cives sanctorum et domestici Dei" ("Now therefore ye are no more strangers and foreigners, but fellow citizens with the saints, and of the household of God"; Ephesians 2:19, King James Version). One piece of evidence of man's temporary exile is language, for the fallen substitute for the paradisal direct communion with, or feeding upon, God is the mediating signs which are themselves, as Dante defines them, *alienus* and *diversus*—strange, foreign, different—perhaps even totally contradictory. Meaning is different from the words that convey it, but to decide that that difference is therefore endless is to leave man in "l'etterno essilio" ("eternal exile")—the fate of Dante's most important source, Virgil (*Purgatorio* 21.18), and of the crucified Caïphas (*Inferno* 23.126)—the one soul in Hell at whom Virgil stares in astonishment, unable to comprehend the meaning of his punishment.[72] However, the model that Dante uses for the *Commedia* and as an explanation for his method of allegory is the story of Exodus, which is the type of the return of the soul to God that, by the laws of typology, promises its fulfillment in its antitype. Dante claims that his own journey is a foretaste of its later repetition and realization, a typological figure which, by the logic of typology, guarantees by referring to the definitive return.[73] Dante's first coming, like Christ's, points to and, by so doing, secures the second. In the meantime, however, exiles speak in language that is *alienus*. Not being fully satisfied with figures is what creates poetry and all human exchanges: Lucifer says nothing, for his mouth is full.

CHAPTER III

The Reformation of the Host

> Then Jesus said unto them, Verily, verily I say unto you, Except
> ye eat the flesh of the Son of man, and drink his blood, ye have
> no life in you. Whoso eateth my flesh, and drinketh my blood,
> hath eternal life: and I will raise him up at the last day. For my
> flesh is meat indeed, and my blood is drink indeed. He that
> eateth my flesh, and drinketh my blood, dwelleth in me, and I in
> him.
>
> —John 6:53–56

Both Augustine and Dante attempt to establish a temperate balance between opposites, based on the model of the incarnation. Letter, or flesh,
and spirit, the outside and inside both of the individual and of poetic figures, are seen as identified but differentiated. In this chapter, I shall be
looking at how the loss of this already delicate balance is represented, tracing the polarization of terms through the works of Rabelais, Ben Jonson,
and Milton. As Dante's journey is from cannibalism to communion, while
Milton's tale of the Fall tells that journey in reverse, I would like to begin
approaching the Renaissance codification of opposition by a brief discussion of one major religious symbol where this process was worked out: the
Eucharist. The symbolism of the Eucharist makes it obviously appropriate
to my discussion; moreover, it is the sacrament which was seen as the ritual
reenactment of the incarnation. To turn to it here enables me to shift my
focus from incarnation to incorporation while emphasizing the connection
between them, and to move from problems of representation into ones
more specifically of interpretation. Moreover, the discussions of the relations between substance and accidents in the Host extend the debate over
the relation between the three persons and one nature of God in the Trinity
that, in response to Arianism, was codified in the Nicene Creed of 325. It
is this debate over the meaning of figures that becomes not only a central
feature of the Catholic/Protestant split, but also the place in which the
modern individual began to be defined.

Like the doctrines of the Trinity and the incarnation, the Eucharist is a
paradoxical relation involving the simultaneous identification and differentiation of opposites. It is a banquet at which host and guest can come
together without one subsuming the other, as both eat and are eaten. Like

the father-son relation created in the Trinity, it potentially eliminates the hostility of the classical pattern of oedipal rivalry, as the antithetical terms are separated by the third substance, either the Word or Host, they both produce and share. It seems ironic, therefore, that the Host is the crux of the Catholic and Protestant debate, the symbol which helped split the two positions apart and set them against each other. The Host became the focus for a fight over interpretation—represented, as in Augustine, as a matter of how one eats—in which a disagreement between critical positions turned into a bloody battle.

The Eucharist was instituted as a representation of the Last Supper described in the gospels, in which Christ offered bread and wine as his body and blood for the redemption of mankind.[1] For the early Church, the meaning of Christ's words and the relation of the substances involved in the sacrament appeared to present few problems. When the bread and wine were said to "represent" Christ, the word *repraesentio* had the significance "to make present," for, as Adolph Harnack argued, "What we nowadays understand by 'symbol' is a thing which is not that which it represents; at that time 'symbol' denoted a thing which is in some kind of way really what it signifies."[2] Through the act of communion opposites are seen as coming together. Different times meet, for the ritual is both a fulfillment of the past meal and a foretaste of the future "Marriage Feast of the Lamb," as well as a present participation in Christ's sacrifice. In the Host, as in the Trinity, different persons meet. The individual bodies of the members of the community are identifed with the corporate body of the Church, which in turn is identified with the individual body of the sacrificed Christ.[3] The two essential characteristics of the early rite are that it is a sacrifice and a corporate act.

The balance between potentially conflicting interpretations may have been maintained by a certain amount of indeterminacy and lack of definition; it certainly appears that it is when the Church began to define the different roles in the sacrament that trouble started. But this definition was itself justified as a response to early schisms and heresies that necessitated the formulation of Church dogma. The definition of the Eucharist was a means of establishing the unity of the Church through the removal of different interpretations inside it and through the exclusion of the pagans outside it. A central goal of the Fourth Lateran Council of 1215 was to define Christianity as a coherent body, a unified faith as it was ultimately defined through Boniface VIII's credo of the *unam sanctam* in 1302, separated off from others who were pushed to the outside as heretics or infidels.[4] As is typical of definitions of social bodies, the difference between two groups—those who are inside and those who are outside—is defined by what or how they eat. But the question of eating here is also explicitly a question of interpretation. The problem raised by the act of communion lay in the actual relation of body to bread and blood to wine. All Christians agreed that there was a relation but differed as to what it consisted of: how, in other words, the body and blood were communicated.[5]

Avoiding both of the two possible extremes—the literalist position, which bloodthirstily maintained that what the communicant ate really was Christ's body, and the spiritualist position, which read the rite as purely symbolic—the Fourth Lateran Council came up with the doctrine of transubstantiation. This stated that while the substances of bread and wine became the substance of Christ, the accidents remained unchanged. By this definition the Church could uphold the reality of the rite without offending sense perception, at the cost, however, of formally codifying a separation between the inner and outer terms of the sacrament.

In fact, this apparent solution, which seemed to establish the temperate balance between opposites, heralded the beginning of further conflict. The relation between accidents and substances became increasingly a point of controversy, which coincided with a growing split between a focus on public ritual and ceremony and one on private internalized worship. Long before the Reformation, the doctrine of the "real presence" of Christ in the Eucharist had been attacked by heretical outsiders reacting against the general materialism of the medieval Church in favor of a more spiritually oriented religion. Against the growing ceremonialism of an increasingly powerful institution, there was a movement toward cults of inner, private devotion that would abolish the need for formal, public ritual.[6]

The changes taking place within the Catholic church, its development as a powerful and unified corporation, had gradually affected the celebration of the mass and ultimately its interpretation. The Church itself began to appropriate for its own body the symbolism previously granted to the Host. Originally the consecrated Host had been referred to as the *corpus mysticum* in order to distinguish it from Christ's historical body, which was *proprium et verum corpus*, and from the body of the Church, which was called the *corpus Christi*.[7] But these different bodies, like those of Dante's thieves, switched places, and ended up defined in totally different roles. Around the time of the early debates over transubstantiation, in reaction against the mysticism of many of the heresies, the Church began to stress the bodily presence of Christ in the bread by referring to the Host as the *corpus verum* or *naturale*. In return, it appropriated for itself the name of *corpus mysticum*. This had the advantage of emphasizing the spiritual side of an institution that was becoming increasingly secularized and commercial.

The growing power of the ecclesiastical corporate body was at the expense of the individual, also produced in part by exclusion, as the layman became gradually eased out of participation in the sacraments and out of direct communion with God. Through an increasing emphasis on ceremony, the role of the communicant was reduced from receptive participant to mere spectator, whose role was not to *eat* but to *see*.[8] A further consequence of this was that the members of the Church became isolated from each other, so that communion was no longer a truly corporate act, but rather a purely private, individual experience, as the consolidation of the ecclesiastical body on an economic level paradoxically led to its own dismemberment on a personal one. In fact, while on one hand the development of Protestantism and individualism seems to be a reaction against the Catholic Church, on the other it is a logical extension of it, produced by an expanding corporation that no longer supported a sense of community and communion.

Furthermore, while the early Fathers had emphasized the eschatological dimension of the mass, later celebrants focused upon its relation to the past in terms of distance and looked back at the passion as a remote historical event that could not be participated in but only remembered. In fact, one of the crucial problems for interpretation became the concept of the supplementation and repetition of an act that was said to be totally unique and sufficient, and to have achieved an absolute reconciliation between man and God. All human action could only be either hopelessly inadequate or simply redundant; as John Donne would later point out: "If the treasure of the blood of Jesus Christ be not sufficient, Lord, what addition can I find to match them, to piece out them! And if it be sufficient of itself, what addition need I seek?"[9]

The first public attack against the mass was made by Luther in April 1520 and was elaborated later that same year. While aspects of Luther's position changed during his life, he generally believed that the sacraments were merely outward signs or tokens of inner faith. Communion was refined to a *convivio*, which gave thanks to God but did not actively participate in or renew the passion. The physical act of incorporation became unnecessary, except as an analogy, as, according to Luther, "no eating can give life except that which is by faith, for that is truly a spiritual and living eating."[10]

As authority for his argument, Luther refers to Augustine who, in his interpretation of John had written, "Utquid paras dentes et ventrum? Crede, et manducasti" ("Why do you prepare your teeth and belly? Believe and you have eaten").[11] As we have seen, Augustine, whose shift of focus here from bodily digestion may be connected to an anxiety about his own Manichean past, tends to oppose spiritual and physical forms of eating. In the writings of many of the reformers who, like Augustus, claimed to be reviving the pure and original form of their beliefs, this opposition becomes consolidated. In general, in order to delineate themselves as one religious body against another, the reformers defined themselves in terms of eating: as those who ate spiritually in opposition to the others who ate

God literally. For the new body of belief, the old, from which it was trying to break away, embodied its own fear of regression and loss of newly won religious identity, so that it became doubly appropriate to represent the Catholics as cannibals who threatened to swallow up both Christ and the true religion. In numerous Protestant tracts, the Catholic mass was turned into a bloodthirsty rite, in which the priests ate God over and over again. As one poet described it:

> As on the whale did Jonas, so they eat
> Him up alive, body and soul, as meat
> As men eat oysters, so on Him they feed;
> Whole and alive, and raw and yet not bleed
> This cookery, void of humanity,
> Is held in Rome for sound divinity.[12]

According to the reformers, bodily analogies degraded the spirit, but it was they themselves who took them completely literally for their own purposes. By cleverly pushing the sacrament to a grotesque extreme unimagined by most Catholics and misrepresentative of the official interpretation of the rite, the reformers made the other extreme, their own position, appear as the only alternative for those who did not wish to be cannibals. This strategy of self-definition against a projected alien group is a version of "colonial discourse," the construction of the savage cannibal as antithesis of civilized man used as a justification for cultural cannibalism, that emerged with the discoveries of the New World.[13]

As defined from a Protestant perspective, therefore, communion could be only one of two opposites: either an analogy for a spiritual process or cannibalism. Milton, for whom the subject of the incarnation and passion causes personal as well as doctrinal problems, insists that the relation between sign and signified can only be that of analogy:

> That living bread which, Christ says, is his flesh, and the true drink which, he says, is his blood, can only be the doctrine which teaches us that Christ was made man in order to pour out his blood for us. The man who accepts this doctrine with true faith will live for ever. This is as certain as that actual eating and drinking sustain this mortal life of ours for a while—indeed, much more certain. For it means that Christ will dwell in us and we in him. . . . Whereas if we eat his flesh it will not remain in us, but, to speak candidly, after being digested in the stomach it will be at length excluded.[14]

To believe that one actually eats Christ's flesh would be to collapse the two terms of the analogy and so literalize a trope, which Milton describes as "a thing which in any way illustrates or signifies another thing," and which is "mentioned not so much for what it really is as for what it illustrates or signifies." He claims, "Failure to recognize this figure of speech in the sacraments, where the relationship between the symbol and the thing symbolized is very close, has been a widespread source of error, and still is today."[15] As it was for both Augustine and Dante, how one eats is a poetic problem, a question of interpretation and how one reads figures. In particular, it is a question of how one takes the copula of metaphor, the word *is* in Christ's claim, "this is my body." According to Milton, *is* does not involve total identity, it really means *as*, being a "figure of speech to denote the class relationship between the symbol and the thing symbolized, and also to show that these spiritual matters are sealed with absolute certainty."[16] Whereas in the early Church the action of the sacrament produced its meaning, for Milton, as for many other of the reformers, the rite is only an expression of a preexisting inner reality, the state of grace, and so it does "not constitute the covenant but only makes it public."[17] To misunderstand the relation of signs to what they signify is, as in the case of Ugolino, to fall into disgusting literalism that degrades the spirit; as Milton notes, with some relish: "the Mass brings down Christ's body from its supreme exaltation at the right hand of God. It drags it back to the earth, though it has suffered every pain and hardship already, to a state of humiliation even more wretched and degrading than before: to be broken once more and crushed and ground, even by the fangs of brutes. Then, when it has been driven through all the stomach's filthy channels it shoots it out—one shudders even to mention it—into the latrine."[18]

It is typical of Milton specifically, although also of many other of the reformers, that in his attack on Catholic materialism he himself cannot resist the temptation of dwelling obsessively on bodily images, especially those related to the "lowest" functions of eating and excretion. His own dualistic definition of communion enables him to indulge in the materialist fantasies he is supposed to be denouncing by projecting them outside of himself onto another group that he then attacks. As cannibalism is projected, communion is protected against literalism and materialism by being introjected, internalized, and transformed into a psychological process that takes place, not in the bread and wine, but inside the faithful. As it can take place anytime, the external act of communion is essentially superfluous, an arbitrary sign that could be replaced by any other. And as it is now a completely personal act, the corporate body of the Church is unnecessary, or at best a temporary congregation of essentially isolated individuals.

I shall be returning shortly to the relation between this process of polarization and the emergence of the modern individual, whose autonomy is founded on an opposition between body and mind. But in order to get to that point, I would like to follow through these thoughts by examining images of eating and internalization in Rabelais, Jonson, and Milton, three writers for whom food plays a significant role in their formulations of their identities as poets and men, and of their concepts of poetic and personal exchanges.

Rabelais

> He that is of merry heart hath a continual feast.
> —Proverbs 15:15

Rabelais takes the Eucharist as a model for the creation and interpretation of his works, which he presents as the means of communion between men. Writing at an early stage of the Reformation, he attempts to use the growing source of division as a means of reunion. The early books establish an ideal of an incarnational and eucharistic poetics that unites both physical and spiritual levels of existence.[19] For Rabelais, writing is the same thing as eating and drinking, and the author insists that the different processes can occur simultaneously:

> à la composition de ce livre seigneurial, je ne perdiz ne emploiay oncques plus ny aultre que celluy qui estoit estably à prendre ma refection corporelle, sçavoir est beuvant et mangeant. Aussi est ce la juste heure d'escrire ces haultes matieres et sciences profundes.

> ("For I never spent or wasted any more—or other—time in the composing of this lordly book, than that fixed for the taking of my bodily refreshment, that is to say, for eating and drinking. Indeed, this is the proper time for writing of such high matters and abstruse sciences.")[20]

Food and inspiration are taken in at the same time, so that the reception of inspiration is revealed to be essentially a form of nourishment. However, in the later books the balance between the two becomes more precarious, and keeping convivial communion from being converted ironically into cannibalism, increasingly difficult.

Rabelais's basic model for incorporation is, even more than eating, drinking. His works are, he claims, a "tonneau inexpuisible" that has a "source vive et vene perpetuelle" ("cask . . . inexhaustible, endowed with a living spring and perpetual flow," *Tiers Livre*, prologue, 43; Cohen, 286). The focus on drinking may reflect one of the shifts in the practices of communion that occurred during the Middle Ages—the change to communion of one kind. As part of the exclusion of the laity from active participation, the chalice was limited to the priest alone, whose consecration and absorption of the blood of Christ the spectator observed. Caroline Walker Bynum has suggested that the blood was appropriated for the priests alone because it appeared to be a more powerful, less defined and controllable, substance than the actual Host.[21] The fact that liquids more than solids overflow and so unsettle boundaries makes them also a useful symbol for Rabelais; they stand for the inexhaustible substances necessary for the drinker/interpreter who finds that drinking is an endless undertaking in a world where appetites are never appeased. As "L'appetit vient en mangeant" ("Appetite comes with eating," *Gargantua*, 5.62; Cohen, 50), so even more, according to Panurge, in drinking wine, "plus j'en boy, plus j'ay de soif" ("the more I drink of it, the thirstier I am," *Pantagruel*, 14.89; Cohen, 214).[22]

Communion provides Rabelais also with an image for an exchange between writer and reader in which the two are identified. As David Quint claims, "To write and read the Rabelaisian text are one and the same spiritual action performed within a community of interpreters."[23] In his prologues, Rabelais invites his readers to a feast, in which the substance shared will be the text, seen as a means of bringing the two together. Creator and interpreter are not antithetical rivals for authority but rather complements, for the meaning of the text is produced in the exchange between them. Their relation is one of reciprocity, involving a movement between the two which, like the alternation between opposites in the *Paradiso*, follows the rhythm of emptying and filling that is part of the continual process of eating and drinking.

In actual practice, however, the exchange between the two terms is not as smooth and free from conflict as it sounds in its ideal formulation; nor is the relation between literal and figurative levels of meaning in perfect balance. Rabelais's humor is produced by an abrupt and often almost violent movement between self-inflation into pretended sublimity and deflation into vulgarity and nonsense. The wondrous Pantagruelion of the *Tiers Livre*, 49–52, for example, is first presented as a transcendental substance that can do anything, and then revealed to be merely hemp. Neither of the poles, the cloak of fiction or the naked truth, alone tells the truth; it is between the inflated description and the deflated referent that both the humor and the significance of the image lie.

But the opposites that resist easy idealizing resolution reveal a potential antagonism, one most apparent in Rabelais's descriptions of his own host, his text. As often has been noted, in the prologue to the *Gargantua* he appears to offer his reader two completely contradictory means of interpreting his work. He first asserts that it has a secret significance and then turns around abruptly to insist that he is actually all "up front," that his meaning is out in the open and right on the surface. Neither statement can in itself be completely adequate; the meaning of the scene lies in the comic movement between the two extremes.

However, this prologue also illustrates the possible polarization of literal and figurative meaning, as Rabelais compares his work to a number of objects, each of which consists of an outside and an inside. In each case, the outside is described as something fraudulent and deceitful which has to be removed, stripped, or penetrated in order to get at the meaning hidden inside. The most elaborate of these examples are those of the Silenus box and of the dog with his bone.

The first recalls the figure of Socrates from the *Symposium* and, in Rabelais's own time, the discussion of the figure of the "Sileni Alcibiades" in Erasmus's *Adages*. Here Erasmus examines duplicitous objects whose ridiculous and lowly exteriors conceal an admirable and valuable interior that is revealed only when the outside surface is cracked open or removed.[24] Erasmus reads Christ, the scriptures, and the sacraments as such Sileni, which teach us that precious objects must be hid from common view: "In living things, what is best and most vital is secreted in the inward parts. In man, what is most divine and immortal is what cannot be seen. . . . the most excellent things are the deepest hidden, and the furthest removed from profane eyes . . . the real truth always lies deepily hidden, not to be understood easily or by many people."[25] What is private and cannot be seen is much more valuable than what is made public and openly displayed. Unfortunately, however, he says, "The greater part of mankind are like Sileni inside out"[26]: attractive on the outside, and empty within, for men live in a world turned upside down, where they prefer "the shadow to the reality, the counterfeit to the genuine, the fleeting to the substantial, the momentary to the eternal."[27] For Erasmus, the image and its inversion suggest a world in which inside and outside are totally at odds. His discussion ends with a plea for the separation of sacred and secular powers that is based on a belief in the total antithesis between the spirit and the flesh: "In this world there are two worlds, at variance with each other in every way: the one gross and material, the other celestial, having its thoughts centred even now, as far as may be, on that which is to come hereafter."[28] There can be no mixing of material and spiritual interests or motives: "Why do we mix up together things which are so conflicting? earthly and heavenly, highest and lowest, heathen and Christian, profane and sacred—why do we confuse them all?"[29] For Erasmus, the figure of the Sileni is an emblem of a world in which opposites are not reconciled in one body, but are opposed, at war with each other, and the outer, lowly, material form must ultimately not merely be cracked and stripped off but totally destroyed.

Rabelais's own text is such an object in which appearance and reality are potentially antithetical. The possible tension, even violence, that may be produced by the disjunction between inside and outside is suggested further by the next figure the author uses for interpretation. Rabelais's image of the dog with his bone is a grotesque version of the exegetical commonplace in which interpretation is imagined as the stripping of a husk or shell to reveal the kernel of truth inside. It looks forward to the prologue of the *Cinquième Livre*, where the reader is encouraged to take the texts "les egoussez" and "devorez, comme opiatte cordialle et les incorporez en vous mesmes" ("shell them," "gulp them down as an opiate cordial and absorb them into your systems," 67; Cohen, 605). But here Rabelais further tells the interpreter to stalk the text like the dog his prey:

> puis, par curieuse leçon et meditation frequente, rompre l'os et sugcer la sustan-tificque mouelle—c'est à dire ce que j'entends par ces symboles Pythagoricques—avecques espoir certain d'estre faictz escors et preux à ladicte lecture.

> ("Then, by diligent reading and frequent meditation, you must break the bone and lick out the substantial marrow—that is to say the meaning which I intend to convey by these Pythagorean symbols—in the hope and assurance of becoming both wiser and more courageous by such reading." 45; Cohen, 38)

The inner meaning will, Rabelais promises, feed the reader and make him wiser, initiating him into "tres haultz sacremens et mysteres horrificques, tant en ce que concerne nostre religion que aussi l'estat politique et vie oeconomicque" ("very high sacraments and dread mysteries, concerning not only our religion, but also our public and private life").

This little scene is obviously ridiculous, as interpretation becomes the revelation of inner truth in order to eat it. The process turns Pythagorean symbols into a bone, and the reader into a dog gnawing away at it. Rabelais's strategy here is one typical of satire, in which a sublime figure is demystified by showing that it simply idealizes a less exalted reality. It is part also of his method of bringing the spirit down to earth and degrading it in order to revitalize it, which Bakhtin has discussed at length. As Bakhtin points out, this method reveals a central ambivalence toward the world, which is seen both as a place of destruction and rebirth. At one level eating is always an act of violence, and interpretation is a place of conflict as well as communion. However, when the relation between literal and figurative meanings of a text is set up as one of total opposition—between outside cloak or shell and inside truth or marrow—interpretation may become a darker sort of feeding, in which the complementary relation between author and reader, host and guest, becomes one of unambivalent antagonism.

In fact, although Rabelais is a convivial host, he welcomes only those who eat and drink, which is to say read, as he does.[30] The list of those he excludes increases with the body of his works, and in the prologue to the *Cinquième Livre*, he not only bans all those who do not take his books in the proper spirit, who are all obviously "les Zoiles emulateurs et envieux" ("little jealous, competitive, envious prigs," 65; Cohen, 604) but encourages them to go hang themselves. But even in the prologue to the *Gargantua*, Rabelais mocks readers who inflate his text by stuffing it with allegorical meanings (45; Cohen, 38). The word Rabelais uses is *calfreter*, a nautical term used to describe ships that are tightly caulked and seaworthy.[31] Rabelais ridicules readers who try to allegorize and idealize, smoothing over the gaps and inconsistencies of the text, which they implicitly imagine as an object full of interpretive holes that must be sealed tight and shut to keep meaning afloat. Yet as he excludes those who try to eliminate differences from the text, Rabelais shows his own authoritarian side as he decides who may or may not come to his feast and tells them how they should eat and drink.

As Bakhtin claimed, feasting—eating and drinking—is an indication of openness. But this openness in turn is a sign of vulnerability, as the reception of external influences can in different ways endanger the self, so that a certain caution on a host's part is perhaps sensible. As we have seen, feasts can be dangerous places, and at the same time as eating and drinking offer Rabelais an image for communion, and for the individual's intercourse with the outside world, he acknowledges the negative connotations that appetite has, especially for those working within the tradition of Genesis. As a child Pantagruel had to be chained in order to keep him from consuming everything in sight; later, the narrator, Alcofribas, informs us, one of these chains was taken to bind Lucifer who—poor devil —was having fits of indigestion from "l'ame d'un sergeant fricassée" ("the fricasseed soul of a sergeant," *Pantagruel*, 4.46; Cohen, 180). While Bakhtin and others have noticed how "the gaping mouth plays a specially important part in Pantagruel. One may say that it is the hero of this book,"[32] Rabelais is aware that the devil also has a large mouth and a notorious appetite.

But appetites are difficult to control, for, as Panurge complains, "plus j'en boy, plus j'ay de soif. Je croys que l'ombre de Monseigneur Pantagruel engendre les alterez" ("the more I drink of it the thirstier I am. I believe that the shadow of my lord Pantagruel makes men thirsty," *Pantagruel*, 14.89; Cohen, 214). Rabelais's book takes its title and omnivorous hero from a little devil whose previous career in mystery plays had been limited to the activity of pouring salt down open throats.[33] Eventually, he came to personify thirst, as in the expression, "Pantagruel le tenoit à la gorge" ("Pantagruel held him by the throat," 6.54; Cohen, 185). Rabelais inflates this devil to gigantic proportions and expands his sphere of influence, as the figure of speech gradually takes on a real life of its own. In the first book, his traditional occupation is pursued, as he pours salt down the Dipsodes' throats, and the author constantly plays on the possible metaphorical and literal meanings of the expression. It is delightfully literalized in chapter 6, as Pantagruel shakes the Limousin student, "qui contrefaisoit le langaige Francoys" ("who murdered the French Language," 6.52; Cohen, 183), by the throat. As a metaphor embodied, Pantagruel knows that one way to deal with those who are slaughtering the language is to use them to restore it to life. The metaphor is regenerated as it is literalized, and old forms are resurrected through parody.

This process is also a part of the ritual degradation, the return of abstractions to the body in order to regenerate them, that Bakhtin has described.

As the books continue, however, Pantagruel's diabolical origin is forgotten, his gigantic body and association with bodily appetites obscured, as he becomes interested in spiritual pursuits and the hunger for knowledge. Knowledge is a substance even more fluid, uncontrollable, and intangible than liquids, which instills an appetite that can be totally insatiable. Rabelais's texts, offered as sources of mental nourishment, are, according to the title page of the *Gargantua*, full, but: "plein de Pantagruelisme" ("full of Pantagruelism"). The barrel of the prologue to the *Tiers Livre* contains liquor compared to "le breviage contenu dedans la couppe de Tantalus" ("that within the cup of Tantalus," 43; Cohen, 286); while the cup may be overflowing, the reader, like Tantalus, may be empty. Though Rabelais claims that "Bon espoir y gist au fond, comme en bouteille de Pandora: non desespoir, comme on bussart des Danaïdes" ("As in Pandora's jug, good hope lies at the bottom, not despair, as in the Danaids' tub"), hope is essentially proleptic and cannot provide a solid bottom. If we take the barrel literally, it is a bottomless pit.

As Bakhtin has noted, Rabelais is fascinated with different sorts of holes, particularly those of which the fundament, like that of the overstuffed Gargamelle, has fallen out. For Bakhtin, it is through the images of holes that Rabelais demonstrates the openness of his own textual body, which reaches out into the world even as it draws the world into itself. More pessimistic than Bakhtin, Terence Cave sees the text as turning itself into one of these abysses, as "Its very celebration of fertility, plenitude, reveals an inverse movement towards emptiness or absence," so that its progress is "an emptying out rather than a filling up."[34] The texts, however, do not decide whether such spaces are empty or full, but rather demonstrate the difficulty of living in a world full of holes which, despite a human desire to plug them up, cannot be easily caulked (*calfreté*) and made secure.

A fear of all spatial and temporal gaps that put men on shaky ground is a part of Panurge's obsession with the difference between the sexes in the *Tiers Livre*. For Panurge, unpredictability and uncertainty become embodied in the single fear that if, as he desires, he marries, he will not live happily ever after but will be cuckolded. His view of women is part of the misogynistic Pauline tradition that had resurfaced in the fifteenth century,[35] in which women were represented as bottomless pits of desire, whose entire bodies were reduced by metonymy to a hole that no single man could ever fill. For Panurge, women represent all differences that can become threatening, as holes that are signs of openness and the possibility of exchange are turned into abysses that devour. Panurge is an interpreter who, like the author himself, foresees the danger in a potential partner and so will enter into relations only when assured of safety and control. In search of a guarantee of future security, he consults a number of figures representing traditional sources of authority—a doctor, a theologian, a philosopher, a sibyl, even a poet—but interprets their answers to suit his own interests. Finally, at the very end of the *Tiers Livre*, he sets off to seek a definitive answer from the oracle of the Holy Bottle, as Rabelais's texts turn into a quest for certainty and protection against all differences, either sexual or interpretive, that are feared to be consuming.

In the course of the quest that takes up the last two books, images of communion and interpretation begin to reappear in distorted forms, and Bakhtin's grotesque body becomes increasingly gothic. In the *Quart Livre* 48, the voyagers pause in the land of the Papimaniacs, who have invested all authority in the figure of the pope, who is for them "L'unicque," "Dieu en terre" ("the One and Only," "God upon earth," 171; Cohen, 550). More dangerously from the perspective of a writer (albeit one who was also a monk, though one holding debatable religious beliefs), they have exalted one book to the position of a transcendental text that contains all significance. The Decretales are described in terms remarkably like the "incomparable et sans parragon" ("incomparable, and beyond comparison," *Pantagruel*, prologue, 30; Cohen, 168) *Pantagruel* and *Gargantua*. They too are said to transform the reader who follows the bishop Homenaz's advice:

> vous [the Decretales] lire, . . . vous entendre, vous sçavoir, vous user, practiquer, incorporer, sanguifier, et incentricquer es profonds ventricules de leurs cerveaulx, es internes mouelles de leurs os, es perples labyrintes de leurs arteres.

> ("to read you . . . to understand you, know you, use you, put you into practice, incorporate you, absorb you into their blood, and draw you into the deepest lobes of their brains, the very marrow of their bones, and torturous labyrinths of their arteries." 51.180; Cohen, 557)

Homenaz takes Rabelais's assertions of the powers of his own texts even further; the Decretales will, he swears, restore the Golden Age and raise men to the heavens:

> vous sentez en vos coeurs enflammee la fournaise d'amour divin: de charité envers vostre prochain, pourveu qu'il ne soit Hereticque: contemnement asceuré de toutes choses fortuites et terrestres: ecstatique elevation de vos esprepritz, voire jusques au troizieme ciel: contentement certain en toutes vos affections.

> ("you feel the furnace of divine love kindle in your hearts; and of charity towards your neighbour as well, providing that he is not a heretic. You feel a fixed contempt for all fortuitous and earthly things, an ecstatic elevation of your spirits, even to the third heaven, and firm contentment in all your affections." 51.181; Cohen, 558)

While the reader is presumably supposed to be able to distinguish Homenaz's claims from those of Rabelais by their tone of hypocrisy and smug certainty, the difference is a shaky one—especially as Rabelais's exclusive invitation to readers to partake of his text did not include heretics, toward whom he was often quite pitiless.[36]

In the first books, the literalization of dead metaphors led to their revival; in the episode of the "parolles degelees" ("Words that have been thawed," 55.192; Cohen, 566), words literally turn into objects that the passengers can see but that when melted prove to be utter nonsense. Panurge is characteristically delighted when he finds that "motz de gueule" ("witticisms") are now really "gueule" ("red"), and Rabelais himself, with his great delight in the way words have a tendency to turn into things, appears to be fascinated by the concept of verbal objects he can actually hold on to. It is Pantagruel, by now the spokesman for the more lofty ideals of the quest, who prefers words that are invisible and heard, and rebukes his friend who is trying to collect them: "disant estre follie faire reserve de ce dont jamais l'on n'a faulte, et que tous jours on a en main, comme sont motz de gueule entre tous bons et joyeulx Pantagruelistes" ("saying that it was folly to store up things which one was never short of, and which are always plentiful, as gay quips are among good and jovial Pantagruelists," 56.196; Cohen, 569). For Pantagruel the real "motz de gueule" cannot be frozen or kept literally "en main," but live in the mouth (also "gueule") where they must be constantly respoken in order to be meaningful. But the different responses of the two friends, although not causing real conflict, suggest a growing polarization of interpretation: words can be taken literally or figuratively, but not both, and all literalness is increasingly threatening.

Like Odysseus meeting Polyphemos, the questors confront a literalized version of their own appetites on the paradisal island of Gaster, "premier maister es ars du monde" ("first Master of Arts in the World," 57.197; Cohen, 570). The body politic here is terrorized by the tyrannical belly, incarnated as Gaster, who demands complete obedience and is deaf to all pleas, for, as the old saying that the belly has no ears takes on a new and grim reality, "sans aureilles feut creé" ("[he] was created without ears," 57.198; Cohen, 571). He is a silent mouth who only takes in food and does not put words forth. Through signs he makes the world serve him; Rabelais takes up a page describing all human and animal activity that has its beginning and end in Gaster, and is done, as he repeats in a mocking refrain, "tout pour la trippe" ("all for the sake of the belly," 199; Cohen, 572).

In the figure of Gaster, Rabelais draws upon a number of traditions. The representation of the belly as the tyrannical ruler of the body politic looks back to the fables of the belly told by Plutarch, Livy, Nicholas Cusanus, and John of Salisbury, in which the stomach is identified with a controlling order—aristocrats in Livy's version, lawyers in Cusanus's, and financial officers in that of John of Salisbury.[37] The image of society as a body can be used as a means of keeping lower orders, identified as members, subordinate to the ruling faction. Furthermore, in Epicurean thought, the belly, *gaster*, is the material motive for all action, the quintessential appetite that literally swallows all energy and invention.[38] The representation of the belly as "Magister Artium" also goes back to classical literature.[39] As the beginning and end of all human activity, the belly replaces both love and God, which appear as more idealized sources for human action and motivation. Rabelais's Gaster is compared to Polyphemos who, according to Euripides (and later Plutarch), sacrificed to no one but himself and his own belly (58.201; Cohen, 574), and his worshippers, to those idolators denounced by Paul for making a god of their own bellies (Philippians 3:18). In fact, he turns out to be an idol, a grotesque image of a "ventripotent" God, with huge head and teeth and, of course, "les oeilz plus grands que le ventre" ("eyes . . . bigger than its belly," 59.202; Cohen, 574). To this grotesque figure are brought the copious quantities of food, described in two long catalogues, as Rabelais's own *copia* of catalogues is set to work, "tout pour la trippe."

As we have seen, Rabelais himself emphasizes the relation between physical and spiritual appetites, which both require satisfaction. As the most basic need, material hunger should be served first, otherwise "the belly has no ears." Furthermore, if all inventions serve the belly, they also come from it:

> Pour le servir tout le monde est empesché, tout le monde labeure. Aussi pour recompense il faict ce bien au monde, qu'il luy invente toutes ars, toutes machines, tous metiers, tous engins, et subtilitez.

> ("The whole world is busy serving him; the whole world labours to do so. But as a reward, he does the world a service; he invents all the arts, all the devices, all the crafts, all the machines and contrivances for it." 57.198; Cohen, 571)

Creation has its source in hunger, the basic physical need that forces men to develop more refined skills. In Rabelais's description in chapter 61, the inventions that emanate from hunger form a kind of chain, each one moving man forward to higher discoveries. But Gaster is a tyrant because he demands that this chain not only begin but also end in him, and he consumes the talents he pretends to have given freely. Like the disguised Odysseus, he reduces all motives to sheer appetite, from which they cannot escape. Hunger is not sublimated when it is redirected into spiritual and cultural concerns, for the belly demands that these too serve it alone. The emanation from and return to a material base become only a vicious circle of production and consumption, as all creation remains bound to the belly by which the beginning and end of all life are subsumed.

Gaster empties Rabelais's ideal of conviviality by literalizing it. The inflation of the belly literally deflates the quest, which, after moving off the island, is brought to a halt as both wind and the questors' spirits fail. The travelers ask a series of questions, to which Pantagruel replies that there is

> une seule solution . . . une seule medecine. . . . La response vous sera promptement expousee, non par longs ambages et discours de parolles, l'estomach affamé n'a poinct d'aureilles, il n'oyt guoutte. Par signes gestes, et effectz serez satisfaicts, et aurez resolution a vostre contentemente.

> ("one single solution . . . one sole medicine. . . . The answer shall speedily be given to you, without any great circumlocutions or any wordy discourse. The hungry stomach has no ears, it can't hear a word. But you shall be answered by signs, gestures, and demonstrations, which will deal with your questions to your absolute satisfaction." 63.218–19; Cohen, 586)

The promise of a single solution and the reference to the earless belly seem somewhat suspicious at this point. Gaster himself replaced words with signs, while in *Pantagruel* 19 the opposition between language and gestures as means of communication was presented and the idea of a more direct method of communication than language ridiculed.

What Pantagruel uncharacteristically (by this point) produces instead of words is food, a literal feast which has, however, a remarkable spiritual effect. It restores the mind as well as the body and causes the wind to return: "Nous haulsons et vuidans les tasses s'est pareillement le temps haulsé par occulte sympathie de Nature" ("As we raised and emptied our glasses, good weather has been raised likewise, by an occult sympathy of Nature," 65.225; Cohen, 591). The ship gets going on a pun, which suggests the renewed ability of the literal to regenerate the spiritual. Suddenly, emptying and filling become a single continuous process that permits progress: the fuller the feeders become, the lighter the ship, and as they drink down their spirits rise up, for by drinking: "sont hault eslevez les espritz des humains: leurs corps evidentement alaigriz; et assouply ce que en eulx estoit terrestre" ("the spirits of humankind are raised on high, their bodies manifestly made nimbler, and what was earthy in them becomes pliant," 65.226; Cohen, 592). They are sublimed by the substances they swallow. Creative energy is released by the return to the body—specifically the belly—and reaches a wonderful climax as, with the salute to the muses, the story, the ship, and Panurge's bowels, move.

This ending, however, is provisional, and, with the continuation of the quest in the *Cinquième Livre*, literalization becomes again deadening rather than regenerating. The "quint essence" of the title page of the *Gargantua* (composed by M. Alcofribas, "Abstracteur de Quinte Essence," "Abstractor of the Quintessence") is actually found (19), roads are literally taken

(25), and the Pantagruelistes' "mespris des choses fortuites" ("scorn of fortune") carried to a ludicrous extreme by the friars on the isle des Esclots, whose whole aim in life is "fustiguer Fortune" ("to give Fortune a beating," 26.263; Cohen, 666). To that purpose, they dress in a way that parodies Fortune, wearing codpieces both in front and behind, as "par ceste duplicité braguatine, quelques certains et horrifiques misteres estre duement representez" ("By this duplicity of codpieces, they affirmed, certain recondite and horrific mysteries were symbolically represented," 26.259; Cohen, 664). Their attitude is frightening, for, as Pantagruel points out, "finesse entendue, finesse preveuë, finesse descouverte, perd de finesse et l'essence et le nom: nous la nommons louderie" ("subtlety understood, subtlety foreseen, subtlety revealed, loses the essence and the very name of subtlety. We then call it plain clumpishness," 26.263; Cohen, 666).

The authorship of these episodes has been debated;[40] their narrative unevenness suggests how the quest itself could become "louderie," as monotonous repetition deadens the story. The danger of the separate but frequent feasts of the texts dissolving into one indistinguishable "grand bouffe" is suggested in chapter 7 on the "Isle Sonante" ("Ringing Island"), where the bells that are meant to mark the time confound it, and all temporal and culinary distinctions are lost, so that the travelers cannot tell if they are eating breakfast, lunch, or dinner. Here, too, the daily rhythm of eating and pausing between meals breaks down into an opposition between feast and famine, as the travelers are forced to fast four days and then are thrust into "un repas, qui duras tout le jour" ("one meal, which lasted all day," 7.105; Cohen, 617). Hunger swallows up all other desire on this island, which is a sterile parasite that swallows but cannot create anything in return. Its only products are the gluttonous and mostly silent birds, parodies of religious orders, who inspire in Frere Jean the desire to curse: "voyant ces diables d'oyseaulx, ne faisons que blasphemer; vuydans vos bouteilles et pots, ne faisons que Dieu louer. Allons doncques boire d'autant. O le beau mot! ("While we're looking at these devilish birds, all we do is to blaspheme. But when we're emptying your bottles and mugs, we do nothing but praise God. Come, and let us drink instead. O the blessed word!" 8.117; Cohen, 622).

Like the saints in the *Paradiso*, and unlike Gaster, Frere Jean opens his mouth not only to take in food but also to put forth words, praising what he eats and its source. As we discover retrospectively, he has indeed spoken "le beau mot"; the answer they seek has been with them all along. Drinking is both the goal of the quest and what keeps it going, as the satisfaction of the belly occurs simultaneously with that of the spirit.

But on Panurge's quest for certainty, spiritual desire appears to be increasingly reduced to sheer appetite, as the hunger of the dog at his bone which Rabelais had used as model for interpretation becomes increasingly bestial and carnivorous. When appetite grows with what it feeds on it may become all-consuming. When we come to the land of the infernal lawyer, Grippeminault ("Clawpuss" in Cohen's translation), we find a more dreadful and infernal version of Gaster: whereas the image of Gaster had eyes bigger than its belly, Grippeminault is compared to a figure with "les yeulx d'une *gueule* d'enfer" ("eyes like hell's throat," 11.135; Cohen, 627; emphasis mine). The polysemous word *gueule* becomes appropriated for and reduced to more sinister meanings in the hands, or claws, of the law, or letter.

The representation of the legal system as cannibalistic is an old topos. Within a Christian framework, the law is associated with the Old Testament and its God of vengeance: it is the letter that kills and which is contrasted with the life-giving spirit and charity of the New Testament (2 Corinthians 2:6). In Plato also, lawyers are attacked as mere rhetoricians who use words to serve their bellies.[41] Centuries of submission to the tortures of legal subtleties have tended to consolidate this negative image; the identification of the law and cannibalism can be found in writers from Cusanus to Dickens, many of whom no doubt had been themselves ensnared in the confusing and consuming system.[42] It is an analogy that implies an identification between the legal and digestive systems, and so plays upon the image of the body politic. So in Cusanus's version of the fable of the belly it is the lawyers who are identified with the belly, while in *Tristes Tropiques*, Lévi-Strauss describes the legal system as the civilized version of cannibalism, the substitution of *anthropemy* for *anthrophagai*, as the alien powers seen as subversive to the body politic are projected rather than assimilated in order to be neutralized.[43]

Rabelais's father was a lawyer, and, beginning with the *Gargantua*, the son depicted the law as an insatiable power self-perpetuated by meaningless rhetoric. The lawsuit of Janotus in chapter 20 is an endless battle of empty words motivated by greed, while the nonsense of Baisecul and Humevesne ("Kissmyarse" and "Suckfizzle," in Cohen) in *Pantagruel* 10–13 is only ended by Pantagruel's equally nonsensical intervention. While these early satires of legal procedure are hilarious, as the lawyers' inflated and abstract rhetoric is reduced by Rabelais to double entendres missed by the speakers themselves, a more ominous aspect of the law is introduced discreetly into the text. Among the books in the library of Saint Victor appears one bearing the telling title "Les Maschefain des Advocatz" ("The Voracity of Advocates," *Pantagruel*, 7.58; Cohen, 189), and Frere Jean at one point describes his own appetite: "j'ay un estomac pavé, creux comme la botte sainct Benoist, tousjours ouvert comme la gibbessiere d'un advocat" ("I have a paved stomach as hollow as Saint Benedict's tun, and always gaping like a lawyer's purse," *Gargantua*, 39.166; Cohen, 123). From Theleme are banished "maschefains practiciens / Clers, basauchiens, mangeurs du populaire" ("lawyers insatiable, / Ushers, lawyer's clerks, devourers of the people," *Gargantua*, 54.208; Cohen, 153). Excluded from the group of convivial readers and good drinkers invited to partake of the *Tiers Livre* are lawyers and pious hypocrites, "que tous soient beuveurs oultrez, tous verollez croustelevez, guarniz de alteration inextinguible et manducation insatiable" ("they are all outrageous drinkers, all scurvy and poxy, all possessed of an inexhaustible thirst and insatiable powers of mastication," prologue, 43; Cohen, 286). The sole exception to these is the simple judge Bridoye, who temporizes by taking literally and throwing the *alea judiciorum*, as the arbitrariness of law becomes embodied as real dice (*alea*). The work of the other lawyers is "vendre parolles" ("selling words," *Quart Livre*, 56.196; Cohen, 569). They are thus the descendants of Augustine's rhetoricians, "venditor verborum," who reduce words to objects that can be sold and used by men against each other to promote the self-interest that is the antithesis of either Augustinian charity or Rabelaisian conviviality.

This pattern of imagery climaxes on the island of the "Chatz fourrez": "chats," punning on "advocatz"—lawyer—and "fourrez"—furry, but also furious—who "mengent des petits enfans et paissent sur des pierres de marbre" ("eat little children and feed on marble stones," 11.129; Cohen, 625), as they are "enragez et affamez de sang chrestien" ("so furiously hungry for human [literally, Christian] blood," 14.153; Cohen, 632). While the well-intentioned Bridoye appeared to regenerate the letter of the law by literalizing it, in less charitable hands—or rather, paws—that literalism becomes murderous. A quotation muttered by Bridoye to give his argument authority, "pecunia est alter sanguis" ("wealth is another blood," *Tiers Livre*, 42.203—an idea found in Cusanus's representation of the body politic) takes on a frightening reality, as the desire for gold and the desire for flesh are identified as one enormous appetite which, like that of Ovid's Erysicthon, absorbs all substances. The desire for money *is* the desire for blood, as the analogy collapses in this body politic, ruled by a figure who embodies all appetites that are no longer differentiated. Panurge's universe bound by a chain of debts, in which debt itself is imagined as a form of Platonic Eros (*Tiers Livre*, 3–4), turns into a world bound by grimmer and ineradicable debts, lawsuits that are "comme toiles d'airaignes" ("like spiders' webs," 12.141; Cohen, 629).

Like a skilled rhetorician, Grippeminault plays with language: he asks a riddle and puns constantly upon the double sense of "or sà," which means both "come on" and "gold here." Yet for him there does not appear to be any real difference between the two, as the two meanings merge into total identity. In his realm, words are not a medium through which men can communicate, but rather reified objects, frozen like the "parolles gelees," that are used as weapons in a contest of wills. The relations among men become polarized into the antithetical roles of eater and eaten. The festive atmosphere of the Pantagruelistes at their symposium of words and wine is gruesomely parodied by Grippeminault, the host who wants to feed on his guests. He is indeed a kind of Hell mouth that sucks everything into itself without bringing forth any new creation; the quest comes perilously close to *Inferno* 34 and the monstrous Lucifer silently absorbed in his continual feast.

The encounter with Gaster momentarily brought the quest to a halt. With Grippeminault, it has reached what is essentially a dead end in the complete perversion of the appetites and total breakdown of communication among men. Rabelais can get out of this place simply by moving the narrative forward, but a nasty aftertaste lingers on, as we have come close to a Hell mouth that could consume Rabelais's own ideals. His ability to reverse this fall, as Dante did, is tested in the final books, where the quest reaches its goal: the oracle of the Holy Bottle.

The temple of the Holy Bottle is described in great detail: its double doors (which inform us "*en oinoi aletheia*" ["in wine lies the truth"], "Ducunt volentum fata, nolentem trahunt" ["Fate leads the willing and drags the unwilling"], and "TOUTES CHOSES CE MEUVENT A LEUR FIN" ["All things move toward their end"], 36.355, 359—a characteristic mixing of tongues, ideas, and sources), the pavement which is so cleverly artful that it seems totally natural, the mosaic of Bacchus, the lamp that lights the temple, and the fountain at its center. In particular, these last two images, neoplatonic commonplaces, suggest the possible upward movement of a text returning to its own source.[44]

The lamp makes the underground cave as light as day; like the emblems on the floor, it suggests an imitation of nature that reproduces exactly without replacing the real thing. Its wicks are made of inflammable substances that recall the Pantagruelion, not present in name or as a "quint essence" that can be extracted, but subtly incorporated as an image of creative energy. The light from these wicks cannot be looked at directly but is seen as it strikes the objects in the cavern and scatters to form a brilliant rainbow. The image suggests an organic relationship between a single source and its many manifestations, and presents as the center of the quest a source that is already in motion—that is already, in fact, a figure. Pointing to the fountain, Bacbuc explains to the questors:

> Vos Philosophes nient estre par vertu de figures mouvement fait; oyez icy, et voyez le contraire. Par le seule figure limaciale que voyez bipactiente . . . est ceste sacrée fontaine excolée, et par icelle une armonie telle que elle monte jusques à la mer de vostre monde.

> ("You philosophers deny that motion can arise through the power of figures. But listen now, and you will admit that you are wrong. Merely by that corkscrew

figure that you see there in two parts . . . this sacred fountain is emptied, and a harmony produced that mounts up to the sea of your world." 42.395; Cohen, 699)

Here it is the figurative that moves and animates the literal, as an image also for the text that feeds the world even as it is fed by it.

As the one light becomes a rainbow, so the water is transformed by the taste of each individual into a different vintage of wine. The word of the Holy Bottle is also taken differently by the various questors. When Panurge finally hears "le beau mot," *Trinch*, he still does not recognize it but is afraid that the bottle has cracked. The transcendental term is in fact utter nonsense. Just as the white light must be broken into colors to be seen, in a playful figurative version of the doctrine of accommodation, "Trinch" needs to be expanded, explicated through discursive language, and realized in the act of drinking in order to be made meaningful. Panurge first takes the explanation orally, as Bacbuc tells him:

Les philosophes, prescheurs et docteurs de vostre monde vous paissent de belles parolles par les aureilles; icy, nous realement incorporons nos preceptions par la bouche. Pourtant je ne vous dy: Lisez ce chapitre, voyez ceste glose; je vous dy: Tastez ce chapitre, avallez ceste belle glose. Jadis un antique Prophete de la nation Judaïque mangea un livre, et fut clerc jusques aux dens; presentement vous en boirez un et serez clerc jusques au foye. Tenez, ouvrez les mandibules.

("The philosophers, preachers, and doctors of your world feed you with fine words through the ears. Here, we literally take in our teachings orally, through the mouth. Therefore I do not say to you: Read this chapter, understand this gloss. What I say is: Taste this chapter, swallow this gloss. Once upon a time an ancient prophet of the Jewish nation swallowed a book, and became a learned man to the teeth. Now you must immediately drink this, and you'll be learned to the liver. Here, open your jaws." 45.411; Cohen, 704)

In this climactic literalization of Rabelais's association of drinking and knowing, Panurge consumes knowledge. He then takes it aurally, as Bacbuc explains, "*Trinch* est un mot panomphée, celebre et entendu de toutes nations, et nous signifie: Beuvez" ("*Trinch* is a panomphean word. It speaks oracles, that is to say, in all languages, and is famed and understood by all nations. To us it signifies: Drink," 45.413; Cohen, 704). The explication unfolds further: drinking refers specifically to "vin bon et frais" ("good cool wine"), because "de vin divin on devient" ("by wine one grows divine") and "pouvoir il a d'emplir l'ame de toute verité, tout savoir et philosophie" ("it has the power to fill the soul with all truth, all knowledge, and all philosophy"). She concludes her speech: "en vin est verité cachée. La dive Bouteille vous y envoye, soyey vous mesme interpretes de vostre entreprinse" ("the truth lies hidden in wine. The Holy Bottle directs you to it. You must be your own interpreters in this matter," 45.413, Cohen, 705).

Interpretation itself is a form of emanation from a source of meaning; a chain is formed from the word to Bacbuc and to the questors and ultimately to the reader. While it took two books to get to the source, the movement away from it is rapid and begins as soon as the characters start to interpret for themselves. Panurge immediately starts to speak in rhyme, announcing that the source has given him complete confidence to go ahead and do exactly what he wants; it appears that he has learned nothing from the bottle but merely used it, like everything else, to justify and confirm his desires. But the bottle cannot be expected to transform the drinkers totally; in a communal and reciprocal relation meaning depends on the receiver or interpreter as well as on the host or writer. Although they can act as guides, neither Bacbuc nor Rabelais is able to control completely how we take things in, either by reading or drinking. Like the Catholic Host, the bottle itself is significant; but the action that it effects, like that of the reformed Eucharist, takes place inside the communicant and so depends on his individual capabilities. Frere Jean, who generally sees life in terms of eating and drinking, thus interprets Panurge's extemporaneous effusion as the result of indigestion, crying, "Que tous les diables a il mangé?" ("What in all the devils' names has he been eating?" 45.417; Cohen, 706).[45] The more refined Pantagruel sees it his own way, explaining, also in rhyme, "Croyez que c'est la fureur poëtique / Du bon Bacchus" ("Believe me, it's the fit divine, / Poetic frenzy"). Whatever it is (and now it's the reader's turn to interpret), it is contagious, and even Frere Jean gets caught up in a fit of rhyme, although only to enter into a match of abuse with Panurge that ends with a pun, as he cries, "Je ne saurois plus rithmer, la rithme me prent à la gorge; parlons de satisfaire icy" ("I can't rhyme any more. The rheum has got me by the throat. Let's talk of giving satisfaction here," 46.423; Cohen, 709).

The kind of satisfaction—revenge—he desires is averted, however, by the intervention of Bacbuc, who offers him a substitute form: "à tout sera satisfaict, si de nous estes contens" ("All will be perfectly satisfactory if you are satisfied with us," 47.425; Cohen, 709). Instead of the physical satisfaction that would end their argument by violence, she offers them the promise of further dialogue. Though the differences between the two perspectives cannot be reconciled, the two points of view are kept from consuming each other by being brought together in the communion of interpretation. Bacbuc returns us to an image which framed the *Gargantua*— that of the resurrection of texts and the partial discovery of meaning—and promises that there is still more "en terre caché" ("hidden beneath the earth," 47.427; Cohen, 709). She moves us from a spatial model for interpretation, in which truth is a bone to be cracked and eaten, toward a temporal one, in which it can be brought to light only gradually;[46] "on temps," as she says, revising Bridoye's naive defense of temporization:

> car par temps ont esté et par temps seront toutes choses latentes inventées; et c'est la cause pourquoy les antiens ont appelé Saturne le Temps, pere de Verité, et Verité fille eut Temps.

> ("For it is time that has discovered, or in due course will discover, all things which lie hidden; and that is the reason why the ancients called Saturn or Time the father of Truth, or Truth the Daughter of Time." 47.428; Cohen, 710)

The temporal metaphor may, however, create its own problems. Saturn is, after all, not known for his paternal kindness; given his past history, his daughter is more likely to be consumed than created. And on the periphery of this final scene are images of violence that suggest the vulnerability of the resolution of any quest for total security, especially one involving the opposite sex. On the walls of the temple surrounding the questors is the mosaic portraying the victory of "le bon Bacchus" over the Indians, in grotesque scenes of violence. Bacchus's followers are mostly hordes of "femmes diverses forcenées et dissolues, lesquelles metoient furieusement en pieces veaux, moutons et brebis toutes vives, et de leur chair se paissoient" ("frantic and depraved women . . . tearing to pieces live calves, sheep, and ewes, and consuming their raw flesh," 38.365; Cohen, 691). Rabelais's god is hardly a hospitable character, but rather an imperialist who is said to fight with fire and thunder, shedding blood in both war and peace. The text's own source, which continues to nourish it, is not communion but murder; we return to the fratricide, the killing of Abel by Cain, from which springs the race of Pantagruel (*Pantagruel*, 1).

Moreover, the old saying quoted by Bacbuc, "en vin est verité cachée" ("the truth is hidden in wine") is a version of the inside/outside hermeneutic for interpretation. In the sacrament of communion, which Erasmus saw as another "Silenus" that opposed appearance and reality, the truth that lies hidden in the wine is the blood of Christ. But in Rabelais's own time, that blood was increasingly the blood of his contemporaries. Many lives were sacrificed in a battle over interpretation, a struggle like the quest of Panurge, to fill holes and make certain the meaning of a dangerously fluid and unsubstantial substance—associated not only with Christ but also with Bacchus and his female followers—to control differences, sexual and otherwise, which, simply because they are different, present potentially consuming abysses. What Rabelais's texts show is that the substance that is supposed to bring men together actually is the thing that sets them at each others' throats, as in the case of the Eucharist, which became the bone of contention between Catholic and Protestant. Rabelais's attempt to use the area of antagonism as a means of reconciliation is daring; the potential danger involved may justify a certain amount of canny wariness on his part: an unwelcome guest might turn the tables by having the host fried for supper, so that some caution concerning who is included and who excluded seems reasonable. Later in the same century, Giordano Bruno's imitation of Rabelais was doomed, and the author finally burnt as a heretic.[47] The differences of interpretation of both sacred and secular texts became too great, so that guest and host easily turned into enemies feeding, not off a text, but on each other.

JONSON

While Rabelais attempts to maintain an identification between literal and spiritual kinds of eating, Ben Jonson insists that the two are polarized. Throughout his works, he contrasts bodily eating with more refined internal processes of internalization. The opposition is evident also in the bifurcation of his own self-images, as he divides himself between his rotund body and his encyclopedic and fecund mind, separating the famous drinker from the voracious reader in order to deny the material base of his own artistic creation. Jonson draws attention to his physical appearance in his poetry, where he represents himself as "Laden with belly" (*Underwoods*, 56.9), a "mountain belly" (*Underwoods*, 9.17) that is comparable in size to "the tun at Heidelberg" (*Underwoods*, 52.6).[48] By exaggerating his own bulk, he makes his bodily image first comical and then nonessential, and so frees the inner man who lives not in the belly but in art and the imagination. The body becomes a mere grotesque husk belonging to the world of appearances; the real Ben Jonson lives in language and is apprehended by hearing rather than vision.

This distinction is one that is obviously made more easily in theory than in practice; when, in *Underwoods* 9, the poet woos by telling the lady not to look at him but to listen to him, he ends by confessing that "My mountain belly, and my rocky face, / And all these through her eyes, have stopped her ears" (17–18). He cannot separate himself completely from his outward appearance, which affects how others respond, or fail to respond, to his words. It seems fitting, therefore, that criticism never seems totally able to get away from discussions of "the bulk of Ben," in which his bodily girth is often read as evidence of his poetical unwieldiness or excess.[49] While dragging in the poet's weight problem may seem to be hitting below the belt, it is significant that the critics try to reassociate Jonson's work with the bodily image and material base from which he tried to detach it.

The most famous of these critical attempts was Edmund Wilson's essay, "Morose Ben Jonson," which used psychoanalysis as a means of reattaching art to its bodily origin.[50] Apparently annoyed by Jonson's reduction of comic characters to "humors," Wilson essentially used the poet's girth as a means of turning him into the modern equivalent of one "humor": the psychological type of the anal-erotic, whose characteristics include pedantry, avarice, and an obsession with food. In most anal-erotics the obsession is sublimated and redirected into a desire for money; according to Wilson, Jonson, who created characters that use alchemical sublimation to get gold, substituted for money the hoards of learning and language that he amassed in impressive heaps.

One response to Wilson, E. Pearlman's essay, "Ben Jonson: An Anatomy," corrected some of Wilson's conclusions but did not question the basic premise that Jonson's anatomy is significant in itself.[51] In Pearlman's reading, Jonson is not merely an anal but a totally corporeal poet, in whom the various drives are not differentiated, and whose truly dominant psychological pattern is an ambivalence to power, which he resisted and yet with which he attempted to identify himself. Pearlman sees Jonson's identification of all appetites as the consequence of "the need to assert strong authoritarian control over disordered impulses."[52] Reason is set up as an internal authority over against all the appetites and passions that threaten to dethrone it. Like Augustine, Jonson uses food as a symbol for all material needs that he wishes to transcend. Throughout his works, he represents all excessive desires as forms of hunger and in particular frequently identifies food and money as objects of corporeal and economic consumption. In *Volpone* and the *Alchemist*, the greed for gold is a kind of gluttony, and the idolatry of the belly-God and Mammon meet in the figure of Sir Epicure Mammon. The two appetites become one when gold is seen as the source and originator of all things and the one substance that can satisfy all appetites. It is the "world's soul," according to Volpone (1.1.3) who, with words that recall Rabelais's description of Gaster, praises "Riches, the dumb god, that giv'st all men tongues, / That canst do nought, and yet mak'st men do all things" (1.1.22–23). Gold is the material motive for human action, which drives men to do and become every and any thing.

According to Mosca, gold also "transforms / The most deformed, it restores 'em lovely / As 'twere the strange poetical girdle" (5.1.100–102). For Jonson, appetite is opposed not only to reason but also to the imagination and the art it produces. Men use gold as a shortcut to a metamorphosis which the imagination achieves through an indirect and internal route. The circle with a dot at its center is both the alchemical symbol for gold and Jonson's own *impresa*, as Jonson suggests that his art is the true form of sublimation. In alchemy, sublimation is the process by which matter is transformed into spirit;[53] for Jonson, it is the imagination alone that effects such a transformation, which in its true form is an internalized process that achieves the humanist ideal of turning nature into art.[54]

Jonson's impresa appropriates also the hermetic image of the God who

is both center and circumference.[55] Jonson's image for his idealized self
that is identified with art and the imagination incorporates the divine position in order to be both securely centered and expansive. The self that is
both its own center and circumference appears able to resist the fixation
and obsession of the isolated ego by going beyond itself, yet without the
possibility of self-dissipation. The centered circumference is an image of a
collected, gathered, and bounded self that stands in direct opposition to
the grotesque appearance of the poet's inflated body.[56] Many critics have
commented on Jonson's horror of metamorphosis and of traveling as images of change that suggest the possible loss of identity through dissipation
of the self.[57] By being both center and circumference, the self can move
safely, thus avoiding either opposing perils of static self-reduction or the
loss of identity—the going native—that is always possible in foreign territory. One may be like John Seldon who, as Jonson tells him, has been

> Ever at home: yet, have all countries seen:
> And like a compass keeping one foot still
> Upon your center, do your circle fill
> Of general knowledge.

(Underwoods 14.29–33)

Jonson's ideal self stays at home while traveling through art. Whereas appetite leads to dissipation in the "febrile thirst for transformation,"[58] art
leads to self-creation, through carefully controlled encounters with others.[59]

Wilson sees Jonson's bodily appetite, the source of his girth, as having a
literary counterpart in his voracious reading. He argues that Jonson's rapacious absorption of literary sources produced a bulky mass of material
that got in the way of his poetry. For Wilson, Jonson's learning appears
either as "an alien and obstructive element" or at best as "a padding to give
the effect of a dignity and weight which he cannot supply himself";[60] in
either case the source is not assimilated to the new textual body. It has,
however, also been argued that the sources were fully absorbed by and at
home in Jonson, who was able to control what he took into himself. John
Palmer, for example, claimed that: "Jonson is most himself in the passages
which come nearest to his sources. His mind and pen follow naturally the
drift of things read and remembered. These old authors have become part
of his imaginative reaction to present life. They are woven into the texture
of his thought. They contain his response, not merely to an historic theme,
but to the people and things of every day. They even determine to a large
extent his feelings and beliefs about himself."[61] More recently, critical discussions of Jonson's mental digestive tract have been placed in the context
of the traditional use of digestive metaphors for poetical imitation, *imitatio*.[62] In the Renaisance especially, a common way of expressing the rela-

tionship between a poet and an earlier source was in terms of eating. In order to create his own poetic identity, the later poet absorbs the substances of his predecessors. So, in his *Discoveries*, Jonson claims that the poet must "be able to convert the substance, or riches of another poet, to his own use. To make choice of one excellent man above the rest, and so to follow him, as the copy may be mistaken for the principal. Not, as a creature, that swallows, what it takes in, crude, raw, or indigested; but, that feeds with an appetite, and hath a stomach to concoct, divide, and turn all into nourishment" (448). In order to be recreated, the source must be fully assimilated and converted into the new writer. Imitatio is anxiously differentiated from mere plagiarism, the theft of poetic property, which, as Dante demonstrates in the canto of the thieves, occurs when substances are taken by but not assimilated to the new host. The product of plagiarism can be compared to the natural results of real digestion, as in Donne's ridicule of the plagiarist:

> hee is worst, who (beggarly) doth chaw
> Others wits fruits, and in his ravenous maw
> Rankly digested, doth those things out-spue,
> As his owne things; and they'are his owne, 'tis true,
> For if one eate my meate, though it be knowne
> The meate was mine, th'excrement is his owne.
>
> ("Satyre II," 25–30)[63]

Donne satirically inverts the idealized version of the process of literary digestion, in which what goes in as food come out refined into words.[64] The miracle of imitatio is, furthermore, that eating ends in procreation, by a sudden switch which avoids the usual outcome of ingestion.[65] The writer devours his models, assimilates them to himself as he digests them, and then, through a clever elision by which the alimentary imagery is superseded by the sexual, brings forth what he has read in a new form, thus also neatly converting his poetic father into his own son.

The concept of imitatio requires the awareness of the existence of individual poetical "I"s, whose substances are differentiated yet capable of identification. It is defined against plagiarism, or theft, a concept which, Spitzer argued, was not available to the medieval writer, who lacked a sense of a separate poetic identity. It is another formulation that establishes opposite terms, host/guest, father/son, in the name of bringing them together, and in the process creates the possibility of potential conflict—theft and cannibalistic rivalry.[66] While the origins of the image go back long before the Renaissance, it is, as I shall discuss further in the next chapter, a peculiarly appropriate way for Renaissance writers to imagine relations. It is a way of representing the relationship between past and present as one of communion, in which oedipal rivalry is suspended through the prolongation of an oral exchange. But it also contains, perhaps by concealing, a potential for aggression.

However, current discussions of imitatio tend to define the relations between opposites in ways that keep cannibalism out. Terence Cave sees the digestive metaphor for imitatio as precisely a means of avoiding conflict between poetic fathers and sons, who are brought together in a reciprocal exchange, "a reciprocal process of incorporation or consubstantiation: the reader is transformed into what he reads . . . at the same time, he converts it into his own substance."[67] For Jonson, it offers the appearance of a literary version of communion, in which he is able to receive and interact with his poetic fathers. According to Thomas M. Greene, in Jonson's dinner invitation poems, the proffered hospitality extends also to the poems' sources.[68] In these works, Jonson "has converted Martial's 'riches' to his own use with a magnanimity that profits the original author," in an exchange which is reciprocal, for "In any act of hospitality, the host receives in one sense and the guest in another."[69]

Such reciprocity may be limited, however, when artistic exchanges are imagined on the model of Jonson's impresa. The movement out of the center is only into an encounter with what is actually, after all, only an expanded version of the self. Stanley Fish has argued that Jonson's invitations are actually exclusive, forming an elite community, a kind of secret society, in which the identification between host and guest is so absolute that no real exchange is possible, and poetry itself, as a medium for communication, redundant.[70] As Fish and Pearlman demonstrate, Jonson idealizes the guest/host relation in a way that works to eliminate not only conflict but ultimately all differences. He creates a fable of identity of a harmonious world of identification and plenitude, a Golden Age world, like that of Penshurst, in which feudal proprietorship is idealized as the elimination of labor and private property.[71] It is a world in which, through the generosity of the lord or host, all partake equally of substances that none are seen to produce; a world of the imagination liberated from material necessity and unruly, antisocial appetites.

The creation through art of a world without loss, without debts, and ultimately without differences, has an obvious advantage for a poet dependent on patronage. Once all men are defined as guests coming together at a communal banquet, the role of host is transferred from the lord to the poet, through the writing of the poem. The king, in particular, is the figure of authority Jonson first ostentatiously acknowledges, then identifies with, and finally replaces. The poor guest turns himself into the host by a strategy Fish admires: "The outsider who must rely on others for favor and recognition imagines himself as the proprietor and arbiter of an internal kingdom whose laws he promulgates and whose entrance he zealously guards, admitting only those he would 'call mine' to an elect friendship."[72]

Jonson's inversion of roles is part of his own imaginative sublimation, through which the hungry guest is turned into the generous host. Whereas alchemical sublimation involves a continuity between lower and higher forms, for Jonson the process is one of simultaneous identification and detachment. He attempts to liberate himself from his bodily appetites by projecting them outside of himself onto parasites and flatterers, like "Captain Hungry," who use words to serve their belly, and false imitators motivated by greed, whose servile imitation of others leads not to self-creation but to self-dissipation.[73] The playwright as host projects his own potential oral aggressivity onto his guests, the lower-class audience whom, as Don K. Hendrick has shown, he represents as cannibals.[74] Detachment from all material motives, finally from the obvious fact that he wrote *poetry* to get *money* to buy *food*, is necessary for Jonson to construct the myth of his own personal integrity. The impossibility of achieving such a separation is shown, however, in his obsessive return to images of food and eating, not only in order to project them, but also as figures for his own work. As Pearlman points out, "Jonson often seems to think of the making of poetry, of creativity itself, in very specific bodily terms."[75] He identifies art and food, as in the masque *Neptune's Triumph for the Return of Albion*, whose cook claims that it was in the kitchen that "the art of poetry was learned and found out, or nowhere, and the same day with the art of cookery."[76]

In Jonson's works, therefore, a tension articulated by Augustine between the two forms of orality—eating and speaking—with their two rival substances—food and words—is intensified through a need for division between the two. At the same time, however, it is subverted by Jonson's orality—his inability to distinguish different drives and appetites, which causes him to identify verbal and edible substances. His attitude toward this opposition results in a deep ambivalence, related to his attitude toward theatricality, the "shows," outer appearances of art, that potentially compromise their inner meaning.[77] Such ambivalence puts the poet in a peculiar position, as in his attempts to sublimate—or effectively excrete—the material origins of his poetry, he is forced to return to them constantly as his subject. Jonson's art, the centered circle, in fact becomes caught up in Gaster's vicious circle of production and consumption.

This paradoxical position is most evident in the masques, both "high" courtly art produced for the upper classes and material spectacles of conspicuous consumption.[78] By the very act of writing masques, Jonson's dependency upon the court, his parasitical position, was revealed, and his myth of integrity compromised. It is in the masques, therefore, that the myth has to be most firmly upheld, through the separation of antitheses. I would like to look now at how this affects a masque presumably about the reconciliation of opposites, *Pleasure Reconciled to Virtue*, which focuses on the absolute distinction between two figures, Comus and Hercules, who are both, however, images of the poet himself.

In his discussion of Renaissance ideals of self-fashioning, Stephen Greenblatt has argued that the construction of identity took place between two poles, "an absolute power or authority situated at least partially outside the self" to which the self submitted, and "something perceived as alien, strange, or hostile," that was also "always constructed as a distorted image of the authority," which "must be discovered or invented in order to be attacked and destroyed."[79] In Jonson's masque, these poles of alien and authority are represented in the figures of Comus and Hercules. Through the course of the masque, the former is projected and the second introjected—enabling Jonson to appropriate authority for himself. Yet the separation of the two, which corresponds roughly to that between food and words, is complicated by Jonson's awareness of the deep identity between them.

According to Stephen Orgel, "The end toward which the masque moved was to destroy any sense of theatre and to include the whole theatre court in the mimesis—in a sense, what the spectator watched he ultimately became."[80] By a more refined version of "you are what you eat," nature is transformed into art. The masque aims to contain completely the reality it represents, incorporating also all media to create what Angus Fletcher has called a "synesthetic feast"[81] that satisfies all senses. But, like all feasts, it ends up inside those who attend it. While Orgel claims that *Pleasure Reconciled to Virtue* succeeds most completely of all Jonson's masques in containing its audience, it is also presented as something to be simultaneously contained by them, through an ideal relation of reciprocal consumption.

However, accounts of the first performance show that, far from becoming what he saw, the king became merely impatient with the delay of the dancers.[82] Ironically, the infamously thirsty James was probably more interested in the images of revelry in the antimasque than in the winding movement of the masque that slowly unfolded outward to embrace and enter the court. However, the difference between the two kinds of representation, the one offering instant gratification both visual and oral, and the other more delayed satisfaction that is ultimately aural, is part of Jonson's construction of two opposing methods of incorporation. The literal banqueting of the antimasque is set off against the indirect process of internalization of the masque, which takes a labyrinthine path in order to refine the material excess of the opening and sublimate it into spiritual nourishment that can inform the audience.

Though the text of the masque is short, it subsumes a surprising number of visual and literary sources; these have been discussed in detail by Richard Peterson, who is mainly concerned with the masque as a series of emblems and with the priority of visual images.[83] While Peterson cautions his reader "lest Jonson's spoken words, through their ears, stop their eyes to his full design,"[84] in "My Picture Left in Scotland" (*Underwoods* 9), it was precisely the poet's visual appearance that was an obstruction to communication, as "all these through her eyes, have stopped her ears" (18). As the famous quarrel with his designer and partner, Inigo Jones, and his "shows, shows, mighty shows! / The eloquence of masques!" ("An Expostulation with Inigo Jones," 39–40) also suggests, Jonson found working with the sense of sight to entail working against it. So Angus Fletcher notes how "Jonson ascribes the role of ultimate vision, not to sight, but to sound," for "Through the ear one can redeem the ephemeral, but not through sight, which loses it in the passing flux."[85] As Walter Ong points out, whereas sight is blocked by surfaces that touch can only penetrate by invasion, hearing permits a more intimate and yet benign encounter with others: "*Sound is a special key to interiority*. Sound has to do with interiors as such, which means with interiors as manifesting themselves, not as withdrawn into themselves, for true interiority is communicative. . . . Sound . . . reveals the interior without the necessity of physical invasion."[86] Or, in Jonson's words, "Language most shows the man: speake that I may see thee" (*Discoveries*; in Parfitt, 435). Through words, ideally, our centers travel to our circumferences and make our minds visible to others; through words, also, others can take our thoughts into their own centers, as they move from our mouths to their ears.

Jonson's differentiation between sight and sound, images and words, looks back to both Plato and Augustine and helps explain the variations between the written and performed text.[87] It is typical of Jonson that the printed "Work" be different from the performed spectacle, suggesting that, as Jonas Barish puts it, "In the poetic kernel of the masque lies its abiding essence, in the theatrical vesture only a disposable shell."[88] The masque becomes a dualistic form divided into its internal essence, words, which exist separate from its external appearance or various incarnations on stage. As Barish points out, the text of *Pleasure Reconciled to Virtue* especially "seems almost to testify to the irrelevance of the spectator's experience."[89]

The audience first saw a struggle between two large men, Hercules and Antaeus, which took place in front of the figure of Atlas. According to Peterson, the appearance of Atlas would probably have reminded the audience of the character in the *Metamorphoses* who was petrified as punishment for his inhospitality to Perseus, Hercules' great-grandfather.[90] The written text, on the other hand, eliminates what was seen, or, rather, revises it in a different medium and so subtly changes it. The wrestling match, the most graphic image for conflict, is omitted, but reappears in a tension between two literary traditions made present through Jonson's use of allusions. Peterson notes that the printed description of Atlas in fact recalls not Ovid but Virgil, *Aeneid* 4.247–51, thus pointing the reader toward another interpretation of Atlas, in which he is the bearer of the world and grateful host and teacher of Hercules. The performed struggle between the two gigantic wrestlers is internalized in the figure of Atlas, who, like Polyphemos before him, belongs to a tradition of man-mountains, huge men whose bodies incorporate the world. These figures are generally viewed with ambivalence; Polyphemos is a perverse primal man whose method of incorporation would by most standards be considered subhuman. For the poet who represents himself as having a "mountain belly" and a "rocky face" (*Underwoods* 9.17), the tradition has a special significance and plays a part in his construction of his own identity as generous host. Jonson consciously appropriates the image for himself and then purifies it, excreting its negative connotations, such as the figure of Antaeus (who never even appears in the written text) and, in the course of the masque, internalizing and, through a form of sublimation, refining Atlas into a figure for the poet himself.

The separation of the two kinds of figures corresponds superficially to the division between the antimasque and the masque. The first revolves around the fat figure of Comus, who is another "Belly-god" (40) and "Prime master of arts," and whose hymn of praise, like Volpone's celebration of money, echoes the celebration of Gaster in *Quart Livre* 57 and 61. In Rabelais, the praise was ironic, for while the belly may be the source of all art, it turns into a tyrant when it claims to be the end as well and forces all inventions to serve it. Similarly, Jonson's catalogue of the arts shows that Comus is interested only in the creation of "Engines" that will aid his appetite. As the Bowl-bearer points out, he is therefore not very interested in poetry; even hymns praising him are not substantial enough to feed his ego, which demands strictly edible tributes. Words are useless to him: "when the belly is not edified by it, it is not well; for where did you ever read or hear that the belly had any ears?" (43–45).

Rabelais's Gaster literally had no ears, but Rabelais himself is aware that, as Pantagruel points out, "L'estomach affamé n'a poinct d'aureilles" ("the hungry stomach has no ears," *Quart Livre*, 63.219; Cohen, 586). A hungry man isn't interested in words; for Rabelais, physical hunger must be satisfied first before the process of feeding the spirit with art can even begin. For Jonson, however, like Augustine, the two appetites are not complementary but polarized; his concern is that physical nourishment will prove satisfying in itself and block the desire for art, and so he reverses Pantagruel's words: "the belly will not be talked to, especially when he is full" (52–53). The complete satisfaction of bodily appetite stupifies the hunger of the imagination, and the full belly has an empty head. For Jonson, to see hunger as a motive for art is to degrade art. Creation that has its origin in the belly is represented as the arts of flattery practiced by parasites, servile imitation that leads to the dissipation of Comus, against whom he must define himself as a purely disinterested, which is to say disembodied, artist.

Peterson and Orgel have both discussed the classical sources for the figure of Comus and the odd expansion of the originally trim god of temperate conviviality into the god of excess whom spectators mistook for a corpulent Bacchus.[91] Behind this belly-god also, as behind Gaster, lie Paul's warnings against the liars who serve their bellies and who are contrasted with the followers of Christ, whose "conversation is in heaven," where they will be refashioned into the body of Christ (Romans 16:18 and Philippians 3:19–21).[92] Here, as in Dante, who similarly drew upon both the Bible and Homer, the belly is associated with fraud, the abuse of language, idolatry, and with a form of metamorphosis. Whereas the man who imitates Christ becomes identified with him and with heavenly conversation, the followers of Jonson's Comus who, like the worshippers of the belly-god, use "fair speeches," undergo a less lofty metamorphosis: "men that drink hard and serve the belly in any place of quality . . . are living measures of drink, and can transform themselves, and do every day, to bottles or tuns when they please" (66–70).

The revelers become what they drink, turning into tuns in a grotesque literalization of Jonson's humanist ideal of inner transformation through the assimilation of art. In fact, they are also grotesque versions of another of Jonson's common images for himself, the "tun" or "pitcher," which Peterson has discussed, noting their relation to a traditional topos of man as a vessel.[93] He notes that the two meanings of vessel, cup and ship (complementary figures, one might note, of mental and physical transport), meet in the figure of Hercules, who made a voyage in a bowl.[94] In the poems, Hercules is a figure with whom Jonson compares himself, in size if not in spirit (see, for example, *Underwoods* 2.2, 30–32). The description with which the text begins informs the reader that the revelers are carrying the bowl of Hercules. The appropriation of the bowl for Comus, himself a vessel and source of transport, suggests a close connection between these two big men. The two opposites form poles parallel to the twin traditions of Atlas, and similarly they begin in identity in order to be separated into the antitheses, Greenblatt's alien and authority, between which Jonson constructs his own self-image.

For the audience, the struggle between these two would have appeared in a much cruder form, beginning with the wrestling match between opposites who then take turns dominating the stage. The dance of Comus ends abruptly with the entrance of Hercules and the replacement of one fat man by another. But whereas the dancers were merely empty containers, circumferences with no centers, Hercules presents himself as a full, weighty center whose presence on the stage puts the antimasque in perspective and brings order out of chaos. His first speech is a tirade against the antimasque that strips it of its illusion of pleasure, revealing it as a degradation of human nature into a base, subhuman existence. Whereas the revelers sang of Comus expanding until "Thou break'st all thy girdles, and break'st forth a god" (34), Hercules explains that this is not a sign of transcendence but of the spontaneous combustion of a bodily container unable to bear the pressure from within itself. Comus becomes identified with assimilation that lacks the creative expression of imitatio; he is a purely material vessel that takes in but can give nothing out. He produces only a mess when, as Hercules foresees, "your swoll'n bowels burst with what you take" (97), and the belly grotesquely breaks forth in the only real way it can.

The stripping of Comus's illusions is enacted dramatically at the conclusion of Hercules' speech, when he commands the grove to vanish. The instantaneous execution of this order must have appeared to the spectators as a fantastic kind of revelation that literally stripped the scene to expose Pleasure and Virtue sitting as if they had been reconciled all along, hidden from view only by false images of pleasure. The scenic effect is a completely conventional one, but Jonson characteristically makes it significant. It becomes the visual equivalent of the act of interpretation seen as the removal of an outer veil to reveal an inner truth, as the disappearance of the grove makes possible the gradual entrance into the Garden of the Hesperides and the discovery of the meaning behind the masque.

There is first, however, a pause in which Hercules is invited by the choir to lie down and "cool awhile thy heated blood" (111). But the sleeping Hercules takes up the exact position of the reclining Comus, and seems suddenly to slide from one extreme to another. While Peterson sees the repetition as an ironic contrast between sleep after labor and sheer insensibility,[95] Hercules may be putting himself in a dangerous spot in which extremes meet and he regresses into the identity with Comus in which he began. The hero identified with labor and, even more in the Renaissance, with choice, the discrimination between opposites, is also a figure of force, associated with violence and excess, even madness.[96] The sudden appearance of Hercules and the abrupt ending of the antimasque may be a premature revelation and resolution, for the hero, like the man-mountain Atlas, contains within himself tensions which Jonson must more fully work through.

The inadequacy of this apparent resolution appears in the hilarious scene that follows, in which Hercules is suddenly surrounded by a troop of pigmies, said to be the brothers of the gigantic Antaeus with whom he wrestled in the opening performed scene. The contrast between the big and little men suggests a movement between opposites toward identification. If Hercules was almost too big for the orderly masque world, he is now in imminent danger of becoming too little: the pigmies plan to cut him up into "small portions" (131). They are so certain of success that they celebrate their triumph before completing it. In a violent fluctuation between extremes, the masque has regressed into its opposite, and suddenly the antimasque world is on stage once more.

A large part of the humor of this scene comes from its ludicrous and almost surrealistically appropriate disjunction. The pigmies are physically truncated, they speak in short disjointed lines, they interrupt the proper movement of the masque, and in turn their premature victory dance is cut short by the arrival of Mercury. For the spectators, the interlude contrasts sharply with the opening scene in which Hercules had physically engaged their brother; he has no contact with them here, and is in fact completely unaware of their presence. In opposition to Comus and Antaeus, the big men who represent the wrong kinds of self-expansion and exchanges, they stand for erroneous self-reduction and separation. The masque has to move away from these bodily based models in order to present an internalized and balanced method of self-creation, the verbal form of the image of the centered circle, which accommodates both expansion and reduction.

This movement begins with the arrival of Mercury, who frightens off the pigmies and wakens Hercules. The messenger has already been anticipated in the written text by means of the opening allusion to *Aeneid* 4.247–51, a passage that describes Mercury landing on Atlas on his way to remind Aeneas of his mission. The point of the opening allusion, which then appeared as simply the spontaneous overflow of superfluous learning, becomes clear in Mercury's speech, which also provides further background to the plot. Atlas is seen to stand behind both the scene and the story, which now unfolds as Mercury explains to Hercules:

> See, here a crown, the agèd hill hath sent thee,
> My grandsire Atlas, he that did present thee
> With the best sheep that in his fold were found,
> Or golden fruit in the Hesperian ground,
> For rescuing his fair daughters, then the prey
> Of a rude pirate, as thou cam'st this way;
> And taught thee all the learning of the sphere,
> And how, like him, thou might'st the heavens up-bear,
> As that thy labor's virtuous recompense.
>
> (151–59)

For most readers this is a surprising description of the relationship between Hercules and Atlas. In the common Ovidian tradition, Atlas is an inhospitable host; he is also said to have been duped by Hercules. Jonson is very deliberate in excluding these associations and insisting on a different version of the relationship between host and guest. Exercising his authorial control over his own text, he keeps some traditions out while letting only the desired ones in. The man-mountain is redefined unambiguously as a generous and grateful grandfather who presides over man's education into moral responsibilities and passes his knowledge down to Hercules.

Thus, through a circuitous route that moves from the opening echo of the *Aeneid* to the arrival of Mercury, Jonson is moving us away from one tradition of Atlas to create another. As the bearer of the world, he becomes associated with Aeneas himself, whose duty it was to found "regno Hesperiae" (*Aeneid* 4.355).[97] Through a chain of increasingly humanized manmountians, figures who carry the world on their shoulders, Jonson is also moving us toward another kingdom in the west that is said to be of Trojan origin: England, and the figure of James as Hesperus himself. The time of the masque and the time of the court come together around James in what, we are told, is a moment long prophesied and now to be fulfilled:

> The time's arrived that Atlas told thee of: how
> By unaltered law, and working of the stars,
> There should be a cessation of all jars
> 'Twixt Virtue and her noted opposite
> Pleasure; that both should meet here in the sight
> Of Hesperus, the glory of the west,
> The brightest star.

> (166–72)

England is traditionally associated with the evening star and island in the west,[98] but it is especially useful for Jonson to turn here to the king's metaphorical identification with the star whose influence reigns over transitions. Jonson's creation of an image of the king as a host who is not treacherous but will respond generously to his guests is connected to a myth of political succession and continuity in which the transition from father to son, like the exchange from host to guest, is represented as free from conflict. While the king is at the very center of the masque, after reaching him it begins to move outward again, as from the audience come twelve dancers, one of whom is James's heir and "shall in time the same that he is be, / And now is only a less light than he" (185–86). The son will become the father, though there is now a temporal difference between them which prevents rivalry while guaranteeing the security of the throne and kingdom. The masque looks forward to that future transformation, foretelling it through the meeting of art and nature, father and son, masque and spectator, that occurs as the court is converted into the garden of the west.

The conversion takes place under the guidance of the figure of the artist Daedalus. He leads the dancers through three interconnected labyrinths that emphasize the circuitous movement of the masque. Their patterns trace the sublimation of the external spectacle into an inner experience that is finally identified with the printed text which remains after the masque is finished.

The transformation begins as the musicians sing, "Ope agèd Atlas, open then thy lap" (196), and the mountain splits. Similar scene transitions had been used in earlier entertainments, from the *Riche Mount* of 1513 to Jonson's own *Oberon* of 1611. In structure the effect is quite similar to the earlier staging of the disappearance of the antimasque world. Here, however, what is found behind the scene is not a spectacle but a text, and the familiar visual device expands to become a written revelation. Atlas turns into a scroll unfolding so that,

> men may read in thy mysterious map
>> All lines
>> And signs
> Of royal education and the right.
>> See how they come and show,
>> That are but born to know.

> (198–203)

A familiar scenic convention is invested with a new significance and subtly turned into a form of poetry. The visual image must be read too, and Atlas turns out to be a text, signifying the rightness of royal authority, by virtue of both birth and education, the very education that the masque claims to represent.

A similar strategy occurs in the first of the three labyrinths, that of wisdom, in which the choice of Hercules is recalled and then recreated. Choice is no longer necessary, however, because Pleasure and Virtue appear in this labyrinth inextricably entwined:

> Come on, come on; and where you go
>> So interweave the curious knot,
> That ev'en th'observer scarce may know
>> Which lines are Pleasure's and which not.

> (224–27)

This labyrinth is said to appeal primarily to the sense of sight, but Jonson turns the spectacle into a text that is seen only to be read:

> So let your dances be entwined,
>> Yet not perplex men unto gaze
> But measured, and so numerous too,
>> As men may read each act you do,
> And when they see the graces meet,
>> Admire the wisdom of your feet.

> (234–39)

For Jonson, vision alone is always potentially perplexing, even petrifying.[99] Properly measured and restrained by numbers, the dancers' feet themselves turn into poetical feet, and the dance itself is no longer merely seen but also must be read. For Jonson as for Augustine, reading becomes the ideal and internalized version of vision, and the means by which the spectator becomes one with what he sees, as the dance begins to move from the dancer's feet into the spectator's mind. The process of internalization leads through a continuous movement to the second labyrinth, of beauty, whose appeal is largely to the ear, the words and music of the masque which are said to "ground" it even "if those silent arts were lost, / Design and picture" (253–54).[100] Defined as music, the masque changes from an external work of art into an inner experience, moving from the audience's eyes to their ears, to enter and become grounded in them.

The goal of the masque is a kind of communion between art and nature, in which the spectators enter the masque as it enters them. In the third labyrinth, of love, the audience begins to move in time with the music, as all desire is sublimated, and even envy, for Jonson one of the most pernicious of vices in being destructive of reciprocal relations, is transformed into pure admiration (286–87). The dancers' feet form labyrinths that are images of the indirect method by which art is internalized to inform the motions of the courtiers. But the labyrinth soon becomes a clue leading out of itself. Mercury, the messenger who brought Aeneas out of a potentially interminable, though very pleasurable, delay with the overly hospitable Dido, once more interrupts the action and reminds the audience of their moral responsibilities. He slowly unwinds the curious knot to send them back to the real world of labor where, he explains, the hard ascent must begin all over again. His speech prepares the audience for the final exit from the hall, and the reader for the closing of the book. The vision has been only an epiphany which should not be confused with a continual mode of existence. The figure of Atlas turns into the rock, in which, "you must return unto the hill, / And there advance / With labor . . ." (302–4). We are sent back to the beginning; after one last dance, the rock shuts, "and was a mountain as before" (319).

While it seems deeply ironic, it may yet be appropriate that the first thing the king did to illustrate how deeply impressed he had been by the masque was to go out and eat an enormous meal.[101] The masque was not the only prevalent form of conspicuous consumption at court. At one level, *Pleasure* is constructed as a means of education, with Jonson as Atlas making the courtiers into the men he represents, and so turning their nature into his art. More generally, it is an attempt to create a network of idealized relations and reconciliation of opposites, by means of a simultaneous identification and detachment that is ultimately impossible. The projection of Comus and the negative aspects of Atlas, and the introjection of Hercules as a type for James, is a means of giving the poet himself authority. Yet Jonson's lack of real control is indicated by his dependence upon his patron the king's approval; when the masque was next performed, it had been substantially revised.

In *Pleasure Reconciled to Virtue*, then, Jonson attempts to reconcile opposites by a form of sublimation in which one is turned into the other. Body becomes mind, guest host, son father. Through this identification, continuity is maintained, which at a political level certainly had a contemporary appeal. Yet the picture of gradated political succession presented in the masque, of the carefully educated Charles succeeding his father, is totally detached from the facts. Jonson is idealizing the British line that had been almost constantly broken and uncertain since the beginning of the War of the Roses. It had been most recently interrupted by the death of Charles's older brother, Henry, Prince of Wales, in 1612—only six years before the first performance of *Pleasure*. As the younger son, Charles had in fact *not* been raised and prepared to succeed his father, as later events revealed only too well. The myth of continuity has, no doubt for reason of its unattainability, a powerful place in English Renaissance literature. It has a further importance also for Jonson, who adopted both fathers and sons and claimed past learning as his rightful inheritance to create an illusion of a genealogical line of unbroken cultural transmission.

The problem for Jonson is that his story of succession depends also on a process of detachment, primarily that of the mind from the body. His ultimate goal is to release the higher, sublimated form from its material origin. So in the printed preface to the *Hymenaei*, he explains the difference in value between a performed piece and written text:

> It is a noble and just advantage that the things subjected to understanding have of those which are objected to sense that the one sort are momentary and merely taking, the other impressing and lasting. Else the glory of all these solemnities had perished like a blaze and gone out in the beholders' eyes. So short lived are the bodies of all things in comparison of their souls. And, though bodies ofttimes have the ill luck to be sensually preferred, they find afterwards the good fortune, when souls live, to be utterly forgotten (in Orgel, *Complete Masques*, 75).

The distinction between the external appearances that perish and the inner essence that survives is typical not only of Jonson but of the general tendency of Christian neoplatonism. The result is an absolute dualism figured in Jonson's own representations of himself as a Silenus box: mountainous and unwieldy on the outside, gathered and gracefully witty on the inside. Repudiating one's appearance is of course easier than going on a diet. But it also suggests Jonson's ambivalence about his motives, and the origin of his art in material bases. Jonson needs to idealize relations to produce images of both a society and poetic tradition that eliminates conflict. A writer from the rising middle class working within an upper-class system with which he needed, both financially and emotionally, to identify, he finds it impossible to admit that art can be produced from material motives—from the need to earn money for food, the two basic substances necessary for survival in society which he repudiates as degrading.

Perhaps this attitude is the most telling and important difference between him and the later Johnson, Samuel, who stoutly asserted that "No man but a blockhead ever wrote, except for money," for "he who does not mind his belly will hardly mind anything else."[102] Ben Jonson represents himself as disinterested, a mind not concerned with its bodily shell, as a means of finally rejecting dependency upon all material hosts, either the king or his sources, who provided him with food. He defines himself as a worthy heir—both son and future father who receives substances and, without consuming them completely, passes them on—in opposition to characters like Volpone who use their arts to gain legacies of gold.

But his vision of the world is derived from an essentially oral or feudal model that is based on antitheses, in which the poet-guest has completely appropriated the role of lordly host. While the masques and many of the poems seem addressed to an ideal audience who are ultimately identified with Jonson himself, other guests, like the theatrical audiences, who are seen as potential ingrates and cannibals, or the false imitators and parasites of the plays and satiric verse, are seen as embodiments of the bodily appetites and mercenary motives that would debase Jonson's art. Like Rabelais, Jonson wants to limit his invitations, to project certain things outside of his sphere. Yet his own material circumstances, his dependence upon others for survival, makes an attempt at total authorial control over what is inside and outside his writing impossible. Jonson was writing during a time of many changes and metamorphoses, including the emergence of the poet as producer rather than consumer,[103] and as an individual whose potential conflict with other poetic individuals would result in the "anxiety of influence," as well as in the midst of the developing social conflict that would erupt in "Intestine War" in Charles's reign. Understandably, any time of rapid changes can generate nostalgia for a simpler life, a life before division, even if that life is always a myth to begin with. For Jonson, adherence to that ideal of harmony paradoxically depended upon his attempted alienation from his own body, although neither he nor his readers have ever been able to get away from the bulk of Ben. The poet who repeated, perhaps with some envy, the rumor that Spenser starved to death, spent the last ten years of his life in bed, trapped in a body weighing almost three hundred pounds.

MILTON

For Milton, as for Rabelais and Jonson, eating provides a model for exchanges between the self and others and for the reception and assimilation
of poetic material. His story of the Fall dramatizes the loss of communion
imagined by Rabelais and similarly is figured as a polarization between
spiritual and bodily forms of eating. Internalization offers him, as it did
Jonson, a refined form opposed to literal incorporation; for Milton, it is
the means of turning the cause of the Fall into the means of redemption.
But for the later writer, the process of internalization has become much
more problematic as a means of refining images—especially images of internalization. Although eating is sublimated in *Areopagitica* into reading,
the devouring of texts, Milton sees the dangers of figurative acts of incorporation, particularly those which involve poetic sources. Whereas Jonson
attempted to identify himself fully with his poetical and political sources of
nourishment and recreate an oral, essentially feudal, fable of identity, Milton provides the paradigm for a rising poetic and bourgeois individual
who sees himself and his work as his own private property. He dramatizes
the tightening of the boundary lines around the self to form the modern
concept of the individual that I will discuss further in the next chapter, in
which relations become expressed predominantly in terms of separation
rather than identification.

When self and others are strictly divided, exchanges need to be negoti-
ated with care and all forms of eating carefully controlled. Milton insists
that he is not an open, passive vessel for influences but is able to determine
and control what he will take into himself. In its most refined form, eating
is "taste," the sense which, as I mentioned earlier, is seen as discriminating
between what the self will incorporate and what it will reject. It is therefore
an image for choice, which for Milton is essential to human free will and
action. Taste for Milton also represents an alternative to experience, a mediated way of assimilating knowledge without being poisoned by it, and
so a means by which the new individual, otherwise totally isolated from
others, can make contact safely with the world outside itself, and even draw
it into itself. Taste is both a unifying experience that brings men together
and a means of division, associated with exclusion, as the tongue becomes
a phallic symbol of separation, distinction between opposites, and control.
In his distinction between taste as identification and taste as choice, Milton
recalls and reinforces Augustine's polarization of spiritual and physical
kinds of eating; in his description of the Catholic sacrament quoted in the
introduction to this chapter, he specifically attacks the confusion of the
two. When the blind Samson tells the staring Harapha that, "The way to
know were not to see but taste" (*Samson Agonistes*, 1091), he defines himself as the last in a line of characters who conflate taste and experience:

Comus tells the Lady, "Be wise, and taste" (*Comus*, 813), and Satan presents knowledge to Eve as an object that can be literally consumed. The result of Eve's taste of knowledge is the loss of Paradise itself which, lest it be absorbed completely by Sin and Death, must be internalized.

However, although Milton warns against the confusion of the two kinds of eating and levels of meaning, he also resists dualism, as his mortalist beliefs suggest.[104] In fact, physical eating provides him, as it did Rabelais, with a useful model for the way in which the literal and figurative levels can interact and feed each other. But mutual nourishment and support depend upon differentiation to keep one level from absorbing or consuming the other. In the tradition of the *Symposium*, drawn upon by Dante in the *Convivio* as well as by Rabelais, food and conversation, bread and the bread of angels, are both present. In the early "Elegia Sexta," addressed to his close friend Charles Diodati, Milton denies that poetry is "refugam vino dapibusque" ("a fugitive from wine and feasting," 13), for "Carmen amat Bacchum, Carmina Bacchus amat" ("Song loves Bacchus and Bacchus loves songs," 14).[105] Because the two subjects are separate, the repetition in the verse is not redundant but is required to stress the reciprocity of their relationship, as well as to guarantee the space between them. Food feeds Diodati's genius only indirectly (29–30), and in the end Milton will advocate for the epic poet the sparse and vegetarian diet of Pythagoras, appropriate for one who must be "scelerisque vacans et casta" ("innocent of crime and chaste," 63).

The model of relation with differentiation subtly underlies Milton's presentation of his own friendship with Diodati in "Elegia Sexta," as well as his relationship with his father in "Ad Patrem." In both poems the banquet, the communal sharing of food and words, provides a place for defining exchanges with others. "Ad Patrem" is the young poet's attempt to acknowledge his debt to his earthly father, whom he compares to Zeus as the giver of all things—all, that is, except heaven, which seems to be the one thing the son really wants. Though the poet appears to be searching for a way to repay his father and avoid potential emotional and artistic rivalry with him, the mythological framework places the two within the classical tradition in which fathers tend to eat their children. Milton's method of repaying his father, a scrivener who supported him in his studies until he was past thirty, takes an indirect route in which his earthly father is first turned into a brother, as both appear as equal sons of Apollo (61–66), and is then replaced by a spiritual father, God. The father's money is sublimated into the son's "talents," whose source is ultimately heavenly; Milton attempts to gain by himself the one thing he desires by claiming that his gifts come from and should be returned to a heavenly origin.[106] By splitting the father into two figures, one earthly, the other divine, Milton is actually able to free himself from acknowledging debts to anyone other than God. This is a strategy I shall return to later in considering Milton's relation to his poetic fathers, his sublimation of sources by absorbing them into himself.

In these early poems, the relation between the poet and his sources is made analogous to that between words and food, and the model for the site of exchange is the feast. In "Ad Patrem" Milton emphasizes that the true center of any banquet is not the belly but, as Cicero says in *De finibus bonorum et malorum*, "caput cenae: / sermone bono" ("the climax of the banquet is good conversation," 2.viii). At the feast the two forms of eating are related by both analogy and contiguity, the characteristics of the tropes of metaphor and metonymy, respectively. In their interpretations of the Eucharist, Protestant theologians frequently substituted the latter for the former in order to avoid the literalization of which they accused the Catholic Church.[107] Milton, who shared their mistrust of metaphor but believed in the unity of body and spirit, combines the two tropes to create a more flexible relation between the two levels of meaning. Metonymy permits him to emphasize the connection between body and spirit at the same time as it "inhibits confusion in metaphor"[108] by making sure that the parallel lines of metaphor cannot meet. The appetites are fed by degrees, and in accordance with their different requirements. At a feast, conversation is the main dish up to which the carnal ones lead, but it is obviously not served or consumed in the same way as the earlier delicacies.

The world of *Paradise Lost* is also described as a banquet of unfallen communion among nature, man, and God. In a world in which work and leisure, learning and lunch, are not yet opposed, talking and eating are intimately related. The copious lunch served by Eve precedes Raphael's *copia*, and the angel uses food as a figure to explain to Adam a number of matters otherwise beyond his understanding, such as the nature of angels. Adam and the reader can apprehend angelic existence only through an analogy in which the exact degree of similarity is left unclear. Angels also eat:

> food alike those pure
> Intelligential substances require
> As doth your Rational; and both contain
> Within them every lower faculty
> Of sense, wherby they hear, see, smell, touch, taste,
> Tasting concoct, digest, assimilate,
> And corporeal to incorporeal turn.
> For know, whatever was created, needs
> To be sustain'd and fed.

(5.407–15)

The precise grounds of comparison are uncertain, as "alike" could modify either "food" or "require." The imprecision of the analogy permits even the possibility that angels might need the same food as man rather than merely having a need for food that is analogous to human hunger.

It is characteristic of Milton to leave the nature of the comparison open. Patricia Parker has shown how Milton imagined Eden as a kind of Twilight Zone, hovering between figurative and literal levels of meaning, and between the promise and fulfillment of figures themselves.[109] Paradise is a "pendant world" (2.1052), suspended on the threshold of meaning that is realized only by degrees and through a system of mediation that Milton represents not only through but also as poetic figuration. Eating is a central image for the simultaneous similarity and difference suggested in the similes that keep Eden balanced, and the relation between word and food provides a basic example of that balance. Milton represents Paradise as a series of distinct elements identified sufficiently to join together and form a mutually supporting and beneficial chain in which "The grosser feeds the purer" (5.416). As Michael Lieb and Geoffrey Hartman have shown, eating becomes a figure for exchange and participation, in which all Eden meets in "an entirely unhurtful, sympathetic, even symbiotic relation."[110] Paradise is an oral world in which eating "is" knowing, but the exact meaning of that copula is kept uncertain. As for Milton to read "is" as "as" keeps communion from degenerating into cannibalism, in Paradise the lack of fixed definition of relations produces a benign symbiosis in which the participants never become fixed into predatory relations. So, as Hartman says, "The relation of innocent knowledge (of the happy consciousness) to reality is this: a feeding on created things which is not a theft or wounding."[111] Invasion and robbery are prevented by the lack of absolute distinction—which is ultimately to say antagonism—between the different terms, which keeps them from forming themselves into rigid binary oppositions.

The fluid relation between the different terms involves the possibility of metamorphosis of one into another. According to Raphael, angels "corporeal to incorporeal turn" (5.413). Digestion itself becomes a model for a process of sublimation, the spiritualization of matter which is part of the gradual ascent of Eden. When Adam thanks Raphael for accepting mortal food that he knows cannot be compared with the bread of angels, Raphael uses his own appetite to explain the circling of the world around, not the belly, but the "one Almighty" "from whom / All things proceed, and up to him return" (5.469–70). The materialist interpretation of a world beginning and ending in Gaster or Comus, has its antithesis in Milton's description of a world moving toward reunion with its divine source, as it is "by gradual scale sublim'd" (483). Raphael uses his tasting of human food to explain:

> Wonder not then, what God for you saw good
> If I refuse not, but convert, as you

To proper substance; time may come when men
With Angels may participate, and find
No inconvenient Diet, nor too light Fare
And from these corporal nutriments perhaps
Your bodies may at last turn all to spirit
Improv'd by tract of time.

(491–98)

Eating provides the model for the sublimation of matter as it is turned from flesh to spirit and the absorption of one lower form into another that could lead to the final identification of all Eden with God.

However, the word *from* in line 497 is ambiguous, as it presents the possibility of agency, an efficacy in the food itself, an idea Satan will seize upon when he presents the fruit to Eve. Furthermore, the exact nature of sublimation in Eden is left unclear, as it is uncertain what it means for an angel to convert matter into "proper substance"—two words with a wide host of possible meanings. Raphael insists upon his own substantiality and the reality of angelic bodily functions such as excretion and intercourse. He sits down to lunch with great gusto:

So down they sat,
And to thir viands fell, nor seemingly
The Angel, nor in mist, the common gloss
Of Theologians, but with keen dispatch
Of real hunger, and concoctive heat
To transubstantiate; what redounds, transpires
Through Spirits with ease; nor wonder; if by fire
Of sooty coal the Empiric Alchemist
Can turn, or holds it possible to turn
Metals of drossiest Ore to perfet Gold
As from the Mine.

(434–44)

The analogies with alchemical sublimation and transubstantiation imply that in the gradual refinement of Eden, matter, the body and food, is not simply excreted, but actually becomes spirit. Yet in this passage alchemical change is presented as a potential illusion, while transubstantiation is, in Milton's view, a gross literalization that turns communion into cannibalism, and instead of elevating the flesh degrades the spirit. It often has been pointed out that the figures and words with which Milton tries to represent the unfallen world are themselves already fallen, tainted by negative connotations, so that his Eden therefore contains within itself the potential for its own destruction. But it is not identical to that potential, as the relation between paradisal processes and the fallen forms with which Milton must of necessity figure them is not defined precisely. The unfallen world is protected by obfuscation, as it is seen only through analogies in which the similarity between a physical model and its mental or spiritual counterpart is deliberately kept from becoming too exact.

The analogy between physical and mental tasting is itself obviously imperfect. Raphael warns Adam against the dangers of consuming knowledge too hastily and greedily, saying,

> Knowledge is as food, and needs no less
> Her Temperance over Appetite, to know
> In measure what the mind may well contain,
> Oppresses else with Surfeit, and soon turns
> Wisdom to Folly, as Nourishment to Wind.
>
> (7.126–30)

Intemperate consumption of food for thought does not produce wisdom or the new poetry created through the digestion of imitatio, but only excrement or hot air. The analogy between thinking and eating enables Raphael to explain Adam's need to control his hunger for knowledge lest he bite off more than he can chew, and metaphor becomes a method of keeping Adam satisfied with his present condition. However, although Adam appears to be content with what he has been told, he points out a crucial difference between spiritual and physical forms of satisfaction. The "as" does not indicate complete identity, for knowledge is not exactly like food, and the mind cannot be filled in the same way as the belly. Conversation has a different effect on one's ears than food has on one's stomach, as Adam explains when he says,

> sweeter thy discourse is to my ear
> Than Fruits of Palm-tree pleasantest to thirst
> And hunger both, from labor, at the hour
> Of sweet repast; they satiate, and soon fill,
> Though pleasant, but thy words with Grace Divine
> Imbu'd, bring to thir sweetness no satiety.
>
> (8.211–16)

The mind cannot be stuffed with words precisely as the belly is with food; its boundaries are more flexible so that it can expand without bursting like Jonson's Comus, which is one of the reasons Jonson claims the mind's superiority.

But the hungry mind is therefore never completely full and must always stay hungry, ready and able to swallow more knowledge. Though somewhat satisfied by Raphael's words, Adam's curiosity has also been fed by them and his appetite increased with what it has fed on; for,

apt the Mind or Fancy is to rove
Uncheckt, and of her roving is no end;
Till warn'd, or by experience taught, she learn
That not to know at large of things remote
From use, obscure and subtle, but to know
That which before us lies in daily life,
Is the prime Wisdom.

(8.188–94)

In this passage also the relation between Mind and Fancy is left ambiguous by Milton's famous use of the word *or*, which can suggest simultaneously choice—the differentiation between alternatives—and the identification of synonyms: both the idealized taste that is discrimination and the literal tasting that identifies eater and eaten completely.[112] It is particularly difficult to define mental territory and keep internal boundary lines straight. Earlier (5.110–13), Adam had described Fancy as the faculty that parodied Reason when it slept, a somewhat subversive imitator which misrepresented its model. Here, however, the two are potentially identified as a single faculty that is a growing and wandering appetite. Adam indicates two possible forms of satisfaction that might stop the potentially endless roving of this drive: on the one hand, example, warning, or education; on the other, direct experience. Adam may indirectly taste reality through the words of others, or, tempted by Satan to turn the analogy between different kinds of taste into total identity, he may try a more direct consumption of knowledge.

Whereas Raphael used figurative language as a means of education by degrees, Satan attempts to use words literally in order to offer a more ready and easy way to taste and be wise.[113] Similes provide a crucial means of identifying while distinguishing two separate terms, which justifies Eden's seemingly hierarchical order. In Eden, not only do differences create meaning, but they also promise, however vaguely, a deferred identity between the different members ascending up the digestive chain of being toward God. Satan seeks to establish a more direct and carnal connection between terms through the radical identification of the differences that produce metaphorical meaning. The existence of such differences makes him uneasy. Like Panurge, Satan is afraid of holes, which he knows only as abysses like the devouring void of the universe, and cannot imagine as holes out of which one might emerge. He is unable to tell orifices apart, and presumably could not distinguish the world's omphalos from its anus, as in *Inferno* 34 Dante's Lucifer may misjudge his position.[114] Lacking the taste that is discrimination, he turns all tasting into complete incorporation, as he cannot stand the suspense of figurative meaning, its imprecision and obfuscation of exact relation. He is threatened by differences, and his aim is "others to make such / As I" (9.127–28)—in other words, to create a world of total identity—his.

Satan therefore presents himself to Eve as a figure with whom to identify in a parodic communion and offers himself to her as a model for imitation. His temptation involves a "synesthetic feast" that inundates all of her senses. As he fills her ears with words, her other senses are also aroused, and come together to create one enormous, undifferentiated appetite:

> his words replete with guile
> Into her heart too easy entrance won:
> Fixt on the Fruit she gaz'd, which to behold
> Might tempt alone, and in her ears the sound
> Yet rung of his persuasive words, impregn'd
> With Reason, to her seeming, and with Truth;
> Meanwhile the hour of Noon drew on, and wak'd
> An eager appetite, rais'd by the smell
> So savory of that Fruit, which with desire
> Inclinable now grown to touch or taste
> Solicited her longing eye.
>
> (9.733–43)

The synesthetic feast turns into what Frank Kermode has called the "banquet of the senses," a "totality of possible temptations," in which one sense automatically leads to another.[115] As the senses come together, order and degree is lost; they dissolve into one another until touch cannot be distinguished from taste, which has subsumed all the other senses.

Furthermore, according to Satan, the fruit not only satisfies the senses but can satisfy the hunger for knowledge in the same way. As well as breaking down the distinctions among the different modes of apprehension, collapsing the drives into one single undifferentiated appetite, Satan turns the analogy between physical and mental hunger into complete identity: knowledge *is* food now, as the saving "as" of Raphael and Milton's similes disappears, and it becomes an object that Eve can directly consume. One substance can conveniently and economically feed both belly and mind. In the digestive metaphor for imitatio, what goes in as food comes out as words; in the *Symposium* tradition, food feeds the genius but is only a forerunner of conversation. Satan abridges these circuitous processes by turning the food itself into the source of *copia* and praises the "best of Fruits" (474),

> Whose taste, too long foreborne, at first assay
> Gave elocution to the mute, and taught
> The Tongue not made for Speech to speak thy praise.
>
> (747–49)

Satan is a parodic version of the saints in the *Paradiso* who come "laudando il cibo che là sù il prande" ("praising the food which feeds them thereabove," 25.24); his fruit is Rabelais's Gaster and Jonson's Comus recreated: the beginning and end of all the arts. It appears as a transcendental substance that can convert the eater at the same time as it economically satisfies all appetites. So Eve wonders:

> Here grows the Cure of all, this Fruit Divine,
> Fair to the Eye, inviting to the Taste,
> Of virtue to make wise: what hinders then
> To reach, and feed at once both Body and Mind?
>
> (776–79)

With these words, Eve convinces herself and makes a god of her belly, which replaces God as the center of her universe. The tree will provide an easier and quicker method of sublimation, and she imagines how she can both eat and praise its fruit, "Till dieted by thee I grow mature / In knowledge, as the Gods who all things know" (803–04). Having discovered such a wondrous and all-purpose substance (the prototype for all labor-saving devices designed to ameliorate our fallen existence), Eve feels completely independent and Adam seems an unnecessary superfluity. She reverses their original relation as presented by Milton, following Genesis, in which Adam was the whole from which she, the part, was drawn.[116] In Milton's version, Adam, created first, realized that he was not perfect and self-sufficient like God but needed others for satisfaction in exchanges and "Collateral love" (8.426). But as the differences between the appetites and senses disappear, all differences, especially sexual ones, come to be experienced as potentially threatening. Eve decides to share the fruit with Adam in order to make him like herself, and she urges him to eat with a veiled threat:

> Thou therefore also taste, that equal Lot
> May join us, equal Joy, as equal Love;
> Lest thou not tasting, different degree
> Disjoin us.
>
> (881–84)

The rhetoric of sharing and equality disguises what is actually a desire to possess the other totally through the resolution of all differences into exact identity. In the unfallen Eden, the existence of differences made possible a vision of a flexible, even symbiotic, relation among the elements, including Adam and Eve themselves. From a fallen perspective, however, all differences are potentially hierarchies, established for the perpetuation of oppression, even cannibalism. Knowledge for the fallen couple is the knowledge of Eden's negative potential and the loss of any alternative, as their tasting involves an irrevocable choice between the opposites previously held in balance. With this knowledge the metonymic relation that differentiated the metaphoric poles disappears. Literal and figurative tastes collapse, and the temperate way of assimilating the external world disappears.

Not surprisingly, therefore, with the disappearance of the veil of innocence and the mediating influence of figuration, mutual nourishment and sublimation degenerate into the cannibalistic encounters between eater and eaten:

> Beast now with Beast gan war, and Fowl with Fowl,
> And Fish with Fish; to graze the Herb all leaving,
> Devour'd each other.
>
> (10.710–12)

Knowledge of an other can no longer be imagined as an act of love but can only be conceived of as an act of aggression, the kind of devouring or penetration already represented, but confined to Hell, in the relationship between Sin and her children. With the Fall, Hell comes to earth, so that exchanges become struggles for power, communion turns into antagonistic intercourse between equal and opposed forces attempting to consume each other. The evenly balanced world moves to extremes, and the sun itself shifts its course:

> At that tasted Fruit
> The Sun, as from *Thyestean* Banquet, turn'd
> His course intended.
>
> (10.687–89)

Eden becomes the world of *Metamorphoses* Book 15 and the "Thyestis . . . mensis" ("feasts of Thyestes," 462) that Pythagoras warns his audience to avoid by adopting a vegetarian diet.

In Ovid, as I argued earlier, figures are completely identified with the forms they have been turned into, so that there is no hole or saving space between sign and meaning: a tree represents a nymph by literally containing her. As a result, there can be no difference between "tasting" the sign and "tasting" the thing signified; even though form and content are in theory opposed, in practice they are completely identified. After the Fall, God's previously balanced system of signification appears to begin to turn into such a trap; but for Milton there is one hope of escape unavailable either to Ovid or the literal-minded Pythagoras. The world of metamorphosis is a closed system created by signs that repeat themselves without the possibility of transcendence, and with the danger of the ultimate disappearance of difference altogether. Within fallen Eden there may be no longer the means of internal reformation or ascent by degrees, but help may still come from without, from the Grace which appears to penetrate the satanic selfhood of Adam and Eve and offer them a new identity. However, that Grace, though ostensibly divine, is ultimately identical with the author himself who, unlike the Ovid who is subsumed by and identified with his text, emerges as the transcendental source of textual meaning. God is subtly displaced by the John Milton who stands as the model of an author and individual who is the origin of his own significance.

Adam had seemed to sense instinctively that God the Father could not possibly provide a useful model for human identity. There is too great a gap between the completely self-sufficient deity and the man who needs others for Adam to imitate Him; when Satan tries to do so, he turns himself into a mere parody god. When man falls, he identifies himself with Satan; but, as Milton suggests, there is a mean between these two extremes. This is to be found in the figure of the Son, who mediates also between God and man, and offers the latter a new identity that comes from the patience and obedience Adam hopes to learn: "Taught this by his example whom I now / Acknowledge my Redeemer ever blest" (12.572–73).

In Milton's famous interpretation of the relation between the Father and Son, the two are not equal but rather complementary.[117] Of all God's decrees, "the first and most important is that which regards his SON, and from which he primarily derives his name of FATHER" (*The Christian Doctrine* 1.3; Hughes, 916): the two gain their identities through their relation with each other. Because the two are represented as separate persons, in Book 3.79–265, Milton is able to create a real dialogue between them, in which he works out a process of redemption that is both literary and historical revision. The Son who is not identical with his Father may seem secondary and subordinate, but he has the power to revise his Father's words, and, where the Father stresses justice and death, the Son emphasizes grace and life. But as a result, where the Son speaks of the redemption of man, the Father focuses upon the exaltation of the Son.[118] While the Son offers himself, "Account mee man" (3.237), the Father moves away from the descent and humanization of God in the incarnation toward the triumphant return of the Son and his elevation, which, significantly, shall involve a new ascent of man also:

> thy Humiliation shall exalt
> With thee thy Manhood also to this Throne;
> Here shalt thou sit incarnate, here shalt Reign
> Both God and Man, Son both of God and Man,
> Anointed universal King; all Power
> I give thee, reign for ever, and assume
> Thy Merits. . . .
>
> (313–19)

Christ stoops to conquer, his humiliation is only a prelude to the ultimate triumph of both himself and man. Through a neat paradox, by being different from God, Christ earns the right to be God,[119] to be finally

> Thron'd in highest bliss
> Equal to God, and equally enjoying
> God-like fruition. . . .

(305–7)

The Son, unlike the Father, is not omniscient and so cannot know the exact consequences of his actions. But Milton does, and the Son's *askesis*, his emptying of himself in order ultimately to "increase in power" and to "know all things" (*The Christian Doctrine* 1.14),[120] provides him with a useful model for self-creation that involves the acquisition of power through deference and deferral. In *Paradise Regained*, the victory through obedience which recovers Paradise for man is represented through neither of the extremes of humiliation and exaltation that can collapse into each other[121] but as the temptation in the wilderness. Christ becomes the example by which man can learn the obedience and patience involved in standing and waiting, the actions which, in his famous sonnet on his blindness, Milton will identify with his own work. However, Milton's attempt throughout his works to figure out how he has spent the "talents" given to him by his heavenly Father is also an indirect consideration of his financial debts to his earthly father, his poetic debts to his literary fathers, and an exploration of the type of poetic identity that is produced from his relations with these sources. His model for himself is the Christ who, while brooding on the meaning of his identity as Son of God, resists the satanic impulse toward self-definition. His identity is held in a new kind of balance by means of a form of what Keats will call "negative capability," which enables him to read his life without restricting it to a single meaning.

This is an ability that Samson, another hero who offers a possible model for human action and identity, lacks. Like Oedipus, Samson is a riddle solver, and his riddle involves an identification of eater and eaten (see Judges 14:14). Milton's Samson, furthermore, looks back to Jonson's Hercules and Comus, and draws generally on the tradition of the poet as a vessel filled with sources from outside himself. Whereas Jonson's Comus took in things too readily and indiscriminately, Samson is too eager to let them out: he is a leaky vessel who spills out his secrets and his power.[122] The punishment for this premature publication is infernal self-containment, as he finds himself "Myself, my Sepulcher, a moving Grave" (102), a blind man locked in, as the chorus tells him, "The Dungeon of thyself" (156). Between dissipation and suicidal self-containment, Samson must find a means of discharging his duty that will also enable God to fulfill equally His promise to him. Unlike Christ, Samson was overeager to interpret the meaning of his life, and overconfident of his ability to read his urges to marry as the "intimate impulse" (223) of God. The hero sure of his inner vision and vocation is finally forced to act blindly, without even inner illumination, and to follow voices whose sources he cannot be certain of. Neither he nor the reader can know what prompts him to his final action, in which he triumphs over his enemies but simultaneously destroys himself. It is his father, Manoa, who claims that "*Samson* hath quit himself / Like *Samson*" (1709–10)—an ambiguous statement that suggests simultaneously a regression into redundancy—the endless self-recreation of the phoenix, with whom Samson is compared, through the collapsing of the two pillars that breaks down all difference between the Israelite hero and his Philistine and hostile hosts—or the recapturing of an ideal "place without boundaries or a name, where the one who eats and the one who is eaten are the same."[123]

Blind men, whether Samson or Milton, learn by listening and must be content with indirect vision through the voices of others; so must the fallen Adam, instructed by Michael. Perhaps because of his own noted early aural sensitivity, as well as his ultimate dependency on the sense, hearing presents Milton with a threat that was less obvious in either Rabelais or Jonson, where it tended to be idealized. Whereas sight preserves the distance between perceiving subject and perceived object, hearing suggests a more disturbing identification between them. Moreover, the ears are apertures which, as Rabelais's Sibyl points out, are always left open, for Nature:

> n'y appousant porte ne clousture aulcune, comme a faict es oeilz, langue et aultres issues du corps. La cause je cuide estre affin que tousjours, toutes nuyctes, continuellement puissons ouyr et par ouye perpetuellement aprendre; car c'est le sens sus tous aultres apte es disciplines.

> ("placed no door or cover over them, as she has done over our eyes, our tongue, and the other openings in our bodies. Her purpose is, I believe, that all day and all night we shall be able to hear, and through our hearing perpetually to learn. For our hearing is the most educable of all our senses." *Tiers Livre*, 16.103; Cohen, 332)[124]

For Rabelais, ears are like mouths—holes through which the external world is absorbed—and their perpetual openness is a sign of hospitality and of the receptivity of the self. But mouths can be shut. While Rabelais may see hearing as a means of education, it subverts the possibility of control over what we take into our body and undermines the power of choice that for Milton is the essence of reason. While Samson complains of the vulnerability of his vision, centralized and so easily destroyed, hearing makes men vulnerable in a different way. To be "all ears" may be to be completely exposed to all sorts of sources, especially if the doors stay open at night when watchful Reason is at rest. At night, Satan whispers in the ears of the angels and Eve, infusing bad influence when they are least on guard. The innocent Eve especially, not used to having to differentiate voices in a world composed of very few characters, cannot tell his voice from Adam's. But Milton's muse also indulges in nocturnal activity, and is described as

> my Celestial Patroness, who deigns
> Her nightly visitation unimplor'd,
> And dictates to me slumb'ring, or inspires
> Easy my unpremeditated Verse.

(9.21–24)

Here the "or" helpfully obscures the precise origin of the poem—it is either divine dictation or inspiration in which the poet presumably takes a more active part—so that God and Milton don't have to fight for copyright. Milton refuses to set himself up as a rival source to God as Satan does and uses indefinition to evade the issue. But this act of poetic inspiration is placed quite close to the climax of Satan's infernal infusions, in which he enters the serpent's mouth and, "possessing soon inspir'd / With act intelligential" (189–90). The metaphor of voice undermines the notion of poetic property. As Milton uses indeterminacy to obscure sources, that indeterminacy demonstrates how difficult it is to control and legislate language. The problem with voices is that they can enter us whether or not we want them to and, furthermore, that their sources are not always clear. As the juxtaposition of the two words in line 189 suggests, it may not be possible to tell possession from inspiration—or from indigestion for that matter—and, in a fallen world particularly, intimate impulses do not always come from God.

When reciprocal feeding turns into mutual cannibalism, it is perhaps justifiable to see all influences as potentially poisonous. Milton's story of the Fall explains the origin of a world in which man is dependent on others but in which all exchanges have a slightly suspicious savour. From this perspective, it is only too easy to spot the cannibalistic conflict lurking under the alimentary metaphor for imitatio, to identify the guest as parasite, or to see cannibalism as the reality underlying Catholic communion. In Milton's case, the suspicion may be produced partially by the tension between his own perpetual dependency—on his father, on his literary sources, and finally on his infamously unfortunate wives and daughters—and his desire for independence and autonomy. For Milton, it is difficult to acknowledge the need for the help of others and to learn to see through another's eyes, as Adam, Samson, and, finally, Milton himself must. Through metaphors such as that of the divinely given "talent," he tries to evade the problem of human debts. By shifting the terms of the discussion from earth to heaven, he differentiates himself from Satan, who privately acknowledges debts as a burden he cannot bear but publicly repudiates them through an assertion of his own self-origination.

However, Milton's natural tendency is to subsume his poetic models so completely that they disappear, so that one is left with the impression of his complete originality. His amazing ability to digest his material and assimilate it to himself was noted frequently by his early critics. Hazlitt commented that "Milton has borrowed more than any other writer; yet he is perfectly distinct from every other writer. The power of his mind is stamped on every line. . . . the fervour of his imagination melts down and renders malleable, as in a furnace, the most contradictory materials."[125] For Dr. Johnson, Milton's absorption of his sources is analogous to a form of sublimation in which the material base is excreted rather than converted: "the heat of Milton's mind might be said to sublimate his learning, to throw off into his work the spirit of science, unmingled with its grosser parts."[126] As part of his attack on the evil and ultimate futility of censorship in the early *Areopagitica*, Milton had argued for the ability of the mind to control what it takes in, quoting Paul and drawing an analogy between the incorporation of food and that of texts:

> "To the pure, all things are pure"; not only meats and drinks, but all kind of knowledge whether of good or evil; the knowledge cannot defile, nor consequently the books, if the will and conscience be not defiled. For books are as meats and viands are—some of good, some of evil substance, and yet God in that unapocryphal vision said without exception, "Rise, Peter, kill and eat," leaving the choice to each man's discretion. Wholesome meats to a vitiated stomach differ little or nothing from unwholesome, and best books to a naughty mind are not unappliable to occasions of evil. Bad meats will scarce breed good nourishment in the healthiest concoction; but herein the difference is of bad books, that they to a discreet and judicious reader serve in many respects to discover, to confute, to forewarn, and to illustrate (Hughes, 727).

Books can serve as warnings to fallen man and provide a way of tasting experience without having to consume it completely. Like the reformed readings of the Eucharist, Milton's argument insists that it is not what goes in the belly that counts—there is no efficacy in food, contrary to Satan's claim to Eve—but the state of the stomach itself, which should be strong enough to control what it takes in.

Perhaps Milton's belief that his blindness had been caused by indigestion is related to his later awareness of the danger of taking substances into the self.[127] However, even in *Comus*, where the young and chaste Milton explores another form of intestinal fortitude, chastity, the possibility of bodily and mental integrity seems more problematic than in *Areopagitica*. At one level, Milton uses the masque to defend his own sexual chastity by giving it a broader significance, as he appears to associate the virtue with autonomy, inviolability, and integrity. At another, the masque, which looks back to Jonson's *Pleasure Reconciled to Virtue*, is an important early formulation of Milton's lifelong exploration of the motives for and possibility of achieving individuation and his concern about the kind of integrity that can be constructed when one is full of others.

In *Comus*, the problem of the assimilation of influences raised in *Pleasure* has become much more complex and threatening. Like Jonson, Milton presents us with two alternative means of incorporation and transformation or conversion. In *Pleasure*, the poet who represents himself as a "tun" splits himself into the ideal and demonic self-images of Comus and Hercules, poles that at times he has difficulty differentiating. Milton's antithesis to his Comus, who has a much larger and more significant role than in Jonson's masque, is not a bulky hero, but the young Lady, creating an even broader range of opposition. However, "The Lady" was Milton's nickname at Cambridge, and she represents one aspect of the poet, as does Comus, whose temptation has more to do with aural than oral excess. But the use of a male/female opposition gains significance also through the redefinition of gender roles that occurred in the seventeenth century, identifying the male with work and the public, and the female with art and the private.[128] For real women, such as Milton's three wives and daughters, the division of labor from labor, production from reproduction, which Milton represents as a consequence of the Fall, resulted in the loss of practical power. However, the association of women with a "higher," spiritual life gave Milton one means of defining himself, as Jonson did, as uncontaminated by economic or materialistic motives or self-interest. At the end of the masque, however, this, as well as Comus, will be a part of himself he cannot fully identify with. The voices of the two antitheses, Milton's apparent alien and authority, are silenced simultaneously in order to release a third term: the voice of Milton in the Attendant Spirit who, like the Son, is a mediator between heaven and earth and, on earth, between poetic opposites.

Comus and the Lady appear as complete opposites, the first being a container that takes in and gives out copiously and indiscriminately, the second, one that is completely sealed and self-contained, the ideal virgin as *hortus conclusus*. As in Jonson's masque, literal and figurative methods of internalization are polarized; but in Milton the terms seem even further set apart, and the latter more sublime. Whereas Comus is associated with literal absorption that leads to a Circean metamorphosis, the Lady is described in terms of an upward and internal conversion, effected by the mediation of the angels of chastity who appear in her dreams (454–63). While the literal transformation takes place through the agency of an external material substance, the spiritual depends upon the inner nature, the strong stomach of the individual. Furthermore, the Lady is petrified not by drinking from Comus's cup, but as a result of her brothers' premature entrance with the magic Haemony. Coleridge read this plant as the Eucharist,[129] picking up on Milton's attempt to differentiate between types of transformation and believing himself that if Comus is what turns men into beasts, the Eucharist would be the means of making them God. But the Haemony fails to rescue the Lady, and the opposites become locked in a paralyzing conflict. To use the Eucharist or any external substance as a remedy is to suggest the efficacy of food, and for Milton the Eucharist specifically is only a symbol with no power in itself. The release of the Lady is brought about by a more internalized change, but one that admits the possibility of external influences entering into both the individual and the poem itself, in order to keep the poet from becoming frozen by his own integrity. The transformation requires a shift of the terms of opposition defined by Jonson as material and aesthetic motives, or bodily and spiritual appetites, to reveal that underneath that opposition, and complicating it, is the struggle between poets that Jonson resolutely denied.

Sabrina, the figure Milton uses to resolve his dilemma, is taken from Spenser's book of Temperance. But—and despite also the dialogue with Jonson—it is Shakespeare whose presence is strongly felt, as his words echo through and seem to haunt the text.[130] In fact, his words have been absorbed so thoroughly that one can scarcely separate them from Milton's. One might once more marvel at Milton's tremendous powers of assimilation but also see the particularly insidious threat that Shakespeare presents to the poet. Milton may have swallowed him so completely that the two can no longer be told apart. This is especially disturbing as they are traditionally considered to be exact opposites. For Coleridge, as for most of the Romantics, the two stand for opposing methods of identification—projection and introjection: "The one darting forth and passing into all forms of human character & passion; the other attracting all forms and ideals to himself, into the unity of his own grand Ideal—Shakespeare becomes all things . . . while all things & form become Milton."[131] Or, as he puts it elsewhere, "Shakespeare was all men, potentially, except Milton."[132] But in the synesthetic feast of the masque these extremes meet, so that it seems difficult to tell the eater from the eaten, just as in "On Shakespeare," the great poet who lives on in the hearts of men may be immortalized at their expense, as he is a monument within that petrifies his hosts with astonishment. Though in *Comus* the later poet appears to be subsuming and controlling the earlier, Milton is aware of the possibility that his mental digestive system could turn into a host that is preyed upon by the foreign substance it has admitted into itself. This possibility seems potentially realized in the final speech of the Attendant Spirit, as he says his farewell in the rhyming couplets of *Comus* which are also the language of Shakespeare.

The Lady tries to avoid contamination by Comus through refusing to take in the food he offers her, but for Milton this does not turn out to be an acceptable alternative to Comus's "swinish gluttony" (776). Although the Older Brother imagines chastity petrifying her enemies, it is the Lady herself who is frozen. The complete rejection of external influences is a direct assertion of independence that Milton will represent later in Satan's repudiation of the gifts that he can experience only as endless and oppressive debt (*Paradise Lost* 4.50–57). The rejection of nourishment from without leads ultimately to solipsism, one characteristic of Satan which makes him the prototype of the Romantic hero, but which for Milton is ultimately defined as the self-cannibalism of the evil of *Comus* that is "self-fed and self-consum'd" (*Comus*, 597). Between the opposites of Shakespearian self-projection and Miltonic introjection, between Comus's indiscriminate inclusion and the Satanic exclusion that turns chastity into self-destructive sterility, Milton attempts to establish a temperate means of assimilation and internalization. To break the deadlock between extremes, he revives Sabrina from Spenser's book of Temperance, but it is his way of resurrecting her that suggests his alternative to perpetual poetic combat.

Shakespeare appears to enter the text on his own volition, echoing in Milton's ears so that the poet cannot choose whether or not to allow him into the poem. But choice is essential to Milton, as it involves the ability to discriminate between opposites, in other words, to "taste." To have freedom of choice is to have control, which is what Milton regains when he chooses to let Spenser into his work. By using Sabrina, he deliberately invokes Spenser's presence; by revising her story from murder to suicide, he not only makes it his own possession, but turns her death into a conscious act involving deliberate choice. Milton receives and extends Spenser's concern with temperance, a virtue he described in *Areopagitica* as the one that governs "the dieting and repasting of our minds; as wherein every mature man might have to exercise his own leading capacity" (Hughes, 727). It is exercised by trial in a world in which one can know good only by evil, where "that which purifies us is trial, and trial is by what is contrary," and is therefore opposed to the innocence that is mere ignorance of evil, which is the mark of "a blank virtue, not a pure; her whiteness is but an excremental whiteness" (728). He praises Spenser as the best instructor of this virtue, but when, in remembering Guyon's descent into Mammon's cave, he brings along the Palmer who Spenser carefully leaves behind, he is rewriting the tale to suit his own definition of temperance, adding the "reason" which "is but choosing" (733; echoed later in *Paradise Lost* 3.108, "Reason also is choice"), which for Milton is an essential part of revision itself. Rather than indicating the fallibility of Milton's memory, the slip shows his inability to merely remember anything without making it his own. As he puts it, his allegiance is not to "Dame Memory and her siren daughters" (*Reason of Church Government;* Hughes, 671) who inspire the "riming parasite," but to the Word, produced by the communion between Father and Son, which Milton represents as the dialogue in heaven in which the Son receives, submits to, and yet ultimately transforms to his own advantage his Father's words.

Milton's substitution of Spenser for Shakespeare as the "source" of *Comus*, his model of temperance, affords him a means of avoiding conflict with his antithesis. In essence, it allows him to have his cake and eat it too—to subsume both precursors while appearing to keep them intact. Furthermore, it is a strategy that makes it appear as if one could choose one's own father, at will getting rid of the earthly father and Shakespeare, and identifying only with the heavenly and Spenser. So, according to Dryden, Milton maintained that Spenser was his "original."[133] While through this tactic some debts are acknowledged, others are eliminated altogether. By appearing to make a choice, Milton has managed to have both alternatives. As Comus is projected from the text, the language of Shakespeare reenters it in the final speeches of the Attendant Spirit who has subsumed his opposite. Introjection is disguised as projection, as it is typical of Milton, most obviously through the negative similes in *Paradise Lost* but even as early as in the banishing of the oracles in the "Nativity Ode," to carefully distance and detach himself from the material he subsumes through a method that Christopher Ricks has described as the inclusion of what is deliberately excluded.[134]

Milton's desire to choose his origins himself coincides with the emergence of the individual and its poetic complement, what Harold Bloom has called the "anxiety of influence," which arises with the discovery of the need to establish a separate authorial identity. Although Bloom's belief that Jonson was free from such anxiety, "for to him (refreshingly) art is hard work,"[135] seems undermined by Jonson's representations of the perils of imitation, it is certainly with Milton's Satan that one finds the model for the modern poet burdened by influence, the oedipal son who is struggling with his poetic fathers.[136] But just as Milton provides two fathers between whom, he claims, it is possible to choose, so he gives us two sons of God. At the end of *Paradise Regained* the antithetical brothers stand together on the temple of their father—giving Milton a choice opportunity to knock one down. Satan, characteristically trying to pin down meaning, tempts Christ to define the sense in which he is the son of God, and falls when Christ neither asserts nor denies his identity but instead answers by quoting from the Bible.

Christ standing on his Father's house provides the central image for the balancing act that is necessary in a world no longer pendant but fallen, the grey Twilight Zone of the end of *Paradise Lost*. Christ's method of response by quotation is, however, ambiguous, as it both defers to his Father's voice and appropriates it. James Nohrnberg has noticed recently also Milton's use in *Paradise Regained* of "The double genitive—the innocent form of the 'infamous double bind' of the Tiresian riddle speech" in repeated formulae such as "my Father's voice," "His Father's business," "Thy Father's house."[137] This deference may not be entirely innocent; although the article is subordinate to the proper noun, it is both prior to it and possessive. Furthermore, as Satan falling is compared to the Sphinx, Christ is implicitly identified with Oedipus in order to complete the analogy. The potential for Christ to be a rival of his Father, and a more insidious one than Satan, is not excluded from the text but incorporated even as it is in some sense projected. As in the case of Shakespeare, the dangerous influence and model is invited in but simultaneously excreted, as the textual body insists upon its own ability to taste without being poisoned.

This projection can obviously never be absolute: in *Comus*, the echoes of Shakespeare, like the implied analogy with Oedipus, remain in the text. But in *Paradise Regained*, neither Christ's self-identification with his Father nor with Oedipus is made explicit; his strength comes from the fact that he, unlike Satan, can stand the suspense. The suspension of choice is necessary for the prevention of tragedy, which involves the discovery of a single identity that was so disastrous for both Eden and Oedipus.[138] The Son refuses to choose; instead he stands and waits, and for his deferral is rewarded by equality with his Father. In Christ, Milton recreates the Edenic suspense of identity imagined through similes that held out the possibility of deferred identity with God through the gradual ascent of Eden. Christ reestablishes an ambiguity in which both communion and cannibalism are equally possible, as Milton attempts to represent once more the moment before identity is discovered and conflict between father and son breaks out. It is Satan who wants to determine identities absolutely, with consequences as disastrous for him as a similar discovery was for Oedipus. The paradox is that the deferral of identity, the suspension of meaning, leads to the acquisition of the most powerful identity of all: God.

If the Son is Milton's model for himself, this process of stooping to conquer anticipates his transformation into a most forbidding father for later poets. The Son who "Recover'd Paradise to all mankind" (*Paradise Regained* 1.3) becomes the poet who, identified not favorably with his own God, refigures Paradise in such a way that other possible representations are covered from later poets' view. According to Bloom, for his followers Milton becomes "a demon of continuity; his baleful charm imprisons the present in the past, and reduces a world of differences into a grayness of uniformity."[139] For Bloom, Milton marks the fall from imitatio into influence, from communal to cannibalistic relations among writers. The anxiety of influence is both a kind of indigestion on the part of later writers whose stomachs are not as strong as Milton's and who are faced furthermore with a greater amount of material to digest, and also a fear of starvation, as "each poet's fears that no proper work remains for him to perform"[140] propel him to imaginative vampirism. All poets "work to subvert the immortality of their precursors, as though any one poet's afterlife could be metaphorically prolonged at the expense of another."[141] The model for the relation between past and present is no longer a feast where both eat simultaneously, but a world in which one must eat or be eaten. As the past may, like Dracula, prolong its life by feeding on the present, the strong poet has to defend himself by "transuming" it.[142]

Bloom's model of influence reveals the oedipal rivalry already within the oral relations of imitatio; Bloom describes it as a form of melancholy, to which I shall be returning momentarily. Oedipus solves two riddles, the answer to the first of which is generic, "man," the answer to the second, individual, "Oedipus."[143] In Milton, to know who one is for certain is always tragic. I shall be arguing further that the discovery of the unique "individual" set off from others involves the discovery of the possibility of conflict within apparent symbiosis and the reification of that possibility as an absolute law. But Milton's suspension of his own identity involves what may be the cleverest form of cannibalism of all. By postponing the revelation of his own meaning and identity, Milton leaves it up to his readers to make the tragic choice by discovering, to their own detriment, that he's actually God.

Or rather, and perhaps more intimidatingly, we see Milton as the modern equivalent of God· the individual and Author, who is seen as origin of his own text and meaning. While Milton himself is always careful to avoid appropriating too much power to himself, and represents himself as as vessel who submits to figures from outside himself—God, his ambiguous Muse, "Patience" in the sonnet on his blindness (who prevents him from saying something he's already said), "wisest Fate" in the "Nativity Ode"—what he in fact provides us with is a myth of the Protestant relocation of authority from outside the self to inside. In his prose defenses of his country and himself, Milton continuously refers his readers to his life as a warrant for his authority to speak and for the validity of what he says. He positions himself as standing behind his texts as a godlike proprietor who guarantees their truth.[144] Moreover, in retrospect, his work seems a coherent whole and his entire life and career a unified structure that appears to have fulfilled his early desire that personal identity and textual identity should be related: "he who would not be frustrate of his hope to write well hereafter in laudable things, ought himself to be a true poem."[145] We inherit from him a model for unified personal and textual identity which seems godlike, and which, as a result, leaves us feeling infernally inferior.

CHAPTER IV

Under the Sign of Saturn

> Through the wrath of the Lord of hosts is the land darkened, and
> the people shall be as the fuel of the fire: no man shall spare his
> brother. And he shall snatch on the right hand and be hungry;
> and he shall eat on the left hand, and they shall not be satisfied:
> they shall eat every man the flesh of his own arm.
>
> —Isaiah 9:19–20

WITH MILTON we have not only moved from communion to cannibalism
but have also come to the emergence of the modern autonomous although
self-divided individual. Milton's central position in seventeenth-century
English literature may be connected with a tendency to read the time itself
as one of a "fall": whether it be seen as a "dissociation of sensibility," a
"breaking of the circle," a replacement of a circular world of resemblances
by a linear world dominated by analysis, or a fall from the symbiotic relations of imitatio into the anxiety of influence.[1] More generally, since Ruskin, the Renaissance has itself been viewed as a fall, in which particularly
the individual as isolated atom was discovered at the cost of an earlier experience of community.[2] As a result, the self came to be defined in terms
of self-identity rather than in terms of identity with a social group.

Bakhtin's description of the transition from a medieval to a modern way
of thinking may prove useful here, as it explains the shift through images
that recall my introductory and all-purpose myth of the primal body whose
dismemberment produces opposition. Bakhtin studies Rabelais's obsession with the "material bodily principle," his use of "images of the human
body with its food, drink, defecation, and sexual life"[3] in terms of his inheritance of the medieval vision of the body as "grotesque"—huge and
open to experience, a place in which the material and spiritual, individual
and society, self and others, are constantly interacting. For Bakhtin, the
Renaissance led "to the breaking away of the body from the single procre-
ating earth, the breaking away from the collective, growing, and continually renewed body of the people with which it had been linked in folk
culture."[4] During the Renaissance, it became increasingly possible to see
the body in a different way, as "a strictly completed, finished product" that
was "isolated, alone, fenced off from all other bodies."[5] In Renaissance art
"The accent was placed on the completed, self-sufficient individuality of

the given body. Corporal acts were shown only when the borderlines dividing the body from the outside world were sharply defined. The inner processes of absorbing and ejecting were not revealed. The individual body was presented apart from its relation to the ancestral body of the people."[6]

Whereas the grotesque body had been imagined as open, with flexible boundaries, orifices, and protuberances that could transgress themselves as well as take others in, the Renaissance anatomy is seen in terms of containment: "All the orifices of the body are closed,"[7] giving an idealized topography of any real body, in which the holes are discreetly smoothed over. The effect is similar to the elimination of textual gaps and homogenization of differences of meaning that Rabelais mocked: in both cases, what is produced is an ideal image of a unified and coherent body. For Bakhtin, the source of this ideal is found in the material body itself when taken literally: "The basis of the image is the individual, strictly limited mass, the impenetrable façade."[8] Whereas the grotesque body had been completely ambivalent, a primal body in which antithetical senses such as birth and death, private and public, material and spiritual, were not yet divided, the Renaissance body is reduced to a single meaning: "It is self-sufficient and speaks in its name alone. All that happens within it concerns it alone, that is, only the individual, closed sphere. Therefore, all the events taking place within it acquire one single meaning: death is only death, it never coincides with birth, old age is torn away from youth; blows merely hurt, without assisting an act of birth."[9] When the ambiguity of the grotesque body is resolved, the anatomy assumes a single, but essentially negative, meaning. The body is simply a body, set aside from other bodies, and ultimately from its own mind.

Bakhtin compares this transformation of the body to a simultaneous controlling of language, the division between familiar and correct speech, proper and improper discourse.[10] At the end of the English revolution, the new middle class emerged as a coherent and powerful force, partially through the controlling of the unruly and subversive forces released during the revolutionary years, as the lower classes, religious enthusiasts, and women were put back into their proper places. This assertion of power included a new monitoring of verbal abuse through a focus upon referentiality, the firm harnessing of words to things, that appears as the program of the Royal Society described by Spratt, and in the writings of Hobbes and Locke, for whom social order seems to be deeply connected with verbal order.

In the last chapter, I argued that Milton represents such attempts to circumscribe meaning and determine relations as disastrous. To reveal identity is to discover, as Dante's envious feared, the worst: that the Son *is* Oedipus, that Paradise *is* already fallen, that Milton himself *is* God the Father. To define relations absolutely is to do what Milton warned against:

to take *is* not as *as* but as literally *is*, and therefore to interpret communion as cannibalism.

According to Jim Swan, Milton lacked a modern sense of identity, but "as poet and revolutionary, was himself a major actor in the drama that transformed what it means, in the Western tradition, to have an identity."[11] In seventeenth-century England, the identity that is discovered with perhaps tragic and certainly oedipal results is that of the modern individual, and it is both source and product of the new bodily image. The word *individual* itself underwent a significant reformation in the seventeenth century. Its original meaning was that which cannot be divided but is one unified whole—a body that cannot be separated from its members.[12] In its early English usage, as in Latin, it was most frequently applied to atoms. When in the seventeenth century it began to be used in reference to people, it reflected a new formulation of personal identity. This rethinking of what defines a person was influenced by the materialist atomism of Democritus, who was used throughout the century as an antidote to the medieval tyranny of Aristotle. Turning to Democritus is to turn the world upside down, replacing an old system in which society is an organism existing prior to its members with one in which each part is now detached and independent, having no essential relation to others. Instead, all are bound only by whatever kind of artificial social contract can be constructed to hold them together.[13] Defined in opposition rather than in relation to society, the identity of the new individual and its relation to itself becomes a question of some concern. For furthermore, from the thirteenth century on, the time of the Fourth Lateran Council, discussions of the relations among the persons of the Trinity became increasingly applied to human persons. The relation between the divine substance and accidents was transferred into questions of personal identity, the relation between a human essence and its properties, and, especially, how much property can be taken from a human being without destroying its identity.[14]

Descartes finds one solution in defining the self or subject as the mind, reformulating the division that began with Socrates at a time when, through the coincidence of a number of scientific, philosophical, religious, and economic factors, it became particularly advantageous. For Descartes, as for Augustine, the mind is superior to the body because indivisibility, or unity, is obviously superior to divisibility, or diversity, and the mind is the enduring and unified essence that is left when all flimsy physical properties have been stripped away.[15] This separation of body and mind frees the mind from the divisible and perishable, and often, as in Jonson's case, simply embarrassing, body. Furthermore, it suits ideals such as Baconian science that elevate the mind over matter to justify man's domination of nature.[16] Before Descartes, knowledge had been seen largely as an act that involved the identification of subject and object; after him, the relation is

seen as one of an original and essential separation that justifies possession.[17] Descartes provides an epistemology appropriate for doctrines also
of self-discipline, such as those found in Protestantism, in which the subject treats its objectified body like any other object in the material world
upon which it imposes its will. The individual becomes reduced to a mind
that cannot be identified with anything outside of itself, not even the body
that contains it, as the microcosmic human being previously identified with
the macrocosm surrounding it becomes, despite Donne's denial, an isolated island. So, in the *Second Meditation*, on the knowledge of the mind
versus that of the body, Descartes broods upon a piece of wax which remains substantially unchanged despite the different forms it takes—a moment that uneasily looks back to *Metamorphoses* 15.169–72, with its wax-
like figures who survive, passing from form to form.[18] In Descartes's
description of the self, the individual as inner mind exists independent of
its various external expressions and incarnations, just as in the political theory that grows alongside this tradition the individual exists somehow prior
to society. The mind transcends existence, and becomes idealized as a
source of meaning *outside* of the physical body (which it is yet, in some
sense, obviously *inside*), and one's essence is seen as distinct from one's
accidents or properties.

This relation is complicated by the fact that the Cartesian split between
mind and body ultimately makes it possible for Protestantism especially to
identify essence with property in both its senses. As I mentioned earlier, in
Homer, the word for substance, *biotos,* meant both one's life and one's livelihood. You are what you have; and Aristotle's term for substance, *ousia,*
also equates man with property, while further including the philosophical
sense of substance, or essence.[19] But it was Protestantism, which, like Descartes, focuses on the individual as an inner essence that exists independent
of its outward material shell, that developed fully the idea of the self-made
man of substance. In fact, as Gilbert Ryle has suggested in his critique of
"the ghost in the machine," the description of the mind as distinct from
the body depends upon an analogy with the body, which is after all, according to Bakhtin, the model for the concept of the individual.[20] At the
same time that the individual is constructed as divided into an inside and
an outside self, the two implicitly collapse, identified through metaphor.
The individual "essence" is defined by and ultimately identifiable with his
"property," and particularly his private property.

According to Alan Macfarlane, the image of the self as a unique, indivisible unity implies that "society is constituted of autonomous, equal, units,
namely separate individuals, and that such individuals are more important,
ultimately, than any larger constituent group. It is reflected in the concept
of individual private property, in the political and legal liberty of the individual, in the idea of the individual's direct communication with God."[21]

The old image of the body politic created the sense of a world of essentially related members whose identities were determined, and controlled, by their social roles. With the rise of individualism, that body is also broken, its members scattered as atomlike individuals, so that society has to be re-membered in a new way, with a new basis and foundation for relations. According to Hobbes and Locke, what brings equal individuals together is the desire to preserve the most essential human right, property.[22]

Behind the theories of Hobbes and Locke, C. B. Macpherson sees the concept of "possessive individualism." Identity is based on ownership, as the individual is defined as "essentially the proprietor of his own person or capacities, owing nothing to society for them"[23]—thus as free from debts as Jonson, and indeed Milton, with his redefinition of debts as talent, wanted to appear. The "possessive individual" who owns himself is free from dependence upon others or relations other than those he chooses to enter into in his own self-interest. A society made up of such individuals must therefore be based on market relations, regulated by laws that at-tempt to determine and preserve the right to private property, "for the maintenance of orderly relations of exchanges between individuals re-garded as proprietors of themselves."[24] Despite its obvious flaws (such as the denial of individuality to most of mankind), this concept was expressed by a wide variety of English seventeenth-century thinkers and has contin-ued to influence our images of the individual and society. It revives and extends the Roman concept of the persona, which was based on owner-ship, and reinforces the focus on *meum* and *tuum* as the primary terms of relation that need social regulation. With the dis-memberment of the body politic by the discovery of the individual, there is a new drawing up of termini: boundaries between people and between other substances that had been seen previously as less substantial, laws regulating exchanges, in-cluding laws of copyright that legalize discourse as a product to be owned and consumed—and stolen.[25]

In England, the redefinition of the national body involved the loss of the dream of a single unified church. The logical extension of the Protestant rebellion against the materialism of the Catholic establishment was the dis-solution of all external religious structures altogether with the investment of all religious authority in the individual. While such an extreme was ad-vocated by only the most radical of sects, the general tendency of Protes-tantism was to isolate even the members who congregated together by fo-cusing on their private and unique relations with God.[26] As Weber showed in *The Protestant Ethic and the Spirit of Capitalism*, capitalism and Protes-tantism are essentially interconnected and play mutually supporting roles in the production of the modern individual. The Cartesian articulation of experience and Locke's image of society were also influential because they were reinforced at other levels of life, as privacy and isolation became possible for the first time for a large group of people—the rising Protestant middle class. The deemphasis in religion of external forms of mediation, leaving the individual alone with God, coincided with an increase in the possiblity of, and therefore an emphasis on, privacy in daily life, reflected in such innovations as the reorganization of the household and the codification of manners that made people keep their bodies to themselves.[27]

Moreover, according to Descartes, minds cannot meet, and it is only through bodies that exchanges can take place. If the body is devalued, even repudiated, as something external and alien to the real self, relations too must be degraded, appearing mercenary and materialistic, and certainly less like communion than cannibalism. Ironically, the kind of impulse that caused Jonson to detach himself from his body to keep his relationships pure, untouched by economic motivation, led to the definition of all exchanges as based on self-interest.

Radically different from Bakhtin's ideal of a cooperative body, such formulations have the effect of representing all relations as not symbiotic but predatory. So Macpherson sees the body politic made up of possessive individuals as "a series of competitive and invasive relations between all men, regardless of class; it puts every man on his own."[28] Whereas certain theorists, such as Bentham and Adam Smith, argued that the individual lust for gain, if left alone, would produce a self-regulating market economy, the result shown more often by history has been the transformation of the body politic into Hobbes's monstrous *Leviathan*, an artificial anatomy whose atomlike members only refrain from consuming each other when it doesn't serve their own interests. According to Hobbes, whose concept of the person is based on the Latin definition of persona, society is only a barely controlled state of nature, in which all exchanges are struggles among rivals.

The reduction of the previously all-inclusive medieval self to a form of private property (which is itself a version of paradise lost) helps explain also the powerful impact that the image of the Enclosure Acts had in England both on contemporary observers and later Englishmen.[29] The dismemberment of the land, which had been previously imagined as a communal body of property, was perhaps the most dramatic representation of my myth, resulting in the fragmentation of the country and a redistribution of bodies within the new developing urban communities. The construction of new termini on the landscape became symbolic of the tightening of the boundary lines around the self, and the loss of communal property suggested the transition into a world in which isolated individuals would be set off and against each other.

Seventeenth-century England is, then, the time of an "Intestine War" that tears apart the body politic so that its organic unity can never be remembered and of revolutions in science, economy, and religion that are all in some way divisive.[30] In his writings, and especially in his treatment of the Fall, Milton reflects a contemporary separation of relations that had been previously less formally defined into binary oppositions. The division between social and individual, public and private, creates an opposition between mercenary and disinterested motives, as, since the seventeenth century, certain areas of life have been idealized as set off from the power systems of the marketplace and made to function as receptacles accommodating the impulses excluded from the working world. However, in a society based on wage relations, all exchanges outside of the norm are ambivalent, both idealized and degraded, like the self-sufficient being outside society which Aristotle saw as either god or beast.[31] One of these realms, as Jonson foretold, is art itself, which, seen as separate from "hard work,"[32] is, especially from Kant on, increasingly defined as disinterested.[33] Precisely at the time that writing was becoming a profession and literature a commodity, art was also being defined as purely aesthetic. In the Romantic doctrine of the symbol, which for Coleridge reconciles inside and outside, the Eucharist is revised into an ideal of aesthetic communion that turns the imagination into the "paradise within thee, happier far" (*Paradise Lost* 12.587). But at the same time, as I shall show further in relation to Coleridge, art also becomes suspected of offering an illusory and regressive escape from reality that is in some sense cannibalistic.

The development of the modern notion of the family and the concept of romantic love are further examples of attempts to create private spheres of uncontaminated relationships.[34] The latter, which was obviously also an effort to find a means of bringing sexual opposites together, developed precisely when social conditions were combining to produce gender roles so completely dissimilar that the possibility of any communication between the two sexes was becoming increasingly unlikely.[35] As Mill was to note later, in marriage two become one, and that one the man, who subsumes the female into his identity, thus legally recreating the original biblical relation between Adam and Eve.[36] With the idealization of love, the female was associated with the private world and bound to home by ties more confining, as they were not mercenary but "sacred." The separation of the family from politics (one of the foundations of Locke's refutation of Filmer) permits the suppression of its own private, inner struggles. In the realistic novel, beginning with *Clarissa*, there is a tension between the representation of an idealized home, the place of harmonious relations, and that of a battle zone for the contest of wills, ruled over by the tyrannical paterfamilias.

The development of Romantic love as a refuge from mercenary relations was preceded in the sixteenth and seventeenth centuries by the revival of the classical ideal of friendship.[37] As a purely masculine relationship, friendship could not resolve the differences between the sexes (which meant it had one less problem to deal with), but focused instead on describing a harmony of fraternal relations, the relations between equal men that would become the center of later seventeenth-century political theory, which could convert potential rivalry and envy into mutual imitation and admiration. The ideal, which has its most significant source in Cicero's *De amicitia*, involves the total identification of two men; a friend, according to de la Primaudaye, "is a second selfe, and . . . whosoever would take upon him this title in regard of another, he must transforme himselfe into his nature whom he purposeth to love, and that with a steadfast and settled minde to continue so for ever. Hereupon one of the auncients speaking of him that loveth perfectly, saith that he liveth in another's body."[38] The greatest Renaissance writer on friendship, Montaigne, describes it as the closest possible form of relation, surpassing marriage and kinship, as it is free from carnal desire and freely chosen, and "In the friendship I speak of, our souls mingle and blend with each other so completely that they efface the seam that joined them, and cannot find it again."[39]

According to the more pragmatic Bacon, a friend is needed to communicate feelings which if allowed to go unexpressed might explode: "A principal fruit of friendship is the ease and discharge of the fulness and swellings of the heart."[40] For him, friendship is necessary as an antidote against the diseases caused by the essential isolation of the individual. To illustrate the dangers of solitude, he quotes a saying of Pythagoras "*Eat not the heart,*" explaining that "those that want friends to open themselves unto are cannibals of their own hearts."[41] I want to return to the subject of friendship in a moment but first would like to say something about its relationship to cannibalism, for it does not seem to me at all accidental that the writer associated with one, Montaigne, should also be interested in the other, nor that he should also be considered one of the early writers on what it means to be an autonomous, independent individual. As an explorer of the self and the possibilities of self-knowledge, it seems appropriate that Montaigne was interested in both ideal and infernal images of identification between self and other.

Montaigne's essay "On Cannibals," which appears as a plea for the toleration of cultural differences, reflects a rise of interest in cannibalism—indeed, the invention of the word *cannibal*[42]—which occurred with the discovery of the New World. But this upsurge of interest coincides also with the emergence of the individual, and ultimately proves a useful tool in its definition.[43] The cannibal is the individual's "alien," against which he constructs his identity, and whose threat to that identity is represented as literal consumption. The construction of the cannibal and New World savage through "colonial discourse" is similar to the Protestant fabrication of the Catholic Black Mass, as both put into pragmatic practice the Socratic method of constructing a dualism in order to justify subsuming the inferior term. In both cases, accusing the other of cannibalism reflects a fear of losing a newly won identity. Having just broken off from the Catholic Church, the Protestants were anxious about turning back into it and so needed to articulate a strict division between their practices and the Catholic ones, while the terror of "going native" in the New World may be related to a fear of losing hold of the new notion of individual identity. As is common in the assertion of cultural and religious differences, the division between desired norm and feared deviant was formulated in terms of how and what the different groups ate. The definition of the other as cannibal justifies its oppression, extermination, and cultural cannibalism (otherwise known as imperialism) by the rule "eat or be eaten." In the case of the New World, a similar logic also justified the appropriation of property: the Indians' lack of a concept of possession, on the one hand, supported comparisons of America with Paradise, where there had been no private property; on the other, it made appropriation totally excusable, as no *individual* was being harmed.[44]

It is not surprising, then, that the fictional character frequently read as a picture of the emerging individual, Robinson Crusoe, discovers himself in alien territory pitted against the cannibals.[45] According to E. Pearlman, whose study of Defoe complements his work on Jonson, Crusoe's unnecessary obsession with cannibalism reflects a group of connected psychological characteristics: infantile orality, ambivalence toward his father and authority in general, and weak "ego boundaries" that need bolstering by elaborate defenses. Pearlman concludes:

> He is a radical individualist and the prototype of new economic man, but he is also an authoritarian of a dangerous kind and an unredeemed, uncivilized colonialist. For when the novel is stripped of its ethnocentric biases, what is left is the essence of the colonial encounter. A weak individual, unable to succeed in his own country, of restless and unstable character, moves to an exotic locale where the technological advantage of his civilization gives him immediate superiority over the indigenous population. There he exploits the land, slaughters the heathens and makes instruments (military and otherwise) of selected converts. He despises the natives, but is also terrified of them, and is prepared to justify massacre if he can fantasize a threat to himself.[46]

Odysseus massacres the guests to regain his original identity as host; the colonist annihilates his hosts for fear of becoming identified with them and in order to set himself up over and against them as the "proper" host. *Robinson Crusoe* looks back to the *Odyssey* and its descriptions of dangerous foreign places that try to absorb the traveler, and forward to *Heart of Darkness*, *She*, and other expressions of the terror of "going native," which, in different ways, represent the imperialist desire for the total mastery of what is foreign and strange by means of complete appropriation and incorporation.

Defoe's novel is also part of the beginning of an intense interest in tales of shipwreck and cannibalism, which becomes most marked in the nineteenth century and in which it is the civilized man himself who turns cannibal. Implicit in the topos of man as vessel had been the identification of shipwreck with loss of identity, an identification Milton plays upon in "Lycidas." Moreover, where shipwreck occurs, cannibalism often follows, as an even more horrifying image for the loss of human identity. In fiction, this motif appears in Byron's *Don Juan*, Thackeray's "Little Billee," and Gilbert's "The Yarn of the Nancy Bell," to which I shall be returning, all comic versions that look forward to the genre of the cannibal joke,[47] and that show in their own ways, as Dante did in his, the relationship between cannibalism and the breakdown of language—in these cases into nonsense. Moreover, reflecting perhaps the late Victorian sense of a crisis of imperial identity, publicity about real cannibalism following shipwrecks escalated toward the end of the nineteenth century, culminating in the famous trial of Regina vs. Dudley and Stephens in 1884.[48] Two men were accused of killing and eating their fellow crewmen in cold blood, not even drawing lots to give the others a sporting chance (which was seen as scandalously un-British), and were condemned and sentenced to death. The sentence was later commuted, but in a very stern editorial the *Times* warned its readers that future cannibals should expect no such clemency.

Such stories, like the cannibal jokes I remember having a brief revival in the early sixties, have retained their popularity in our own century, though in recent years they have appeared, not surprisingly, more frequently in relation to plane crashes. The tale of the 1972 plane crash in the Andes became a bestseller as *Alive: The Story of the Andes Survivors*,[49] an account which focused on the psychological effects that cannibalism had on the survivors, a group of Catholic boys, and the defenses by which they represented their actions to themselves. Forced by hunger to eat their dead friends, the survivors sublimated to themselves their experience, converting an act that represented the survival of the fittest in its crudest form into a kind of communion. Reports in the London *Times* (which, almost a hundred years after Dudley and Stephen, had apparently learnt clemency) quoted the boys as saying: "If Jesus, in the Last Supper, offered his body and blood to all the disciples, he was giving us to understand that we must do the same," "what we did was really Christian. We went back to the very source of Christianity," and "We swallowed little bits of flesh with the feeling that God demanded it of us. We felt like Christians."[50]

These stories exert a lurid fascination, for they suggest, as Montaigne had already pointed out, how fragile the boundary between cannibal and Christian is, and how difficult it is to tell where communion stops and cannibalism sets in. For the Andes survivors, cannibalism is an act that makes the flesh symbolic, that in effect turns matter into spirit, which is precisely what Peggy Reeves Sanday has claimed is the role of cannibalism in other societies.[51] The story of the Andes survivors concerns a group, however, and it is the tales of the lone survivor, like Crusoe, that are the most interesting in terms of what they say about the underside of the ideal of the self-sufficient, independent individual, as they literalize the belief that the individual is an island.[52] Stephen King has written the twentieth-century version of *Robinson Crusoe* in his short story, "Survivor Type," which tells of a corrupt doctor, in whom the Baconian pragmatic and gothic mad scientist are shown to be the same, who, after clawing his way out of the gutter to the top of his profession, is ruined by the exposure of his drug connections.[53] In order to make a comeback, he tries to smuggle in heroin from Saigon but on the way back is shipwrecked on a rock, with only the heroin and a sharp knife. Like Crusoe, he is very enterprising and self-reliant. In fact, in the end he's totally self-sufficient: he survives by taking the heroin, amputating bits of himself, and eating them. Robinson Crusoe, eat your heart out. A neat solution, too, to the problem of the relation between substance and property. The detachment of this objective scientific mind from its own bodily members means that they can be literally detached; in the end, however, the opposites collapse when they become absolutely identical through an extremely economic recycling.

As King's story cleverly illustrates, the desire for absolute self-reliance and independence from all external influences would be best satisfied by self-cannibalism, in which one doesn't even need to rely on the world outside for food. The modern definition of the self in terms of self-identity and self-knowledge is parodied as being not only narcissistic but self-cannibalistic. In his self-consuming self-possession, King's doctor looks back to Ovid's Erysicthon, and to the iconographical representations of Envy which Erysicthon himself incorporates. In her works on early child development and the formation of identity, Melanie Klein has read envy as an oral trait, associated with the loss of identity with the mother (represented as the breast, which is for the infant the source of all nourishment) that marks the transition from an oral phase of symbiosis to one of cannibalistic aggression.[54] For Klein, the characteristics of envy are a fear of being robbed, a suspicion of gifts, and, above all, an antagonism toward creativity, all of which are connected with an ambivalence about the exchange of property that is the result of an inability to accept the alterity of the other. It is "the ability to assimilate the loved object—not only as a source of food—and to love it without envy interfering"[55] that is the basis for the gratitude which Klein sees as the antithesis of envy which yet grows out of it. Whereas envy aims at appropriating a source of plenitude for itself, gratitude pays tribute to it. In Klein's description of individual development, envy and gratitude become the two poles representing the possible relations one can have with others, and both are constructed during the oral phase.

In the Renaissance formulations analogous to Klein's terms, envy is opposed to friendship. According to Robert Burton, envy is a perverse form of imitation, in which emulation has turned into rivalry.[56] For Bacon, as I mentioned, the alternative to invidious self-consumption is friendship as a more amicable form of identification. For Montaigne, the ideal of friendship is both a refuge from more mercenary and hostile relations (including those within families and marriages) and also a way of combating the solitariness and isolation that he sees as defining the individual. But there is a tension between Montaigne's idealization of friendship and his affirmation of not only introspection but independence, his focus on self-knowledge and self-sufficiency, a tension that reenacts an inconsistency in his essay "On Cannibals" between his plea for toleration of the different and unfamiliar and his appropriation of the figure of the savage for a familiar classical ideal.[57] Knowledge, even of the other, is difficult to separate from self-knowledge, which Montaigne represents as self-cannibalism,[58] for the isolated mind works to eliminate the category of otherness and alterity. For Montaigne, a friend "is myself":[59] the other becomes Montaigne, just as ultimately the cannibals themselves become identified with Montaigne's own ideal. The strange is in fact domesticated by the strategy familiar to colonial discourse.

Moreover, the representation of friendship in Montaigne begins with loss, the death of La Boétie.[60] But although writing about friendship involves nostalgia for a lost unity, in fact the death of La Boétie allows a greater unity between the two friends, as he lives on through Montaigne, who wrote "In truth, he is still lodged in me so entire and so alive that I cannot believe he is either so irrevocably buried or so totally removed from our communication."[61] The death of one friend in fact permits a greater intimacy, as he is totally absorbed into the identity of the survivor.

In the rest of this chapter and in the following one I shall be looking at fantasies of incorporation which involve the denial of loss, especially the loss of unity that, I have been arguing, appears to be echoed throughout descriptions of the Renaissance. This will include a discussion of the gothic and its representations of the desire to revive the dead and keep the past present (which Stephen King has once more captured in *Pet Sematary*), and of the incremental visions of Coleridge and Melville. In my conclusion, I will look briefly at Freud and Frye as examples of twentieth-century psychoanalytical and critical readings of internalization as a method for the formation of personal and poetic identity.

I will start with a last look at the seventeenth century, focusing on a strange and eccentric book to which I have just referred, Burton's *Anatomy of Melancholy*. Burton's text looks back to earlier forms of literary relations and attempts to prevent divisions as they are occurring by recreating Bakhtin's grotesque body as a work that is huge, open, and structured on a basic ambivalence. It is a text that draws attention to its own analogy with the human body as an "anatomy," a term taken from medical analyses, in which it referred to the act of dissection.[62] In the sixteenth century, the word was appropriated to describe a specific kind of literary work, one that generally incorporated a great deal of material under the rubric of a unifying transcendental term. To call a book an anatomy might suggest one way of re-grounding meaning and the mind in the literal, physical world of the body from which it was becoming detached. Yet anatomies tend to appear as completely fanciful fictions, and "forms that have no reference"[63] beyond the minds that create them. As we shall see, as autonomous verbal structures par excellence, they provide Northrop Frye with a fitting model for the shape of literary tradition. Still, in a Cartesian world consisting of minds cut off from each other, in which only bodies can connect, a book that is at least said to be a body may offer a different opportunity for individuals to meet, and in his *Anatomy*, the last great work of its kind, Burton attempts to create a place where opposites that were becoming increasingly polarized can come together. However, the term with which he hopes to restore loss is the one that both Freud and Klein will associate with the denial of loss and with the failure to properly internalize the lost object that leads to a self-consuming identification with it.[64]

ANATOMY OF MELANCHOLY

In his opening address to the reader of the *Anatomy*, "Democritus Jr." describes the philosopher whose name he has appropriated as, "a little wearish old man, very melancholy by nature, averse from company in his latter days, and much given to solitariness" (1.12). According to different sources, the original Democritus was a great philosopher, theologian, physician, mathematician, natural scientist, and "In a word, he was *omniafariàm doctus*, a general scholar, a great student" (1.12–13). As the writer explains his decision to identify himself nominally with this omniverous thinker, he claims that he too has led a solitary life and has suffered greatly from melancholy.[65] Moreover, though by profession a divine, by constant study he has become *omniafariàm doctus* as well:

> yet *turbine raptus ingenii*, as he said, out of a running wit, an unconstant unsettled mind, I had a great desire (not able to attain to a superficial skill in any) to have some smattering in all, to be *aliquis in omnibus, nullus in singulis*, which *Plato* commends, out of him *Lipsius* approves and furthers, *as fit to be imprinted in all curious wits, not to be slave of one science, or dwell altogether in one subject as*

most do, but to rove abroad, centum puer artium, *to have an oar in every mans boat, to taste of every dish, and sip of every cup* . . . (I.14).

Through the use of this persona, the masking figure of Democritus Jr. with which Burton is identified but which still is separate from and covers the identity of the real "I" of the author, Burton, one of the most isolated of writers, is able to inflate his own individual identity to create a grotesquely huge and open anatomy that can incorporate all men and knowledge. But while Burton finds a place for all under a single heading that is also imagined as a single mind, the only transcendental term that can subsume, and perhaps consume, all meaning is "melancholy."

From the Middle Ages on, there had been an increasing interest in melancholy, which in many ways anticipated the studies of Freud and Klein. The traditional concepts of melancholy have been discussed frequently and thoroughly enough not to necessitate any lengthy discussion here.[66] Associated with theories of stellar influence, the infusion of external powers into the body, melancholy looks forward to theories of poetic influence[67] and from its beginning was identified with the artistic personality, which was seen as essentially ambivalent. Melancholy was seen as both a humor and a disease, and, through the merging of the originally opposed theories of Galen and Aristotle, as both curse and blessing. It was a sign of both a *genius* and of a vicious *daemon*, both in the older sense of good and bad presiding spirits and later in the modern sense of innate qualities. It is certainly a loaded word to choose in order to identify all mankind. Potentially indicating, perhaps even collapsing beyond the hope of differentiation, insanity and inspiration, it is also associated with Saturn, the ambivalent god of the Golden Age who devours his children. While Marsilio Ficino, a sufferer of melancholy who attempted desperately to emphasize its redeeming features, claimed that those born under the sign of Saturn were truly geniuses, he knew very well that the melancholy mind is fed not only by outside influences, but also by and on itself, so one should "beware of Saturn; for he often devours his children."[68]

For Burton, melancholy is essentially ambivalent, a primal word that is the source of both good and evil. Like Gaster and Comus, it is the beginning and end of human endeavor; like Derrida's *pharmakon*, it is both disease and cure, as Burton writes "of melancholy, by being busy to avoid melancholy" (1.17).[69] It is a source in which, according to the opening "Author's Abstract of Melancholy," pleasure and pain are identified, a place in which ultimately all extremes of meaning can meet. While this annihilation of differences and identification of opposites ultimately threatens the possibility of any meaning at all, in the act of writing Burton attempts to find a mean, not only between the opposing poles of melancholy itself, but also between the oppositions of mind and body, self and others, unity and diversity. He attempts to create a single textual body that is big enough to incorporate all differences but still keep them apart. The anatomy that Burton constructs looks back to Bakhtin's grotesque body, for it is in fact an ambivalent anatomy in which the tension between coherence and diversity is never resolved in such a way that enables one to subsume the other.

The text presented as a body also represents a single mind, that of Democritus Jr., and so acts as a kind of antidote to the Cartesian separation of the two, which attempts to restore the imagined earlier unity of individual being. As melancholy is encouraged by isolation, the Cartesian insular mind is by definition melancholy, trapped in private experiences that are inaccessible to other minds. It is only through bodily exchanges that men can truly meet. However, the text's status as both body and mind suggests the problems involved in attempting to imagine the two as analogous. Before the beginning of each of the three partitions, Burton provides a synopsis that represents the text as if it were a body that, like a real human body which Descartes defined in terms of extension in space, could be taken in at a single glance even as it consists of stable units and partitions that stay apart. The promise of an organized coherence of diversity disappears, however, as the text begins to unfold through time, the dimension in which the mind extends itself. The boundaries set up by the synopses are blurred and broken until the plan appears to have little to do with the finished text.[70] Through the repetition of stories, figures, and themes, categories become confused, and the possibility of straightforward analysis seems lost. The melancholy mind does not appear to order the material it subsumes but seems to go around in circles until finally, having subsumed everything and digested it to a single undifferentiated lump, it revolves only around itself. Unlike the spatially oriented body, the temporally defined mind cannot actually take in opposites at once without collapsing them, not merely into nonsense, but even total insanity.

Burton's famous description of the course of melancholy follows the mind as it loses control. Those who indulge in melancholy and "Voluntary solitariness" are lured by a "Siren" to an "irrevocable gulf" (1.283) in which they become completely consumed by their own habit. The obsessed mind cannot control its imaginings any more than Burton apparently can control his own narrative, and suddenly the melancholy man discovers that he has crossed an immutable boundary that marks the point of no return, and repeated pleasure has turned into endless pain. The curious wandering mind has a tendency to go too far, to poke into corners that turn out to be traps. As in the world of the *Metamorphoses*, transgression, even that which is apparently innocent, has strict consequences; the melancholy man left too much to himself becomes obsessed with his "destructive solitariness" so that unwittingly "These wretches frequently degenerate from men, and of sociable creatures become beasts, monsters, inhuman, ugly to behold, *misanthropoi*, they do even loath themselves, and hate the company of men, as so many *Timons, Nebuchadnezzars*, by too much indulging to these pleasing humours, and through their own default" (1.286).

However, in the midst of this lengthy warning against the hideous dangers of self-indulgence in pleasing melancholy, Burton suddenly remembers: "I may not deny but that there is some profitable meditation, contemplation, and kind of solitariness to be embraced, which the Fathers so highly commended . . . a Paradise, an Heaven on earth, if it be used aright, good for the body, and better for the soul . . ." (1.284). If melancholy can turn men into beasts, it may also lead them to God, for it is, after all, a kind of primal word that has antithetical senses. Burton briefly attempts Ficino's method of claiming that an apparent curse is really a blessing in disguise when he writes: "I was not a little offended with this malady, shall I say My Mistress *Melancholy*, my *Egeria*, or my *Malus Genius*? & for that cause, as he that is stung with a scorpion, I would expel *clavum clavo*, comfort one sorrow with another, idleness with idleness, *ut ex Viperia Theracium*, make an Antidote out of that which was the prime cause of my disease" (1.18). However, Burton's method is not to exchange one form of melancholy for its opposite, for the two extremes are too difficult to tell apart. Instead he uses the restless movement of the melancholy mind in order to protect itself against its own tendency to be overmuch *in singulis*. To prevent the melancholy mind from fixing obsessively upon a single object until it ultimately preys upon itself, he keeps it in motion, sending it outside of itself through the acts of writing and reading of the text. However, the only movement possible for such a mind, represented by the narrative as well as the opening poem, is a manic depressive flux between extremes that, even as it keeps them apart, threatens to identify them.

The body of the text also has at times a manic depressive relation to its own members. The text that is an anatomy ideally creates a space for encounters with others to take place as an alternative to isolation and solipsism that lead not to individuation and self-knowledge but to madness and meaninglessness. A host of sources are drawn inside, and even the reader whom, Burton tells, "Thou thyself art the subject of my discourse" (1.12). The use of a persona creates the impression that the author himself also is contained completely within his own work. Although at the end of the first edition of the text, Burton revealed his identity, unmasking the true self and authorial presence behind the persona, in later editions this revelation was omitted and replaced by a number of clues within the work that hinted obliquely at the writer's identity. The result is a tightening of the identification between persona and author that prevents the possibility of locating a source of meaning outside the work itself. Like Ovid, Burton represents himself as absorbed by his work, subsumed by melancholy along with everything else.[71] But at the same time as the speaker draws outside material into his text, the process of writing is one that involves the externalization of the inner mind onto the surface of the anatomy, and Burton claims, "I have laid myself open (I know it) in this treatise, turned myself inside out" (1.25).[72] The melancholy mind's introjection of material, including itself, is countered by its own self-projection, creating a rhythm of exchange between inner and outer realms similar to that represented by Rabelais through images of eating.

The absorption of the author into his own text holds out an obvious advantage for an isolated reclusive scholar who in many ways literally lived in books. Burton's is a totally textual universe, in which the only bodies with which one can come into contact are textual ones. By reading alone he experiences others and takes in the world outside himself. The text enables him to encounter others, to move out of his own singularity in a rhythm of expansion and contraction, which often creates an effect of comic self-deflation. While critics have emphasized the centrality of Burton's persona, whose mind holds the mammoth work together, that "I" also stands on the border of the world it sees, dilating itself, like Jonson, between center and circumference. As his mind assimilates experience, it remains forever on the periphery, peering in: "A mere spectator of other mens' fortunes and adventures, and how they act their parts, which methinks are diversely presented unto me, as from a common theatre or scene" (1.15). Burton frequently calls attention to his own inexperience in certain matters in order to avoid total authorial responsibility: "I confess I am but a novice, a Contemplator only . . . what I say is merely reading, *ex aliorum forsan ineptiis*, by mine own observation, and other's relation" (3.212). A bachelor, his use of the "modesty *topos*"[73] is largely in discussion of sexual relations and desire; the only intercourse he knows is textual. Drawn toward others by means of books, he still remains separated from them, a *spectator ab extra*, looking down on the world even as he tries to draw it into the circumference of his mind, from his library tower, "in some high place above you all, like *Stoicus Sapiens, omnia saecula, praeterita presentiaque videns, uno velut intuitu*" (1.15).

Because Burton's experience is mediated through books, he travels only in his mind. But mental travel has one advantage over bodily in that it is not encumbered by space and indeed seems able to take in all ages and places at once. Mediated experience makes it possible for a man to visit "all the remote Provinces, Towns, Cities of the World, and never to go forth of the limits of his study" (2.103). In the "Digression on Air" he takes off on a flight of fancy that increasingly violates chronological and geographical limtiations by juxtaposing heterogeneous figures and countries. The mind begins to replace an external order with its own internal concept of coherence. But as he gets carried away in a tirade against the excess speculation of minds who "soar higher yet, and see what God himself doth" (2.67), he suddenly realizes that he himself has gone too far and pulls himself back down to earth: "But hoo! I am now gone quite out of sight, I am almost giddy with roving about: I could have ranged farther yet but I am an infant, and not able to dive into these profundities, or sound these depths, not able to understand, much less discuss" (2.69). His self-expansion bursts into comic self-deflation with the reminder that no single mind can contain everything.

While the abruptness of the movement between extremes has a comic effect here, elsewhere it appears to be potentially more disturbing. A complete inversion of values occurs in Book 2, in which all of the evils denounced in Book 1 are reevaluated and converted into comforts. So, for example, a sick body should not be a cause for despair, as it is the sign of a healthy soul, imprisonment is not so disastrous, as all men are in reality prisoners, poverty is a blessing in disguise, as it frees us from inessential burdens and the cares of wealth, while melancholy itself is not the worst of diseases and has some redeeming aspects. The transition is done in a spurt of stoicism that floods through the partition and results in the claim that the mind is inviolable and can control mere matter and circumstances. However, the problem with such a consolation is that it is precisely the mind which is melancholy and diseased; that stripped to its essential self and freed from all the properties that distract it, it is hopelessly mad.

Moreover, this hopeful metamorphosis seems suspicious in a world described in the "Author's Abstract" as the perpetual alteration between joy and pain, and is potentially a product of the self-delusion of the melancholy mind. The total inversion in Book 2 calls attention to the difficulty of maintaining differences under the power of the melancholy mind in which extremes can meet. Opposites can come together too easily, as in the case of Burton's discussion of tobacco: "*Tobacco*, divine, rare, superexcellent *Tobacco*, which goes far beyond all their panaceas, potable gold, and philosopher's stones, sovereign remedy to all diseases. A good vomit, I confess, a virtuous herb, if it be well qualified, opportunely taken, and medicinally used, but, as it is commonly abused by most men, which take it as Tinkers do Ale, 'tis a plague, a mischief, a violent purger of goods, lands, health, hellish, devilish, and damned *Tobacco*, the ruin and overthrow of body and soul" (2.264). Such sentences are not only manic depressive, they're suicidal, as their ends turn upon and undo their beginnings.

While the second book turns the first inside out, the self-contradictory and perhaps consuming nature of Burton's text is most apparent in the third partition, on love and religious melancholy. Speaking of love, Burton careens frantically back and forth between denunciation and praise of marriage. Tales of connubial bliss turn suddenly into stories of rape, or of female insatiability. The distinction between lust and love with which he began dissolves as he moves too quickly from one to another and further describes them in identical ways: after describing a vile love that debases lovers, as examples of which he cites the metamorphoses of gods into beasts, he speaks of a noble love that elevates by making lovers clever, using Jupiter's transformation into a swan to woo Leda (2.200). Thus sublimation and degradation meet. Moreover, the very nature of desire seems to put us in a state of endless manic depressive flux, for the simple reason that one desires what one lacks. Therefore the single man wants to be married, but once married wants to be single again; we're caught in a double bind, as no matter what we have, we'll want something else. The stoic advice of the second partition, be content with what you have, seems in this predominantly neoplatonically oriented book woefully inadequate, as it is always what you have that makes you dissatisfied.

The discussion of love ends with a sudden assertion that everyone should get married: "God send us all good wives, every man his wish in this kind, and me mine!" (292)—an ambiguous statement, especially considering Burton's enforced celibacy—and an attempt to sing an *Epithalamium*. In a note, Burton refers his reader to the end of Chaucer's *Troilus and Creseide* as a model for his hymn. Those who know the real conclusion of the poem may wonder at the slip in Burton's memory. But Burton does many other strange things to his sources in these sections. As he subsumes stories and figures, they lose their original identities. Apparently arbitrarily connected by the associative power of Democritus Jr.'s mind, they begin to blur into one another. One tends to lose track of figures who appear throughout the text, and attempts to trace coherent patterns in their different appearances prove rather puzzling, as their characters seem completely unstable. Someone like Seneca may be either an authority or an exemplum, while Helen is sometimes a femme fatale and sometimes a sedate matron who at different times appears happily married to both Menelaus and Paris. Figures keep switching roles and contradicting themselves or their usual connotations: Orpheus, for example, appears as a type for wedded bliss (3.58), and in the *Epithalamium* the odd couples of Helen and Menelaus, Aeneas and Dido, Echo and Narcissus, join Troilus and Creseide as examples of connubial happiness (3.292–94). Perhaps the most striking instability is that of Burton's namesake, Democritus, the origin of whose blindness is told four times. In the opening address, after the description of Democritus we are told, "to the intent he might better contemplate, I find it related by some, that he put out his eys, and was in his old age voluntarily blind, yet saw more than all Greece besides, and writ of every subject" (1.13). Here, blindness is a source of inner vision, as the mind is freed from material distractions. In the second partition, typically, this story is inverted, as the tale of Democritus's blindness is given as an example of someone whose loss of physical sight was afterward recompensed by greater insight (2.155). Then, in the third partition, we are told that he blinded himself, first, in the section on jealousy, "because he could not look on a woman without lust, and was much troubled to see that which he might not enjoy" (3.357), and second, in the section on despair, "because he could not abide to see wicked men prosper, and was therefore ready to make away himself" (3.454). Burton seems to be deliberately not getting his stories straight to demonstrate how the melancholy mind, isolated from direct experience and unencumbered by reality, is able to revise all stories to suit its own desires of the moment.

In other words, though sent outside of itself, the melancholy mind, like Montaigne's, keeps returning to itself, as it strives to subsume and reduce everything to itself. As one form of melancholy merges with another, even the distinctions between categories break down. Melancholy is everything, everything is melancholy. The reader has nothing solid to hold onto—no nice, simple, straightforward plot with a comforting Aristotelian beginning and end—but only a swirling mass of related facts and stories tossed up and down in the fit of the narrative. Burton's text contains 1,250 sources from a wide variety of fields—philosophy, theology, medicine, science, and literature, which represent very different points of view and often support contradictory arguments. Such contradictions do not appear to worry him, as all opposites are reconciled in the word "melancholy." No authority is privileged, not even Scripture, and authorial identity is often obscured by the use of the vague "he" and by quotation without sources.[74] Burton sometimes misquotes as well, estranging words from their original form as he appropriates them for himself. Melancholy subsumes everyone, and within its anatomy there often appears to be little to distinguish the different members. The irony of melancholy is that it is what makes men unique and individual by isolating them completely from each other, but it is also what makes them indistinguishable because it identifies them all. The text that "anatomizes" its parts in order to reunite them as a single anatomy, that tries to reduce everything to forms of a single unifying principle, the transcendental term "Melancholy," potentially eradicates all distinctions. As Burton constantly cries: "who is not a fool, melancholy, mad?—*Qui nil molitur inepte,* who is not brain-sick? Folly, melancholy, madness, are but one disease, *delerium* is a common name to all. . . . take melancholy in what sense you will, properly or improperly, in disposition or habit, for pleasure or for pain, dotage, discontent, fear, sorrow, madness, for part, or all, truly, or metaphorically, 'tis all one" (1.39–40).[75] In other words, everything is everything else, and can be reduced to one sentence: "To conclude, this being granted, that all the world is melancholy, or mad, dotes, and every member of it, I have ended my task, and sufficiently illustrated that which I took upon me to demonstrate at first. At this present I have no more to say" (1.137).

However, the fact that he has just said everything doesn't shut him up, even for a moment. Moreover, while Burton anticipates and even encourages reductive readings, he subverts them by preventing the text from becoming too perfectly unified and coherent. The desire for coherence—similar to the desire to plug up holes and, effectively, to idealize the grotesque body that Rabelais ridicules—is a sign of melancholy that, as I will show later in relation to Northrop Frye, connects it to forms of criticism that seek in the text a unified body without contradictions or open and unfilled gaps. But the textual body that Burton creates is one that is not smoothed over and idealized. The homogenization of voices cannot in reality be complete, for Burton's style alone forces us to see the differences. According to Stanley Fish, "Nothing stands out in Burton's universe, because nothing— no person, place, object, idea—can maintain its integrity in the context of an all-embracing madness. Even syntactical and rhetorical forms—sentences, paragraphs, sections—lose their firmness in this most powerful of solvents."[76] However, swept along as we are by Burton's prose, which he himself compares to a river, we are constantly being obstructed by grammatical difficulties, such as clauses in apposition that do not agree. In a characteristic passage, Burton's description of Democritus with which I began, English alternates with Latin, analogies jar, while authors are assimilated by different means: Plato and Horace are directly named, Horace is quoted, Scaliger is identified in a footnote as this time occupying the indefinite "he." While these elements create the impression of a unique and consistent style, one of its essential characteristics is a tension among its units which are never allowed to merge perfectly. The different members of the sentences are somewhat disjointed, even dismembered, as they are set in odd and inconsistent relations to each other.[77]

The stylistic lack of homogenization is reflected also in Burton's incorporation of authors. Burton's method is based on the Renaissance ideal of collation that was part of the early humanist attempt to recapture and restore the past.[78] The act of collation itself was often imagined as the remembering of a past which, like the primal man, had been fragmented: "the text is a beautiful body, a 'corpus' whose limbs are scattered, a body mutilated and mangled,"[79] which the collator restores to its original wholeness. In the process he also creates himself as a unified entity.[80] Burton's own model for the act of collation was Erasmus, whose works are among his most common sources. *In Praise of Folly* provides one type for Burton's text, as it too tries to trace all human activity to a single source. For Erasmus, that source is found in the word *Folly*, which, in the world of the early Reformation that is beginning to question the status and efficacy of signs and symbols, is the one transcendental term that can contain everything. But obviously the entire enterprise itself is seen as pure folly: the all-purpose signifier is meaningless, as, for Erasmus, to mean everything is to mean nothing, and Folly's vision is of a world that finally consists of a mass of almost indistinguishable idiots.

Burton surpasses Erasmus and subsumes his term by claiming that folly and madness are only subsections of the truly all-meaningful word and ultimate source, "melancholy." But while the *Anatomy* is a *Praise of Folly*, a dilation upon a single word that calls into question its own activity, it is Erasmus's *Adages* which not only most obviously feeds Burton's work, providing it with an almost endless supply of proverbs,[81] but also gives it a different model for itself that helps it imagine both differentiation and meaning.

The aim of the *Adages* was to make the past accessible to the present; as one translator writes, "to recapture, in this handy, portmanteau form, the outlook and way of life of the classical world, through its customs, legends and social institutions, and to put within reach of a modern public the accumulated vision of the past."[82] The revival and restoration of learning becomes for Erasmus the type for all great labor, as the modern Hercules is Aldus Manutius and, finally, the collator himself. The task of collecting the *Adages* and re-membering the past in a single body is the most arduous of all, the most beneficial to mankind in general, and the least beneficial to the collator himself, who finds himself embroiled in endless work. He must constantly struggle to make sense of conflicting sources and versions of his material, and Erasmus complains, "there is so little agreement between these authorities that they very often write things which cancel each other out, and the additional burden is laid on one of consulting different commentators on the same thing, and—over and over again—of examining, comparing, pondering and judging" (198). As a series of proverbs the work is potentially literally endless; Erasmus defended its apparent lack of order as part of a strategy to facilitate expansion, and in his lifetime it grew from 818 to 4,251 proverbs. Its growth ended only with his death. Ideally, however, even that conclusive event need not have put an end to the work, for Erasmus saw himself as part of an ongoing community of humanist scholars working together for the benefit of all men. Such an encyclopedic work is beyond the power of any single man, and so Erasmus defines himself as a link in a chain of collaborators: "I have done my work and am handing on the torch. Let someone else take up the succession" (206). For Erasmus, to be a collator of sources is to be defined less as an individual than as a member of a group of scholars, a community of friends whose bond is formed by a mutual love of learning, for "Indeed, neither family connections, nor blood relationships bind the soul together in a closer and firmer bond of friendship than does the shared enthusiasm for noble studies" (312). The isolated scholar is absorbed into a group made up of members who partake of a single substance: knowledge.

For Burton, as for Erasmus, one man alone can do nothing; it is only through the combined efforts of men that achievement is possible. He quotes Scaliger, "*Nequaquam nos homines sumus; sed partes hominis; ex omnibus aliquid fieri potest, idque non magnum, ex singulis ferè nihil*" ("for by no means are we men, but parts of a man; from all of us something may be done, itself not much, from one alone scarcely anything"; 2.29). However, the context within which the collator is working has changed greatly, as Burton is not part of an active international intelligentsia but a solitary scholar, working on his own, who only encounters the dead through texts. When the contemporary world outside of the text seeps through, it is to present us with a glimpse not of a community of kindred spirits feeding each other, but a Hobbesian world of competitive men, feeding off each other, a "market . . . in which kill or be killed; wherin every man is for himself, his private ends, & stands upon his guard" (I.68–69), in which also "we maul, persecute, and study how to sting, gall, and vex one another with mutual hatred, abuses, injuries; preying upon, and devouring, as so many ravenous birds; and, as jugglers, pandars, bawds, cozening one another; or ranging as wolves, tigers, and devils, we take a delight to torment one another; men are evil, wicked, malicious, treacherous, and naught, not loving one another, or loving themselves, not hospitable, charitable, nor sociable, as they ought to be, but counterfeit, dissemblers, all for their own ends. . . " (1.320). Such denunciations echo those of Erasmus on war; for Burton this is daily life, where men are in conflict, usually over money.[83] Perhaps this accounts for his retreat into books, as well as his own guarded encounter with the reader, to whom he will not reveal himself. His attitude toward his reader reenacts with greater ambivalence that of Rabelais, as he both includes and excludes everyone at the same time. After rather rudely beginning with a warning that we should not hope to know the author, he attempts to draw us in with, "Thou art thyself the subject of my discourse" (12). But soon after he will tell us abruptly, "if you like not this, get you to another Inn: I resolve, if you like not my writing, go read something else" (26–27). At the end of the preface, he suddenly pushes us away, "I owe thee nothing (Reader), I look for no favour at thy hands, I am independent, I fear not," only to suddenly turn around, "No, I recant . . . and now being recovered and perceiving my error, cry with *Orlando, Solvite me*, pardon (*O boni*) that which is past, and I will make you amends in that which is to come; I promise you a more sober discourse in my following treatise" (140). While the text itself tries to identify us all, it is simultaneously (especially to a modern reader) an alienating experience.

Perhaps this is because, as the stories of mixed marriages and unholy unions (some of which are told discreetly in Latin) in the third partition also suggest, Burton is ambivalent about the concept of identification. Whereas for the early humanist Erasmus the collators' Herculean task was one of gathering, for the later writer it is one of finding a means of separating and maintaining distinctions. Margaret Mann Phillips points out that in the *Adages*, Erasmus often does not bother to sort out his sources, giving various versions and letting the reader choose. While Erasmus leaves the questions open so that the reader can exercise his freedom of choice, Burton appears to offer alternatives because there is no possibility of choice. So Fish once more complains that "Clearly Burton's 'ors' are to be translated 'it doesn't matter which' ";[84] clearly also, Fish intends them to be compared with those of Milton, for whom reason is but choosing, and whose "Penseroso" world is an alternative to that of Burton's opening "Abstract," which rewrites Burton by adding the possibility of real alternatives. However, Rosalie Colie has argued that Burton refuses either/or decisions in order to demand all alternatives,[85] while Ruth Fox points out that "whenever the book displays a series of oppositions or a sequence of theses and antitheses, it does so by making confused categories and doubtful equivalents fit into the artificial neatness of the structure."[86] While the critical mind (being melancholy) often tends to create coherence that does not exist, by first isolating easy oppositions and then resolving them through the subsumption of one by the other, the apparent antitheses are in fact not always exact opposites. The lack of exact parallelism is necessary in a structure created by a melancholy mind that reconciles all oppositions—even those between interpretations. Like Milton, Burton attempts to prevent the formulation of relations in terms of binary oppositions.

Furthermore, in the *Anatomy*, the differences between authors are upheld in ways that offer an advantage for an author who does not create ex nihilo but explicitly relies upon past texts which he re-members into a new textual body, and who therefore must define himself through relations with sources. Whereas Erasmus felt the need to create a sense of continuity with the past, for Burton that past is constantly present, and so a potential rival. Burton admits that *"Nihil est sub sole novum"* (2.69), and that in writing there is no hope of absolute originality. He anticipates criticism of his own work, "that this is *actum agere*, an unnecessary work, *cramben bis coctam apponere*, the same again and again in other words. To what purpose?" (1.19). He even denounces the exemplars of "this scribbling age" (1.20), who write anxiously to prove they have been alive, but then admits his own complicity as, amid a stream of abuse against what *they* do, he appears suddenly among them: "As Apothecaries we make new mixtures every day, pour out of one vessel into another; and as those old *Romans* robbed all the cities of the world, to set off their bad sited *Rome*, we skim off the cream of other men's wits, pick the choice flowers of their tilled gardens to set off our own sterile plots. . . . they pilfer out of the old Writers to stuff up their new Comments, scrape *Ennius'* dung-hills, and out of *Democritus'* pit, as I have done" (1.20–21).

Characteristically, the figures, analogies, languages, parts of speech, do not completely harmonize, and their eccentric union suggests his own method of self-differentiation. Brought together into a new whole, the different parts do not merge together perfectly: there is a slight tension among them, though one that is kept from turning into an opposition that could collapse into total identity. Burton identifies himself with the others, then sets himself slightly apart, "For my part I am one of the number, *nos numerus sumus*, I do not deny it, I have only this of *Macrobius* to say for myself, *Omne meum, nihil meum*, 'tis all mine, and none mine" (1.22). He confesses complicity, and then sneaks out by the devious method of making another author speak in his defense. Even as he is drawn into the new context of Burton's work, Macrobius speaks in his own words, creating the favorable impression that another authority, not merely the author himself, is vouching for him.

Moreover, this other voice defines the nature of Burton's authorship: "*Omne meum, nihil meum*," an evasion of the problems of poetic property rights that moves us swiftly away from the image of theft on the previous page. Burton distinguishes himself from the looting Romans by claiming he respects the property of his sources: "I have laboriously collected this *Cento* out of divers Writers, and that *sine injuriâ*, I have wronged no authors, but given every man his own; . . . I cite and quote mine Authors . . . *sumpsi, non surripui*. . . . The matter is theirs for the most part and yet mine, *apparet unde sumptum sit* (which *Seneca* approves) *aliud tamen quàm unde sumptum sit apparet*; which nature doth with the ailment of our bodies, incorporate, digest, assimilate, I do *concoquere quod hausi*, dispose of what I take" (1.22–23). He doesn't *steal* their property, but rather *eats* it; by shifting from metaphors of personal possession to those of food, and so into the digestive metaphor for imitatio, he is able to claim that he assimilates their property while it still remains their own. They can have their cake and let him eat it too; the words are both theirs and his: theirs in substance, although incorporated now also into the body of Burton's text, where they create a new meaning.

Burton sees the possible conflict over the poetic property rights but attempts to evade it by turning to the model of imitatio which allows him to feed innocently on others. This, along with the elimination of the identity of the author from the text, creates the impression that his anatomy is ultimately a communal banquet of voices coming together, a truly democratic body politic of equal brothers. In Klein's terms, Burton appears to have established a relationship with his sources based not on envy but gratitude. According to Klein, when its separateness is acknowledged and accepted, the past can be internalized and re-membered into a new whole that nourishes the present. While a text, especially one modeled on a single melancholy mind, cannot literally contain alterity, it can at least try to represent its own ability to imagine and entertain it, which in Burton is figured through the presence of unresolved differences.

A literary anatomy is obviously very different from a physical anatomy, for it represents not a body but a mind. Like a body, Burton's text has a beginning and end and is divided into distinct and separate members that yet exist simultaneously within a unified whole. But its narrative unfolds through time, following the wanderings of a mind that cannot imagine its own beginning or end. The mind cannot incorporate as the body does, by completely consuming the minds of others. Even when internalized, these still remain somehow alien and not perfectly identifiable with the self—as Freud will explore further. All minds remain ultimately separate, and therefore melancholy, as in their estrangement from each other they create their own isolated universes. The Cartesian individual, both subject and object of its own knowledge, is involved in the self-cannibalism that Burton's contemporary, Thomas Browne, saw as an essential characteristic of human identity: "we are what we all abhor, *Anthropophagai* and Cannibals, devourers not onely of men, but of ourselves; and that not in an allegory, but a positive truth; for all this mass of flesh which we behold, came in at our mouths; this frame we look upon, hath been upon our trenchers; in brief, we have devour'd our selves."[87]

Burton dilates his own mind and that of his readers outside of themselves to keep them from returning and preying upon themselves. He attempts to offer an alternative to radical alienation through the creation of a space for exchanges between minds, which he embodies as an anatomy. Different minds meet as one yet retain their singularity, and so are able to know each other. Yet this may be only an illusion created by the one member who, in this democratic text, represents the rest and so may subsume them: Democritus Jr. The single mind of Democritus Jr., the everyman and Nemo whose relationship to Burton is one of identification and separation, is still melancholy and can imagine nothing beyond itself, and no end to its own restless flux between extreme states except through their merging in total madness. Like a physical body, Burton's text grew through time. As it passed through six editions, very little was changed, though a great deal of material was added.[88] For Burton, revision is not internal change but rather addition: " 'tis much better to build a new sometimes than repair an old house; I could as soon write as much more, as alter that which is written" (1.32)—a statement anyone who has had to rethink old ideas and beliefs will sympathize with fully. His relation to the past is that of a dwarf standing on a giant's shoulders (1.23), a situation from which he may see farther without affecting or explicitly challenging the giant's original position. Within the world of the text there is no possibility for real reformation, and Burton's constant search for a Hercules who will reform the error of men's ways repeatedly fails. No single, individual hero emerges out of the stories of the *Anatomy* to free the world from its self-bondage, as all heroes are equally infected with melancholy. Therefore, "there is no remedy, it may not be redressed" (1.109); man can ease his misery but not end it, except by suicide, a somewhat dubious strategy.[89] The text that identifies itself with melancholy is similarly helpless: alternating between disease and cure, it offers a way of tempering melancholy but contains within itself no principle of redemption or even narrative closure: like Erasmus's *Adages*, it ends only with its author's death.

In some ways the *Anatomy* seems almost medieval, a recreation of a grotesque body that attempts to recapture an oral tradition and a time before experience became perceived in terms of binary oppositions. In others, it seems strangely modern, formulated precisely in terms of such oppositions, a text that could only have been written by a man who was almost as insularly isolated as Robinson Crusoe, and whose experience of reality was totally mediated by and dependent on printed texts. It points back to Rabelais and forward to Melville, through Hobbes and Locke, whose visions of a social body formed by atomistic members brought together by an effort of human will it oddly anticipates. At any rate, it is individual in the sense of "eccentric," a work that defies easy classification and sits uneasily on the fringe of the canon, even when that canon itself is articulated by Burton's twentieth-century descendant, Northrop Frye, as an "anatomy." It describes a vision that is intensely incremental, that denies change and refuses loss, adding more and more material as if it could get everything inside of itself. Yet its only hope, a hope which it fears is vanishing, is that there still is something it cannot know and contain, some genuine image of alterity outside the self with which it cannot be identified, and which has not been contaminated and consumed by melancholy. For Burton, this is the remote deity in whom, he imagines, all alternations are grounded and will finally be resolved: "God often works by contrarieties, he first kills, and then makes alive, he woundeth first, and then healeth, he makes man sow in tears, that he may reap in joy; 'tis God's method: he that is so visited, must with patience endure and rest satisfied for the present" (3.489). While Christ appears throughout the third book as the epitome of whatever virtue or attribute Burton is upholding at the moment, Burton's God is very far away. But this distance may be necessary in order to keep the melancholy mind from consuming Him too, thereby reducing Him to the Saturn who devours his children.

CHAPTER V

The Reformed Deformed

DISCUSSIONS of the century of revolution in England, then, tend to char-
acterize it as the time of a fall, in which, as in Milton's version, terms previously held in a more flexible relation to each other became consolidated
as binary oppositions. The product of this fall is the individual, a unified
and coherent being defined by and against others who appear less coherent, even fragmented: society (especially when represented as the mob),
women, social and religious deviants, cannibals—others whose very existence threatens the unity of the individual. The subject overcomes duality
and creates itself as a unified being by knowing these others as separate
objects that it can master and possess. Even as the subject is dependent on
such objects for its sense of identity, it defines what is different as an antag-
onist that must be appropriated and consumed, something strange that
must be made familiar. For Burton, however, the hope that there is still
something "outside" that his text cannot assimilate is what differentiates
the world of melancholy from that of Ovid's metamorphosis. But the Protestant internalization of religion is part of an incremental vision of reality
that will lead to the subsumption of any external transcendental term and
the replacement of God by the individual, both person and author, as
source and guarantee of meaning—a replacement foreseen in Milton. God
Himself is appropriated by a strategy of colonial discourse, as the ultimate
Other and Authority becomes internalized and ultimately identical with
the self.

I want to look now at some works of the eighteenth and nineteenth
centuries that reveal an incremental vision of experience, to explore some
of the effects of the modern emphasis on the concept of the "inside" and
its connection with a nostalgia that is indeed also melancholy, since, by
denying the existence of anything "outside," it refuses to accept loss. I shall
begin with a discussion of the gothic novel, an ambivalent form peripheral
to and parasitic on the canon proper that dramatizes its own position; then
I shall turn to the works of Coleridge and Melville, in which ideals of
purely internalized—that is, mental or textual—incorporation potentially
cloak more cannibalistic encounters. But first, I would like to return to the
Renaissance for a moment to discuss its representation of itself as a revival.

The "Renaissance" was by definition a time of rebirth. The first awareness of the difference between a historical past and the present has often
been attributed to Petrarch, who also has been regarded frequently as the

first modern individual.[1] The identity of both the individual and the Renaissance involves the perception not only of difference, but of loss and discontinuity, which the individual humanist tried to repair. Renaissance writers attempted to bridge the distance they felt from their classical sources through a revival of learning idealized through the imagery of imitatio as a communal banquet. However, while the digestive metaphor for imitatio and the identification of collation as a re-membering of the past evade the problem of time, since they represent past and present as simultaneously present, another metaphor used to explain relations draws attention to temporal difference and then attempts to overcome it. This is the "necromantic metaphor" "of *disinterment*, a digging up that was also a resuscitation or a reincarnation or a rebirth,"[2] which is the humanist version of the apocalyptic promise that the dead shall be raised. The humanist, trying to achieve his own revelation of meaning, played the part of necromancer, calling the dead back to life, so that Petrarch could even write letters to them.

According to Harold Bloom, Romanticism is a "renaissance of the Renaissance."[3] However, although English Renaissance authors saw discontinuity with and loss of the past, later writers appear to be acutely aware of the survival and burden of the past. Renaissance forms and traditions were perceived not as lost but as perpetuated by a process of internalization comparable to that which was begun with the Reformation. The anxiety of influence began when writers, following the example of Milton, felt a new need both to assimilate previous works and yet create for themselves a unique and coherent individual and authorial identity. But the emphasis upon originality in poetry, beginning in the eighteenth century as an extension of the new interest in individualism, occurred at the moment its possibility seemed lost, and writers condemned simply to repeat past forms over and over. Between the Renaissance and Romanticism there is no radical discontinuity in intellectual, literary, or political development. This is not to say that there were no actual breaks or changes, but rather that later writers imagined themselves as heirs to Renaissance culture in a way that was different from the relation which Renaissance writers envisioned themselves as holding to their classical sources. As Bloom's theory suggests, after Jonson, to be a son is an increasingly oedipal undertaking. One of the consequences of this is that the idea of return itself becomes even more explicitly suspect: it appears less as a dream of recovering a past inheritance that has been lost than a nightmare of being unable to escape from a burden that will never be lifted. While an obvious symbol of division between the two times and perspectives would be the climax of the Enlightenment, the French Revolution, the Revolution ultimately did not break definitively with tradition but also internalized it, participating in a general reorienting of attention downward and inward, from higher to lower classes and faculties.[4] Any revolution that accepts the assumptions and values of the system it is trying to overthrow ends up being a new version of the old authority, as the binary opposition between powerful and powerless is simply reversed. The shape of the English literary tradition from Milton to Blake is commonly explained as an indication that the failure of the external revolution in England led to its introjection and redefinition in terms of an internal revolution of the imagination, idealized in Romanticism. English literature, with its increasing focus on parodic genres such as, for instance, the gothic, demonstrates how the old ideals and conventions were neither lost nor completely revolutionized through this internalization. Past forms went underground, only to reemerge in new and strange and powerful figures.

Psychoanalysis will offer a number of possible readings for the role internalization plays in the sublimation of desire in psychic development. In an article I alluded to in my introduction, "Introjecter-Incorporer," Nicholas Abraham and María Torok differentiate between the two processes. The first they define as a process of metaphorization, a putting of the mouth into words, which is involved in the sublimation of our early experiences. As such, it is similar to Melanie Klein's description of the way in which an infant's earliest desires are revised. Klein, noting sensibly that the actual realization of the child's early incestuous and cannibalistic impulses would be disastrous, argues for the possibility of satisfaction through deferral and a form of metaphorical substitution, in which the adult allows another figure to represent the mother. By delaying satisfaction, the adult can revise the desired relationship internally and sublimate it.[5] For Klein, as for Milton, deferral provides a way of avoiding the antagonism between parent and child that is at the center of Freud's theory and that accounts for the intestine war between the ego and the murderous and authoritative superego. Klein presents a positive model for recreating the past within the self through the transition from envy to gratitude, which she explicitly compares to the transformation of Paradise Lost into the paradise within.[6] While the first part of internalization involves an act of aggression, in which the introjected object is imagined as being torn to pieces, the resulting guilt can be atoned for through the reassembling of those pieces in the self. The lost objects are re-membered and restored, even redeemed, through an act of gratitude. Thus the dead can be recalled to a new life without haunting us.

For Klein, the process of mourning loss begins with a belief that the lost loved object can be preserved within. But Klein's more positive formulation of the possible relations between past and present has been less influential than Freud's, for it is less compatible with the vision of experience prevalent since the seventeenth century and connected with ideas such as possessive individualism, which Freud supports by claiming that oedipal conflict is both necessary and central to the formation of identity. I shall return to this later in my conclusion, where I shall discuss Freud's ambivalence toward psychic internalization, which he sees both as a means of creating individual identity and as a threat to that identity.

For Torok and Abraham, the distinction between introjection and incorporation is a means of differentiating between these positive and negative aspects of internalization. They argue that the opposite of the positive process of introjection is a fantasy of incorporation. This is a regressive substitution that denies loss and attempts to keep the past alive inside, even suggesting that the internalized object was lost or killed in order to survive more fully and authentically in the mind of its host. Incorporation, defined as literalization, or an "antimetaphor" that puts words into the mouth, is described as a perversion of sublimation, in which the flesh, or letter, is annihilated in order to allow the host to possess totally whatever it defines as the spirit of the internalized object.

This denial of loss is a form of melancholy, which Pierre Fédida describes as a "*rêve* cannibalique" ("cannibalistic fantasy") of "le désir inconscient d'annuler ce qui sépare et distingue pour ne perdre jamais, au nom d'une illusoire identité du *même*, ce qui ne peut être que *l'autre*" ("the unconscious desire to abolish everything that separates and distinguishes in order to keep from losing, in the name of an illusory identity of the *same*, that which can be nothing but the *other*")[7]—in other words, to have one's love and eat it too. I have suggested already that there is an element of such annihilation of the other in Montaigne's ideal of friendship, a possibility that emerges vividly later in Genet's *Pompes funèbres*, in which, as Leo Bersani notes, "death is the happy condition for a total possession. The loved one's presence no longer interferes with the lover's assimilation of him . . . [which is] expressed in fantasies of eating him," so that mourning becomes mere cannibalism.[8] This is the gothic love relationship Lawrence recognized with horror in Poe, in which knowledge of another becomes the complete possession of him or her in death.[9] But in Torok and Abraham's description, the mind of the survivor, the consuming host, becomes a gothic graveyard full of undead spirits ready to exert their power when least expected, as,

> Il arrive cependant que, lors de réalisations libidinales, "à minuit," le fantôme de la crypte vienne hanter le gardien du cimitière, en lui faisant des signes étranges et incompréhensibles, en l'obligeant à accomplir des actes insolites, en lui infligeant des sensations inattendues.[10]

> ("It happens, however, that at the time of the fulfillment of libidinal desires—midnight—the phantom from the crypt comes to haunt the keeper of the cemetery, making strange and incomprehensible signs, forcing him to perform unfamiliar acts, by stirring up in him unexpected sensations.")

To "incorporate" the past in this sense is not to redeem it but to be haunted and possessed by it.

I have referred to these various psychoanalytical models as a means of moving toward a look at the gothic because psychoanalysis itself is a fulfillment of the process of internalization I have been describing.[11] When sources of motivation previously located outside of man (in spirits, geniuses and daemons, and ultimately God) become located inside (as innate genius, an inner light, or the superego), the analyst becomes the new necromancer digging up the past within.[12] But the gothic emerges on the threshold of this shift and involves sources that are potentially both supernatural and natural, so that inside and outside are eerily confused. Norman H. Holland and Leona F. Sherman describe the gothic as a recreation or representation of the oral phase of sexual development, "when the boundaries between inner and outer, me and not-me, are still not sharply drawn, and self cannot distinguish itself from the mother who is the outside world."[13] They also note how a central theme of the gothic is the fear of nonseparation, annihilation, and the loss of identity. Whereas Milton had been able to afford to keep relations indefinite in order to prevent the eruption of conflict, the gothic represents the more sinister possibilities of indefinition and obscurity. It enacts a return of a repressed past—personal, cultural, and literary—in which an earlier ideal form of relations comes back as something sinister and suspicious. What once was perceived as familiar and canny is revealed as extremely uncanny. In a world in which definition and the establishment of individual autonomy are now seen as necessary but difficult, as the existence of others represents a potential attack on personal territory, any "oral phase," or symbiotic relation like that associated with the Golden Age, is bound to appear cannibalistic.

THE GOTHIC

The gothic novel begins where *Paradise Lost* ends, in a shadowy world of suspense that is also the dark wood of *Comus*. As in the dark of night nothing can be seen clearly, hearing becomes the primary means of discrimination, and all interpretation requires the balancing act of Christ to enable the reader to endure the suspense until the final moment of revelation. But as Milton's fictional world enters the gothic, it is subtly metamorphosed. The gothic, too, incorporates past tradition, especially literary tradition, and, as in the digestive metaphor for imitatio, recreates it in a new form.

The strangeness of these new forms strikingly reveals the peculiarity of the way in which the eighteenth- and nineteenth-century writers revived the idea of revival itself. The resurrection of a past time that was idealized earlier as a "Renaissance," is transformed into the unearthing of buried bodies and the exhumation of deeply submerged or unconscious terrors. The resurrection of the body, part of the promise of apocalyptic revelation, and its secular type, the necromantic metaphor for imitatio, which promises a revelation of meaning, is revised and literalized in the widespread theme of the past that is "recalled to life," which haunts especially writers of the late nineteenth century.[14] Browning, for example, claims in his recreation of a Renaissance murder mystery that he can reanimate figures from the past:

> man, bounded, yearning to be free,
> May so project his surplusage of soul
> In search of body, so add self to self
> By owning what lay ownerless before,—
> So find, so fill full, so appropriate forms—
> That, although nothing which had never life
> Shall get life from him, be, not having been,
> Yet, something dead may get to live again.
>
> (*The Ring and the Book*, 1.722–29)[15]

Browning's poems are filled with suggestions of buried things, figures and feelings submerged beneath the monologues, which struggle to emerge and express themselves, often against the speaker's conscious will. The poet who cannot create ex nihilo but rather recreates, frees these suppressed forces by appropriating and assimilating them. Through his act of revision he "Makes new beginning, starts the dead alive, / Completes the incomplete, and saves the thing" (734–35). This is a vision of resurrection imagined as redemptive recreation, which looks forward to Klein's formulation. It is a useful model for revision as a means of evading anxiety about influence, as it gives the present complete control over the past it revives. But Browning's works still ooze with an uneasy energy that often cannot be kept down or controlled by the author, who seems at times possessed by forces beyond his control. The gothic shows that revival, like all acts of incorporation, is difficult to control absolutely and that any attempt to distinguish positive introjection from negative incorporation is a tenuous one. To bring back the past is always potentially to be possessed by it, and when in the gothic the dead return, they are not re-membered as a classically coherent wholes, but rather as grotesquely fragmented, incoherent bodies: Frankenstein's monster—an anatomy created by a perverse collation of sources, or the reanimated but still mutilated corpse of W. W. Jacob's classic tale, "The Monkey's Paw."

The ideals of rebirth and recreation are grotesquely literalized in these gruesome figures, as well as in such others as Dickens's "resurrectionists" and the hordes of vampires and "undead" who haunt the gothic. Figures like Melmoth, She, and most famous of all, Dracula, suggest the power of a past that has not perished but has gone into hiding and gained power until it emerges to threaten the fate of the present. Vampirism is the gothic definition of symbiosis and communion, as Dracula takes on the role of Christ, offering his own breast and blood to Mina.[16] He is both victor and victim, but consumes others by offering himself to them: the reciprocity of exchange is thus shown to be an illusion, for he is an alien who possesses those who have let him into their bodies. Dracula is also therefore a gothic version of both the digestive and necromantic metaphors for imitatio, the literalization of an idealized formulation for relationships that appears to strip the pretense from these relations, revealing them to have been always essentially infernal. He is a figure for a past that feeds on the present because it is, like any good vampire, "undead." Like the figures in Ovid's text, this continuing past has perpetuated itself by metamorphoses, and finally by the assumption of more and more grotesque forms. Its undying survival is the gothic's alternative to an apocalyptic revelation and re-membering, in which the promise that the dead shall be raised is shown to really mean that they cannot be kept down at all.

In English literature the ghost of Milton in particular has taken on a life of its own, surviving by transforming itself into new literary forms. While *Comus* is the last masque, it is a source for the birth of the novel, whose very name connotes newness but which reveals traces of earlier forms.[17] The Lady is revised to comply with new conventions of realism and becomes Clarissa, who resists invasion by a satanic seducer and who, when violated, kills herself by starvation. The heroines of Ann Radcliffe's novels appear to maintain their integrity without resorting to such drastic measures, partially because the author ultimately insists upon the rationality of the universe and the consequent rewarding of virtue and punishment of vice. There is a reasonable explanation for every mystery—except, perhaps, for the author's obsessive quotation of Milton, especially "Lycidas" and *Comus*, works concerned with the restoration of loss and the problem of voices. As Jay Macpherson has noted, quotations from Milton often appear in Radcliffe's works just before a character hears voices;[18] the impression created is that it may be Milton, and not, as Coleridge claimed, "truth," who is a "divine ventriloquist."[19]

As the gothic is a consciously literary genre that feeds on earlier traditions, I would like to concentrate on the theme of possession from a textual level. I shall look at ways in which works represent their own haunting by what they cannot fully remember, in order to make a few suggestions about how the gothic indicates the vulnerability of modern concepts of personal and textual autonomy. My primary focus will be on Charles Brockden Brown's *Wieland, or The Transformation* and its unfinished sequel, *Memoirs of Carwin the Biloquist*. The problem of the reception of influences, the tracing of one's sources, becomes complicated for the American writer working in a new world with a new, "novel," form. However, both country and genre have their roots in the past, which has not fully been left behind, but rather carried from the old world to the new, like Anchises and the Trojan Penates on the shoulders of Aeneas. Any insistence on newness and originality reveals the vulnerability of the present, as those who do not remember the past really do—in the gothic at least—seem to repeat it.

While focusing on Brown's text, I should also like to discuss briefly William Godwin's *Caleb Williams* and Mary Shelley's *Frankenstein*, for the three texts are related historically and thematically in ways that suggest the intimacy of literary relations often represented in the gothic through the image of incest. *Frankenstein* was written by Godwin's daughter, *Wieland* by a great admirer of his works. In turn, Godwin cited Brown as an important influence on one of his later novels.[20] But in some sense all these novels are equal siblings, looking back to a common father, Milton, as all are versions of a fall involving a trespass across a boundary into some area of forbidden knowledge and motivated by excessive curiosity. This, however, is not the original Edenic Fall as described by Milton but a repetition that takes place in a world already fallen, which resembles the *Metamorphoses* more than Paradise. In this later world, categories appear to be collapsing, boundaries are badly marked though still immutable, and, because of the difficulty in defining identities, God and Satan are increasingly indistinguishable. The paradisal balance imagined by Milton has turned into the suspense of mystery, so that mediation and continuity appear as sources not of reassurance but of confusion and terror. Indirection, including that of figurative language, is seen as suspect, leading only to a continuing fall. A single error seems to have irrevocable consequences, as Brown writes in his epigraph:

> From Virtue's blissful paths away
> The double-tongued are sure to stray;
> Good is a forth-right journey still,
> And mazy paths but lead to ill.[21]

Life, and narrative, must follow the straight and narrow path in this world where deviation is equated with inevitable disaster.

The relationships of Frankenstein to his monster, Falkland to Caleb, and, in the *Memoirs*, Ludloe to Carwin, revise that of Milton's God to his created son, Adam. But in this later fallen world communion between father and son has been thrown off balance, so that the two are simultaneously identified and opposed, two rivals struggling for a single identity.[22] Relations previously represented as benign, even symbiotic, are revised in a world of possessive individuals. While the image for relations is still basically oral, through the introduction of oedipal conflict, orality is seen as pure aggression and cannibalism. As the young orphan of Godwin's *Mandeville* (the novel he claimed was influenced by Brown) describes his idea of the world he inhabits: "I had hardly a notion of any more than two species of creatures on the earth,—the persecutor and his victim, the Papist and the Protestant; and they were to my thoughts like two great classes of human nature, the one, the law of whose being it was to devour, while it was the unfortunate destiny of the other to be mangled and torn to pieces by him."[23] This is a world of isolated and introverted selves, whose minds are cut off from each other so that relations involving the crossing of individual boundaries are interpreted as acts of violation. All exchanges are regarded as governed by self-interest, which is ultimately the law of the survival of the fittest. The avoidance of oedipal rivalry through communal imagery is no longer possible, because communion itself has been revealed to harbor cannibalistic possibilities, to be a method of permitting the past to feed on the present. The primary relation is no longer the complementary model of guest and host but the complete opposition between eater and eaten, victor and victim, relations, furthermore, which in *Caleb Williams* and *Frankenstein*, seem irresolvable because endlessly reversible.

At the end of *Caleb Williams*, however, Caleb appears to achieve a sympathetic identification with Falkland that might break the chain which had bound them in antagonistic identity.[24] Initially obsessed with establishing his own identity as victim through the narration of his persecution, Caleb concludes by transforming his tale into the story of Falkland, which he will survive to tell. The purpose of the narrative, revenge and self-justification, is subverted by sympathy, and he concludes, "I began these memoirs with the idea of vindicating my character. I have now no character that I wish to vindicate: but I will finish them that thy story may be fully understood."[25] The son defers to the father, and the two replace their earlier curses with mutual blessings.

The ending, which attempts to revive an earlier model for family and literary relations, is still ambiguous, however, as the father immediately dies and the son survives only to repeat the father's story, with which he now identifies himself. It seems that past and present, father and son, cannot be simultaneously present without one subsuming the other. Godwin's own daughter, Mary Shelley, describes a much bleaker version of the parent-child relation. Frankenstein essentially disinherits his creation; "Victor" and his victim become bound in a vicious circle in which it is ultimately impossible to tell who is chasing whom, and which ends in the annihilation of both in an infernal apocalypse of fire and ice.[26]

In Shelley's novel, authority, and especially parental authority, is explicitly associated with Milton, whose work the monster reads and echoes in his own speech. He is in an exaggerated version of the position of the post-Miltonic reader, as he literally discovers his own voice through listening to

Milton's but finds himself limited to the roles of *Paradise Lost*, none of which seems to fit him. Although he sees himself as Milton's Adam, to his creator, the monster who absorbs the voices of past authority seems to represent a forbidding father. While imitatio claims that the son can re-create and give birth to his own father, Shelley seems to suggest that all the scientist can create is a figure who in his eyes embodies the perpetuation of past authority, as in chapter 21 Frankenstein confuses the monster with his most unmonstrous father. The past is re-membered in a gruesome and op-pressive form through the creator's lack of imagination and sympathy. In the figure of Frankenstein, Shelley criticizes not merely the scientific spirit but the whole enlightenment tradition of rationality (for which her own father was a spokesman), which upholds oppositions that ensure the dom-ination of mind over matter—and, equally significant for a woman writer, of male over female—and sees relations in terms of rivalry, the struggles between opposites motivated only by self-interest to subsume power. So Shelley's novel is a *Paradise Lost* set in her own times, in which the Father and Son have become polarized, so that the figure of Christ as mediator disappears. Instead, both poles claim for themselves one role of Christ, that of victim, and turn the subordination of Milton's Son into Satan's sense of persecution. Each accuses the other of being the attacker, and so they not only define each other as forbidding fathers but irreconcilably perpetuate the antagonism between them.

If the presence of Milton is most obvious in *Frankenstein*, it seems least so in Brown's *Wieland*, which points back to *Caleb Williams* as an obvious source that Brown himself acknowledged. But for Brown it is much more difficult than it was for Milton to choose one's own father. The gothic hero or, even more often, heroine, is frequently an orphan, and the structure of the novel recalls the Greek romances, in which the narrative moves toward the revelation and restoration of identity. But as I suggested earlier, some-times, as in the case of Oedipus, the revelation of identity is disastrous. The gothic hero or heroine is both isolated and alienated by being orphaned, but also finally bound rigidly by family ties he or she cannot know about and discovers too late. The past takes on even more terrifying and mon-strous forms when it remains buried and unknown, when one cannot tell where one has come from or who one's father is but is still tied to a source one cannot see or remember.

Wieland and its unfinished sequel represent the problem of knowing or-igins through the use of voices that are cut off from their sources. In the text, knowledge is assimilated primarily through hearing. So Pleyel de-nounces Clara after overhearing her conversation with Carwin on a night too dark for seeing, in which, therefore, "Hearing was the only avenue to information" (154). But what he hears has a different source from that which he imagines. He makes the error of believing that he can reason where voices come from, falling into the trap of taking voice as a guarantee of authenticity and presence. As Derrida has shown, voice has been idealized as a place where inside and outside meet.[27] In Milton, the fact that hearing enabled the incorporation of an outside source is what made it dangerous. In *Wieland*, the dangers are even greater, for voice is what both polarizes and confuses inside and outside, source and projection, not only because all sources are mysterious, but because there is a ventriloquist on the loose.

The problem of the relation between inside and outside, words and source, is embodied in the figure of Carwin, who is able to throw his voice and thus create disjunction and division between the poles. As Carwin represents the problem of voice, however, he also seems to offer a rational explanation for it, providing disembodied voices with a reassuring and comprehensible source. But while in one of Ann Radcliffe's novels he would have been used to explain the mystery, in Brown's he serves only to confuse and deepen it. No single voice is revealed as the cause of events; all alternatives are suggested, but no one is privileged. Although the heroine, Clara, assumes that all voices can be traced to Carwin, there appears to be little relation between the voices he throws and those that Wieland hears. Although it is suggested that his actions "indirectly but powerfully predisposed [Wieland] to this deplorable perversion of mind" (268), his influence is intangible; he may even be superfluous to the main plot, merely a peripheral complication that distracts us from the central story.

In fact, there is no causal connection among the characters, or between the two main plots; instead, the novel suggests that the gothic world works by correspondences, analogies which contaminate each other.[28] The relation among figures appears completely metaphoric rather than metonymic, but the parallel lines seem to influence each other oddly, even infect each other. Furthermore, the novel, and the gothic in general, suggests one complication that arises from the internalization of reality and the transition from belief in demonic possession to belief in neurotic obsessions.[29] The gothic is suspended between the two, so that voices may come from outside, from daemons or God himself, or from inside, from the human mind, which is prone to "hear things." Inside and outside are not only analogous but easily confused, as it is difficult to tell for certain where things, including the text itself, are coming from. Carwin learns to throw his voice when he reads *Comus* and copies an echo; one cannot tell if the source of his talent and of the novel is in nature or in the echo of Milton, ringing in both Carwin's and Brown's ears.

Clara, Brown's heroine, is certainly a descendant of Milton's Lady (filtered obviously through Clarissa), who has faith not only in the strength of her own integrity but also in the powers of her enlightened mind. At the opening of her story she maintains a firm belief in clarity and her ability to draw definite distinctions and make Miltonic choices. Her diction is "proper," precise and logical—but as a result totally "improper," inappropriate and almost ridiculously inadequate for describing her situation.[30] But her language reflects her misconceptions about the world she inhabits and the possibility of her own innocence. Carwin appears to her as a seductive version of Socrates, as his ugly appearance seems at odds with his beautiful voice, which suggests to her, though it does not ultimately signify, an inner essential beauty. The gap between his outside and inside fascinates her; she is attracted by Carwin's ambiguity because she wants to resolve it by discovering "whether he were an object to be dreaded or adored, and whether his powers had been exerted to evil or to good" (80). But, like Pleyel, she constantly misinterprets intentions through an overreliance upon deduction from empirical evidence, which also leads her to believe that she can reason backward from effect to cause, voice to source. The actual disjunction in the sequence revealed by a text in which voices are literally thrown means that human nature and motives for action are always mysterious and ambiguous. Identities, either of persons or texts, cannot be pinned down as clearly and neatly as Clara would wish. While in *Wieland* Carwin seems to be Satan, in the *Memoirs* he appears as Adam or Caleb. His mentor, Ludloe, shares the ambivalence of Godwin's Falkland and, as the novel is unfinished, we can never know if he plays God or Satan to Carwin—or whether there can be any real difference anymore. Brown himself seems unable to decide; moreover, at the end of *Wieland*, when Clara's life is threatened, the attempt to resolve ambiguity becomes completely beside the point, as looking at Carwin she realizes, "Whether he were infernal or miraculous, or human, there was no power and need to decide" (254).

Clara's belief in a coherent rational world is finally undone through her curiosity about Carwin, which also causes her misunderstanding with Pleyel and her willful blindness to her brother's guilt. *Curiositas*, the crossing of prescribed boundaries, is a central element in any story of a fall. It is the ruling passion of Caleb Williams who, according to Godwin, was modeled on Bluebeard's wife,[31] and the dominant characteristic of Carwin, who begins his *Memoirs* with a description of his early insatiable desire for knowledge: "My thirst of knowledge was augmented in proportion as it was supplied with gratification. The more I heard or read, the more restless and unconquerable my curiosity became" (275). Appetite grows with what it feeds on and, as in the case of Caleb, youthful customs develop into binding and incurable habits.

Carwin's curiosity has further consequences, for it leads to the discovery of the peculiar talent that ultimately possesses him entirely. His literal appropriation of other voices becomes not a means of self-creation but of a dissipation of identity, as he becomes a vocal chameleon who can turn into any character by means of ventriloquism. But, able to be everyone, he himself is no one. Whereas early Renaissance humanists frequently idealized the limitlessness of human potentiality, man's ability to be anything, writers from the seventeenth century on see endless "self-fashioning" as more like the dissipation of Comus or a form of vampirism.[32] Carwin is a constant metamorphoser, he changes nationalities and even uses religious conversion, the most radical form of metamorphosis, as a means of blending into his situation. Curious as he is, his protean shifting of shapes never settles into a single form that tells the truth about him. There is no stable self he can return home to beneath the forms he assumes, and he becomes an anti-apocalyptic force, a Ulysses who has become the Circe or her son, Comus—figures who use transformation to keep questors from arriving at a home where they will discover their true identities. He creates mystery and confusion, keeping both Clara and the reader from understanding what's going on in the novel.

The difficulty in figuring out the plot is increased, however, by the fact that there are actually three different stories being told, all dealing with the dangers of curiosity and all offering different resolutions. In Clara's story, curiosity about Carwin is ultimately redirected to a more appropriate male partner, Pleyel, whom she finally marries. After prophesying doom and total destruction, Clara's narrative ends, like a comedy, with marriage, a conclusion that is not altogether satisfactory, as it seems an artificial device imposed by an author obliged to fulfill conventional expectations. In Carwin's case, curiosity compulsively indulged is unredeemed, as his habit cannot be broken. His narrative does not end at all; it continues beyond *Wieland* into the *Memoirs*, and finally the mazy way of error winds on forever, endlessly deviating and complicating the plot of the *Memoirs* beyond the possibility of resolution, so that Brown can only break off abruptly. But the truly terrifying curiosity in the novel is that which provides it with the possibility of a resounding conclusion in an apocalypse that comes as annihilation: the colossal curiosity of Wieland himself, who hungers to know the will of God.

Whereas Clara believes that Carwin is the natural source of all voices, Wieland is absolutely certain that his intimate impulses come from God. Like Milton's Samson, he is a vessel certain of the source of his inspiration and the nature of his calling or vocation.[33] But both Clara's reason and Wieland's faith may be equally misleading, or at least as ambiguous as the voice that calls Samson to the destruction of both himself and his enemies. Near the end of the novel, Clara's uncle suddenly explains that some of the members of the house of Wieland have a peculiar tendency to hear voices that demand destruction. The implication is that this is some sort of inherited mental illness, the psychological equivalent of the old family curse, which is never discovered until after it has already taken effect. This sudden revelation seems to shed light on the story of Clara and Wieland's father's strange death, with which the narrative opens. Both sequentially and thematically, the father's story provides the background for Clara's, and for that of the son who shares his name, and finally, as if the two were irrevocably linked, his fate.

As an (inevitably) orphaned and isolated boy, Wieland Sr. underwent a conversional experience modeled upon that of Augustine. The text he turned to was not, however, the Bible, but a book of the Albigenses, a secret Gnostic heresy with dualistic beliefs that may have provided him with a more dubious source of authority.[34] Browsing through the text, he comes to a passage that he takes as a voice speaking directly to him, which tells him "seek and ye shall find." As a result, "His curiosity was roused by these so far as to prompt him to proceed" (9)—unlike either Augustine or Dante's Francesca, he keeps on reading obsessively. As his daughter later realizes, "His mind was in a state peculiarly fitted for the reception of devotional sentiments. The craving which had haunted him was now supplied with an object" (9). Particularly susceptible to this kind of influence, he is absorbed by it, as his previously restless mind becomes fixed on a single object.

But his obsession with "the awe-creating presence of the Deity" (10) makes him not merely melancholy but totally paranoid. A personal God is too close for comfort: He not only calls but completely possesses his vessels. As Wieland Sr. fails to fulfill his vocation as a minister, to be called seems increasingly to be threatened, and to be possessed, to be destroyed. His fate is a nice allegory of the dangers of the internalization of religious fervor. Unable to express his allotted role publicly, he internalizes his worship, transforming it into a completely private act that he keeps hidden even from his own family. The energy denied expression through normal social channels is driven back upon itself until it literally explodes him.

What powerful forces move inside his mind we never know, nor what impossible tasks his deity demands and how closely they resemble those his son executes. The reader never hears what father and son do, as the voices inside others are kept hidden from us, so that their motivation is always mysterious. We do hear about the father's strange and dreadful fate, which he had anticipated, hinting that he had deviated from duty and delayed until it was too late. Deferral can have negative consequences when continued too long without a sense of an ending. The forces inside Wieland Sr. build up until the pressure is too great: one midnight he retreats to his private temple and spontaneously combusts.[35]

This bizarre story haunts Clara's, providing the gothic background out of which her enlightened voice emerges. She puzzles over the mystery and its possible meanings:

Was this the penalty of disobedience? this the stroke of a vindictive and invisible hand? Is it a fresh proof that the Divine Ruler interferes in human affairs, meditates an end, selects and commissions his agents, and enforces, by unequivocal sanctions, submissions to his will? Or, was it merely the irregular expansion of the fluid that imparts warmth to our heart and blood, caused by the fatigue of the preceding day, or flowing by established laws, from the condition of his thoughts (21–22).

Clara's rational mind is open to all possibilities, but in this passage the equation of supernatural revenge with heart failure as equally plausible solutions seems ludicrous. Brown himself, however, entertains alternative explanations, as he supplies the reader with documented cases of spontaneous combustion as well as with a report of a real murder similar to that later committed by Wieland. There is a natural explanation for everything—the only problem being that it is probably not the right one. Supernatural revenge and heart failure are both possible alternatives, but neither is revealed to be the ultimate cause. Even the uncle's story of the earlier suicide, this time of their *mother's* father—who was not even related by blood to their unfortunate father, though this may suggest a double evil inheritance—does not reveal the cause of Wieland's actions, but only suggests an analogy for it.

However, as analogy usurps the role of causation in the gothic world, the opening mystery lingers on through the novel, a narrative specter that exerts a peculiar kind of influence upon subsequent events. The memory of the life and death of the father obsesses the son, who is said to resemble him strongly, though possessing a mind more expanded by advanced education. The son, whose leisure and intellectual pursuits are, as Milton's were, founded on the father's physical labor, potentially repeats the father in a finer tone. He sublimates and refines his inheritance by turning money into learning, as Wieland appropriates his father's place while making some significant transformations.

After his father's death, Wieland turns the temple of worship into a kind of humanist bower that shelters a small intellectual community. The presiding deity is the august Cicero, the author who, in Renaissance debates on the appropriate models for imitatio, was held to be worthy of imitation beyond all others, and whose authority was so great as to render potentially superfluous the need for any others.[36] For Wieland, Cicero becomes "the chief object of his veneration" (27), and he embarks upon the traditional humanist endeavor of "settling and restoring the purity of the text" (27) in order to create a definitive edition. This is, however, an act of essentially nonrevisionary recreation, in which the later writer tries to return the work to the state intended by the author, without himself adding to or changing it. Ideally, the text is reformed into its original condition, as if it had never been lost or broken or been in some sense dead to the world. For Bakhtin, it was just such an attempt to revive Ciceronian language that killed Latin, as the quest for perfection and completion led to a dead end.[37] In fact, all such attempts at perfect revival, or at recapturing authorial intention, are bound to fail or, perhaps even worse, to succeed through an illusory eradication of difference and loss. Wieland's resurrection of Cicero is even more ambitious and dangerous, however, as he is not content with the reconstruction of the printed text but aims at its complete reanimation. He tries to invoke the dead writer by assuming his voice, as he practices all the speeches out loud: "He was very scrupulous in selecting a true scheme of pronunciation for the Latin tongue, and in adapting it to the words of his darling writer. His favorite occupation consisted in embellishing his rhetoric with all the proprieties of gesticulation and utterance" (27). While total recreation is literally impossible, in Wieland's mind at least, his voice and Cicero's meet, and something dead gets to live, and even speak, again.

The other scholarly work in which Wieland is engaged is that of "collecting and investigating the facts which relate to that mysterious personage, the Daemon of Socrates" (55). For a man who hears voices, this is a highly appropriate project. Wieland obviously has a vested interest in proving that Socrates' Daemon is an external *genius*, in the old sense of the word, rather than a sign of an innate mental quality, the modern meaning that was becoming common in Brown's own time. When Wieland himself hears voices, he is certain not only that they come from outside of himself but that they come from God. Sure of his source, he claims to know God's will fully. At his trial, he turns from his judges to address the God with whom he imagines himself to be in private communion: "Thou, Omnipotent and Holy! Thou knowest that my actions were conformable to thy will. I know not what is crime; what actions are evil in their ultimate and comprehensive tendency or what are good. Thy knowledge, as thy power, is unlimited. I have taken thee for my guide, and cannot err" (199). The Protestant emphasis upon a direct communication between the self and God had led to debates on the rights of the elected individual to kill another; according to Tyndale, "To steal, rob and murder, are holy when God commandeth them."[38] Like Clara, Wieland asserts his own innocence and integrity, which he, following Tyndale's argument, bases on the purity of his motives that only an omniscient God can know. He rebukes his judges for presuming to see into his mind: "You say that I am guilty. Impious and rash! thus to usurp the prerogatives of your Maker! to set up your bounded views and halting reason as the measure of truth!" (199).

Ironically, however, this is his own error. Wieland claims to submit to the will of God, as Milton's Christ did, but this is in fact to act *as* God and usurp the divine prerogative,[39] and so to act as Satan. The Protestant impulse to internalize God within the individual can be as cannibalistic or at least as infernal as its idea of the Catholic Black Mass, as Hogg most famously shows in his *Private Memoirs and Confessions of a Justified Sinner* (1824). To internalize God so as to identify Him with the self completely is to make oneself into God at the expense of any image of a transcendent, or even ultimately different, principle outside of the self. Milton's Christ managed to avoid such total identification through the refusal to define his own identity. Wieland's error is believing that he can define himself and his identification with God. Having sought all his life for divine revelation, he believes he has been given signs that he can totally explicate and claims divine powers of interpretation that allow him to see sources, including the sources of his own actions.

But at the very moment at which his final project verges on completion with the murder of Clara, Carwin's voice breaks in to interrupt whatever voices Wieland has been hearing, crying: "Man of errors! cease to cherish thy delusion: not heaven or hell, but thy senses have misled thee to commit these acts. Shake off thy phrenzy, and ascend into rational and human. Be lunatic no longer" (257). Wieland is totally unable to distinguish this human voice from the one he believed to come from God and submits to both as equally authoritative with complete and immediate obedience. When a voice tells him to kill his family, he obeys; when one tells him he was mistaken, he believes that too and kills himself. Like his father, he is finally (though in a more refined and internally expressed form) the receptacle for influences he cannot control—in his case, because he does not question their source. Despite his assertion of certainty, he cannot tell where things come from. He believes too much in the arguments of the belly of *Aereopagitica* and of chastity from *Comus*: in the power of his individual integrity and purity of motives to guarantee his innocence. But the ultimate error in the novel is to believe one knows for certain one's own motives. These remain mysterious, for the individual can never know for sure where things inside the self originate.

The death of Wieland reveals to Clara her own guilt. The impulse to kill her brother, even in self-defense, causes the previously self-proclaimed innocent victim to cry: "I acknowledge that my guilt surpasses that of all mankind: I confess that the curses of a world, and the frowns of a deity, are inadequate to my demerits. Is there a thing in the world worthy of infinite abhorrence? It is I" (249–50). The hyperbole may seem a little silly, especially when rendered in Clara's pure and rather prissy prose, and it indicates the characteristic tension between her assumptions about reality and her actual situation, which causes the content to strain the form. Against her will, she has been contaminated by an evil which, when tasted, enters into and infects the self. The very vulnerability of innocence constitutes its guilt, as it ignorantly exposes itself to dangerous influences. For all her appearance of integrity, Clara has been infiltrated: by the social and literary conventions that shape her behavior and narrative; by Carwin, who sneaks into her closet and with whom she is obsessed; by Pleyel, whom she loves (although she is forced to hide her feelings) and finally marries; and by the brother for whom she cares most of all, and whose story almost entirely, and fatally, dominates her own. The opposition between guilt and innocence dissolves when victor and victim are as intimately involved as the Wielands. In a novel subtitled, ambiguously, *The Transformation*, the small circle of friends is too closely related and their fates too tightly bound together for such a thing as a truly separate and autonomous self to exist. Any assertion of integrity is a delusion when identity is represented as unstable, and figures can change parts until one cannot tell for certain who's who. Clara's tendency to confuse Pleyel, Carwin, and her brother creates the impression that they are essentially one man who simultaneously incorporates the roles of lover, enemy, and brother. In the end, all parts merge into the title figure of Wieland.

Looking back, Clara tries to determine where she and her brother went wrong and deviated from the straight and narrow path of safety, suggesting that, "If Wieland had framed juster notions of moral duty, and of divine attributes; or, if I had been gifted with ordinary equanimity or foresight, the double-tongued deceiver would have been baffled and repelled" (273). But the point of fatal error and trespass can never be seen clearly in the world of suspense where boundaries are not well marked. Moreover, to whom or what does "the double-tongued deceiver" refer? Those who stray from "Virtue's blissful paths" in the epigraph? Satan, often represented as literally double-tongued, or Carwin, more figuratively so? The origin of the evil is unclear, although agents—Wieland and, to a lesser degree, Carwin—can be indicated. But the sources and motives of their actions are obscure; we never know exactly what "got into" them to make them act as they did. Perhaps this uncertainty has its redeeming aspect for the reader; the real evil represented in the text is faith in the certainty of one's own interpretations, which could reduce anything ambiguously "double-tongued" to a single, and no doubt murderous, meaning.

Wieland, then, recalls Milton's attempt to postpone the catastrophe that occurs with the discovery of identity. But the impossibility of representing what lurks in the hearts of men also corresponds to the text's own inability to tell what has got into it, which suggests the dangers of unresolved ambiguity. The Miltonic elements in Wieland raise the problem of locating literary sources and voices, and knowing whether they are consciously invoked, or whether they are subconscious expressions that indicate the alien author has crept so far inside us that we think he *is* us. In *Comus*, Milton insists upon his own ability to assimilate the past without being possessed by it, through the maintaining of an authorial control that enables him to choose his own sources, the voices he will listen to. Yet in practice this is obviously an illusion sustained through Milton's powerful and authoritative assertion. Shakespeare's voice still remains in the text, and in fact, as Milton saw, to use the metaphors of voice and hearing is to raise the problem of influence, the inflowing of others that renders any act of incorporation hazardous and potentially uncontrollable. Even when circumscribed by copyright, words are always crossing boundaries, entering into ourselves and others whether we want them to or not. What the gothic demonstrates is the unsettling vulnerability of those things we tend to think of as autonomous and self-sufficient: both texts and our selves.[40]

Carwin reads *Comus* on the night when, by imitating a natural echo, he learns to diffuse and throw his voice in order to disguise its source. Within the text itself, the voice of Milton is naturalized and hidden behind the pretext of Godwin, perhaps as a means of suppressing a forbidding father who might prove to be a petrifying source whom no son would care to oppose directly. However, to make Milton part of the landscape is to confer on him a tremendous power that it will be hard for any but the strongest of writers to question. It is precisely the suppression of Milton, his metamorphosis into, if not literally the natural landscape, certainly our literary one, which turns him into the truly protean ventriloquist who disguises his voice in those of other writers. Introjected into their works, he becomes a specter who cannot be conquered because his traces have been so cleverly disguised that those who follow mistake them for their own. Milton's influence demonstrates on a textual level the danger of oversuccessful internalization becoming a form of perpetuation of the past. He has become completely absorbed into our stories and our lives, turning into an echo which rings so constantly in our ears that we cannot always tell where the music is coming from. As the gothic novel demonstrates, it is difficult to discriminate alien influences when they have found their way into our poems, homes, closets, and minds.

COLERIDGE AND THE ANXIETY OF EVERYTHING

The gothic makes the familiar very strange, the canny extremely uncanny, a conversion we also associate with Romantic revolutionary art. In the *Lyrical Ballads*, the estrangement of the normal was the task of Wordsworth; it fell to Coleridge to make the strange familiar, the tactic identified with both colonial discourse and bourgeois art.[41] But the relations between the two poets and their poetry do not fit into easy antitheses. By discussing some aspects of Coleridge's theory of art in respect to his own writing, I hope to make a few suggestions about the relationship between Romantic idealism and the image of cannibalism, a connection I will explore further through the work of Melville. As in *Heart of Darkness* Conrad will show vividly that even, or perhaps especially, the most idealistic imperialism is a form of cannibalism, so Coleridge demonstrates how even mental acts of appropriation can be subverted by their own appetite, particularly the act in which a subject knows and possesses objects. For Coleridge, any act of internalization is undermined by his inability to keep opposites apart, as an ambivalence about appropriation and a deep desire to resolve oppositions within a single coherent system lead to an annihilation of all differences that are simultaneously seen as making meaning and identity possible.

Like the gothic with which it is contemporary, Romanticism in general involves the resurrection of past forms and ideals, and therefore also includes the anxiety of influence that accompanies this inheritance. As has often been noted, it revives certain elements of neoplatonism, one of which being the idea of the *coincidentia oppositorum*, by which all oppositions are imagined as being ultimately reconcilable in a harmonious whole.[42] Coleridge was fascinated by the saying "EXTREMES MEET," "a proverb, by the bye, to collect and explain all the instances and exemplifications of which, would constitute and exhaust all philosophy."[43] In his notebook of December 1803, he actually began such a collection, which included the torment of the devils by fire and ice in *Paradise Lost*, Book 2, and other examples such as "Dark with excess of Light," "Self-absorption & Worldly-mindedness," and "Nothing & intensest absolutist Being."[44]

To identify nothing with absolute being might appear somewhat suspicious, but ambiguity and ambivalence are obvious characteristics of a doctrine in which two antithetical forces are conflated into what appears as primal unity. For Coleridge, the return of opposites to an original state of wholeness, the re-membering of the primal body, is the aim of art. Art reunites man and nature, subject and object, for "In every work of art there is a reconcilement of the external with the internal."[45] Art that strives "To make the external internal, the internal external, to make Nature thought and thought Nature,"[46] works against the modern systems of division and separation, finding a way of compensating for the loss of the medieval correspondence between microcosm and macrocosm, an earlier harmony between man and nature, by recreating that original unity within the individual imagination. The unity earlier associated with an external Paradise or Golden Age became internalized by means of a focus on the imagination as a Paradise within that makes up for the Paradise Lost.

The central means for this identification is the symbol that, as Thomas McFarland has noted, originally connotes "a putting together of something torn apart."[47] Coleridge's definition of the symbol is a kind of revival of a pre-Reformation concept of figuration which, as I will show later, complements his ideal model for harmonious personal and poetic relations. He imagines symbols to be parts that both represent and partake of the whole, being "consubstantial with the truths, of which they are *conductors*."[48] In a famous passage he contrasts symbols with allegories, which are "but a translation of abstract notions into a picture-language which is itself nothing but an abstract for objects of the senses" and are "unsubstantial," and with metaphors, which he claims are also allegorical, as they mean "other" than their words literally signify. A symbol, however, is what he calls "tautegorical," "expressing the *same* subject with a difference," and it "is characterized by a translucence of the Special in the Individual or of the General in the Especial or of the Universal in the General. Above all by the translucence of the Eternal through and in the Temporal. It always partakes of the Reality which it renders intelligible; and while it enunciates the whole, abides itself as a living part in that Unity, of which it is the representative."[49]

For Coleridge, the symbol is further described in terms recalling the Host, as a substance that can satisfy spiritual hunger and thirst: "the bread which was given from heaven that we should eat thereof and be strengthened" and "that water which, instead of mocking the thirst of him to whom it is given, becomes a well within himself springing up to life everlasting!"[50] Pater, commenting that Coleridge hungered too intensely for eternity, quoted de Quincey's canny comment that "he wanted better bread than can be made from wheat."[51] In his critique of the Romantic privileging of symbol over allegory, Paul de Man argued that the symbol is not a solution to the subject-object problem but rather its source, which, by offering a fallacious promise of an end of dualisms in fact reinforces them.[52] McFarland makes a similar point by placing the Romantic ideal of the wholeness and integrity of art, upheld through theories of the symbol and organism, in the context of a poetic practice that is widely fragmented.[53] In Coleridge's writing, an ideal of communion and satisfaction is complemented by a sense of alienation and emptiness. The myth of plenitude and of communion created by the ideal of the symbol as reconciler of opposites, seems bound to its opposite, a hunger that causes Coleridge to use substitutes, both chemical substances and people, in order to fill himself up. However, for Coleridge such attempts at reparation are never satisfactory or satisfying, for they produce only an illusory restoration that increases his sense of hollowness. The nostalgia for a restoration of lost unity leads to an imaginary abolition of differences that ultimately feeds further his despair.

Coleridge's self-representations constantly return to images of emptiness and incompletion that suggest a feeling of an inner lack that needs to be filled and made whole. He believed "There is something, an essential something wanting in me,"[54] and used the image of a huge hollow tree to describe his sense of his own weakness and hypocrisy: "A sense of weakness— a haunting sense, that I was an herbaceous Plant, as large as a large Tree, with a trunk of the same Girth, & Branches as large & shadowing—but with *pith within* the Trunk, not heart of Wood/—that I had *power* not *strength*—an involuntary Imposter—that I had no real Genius, no real Depth."[55] Applied to himself the organic metaphor fails to guarantee wholeness, suggesting instead a total separation of inside and outside man that leads not to the liberation of Jonson but to a picture of himself as a fake, a hollow fraud. Physically large on the surface, Coleridge sees his inside as an empty space, which he often appears to have experienced as a vessel invaded by violent forces. He suffered frequently from "frightful Dreams with screaming—*breezes* of Terror blowing from the Stomach up thro' the Brain/ always when I am awakened, I find myself stifled with wind/ & the wind the manifest cause of the Dream/ frequent paralytic Feelings—sometimes approaches to Convulsion fit."[56] The polarization of his inner and outer selves generates a sense of his own hypocrisy and guilt and produces also a complex relation between body and mind in which the two antitheses act upon each other. The physical torment causes mental anguish but in turn is caused by it. In one dreadful notebook entry, he describes his physical agony as: "the dull quasi finger-pressure on the Liver, the endless Flatulence, the frightful constipation when the dead Filth *impales* the lower Gut—to weep & sweat & moan & scream for the parturience of an excrement with such pangs & such convulsions as a woman with an Infant."[57] The body becomes symbolic of the mind in such a way that the two are almost identical, interacting upon each other in a frightful reciprocity. The sensation of constipation is experienced as a gruesome parody of poetic inspiration and creation, in which the inspiring breath leaves the poet "stifled with wind" that he is unable to express. The material he, unlike the woman, cannot give birth to, turns instead into excrement, torturing him from inside. Body and mind are hollow places that receive material but lack the strength to recreate it, and instead are eaten away from within by what they have taken inside themselves. Unlike the wind that plays on "The Eolian Harp," or the Romantic image of the "correspondent breeze" that unites the mind and nature,[58] the wind that fills the poet does not free poetic voice but suffocates it. Coleridge is turning his own body into an allegory of perverted inspiration—the possession of a weak, exposed self by external influences—that recalls Dante's description of the falsifier Master Adam in *Inferno* 30, to suggest that he, like Master Adam, is a hollow sham. To be self-divided and lack a coherent being is, for him, a sign of guilt. For Ben Jonson, the very polarization between appearance and reality could offer a potential means of achieving freedom from the prison of the body, relegated to pure appearance. For Coleridge, however, this opposition reveals only his own hypocrisy and falseness while suggesting also that all communion between inner and outer being is bound to be mutually aggressive, as mind and body feed upon each other.

According to Coleridge, these physical attacks were the source of his personal fall, his descent into falsehood, for they forced him to eat the opium which he blamed for all his failings:

> What crime is there scarcely which has not been included in or followed from the one guilt of taking opium? Not to speak of ingratitude to my maker for the wasted Talents; of ingratitude to so many friends who have loved me I know not why; of barbarous neglect of my family . . . I have in this one dirty business of Laudanum an hundred times deceived, tricked, nay actually & consciously LIED.—And yet *all* these vices are so opposite to my nature, that but for this *free-agency-annihilating* Poison, I verily believe that I should have suffered myself to be cut to pieces rather than have committed any one of them.[59]

However, such protestations that his essentially pure self was contaminated by an evil influence he had depended upon to ease his pain are not totally to be trusted; opium taking probably preceded and aggravated, if it did not completely cause, his internal disorders.[60] The original impulse to take opium was more likely bound up with his need to compensate for the sense of inner emptiness that he took as a sign of his own falseness and lack of genuine being. In his own personal mythology, his fall into addiction is traced back to a single source, a famous incident that dramatizes his own hunger for wholeness and the sad consequences of his inability to bear fragmentation and incompletion. As a child, Coleridge fought constantly with his older brother, Francis. One day he requested from their nurse and received what was for him a real treat: a perfectly whole piece of cheese. Francis grabbed it from him and proceeded to tear it into bits. Totally devastated, Coleridge ran away and spent the night outdoors, gratified to think that his family would be desperately worried about him. Early the next morning he condescended to return home, meeting on his way a party who had been out searching for him all night. But the hours spent out in the open caused a fever that became quite serious and left permanent damage, causing a condition which later, he claimed, forced him to take opium. Whether or not this story is true, it stands as a nice allegory, constructed by Coleridge himself, of his impatience with all imperfection and fragmentation, which he associates with his personal fall. Lack of wholeness is the proof of his essential falseness, his lack of a real, that is inner, self, which in turn generates a need to fill himself not only with drugs but with others.

Coleridge's acute dependence upon and desire for identification with others is evident in all his personal relations, and particularly in his idolatry of Wordsworth, to whom he cries out silently in his notebook, "O that my Spirit purged by Death of its Weaknesses, which are alas! my *identity*, might flow into *thine*, and live and act in thee, and be Thou."[61] His own identity he sees in terms of weakness, which requires him to use others outside of himself to gain strength. His need to fill himself with others in his work has been discussed by McFarland, who sensitively examines the problem of the plagiarisms.[62] McFarland relates Coleridge's blatant appropriation of the literary property of others to his desperate desire for support, and to his insistence that truth is a "divine ventriloquist" who speaks through different men and is therefore not the personal possession of a single individual.[63] Such a belief looks back to a medieval lack of a sense of poetic property and circumscribed individual identity, and to the hope, still entertained by the early humanists like Erasmus, of a community of writers whose individual identities have been transcended, as they are all identified by common concerns. As in his description of the symbol, Coleridge is turning back to models for relations that predate total polarization and the eruption of conflict.

According to Harold Bloom, "Coleridge hungered also for an eternity of generosity between poets as between people," at a time when such a relation was no longer possible, as "each poet must struggle to individuate his own breath, and this at the expense of his forbears as much as his contemporaries."[64] The attempt to circumvent the issue of ownership by tracing all texts back to a single divine source, a technique that worked for Dante, in the nineteenth century looks too much like the strategy the colonists used to justify the appropriation of Indian territory through invoking the natives' lack of a sense of private property. For Coleridge, as for many of the colonists, the result is a mixture of guilt and terror of retaliation. Bloom suggests that Coleridge was attracted to the organic metaphor for poetic creation because it appears to preclude antagonism, suggesting rather that poets grow naturally and not at one another's expense. But for all its organic wholeness and originality, the imagination is, according to Coleridge, an "assimilative" power. The word *assimilative* was, at this time, newly taken from biology, where it meant "the process by which an organism converts food into its own substance."[65] Even natural organisms (as Sade showed) need to absorb things from outside themselves and turn them into themselves, and so natural consumption involves the possibility of conflict and guilt. Coleridge uses idealized formulas to try to repress the truth that, in certain obvious ways, he was nourished at the expense of others. The result of this repression is similar to that of Melanie Klein's manic-depressive who is unable to acknowledge his own aggression toward his sources and so turns it masochistically upon himself, and chooses failure, "because success always implies to . . . [him] the humiliation or even the damage of somebody else."[66]

At many times, Coleridge's powers of imaginative assimilation seem to turn against him: all sorts of odd things get into the *Biographia*. The most puzzling of these are long passages that appear to be translated directly from sources which Coleridge not only does not note but with which he ultimately disagrees.[67] At times the text seems completely open and exposed—the passive dummy not of truth but a host of foreign voices who invade it and speak through Coleridge. As McFarland suggests, while the plagiarisms reflect a need to fill the self with others to gain strength and wholeness, the actual result is a masochistic *askesis*, in which Coleridge, in a kind of parody of Milton's Son who empties himself to "increase in power" and "know all things" (*The Christian Doctrine*, 1.14), completely empties himself in subordination to these others. As a means of denying further aggression and guilt, he rejects Milton's authorial stance of choosing and controlling what is incorporated; he lets everything in without asserting control and so seems to be more eaten than eater.

For this reason, among others, one can easily see that the project of the *Magnum Opus* was doomed. In this encyclopedic *summa*, Coleridge planned to synthesize all previous philosophical systems while differentiating among them and putting them into their proper perspective so that they could form a new coherent whole. But, as he admitted, like Burton he had great difficulty in discriminating differences, "I feel too intensely the omnipresence of all in each, platonically speaking—or psychologically my brain-fibres . . . is [sic] of too general an affinity with all things and tho' it perceives the *difference* of things, yet is eternally pursuing the likeness."[68] Coleridge's general tendency is to resolve rather than sort out sources, in fact to obscure the existence of human sources altogether in favor of the transcendental source—truth. The reader of the *Biographia* who is not conveniently provided with the massive footnotes that the text requires in order to clarify the origins of the material, hears only one voice speaking through the text. The other authors have been incorporated so completely that, without scholarly apparatus rushing to the rescue, the reader has no means of telling them apart. Coleridge has filled himself up with others so that, by the principle you are what you eat, they are completely identified and all notions of authorial and personal identity negated.

For another famous Romantic opium-eater, Thomas de Quincey, Coleridge's absorption of sources was simply kleptomania. As McFarland points out, psychoanalytical interpretations of kleptomania see it as an attempt to compensate for the loss of the source of primal satisfaction: the mother's breast.[69] For Augustine, the image of the baby at the mother's breast represented man's symbiotic communion with God and also showed his essential weakness, incompletion, and dependency. For Coleridge the image has equal significance, but it is much more ambivalent. In many ways he anticipates Klein's concern with the significance of the oral phase, especially her description of the child's ambivalence toward the breast, which it both desires and fears, seeking to incorporate it as a means of establishing its own identity, yet fearing to do so lest in the act it destroy the external object that guarantees fulfillment. Kathleen Coburn has studied Coleridge's use of the image of the infant at the breast in relation to other figures for self-reflection, such as that of the mirror.[70] Coburn sees the breast as an ambivalent image for Coleridge, for it suggests both identification and alienation: "A tactual mirror in which the infant first senses himself, the breast also is the first means by which he senses himself as something other than something else bigger and more powerful, which he, however, learns to use."[71] The breast is both a means of identification and of the discovery of individual identity; for Coleridge it would seem to represent in part what Lacan will identify with the mirror stage, the point at which the infant through the discovery of images of itself imagines itself to be a unified, coherent entity.[72] Coburn connects Coleridge's interest in the image of the baby at the breast to his concern with following the Socratic dictum: "KNOW THYSELF,"[73] an injunction important also for both Ovid's Narcissus and Descartes, and which Coleridge repeatedly emphasizes as the beginning of all knowledge. She identifies his fascination with images of both breasts and mirrors with his reading of Francis Quarles's "Emblem XII," which shows two idiotic-looking children sucking the round and mirrorlike breasts of the world. The caption is a quotation of Ovid's Narcissus as he recognizes the paradox of his position of self-knowledge, "inopem me copia fecit" ("my plenty makes me poor")—a line that appears enigmatically in *Notebooks* 1.1383. In the emblem, the food absorbed is not a source of satisfaction, and self-knowledge is identified with the self-dissipation of Narcissus who was warned *against* knowing himself. For Coleridge, as for Narcissus, the fact that one can know oneself, be both subject and object of one's own thought, reveals further the deep division within the individual. Self-knowledge is by definition an illusion, as is, according to Lacan, the sense of a unified self that an infant acquires during the mirror stage. For Coleridge, it is ironically the lack of the *illusion* of autonomy that convinces him of his own fraudulence and generates in him a desire for wholeness, an end to self-division that is deeply, and destructively, narcissistic.

For this reason, the image which may more accurately represent Coleridge's desire for a unified autonomous self than that of the baby at the breast might be the figure of the uroboros. To equate the two may sound rather grotesque, but the serpent with its tail in its mouth forms a perfectly narcissistic self-circumscribing, if also self-consuming, system, that surpasses the relation of mother and child by its complete identification of eater and eaten. Like other images of self-cannibalism, it offers a nicely literal picture of self-sufficiency and the self-reliance of the closed system that economically, if redundantly, recycles itself. John Beer has discussed Coleridge's use of the image, its neoplatonic and hermetic roots, and contemporary popularity.[74] The archaeologist William Stukely, for example, interpreted the Druidic form of the symbol as a version of the Trinity, saying that, "A snake proceeding from a circle, is the eternal procession of the Son, from the first cause."[75] Beer points out the Romantic fascination with the ambiguity of the serpent: mythologists were fond of noting that the Hebrew word s'R'PH could mean either serpent or angel.[76] The uroboros is traditionally associated with antithetical meanings and is used to refer to both time and eternity. In Milton's "On Time," for example, Time is a snake with its tail in its mouth who will finally, in the fulfillment of Milton's vision of evil recoiling on itself, completely swallow itself. For the mystic Boehme, however, the image represents the return of all life to eternity from whence it came: "For all beings move onward until the end finds the beginning; then the beginning again swallows the end."[77] Beer interprets the image as a figure for ideal creative energy and the transcendence of sexual differences by a return to an original state of androgyny. The latter reading has descended from the mystics down to Jungian analysis, where the uroboros reappears as a variation on the figure of the hermaphrodite.[78] Extremes meet in this figure, which provides another emblem for the transcendence of alienation and the recreation of an original state of wholeness and total satisfaction.

However, as an image for a state of original identity, the uroboros seems too close to chaos for comfort. If the Saturn who devoured his children appears as a dubious model for transcendence, there may be something even more suspicious about a figure that glorifies self-cannibalism. Even more than the father who devours his sons, the uroboros suggests the perverseness of an ideal of self-knowledge and self-sufficiency that involves the self-cannibalism of a solipsistic ego so wrapped up in itself that it denies all alterity, rejecting external influences and refusing to see the other even as food in order to, in the fulfillment of Montaigne's image for self-knowledge, feed only upon itself.

For Coleridge, however, the figure suggested not only an intensely desired union, but also the ideal narrative structure defined by Aristotle, which he himself, of course, rarely achieved. In a letter to Cottle he expanded on Aristotle, to explain that "The common end of all *narrative*, nay of *all*, Poems is to convert a *series* into a *Whole*, to make those events, which in real life or imagined History move on a *strait* line, assume to our Understandings a *circular* motion—the snake with its Tail in it's Mouth."[79] In *Biographia Literaria* 1, in a note which included a number of self-parodies, Coleridge amusedly quotes a bit of doggerel that he himself had anonymously submitted to the Morning Post as a prank. These were addressed to the author of "The Rime of the Ancient Mariner":

Your poem must eternal be,
Dear sir! it cannot fail,
For 'tis incomprehensible
And without head or tail.[80]

This odd bit of nonsense, written circuitously by and to himself,[81] turns the poem into a parody of the eternity that is described as being without beginning or end, and specifically the uroboros, whose endlessness is identified here with sheer meaninglessness. And in fact, in a later parody written not by Coleridge but by W. S. Gilbert, the "Ancient Mariner" becomes very much like a narrative version of the uroboros, which is revealed to harbor a rather sinister fable of identity.

I want to look briefly at Gilbert's parody, "The Yarn of the Nancy Bell," as a grotesque and even gothic version of the "Ancient Mariner," before approaching the original to see what a nonsense writer makes of the work of a Romantic metaphysicist. For one thing, Gilbert's poem pushes the gothic world of Coleridge's into the realm of nonsense and suggests how fine the line between the two territories is. A world full of too much meaning seems ultimately senseless. I have been claiming that cannibalism as an image is related to the breakdown of certain notions of identity and language, and this is precisely, of course, what doggerel aims at as well. In fact, Gilbert, a greatly underrated writer, plays with many of the themes I have been discussing and undermines "normal" (or at least Victorian) definitions of identity.[82] His characters can simply switch selves, like the two babies in "The Baby's Revenge" and the soldiers in "General John"—a short poem that provides the model for the twist at the end of *H.M.S. Pinafore*. In the operetta, the change furthermore plays havoc with time and flirts with nominal incest, as Josephine's lover turns out to be really her father—the two having been exchanged at birth. Gilbert disrupts conventional principles of order and of regulating identity. Time is made meaningless as a measure in *The Pirates of Penzance*, where it will take Frederic, a leap-year's baby, fifty-one more years to reach his twenty-first birthday. It is further disordered in Gilbert's very ironic version of the Romantic idealization of the child and the belief that the child is father to the man: the *Bab* (a diminutive for baby) *Ballads* are populated by demonic infants who either age and die prematurely or end up as infantile old men. In Gilbert, the confusion of identities and telescoping of stages is treated without the horror it raises in writers such as Ovid, Dante, and, of course, in the gothic, but still with a suggestion of potential threat. Gilbert makes names useless as a means of differentiation, and, in a move that occasionally surpasses Rabelais, uses catalogues to create utter confusion—most notably, perhaps, in "King Borria Bungalee Boo," which consists almost entirely of the chaotic repetition of nonsense names of cannibals who finally eat each other up, so that differentiation is totally pointless. In an apparently light-hearted yet also sinister way, Gilbert indicates, as the writings of not only Stoker but also Rider Haggard and Conrad reveal in more gothic forms, that the time of the late empire was one in which the threat of losing personal and national identity broke out with renewed vigor.

As I have mentioned, Coleridge's task in the *Lyrical Ballads*, in which the "Ancient Mariner" first appeared, was to make the strange familiar. His aim is achieved partially by the emphasis upon details which, in the midst of this strange story, seem recognizable. Gilbert's job is to make the strange banal—to draw attention to the rhythm of Coleridge's poem and normalize it until it becomes a rollicking ballad bouncing along with comic predictability, and to introduce details from everyday life that are totally inappropriate to the gruesome tale he is telling. The discrepancy between form and content, outside and inside, which appeared in *Wieland*, and which in Coleridge is identified with fraud and hypocrisy, here produces a wonderfully ridiculous effect. The mysterious Ancient Mariner is metamorphosed into an "elderly naval man," whose "hair was weedy, his beard was long / And weedy and long was he" (4–6).[83] The Wedding Guest becomes a polite, soft-spoken young man who, as the elderly naval man melodramatically shakes his fist and tears his hair, becomes slightly perturbed, "For I couldn't help thinking the man had been drinking" (15). The scene is enhanced by Gilbert's drawing of a woolly sailor perched on a stone and gesticulating at a bespectacled, bowler-hatted, and clerical-looking character carrying an umbrella.

Gilbert's real insight, however, lies in his recreation of the events that take place at sea, a revision which suggests that his poem is in fact an extremely perceptive comment, not only on the "Ancient Mariner," but on Coleridge's version of the Romantic aspiration for totality. His elderly naval man recites ("in a singular minor key," 8):

> Oh, I am the cook and a captain bold,
> And the mate of the *Nancy* brig,
> And a bo'sun tight, and a midshipmite,
> And the crew of the captain's gig.

> (9–12)

The narrator is politely bemused by this assertion of multiple personalities and asks the man how he can manage to be so many people at once. The naval man's explanation indicates one way in which one man can contain multitudes, in fact, the simplest and most direct way: by eating them all.

Gilbert draws upon an interest in tales of shipwreck and cannibalism which, as I mentioned, was experiencing a revival in the late nineteenth century. But he avoids the gruesome side of the situation, so that the gothic is reduced to mildly grotesque nonsense. The gambling between Death and Life-in-Death for Coleridge's Mariner becomes the drawing of lots among the shipwrecked crew to see who's for dinner. The victims are tidily disposed of: the Nancy's mate made "a delicate dish" (46) and the bo'sun tight "much resembled pig" (50). The elderly naval man is finally left alone with the cook (a nicely nonsensical version of the showdown between poet and chef in Jonson's masque *Neptune's Triumph*), and they fight it out with puns, crude figures of speech that take on a comically literal meaning because of the rather bizarre circumstances:

> "I'll be eat if you dines off me," says TOM,
> "Yes that," says I, "you'll be,"—
> "I'm boiled if I die, my friend," quoth I,
> And "Exactly so" quoth he.
>
> (73–76)

The verbal play not only makes words mean *more* than they are intended to but turns them into the *opposite* of the intended meaning, making would-be eater into eaten. Pointing out with fine practicality that "you can't cook me / While I can—and will—cook *you!*" (79–80), the cook gets things ready—boiling water, seasoning, shallots, sage, parsley—ludicrous details that Gilbert again focuses on to heighten a humor that, like the horror of the gothic, is produced by an incongruity between subject matter and the way in which it is represented. But as the cook thoughtfully brings his friend over to the pot to "see" "How extremely nice you'll smell" (88—a fine parody of synesthesia), our hero swiftly "Ups with his heels, and smothers his squeals / In the scum of the boiling broth" (91–92). With a deft twist that recalls the poetic justice Dante uses at the end of *Inferno* 22, the cook is cooked.[84]

Just as he is polishing off the last remains of the cook, the naval man is rescued, and his version of the mariner's penance begins:

> And I never larf, and I never smile,
> And I never larf nor play,
> But I sit and croak, and a single joke
> I have—which is to say:
>
> "Oh, I am a cook and a captain bold,
> And the mate of the *Nancy* brig,
> And a bo'sun tight, and a midshipmite,
> And the crew of the captain's gig!"
>
> (97–104)

Gilbert's poem itself forms a uroboros as it returns to the refrain with which it began. While at the beginning the chant sounded like utter nonsense, the tale has explained quite logically the means by which one man can be cook, captain, and all. Gilbert's stroke of genius lies in his presentation of cannibalism as a form of identification, which implies conversely that Coleridge's fable of identity has some kind of cannibalism lurking beneath it.

Although Coleridge's poem has been read as a description of a sacramental universe where everything is, in his words, "*one Life*,"[85] it is a world like that of the "Nancy Bell," in which identification is an ambiguous concept. At the time Coleridge was writing the "Ancient Mariner" he still professed to be a Unitarian. Like Augustine, he resisted the idea of the incarnation, preferring the concept of an impersonal, transcendent deity to one who might be overly involved in and perhaps contaminated by the world he had entered.[86] Coleridge ultimately rejected Unitarianism, however, because he believed that it led to pantheism and the ultimate equation of God and nature. In a pantheistic universe, there can be no transcendent principle outside the natural order, for, as Schilling put it, "All is one and One is All."[87] As McFarland notes further, in a world where God is immanent there cannot be such a thing as personal identity: everyone is merely a metamorphosing form of a world substance called God.[88] As in the *Metamorphoses*, everything turns out to be everything else; each man is everyman and therefore nobody, *nemo*, both universal and completely characterless. It is in such a world that the story of the Mariner takes place, a closed system in which the Christian circle of fall and redemption has been revised into the figure of the all-consuming uroboros, endlessly turning upon itself, for there is nothing left beyond itself, no place outside to which man may finally return.

The topos of the voyage immediately suggests the theme of quest and return that has its classic expression in the *Odyssey*, read by neoplatonists as a type for the soul's return to God. But in more than one way, Coleridge's poem is "Without head or tail," for it shows no real beginning or ending, but only endless repetition of the middle. The narrative revolves around moments of suspense, in which willed action is completely paralyzed. After the killing of the albatross, the ship becomes becalmed and "As idle as a painted ship / Upon a painted ocean" (117–18).[89] To be paralyzed appears here to be identical with being a work of art, and from the beginning the Mariner has been stuck in the middle of his own story, which is a medium that cannot get him anywhere but, like its model the uroboros, always circles back upon itself. In the practice of the poem, the imagination is revealed, not to restore an ideal harmony between opposites, but to construct a more sinister and gothic meeting that results in endless suspense.

The stasis of the ship is followed by a release in which the story moves forward violently, but only as if propelled by a kind of repetition compulsion. At the very moment when the sailors expect rescue, they encounter Death and Life-in-Death. The latter wins the Mariner; the former takes the others, who curse him as they die. He is left alone, the knowledge of his guilt increasing his sense of isolation and alienation and further paralyzing him, as it prevents prayer for release and so perpetuates itself in a vicious circle. The effective action in the poem is not willed but unconscious or even simply thoughtless, as in the case of the killing of the albatross. The

Mariner's passivity, about which Wordsworth complained, is intensified by
the fact that the actions he does instigate appear to come from sources
inside himself over which he has little control. It is when we do not know
what we are doing that our actions prove most significant, and when the
Mariner unconsciously blesses the creatures of the sea, the albatross falls
from his neck.

However, if the Mariner is impelled by forces from within himself that
he cannot control, he is also open to invasion by alien forces. Like other
gothic works, the poem shows attacks from both inside and outside, which
are seen as equally uncontrollable and perhaps ultimately indistinguishable. The ship becomes inspired by spirits, who also reveal their interpretation of the killing of the albatross. However, their explanation does less
to reveal the significance of the crime than to prophesy its punishment: the
Mariner just happened to kill a bird loved by the daemon who has now
taken over the ship, and therefore he must do further penance. In order to
continue both voyage and punishment, the sailors are revived, though they
are not actually resurrected but only possessed by spirits. This does not,
however, prevent them from accusing the Mariner of their murder, thus
once more paralyzing his prayer for release:

> The pang, the curse, with which they died,
> Had never passed away:
> I could not draw my eyes from theirs,
> Nor turn them up to pray.
>
> (438–41)

The Mariner has just awoken and, the gloss informs us, "his penance
begins anew." In the very next line, however, we are told, "And now this
spell was snapt" (442), which the gloss elaborates as "The curse is finally
expiated," for the Mariner is approaching home. But if *this* spell ends, another begins, and the return home provides an inadequate resolution—as
it did, of course, for Odysseus. While the Mariner anticipates that the Hermit who rescues him will absolve him of his sin, on seeing him the Hermit
recoils, the pilot boy has conniptions, and, the gloss explains, "The penance of life falls on him. And ever and anon throughout his future life an
agony constraineth him to travel from land to land." The Mariner is condemned to endless wandering, an exile that is identified with narrative itself, as it consists of telling his tale again and again. Whereas Gilbert's naval
man spoke what sounded like utter nonsense that bounced along as if it
could keep going indefinitely, the Mariner claims "strange powers of
speech." However, his fate is not to transcend language but to remain
caught in it, and the final curse is the perpetuation of the narrative, which
leaves the Mariner forever suspended in his own story.[90]

The "Ancient Mariner" describes a world of total "insideness," in which everything is incorporated with rather sinister results. Yet it does leave something on the outside—the marginal glosses which, along with the epigraph and some revisions, were added to the poem when it was reissued in *Sibylline Leaves* in 1817—the same year that the *Biographia*, with its own odd obfuscation of sources and inside and outside, came out. These added comments, which lead a strange peripheral life, external to the poem proper and yet a part of the total text, would seem to offer the reader one possible interpretation of the poem—and one that, coming from the author, might be expected to be authoritative. But their amphibious status makes them somewhat unclear. Who, after all, is supposed to be writing these glosses? Is Coleridge explaining himself directly like the Dante of the *Vita nuova* and *Convivio*, or is he creating a fictitious interpreter? If the answer is the latter, who is he and how far can he be trusted?

As I argued in the last section, the emphasis on the mysterious origin of voices in the gothic is related to the difficulty of distinguishing sources behind both texts and individuals that present themselves as the self-contained origin of their own meaning. The Mariner hears voices that appear to explain the mystery but do not give an adequate account of the significance of his crime, reducing it to the inadvertent murder of some spirit's favorite pet. And the very presence of these beings deepens the sense of the inscrutability of a world filled, as the epigraph (also added in 1817) warns us in advance, with invisible presences.

The glosses similarly complicate rather than simplify the act of interpretation. One cannot know where they themselves are coming from: they are both inside and outside the text, a later addition that shares the same page as the poem but runs parallel to it, and so provides an analogue or imitation of the story rather than an explanation of it. Judging by their diction and tone, they might have been written by a medieval commentator who is anxious to impose a Christian coherence upon the poem and force it into an allegorical frame. But the medieval assumptions about the nature of things seem inadequate to the romantic text. The glosses draw the reader's attention to the natural imagery in the poem, as if to suggest a harmonious correspondence between man's life and the natural cycles. So, for example, the longest gloss explicates the scene described in lines 263–71: "In his loneliness and fixedness he yearneth towards the journeying Moon, and the stars that still sojourn, yet still move onward; and every where the blue sky belongs to them, and is their appointed rest, and their native country and their own natural homes, which they enter unannounced, as lords that are certainly expected and yet there is a silent joy at their arrival." The desired correspondence between man and nature, as both "one life," does not hold, except by parody. The moon and stars are at home everywhere, the Mariner nowhere; they, like Jonson's ideal of centered dilation, reconcile rest and motion, moving forward as they "still sojourn," while he knows only restless movement that gets him nowhere. While the glosses encourage us to read the poem as one of crime and expiation, the poem itself describes the perpetuation of punishment with no foreseeable end.

The world of the "Ancient Mariner" still could be considered sacramental in its assertion that the physical world has a spiritual meaning if one keeps in mind the fact that *sacer* is a primal word that unites the antithetical senses of blessed and cursed. The return to total identity and the recreation of a world in which everything is seen as "inside" is viewed with ambivalence, as it involves a loss of anything "outside," and in particular a transcendent principle associated with God the Father. For Coleridge—as for Augustine, Dante, and Burton—God represents a principle of separation and alterity which, in order to guarantee meaning, must be projected lest it too be consumed and made identical with everything else. But working against this need for difference is Coleridge's powerfully oral and incremental vision, which subsumes all oppositions to create a closed-circuit world of immanence with no hope of transcendence, a world that recalls not the writings of the early Christians but the pagan cosmos of Ovid, in which identity is constructed only to be violated and consumed.

As in the *Metamorphoses*, the fact that nature is full of meaning is a mixed blessing. Coleridge asserts the significance of the natural world in such poems as "The Destiny of Nations" (1796), in which he claims: "For all that meets the bodily sense I deem / Symbolical, one mighty alphabet / For infant minds" (18–20). As one means of making nature significant, Coleridge, like others among his contemporaries, revives the topos of the world as text; unlike many of the Romantics, however, he reaffirms its origin in a divine, transcendent author. In the "Hymn Before Sun-Rise, in the Vale of Chamouni" (1802), a catechized nature cries out triumphantly that its author is "GOD!" However, in this poem, as in any textual universe, it is difficult to tell where voices come from. The poem insists upon its own spontaneous and inspired creation and attempts to trace artistic creation back to an original source. In the *Purgatorio*, Dante used a similar tactic as a means of avoiding poetic rivalry. But in the nineteenth century the strategy suggests a fallacious obfuscation of individual identity and the property rights that have been formally recognized and even legally defined. Furthermore, the technique fails here also because a human source is too easily identified: the real author of the poem is neither Coleridge nor God but Frederika Brun, whose "Ode to Chamouny" Coleridge expanded and translated. To point to one divine author behind all work seems like a clever but deceitful move when one is indulging in what has by this time become identified as plagiarism. But the appropriation is too obvious; it cannot solve or transcend the problems of individual identity and private property but can merely pretend to ignore them through the recreation of an idealized myth of a communal sharing which is in fact self-serving.

When nature speaks in the undated manuscript poem "Coeli Enarrant," however, it is to give utterance to a blank page:

> all is blank on high,
> No constellations alphabet the sky:
> The Heavens one large Black Letter only shew . . .
> The groaning world now learns to read aright,
> And with its Voice of Voices cries out O!

$$(5–7, 10–11)$$

The climactic cry of surprise corresponds to an emptiness now seen to be behind all signs, including nature. However, the poem itself is not empty but rather full of voices, as the words "read aright" echo Collins's "Ode on the Poetical Character," a poem Coleridge claimed to admire very much. This ode constructs a genealogy of English poetry from Spenser and Milton down to the present, in which, Collins claims, there is no one to take over the "magic Girdle" of poetry. Milton, with "His Ev'ning Ear" (64), has exhausted the sources of poetic material so that "Heav'n" and "*Fancy*" "Have now o'erturn'd th'inspiring Bow'rs, / Or curtain'd close such Scene from ev'ry future View" (75–76). The ironic "or" here suggests not the possibility of Miltonic choice but the preclusion of it: Milton's Son's "recovery" of Paradise has completely covered it from the direct view of later poets. For these, any vision of the original source of poetry is so heavily mediated, filtered through Milton's texts, that it appears as the universal blank passed by him to them as his ironized version of the book of nature.[91] Nature appears as an empty blank precisely because it is too full, not of divine voices, but of human ones.

Because the world of the Mariner is full of mediating spirits, all action is significant. In response to Mrs. Barbauld's complaint that the tale had no moral, Coleridge insisted that it had too much, and that "It ought to have had no more moral than the Arabian Nights' tale of the merchant's sitting down to eat dates by the side of a well, and throwing the shells aside, and lo! a genie starts up, and says he *must* kill the aforesaid merchant, *because* one of the date shells had, it seems, put out the eye of the genie's son."[92] Coleridge's emphasis upon necessity and causation seems incongruent with the apparent arbitrariness of the crime; this is a world, like Ovid's, in which laws are strictly enforced, but unfortunately one is never told what they are. And his complaint is ironic, for while the "Ancient Mariner" ends with a moral—love all creatures great and small—it is one that not only seems banal in context but also offers no practical guide for action in a world that is too much *like* that of the *Arabian Nights*. The consequences of action are impossible to calculate in a world populated by invisible beings who may be injured by any move one makes. This is very much like the world of the *Metamorphoses*, in which no action is innocent, for everything one does—especially the meaningless movements—means too much, until everything borders upon nothing, the total breakdown of mediation, in which signs are seen as pointing only to the hollow "O!" of "Coeli Enarrant."

In general, then, Coleridge's imagination, which works to repress conflict and restore harmonious relations through the reconciliation of inside and outside, does its task too well. His mind appears like a gothic text, so full of other voices that all mental activity is liable to call them up and let them possess him from within. Unlike Milton, who reduces everything to himself, or the egotistically sublime Wordsworth, Coleridge is never capable of controlling the material he incorporates: he is an open and hungry mouth that is easily invaded and influenced. As a result, he appears, not as a unified author or individual standing outside of his own texts and controlling their meaning, but more as a Burtonesque writer whose life is indistinguishable from his work (as the *Biographia Literaria* suggests), which, nevertheless, often seems the property of others.

One further example of the way in which Coleridge is taken over by what he takes in can be seen in "The Picture, or The Lover's Resolution." This is a poem full of Miltonic echoes, and which attempts to imitate Milton's characteristic technique of including material by negation. In Milton, the effect of including what is excluded (as Ricks describes it) is often achieved through the use of negative constructions, as in "Not that fair field / Of Enna" (*Paradise Lost* 4.268–69). Wordsworth assimilated this technique but carried it even further by using double negatives to blur the line between what is banished and what is incorporated, as, for example, in "Tintern Abbey": "Nor perchance, / If I were not thus taught, should I the more / Suffer my genial spirits to decay" (112–14). It is hard to unravel what is being positively asserted through these negatives, which enable Wordsworth to create his own later version of Milton's suspension of definition. When Coleridge attempts the technique, it is already burdened by Wordsworth's successful assimilation and transformation. Moreover, it is genuinely not compatible with Coleridge's mind, which lacks the strength to keep things outside of itself. Images that are banished invade the poem, for he lacks Milton's firm control and ability to exclude as well as include. When Coleridge says things are "not" he doesn't mean it, and the moment they are conjured up, even negatively, they take on a life of their own. He confessed to Godwin that, "Of all words I find it most difficult to say, *No*";[93] like Freud's unconscious, Coleridge knows no negation or contradiction—which is why he can easily imagine extremes that meet.[94]

The syntax of "The Picture" is even more tortuous than usual, as it follows the serpentine movement both of the speaker's thought and of his consciously "penseroso," or melancholy, walk through a forest. The paths of mind and nature, inner and outer worlds, run parallel but strive to meet, as the narrator's thoughts struggle to get loose and enter the world outside. He shows a tendency to personify abstractions and imagine characters who then become instantaneously embodied. His own situation is not directly described but is suggested by an implicit analogy, as his thoughts wander constantly toward a figure of a "love-lorn man," a melancholy misanthrope who, tired of company, might find such a place a congenial retreat, for,

> He would far rather not be that he is;
> But would be something that he knows not of,
> In winds or waters, or among the rocks!
>
> (23–25)

This figure who dreams of dissipation and the dispersal of his own identity into nature is only a figment of the speaker's imagination. But he suddenly attains an astonishing degree of reality, for it takes the very elaborate exorcism of lines 26–45 to get him to go away. Moreover, he shows remarkable tenacity—once created, he keeps popping back into the poem, pursuing and finally merging with the narrator.

The speaker himself dreams of merging with nature, as he had imagined the lovelorn man desiring to do. He pictures himself sitting in the shade of an oak, listening to the sounds of the brook and bees, feeling the gentle breeze that—and suddenly the vision of harmony is disrupted—"was never Love's accomplice" (59):

> Ne'er played the wanton—never half disclosed
> The maiden's snowy bosom, scattering thence
> Eye-poisons for some love-distempered youth,
> Who ne'er henceforth may see an aspen-grove
> Shiver in sunshine, but his feeble heart
> Shall flow away like a dissolving thing.
>
> (62–67)

Just as the earlier exorcism is not firm enough to keep the figure of the youth out of the poem, the negatives here are too weak to prevent that other breeze from entering and contaminating the scene. Before the Fall, Milton's Adam tells Eve that:

> Evil into the mind of God or Man
> May come and go, so unapprov'd, and leave
> No spot or blame behind.
>
> (*Paradise Lost* 5.117–19)

For the later poet, living in a definitely fallen world, negatives appear to be taken in fully, even when merely imagined or "tasted." The hypothetical youth who is pining away from unrequited love infects the speaker who has dreamt of dissolving into the landscape.

Furthermore, when the speaker looks into the stream, he exclaims,

> no pool of thine,
> Though clear as lake in latest summer-eve,
> Did e'er reflect the stately virgin's robe,
> The face, the form divine, the downcast look
> Contemplative!

(72–76)

Milton's "penseroso" Nun is not only evoked through allusion but suddenly present, as in the place where she is not she instantly appears,

> Behold! her open palm
> Presses her cheek and brow! her elbow rests
> On the bare branch of half-uprooted tree,
> That leans towards its mirror!

(76–79)

Next, the vague relative pronoun "who" momentarily disorders reference and identity so that the youth slips back in to complicate the situation:

> Who erewhile
> Had from her countenance turned, or looked by stealth
> (For Fear is true-love's nurse), he now
> With steadfast gaze and unoffending eye
> Worships the watery idol, dreaming hopes
> Delicious to the soul, but fleeting, vain,
> E'en as that phantom-world in which he gazed,
> But not unheeded gazed.

(79–86)

Like Medusa, this lady of the lake can be seen safely only in reflection. Yet this reflection appears to take on an unnatural autonomy of its own, for it gazes back at the youth and then appears to destroy itself by tossing flowers on water:

> Then all the charm
> Is broken—all that phantom world so fair
> Vanishes, and a thousand circlets spread,
> And each mis-shape the other.

(91–94)

The scattering of flowers is a traditional romance image for writing found, for example, in Spenser's "Prothalamion" and Milton's "Lycidas," and one that suggests the fragility and ephemerality of poetry. Coleridge is creating a negative, even masochistic, version of the gesture: through the casting of flowers on water, an image is not created but destroyed—and apparently by itself. The very poem seems to be subverting the poet's attempt to contain it.

A similar kind of poetic spontaneous combustion would seem to be responsible for the fragmentation of "Kubla Khan"—despite Coleridge's attempt to blame external circumstances in the form of the intruding man from Porlock. The two poems are closely connected: Coleridge used the next six lines as the epigraph for "Kubla Khan." Suddenly the narrator breaks in and cries out to his own character, in a gesture that recalls while inverting Ovid's attempt to warn Narcissus:

> Stay awhile
> Poor youth, who scarcely dar'st lift up thine eyes!
> The stream will soon renew its smoothness, soon
> The visions will return! And lo! he stays:
> And soon the fragments dim of lovely forms
> Come trembling back, unite, and now once more
> The pool becomes a mirror.
>
> (94–100)

The speaker's imagined character appears to hear and obey. But the lines that follow—not included in the epigraph to "Kubla Khan" but reinacted within that poem—show that the invoked image does not return. The mirror reflects only the woods, showing neither the lady nor even the youth himself, who at last dares to look behind him for the source of the reflection only to find that it is gone. Again the narrator cries out, as Ovid did to his Narcissus, and in fact exhorts him to be a kind of Narcissus, pining away at a water's edge, consumed by his inability to embrace a mere reflection:

> Go, day by day, and waste thy manly prime
> In mad love-yearning by the vacant brook,
> Till sickly thoughts bewitch thine eyes, and thou
> Behold'st her shadow still abiding there,
> The Naiad of the mirror!
>
> (107–11)

The image this youth yearns for is not his own, but it is still an image, a reflection that oddly takes on a character of its own, becoming finally embodied as the "Naiad of the mirror." While we assume that a real woman must have been there in order to cast the reflection, the poem shows us only a mirror-image, which itself becomes an object of desire. The scene reenacts the pattern of loss and return. But Coleridge's image for the fragmentation and restoration of unity here is that of a temporary loss, brought about through the force of the flowers of poesie itself, of a wholeness that, like Lacan's infant's imaginary self, is an illusion seen only in a mirror; when the unity of the mirror is restored the individuals are lost altogether.

However, as soon as he has urged the youth to fade away, the speaker attempts to make the whole scene disappear, crying out Miltonicly as if to banish all these intrusive images: "Not to thee / O wild and desert stream! belongs this tale" (112–13). He tries to purge the scene before him of these characters from his own mind and bring us back to the original action of the poem by returning to the walk in the woods and arriving at a lake. But while the return to the external landscape is supposed to counterbalance the tendency of his mind to replace what is in front of him with a fictitious situation, the reality here (if, of course, it really *is* here—we have only his report to go by, and he is not the most reliable of witnesses) becomes assimilated by his obsessed and melancholy mind. In the center of the lake is an island over which the waves, approaching from opposite directions, strive to meet, and then

> Dart off asunder with an angry sound,
> How soon to re-unite! And see! they meet,
> Each in the other lost and found.
>
> (125–27)

As in Ovid, water is the place in which extremes meet with the loss of all means of differentiation. The final collapse toward which the poem has been moving is that of the difference between art and nature, and what is inside the speaker's mind and what outside. Coming to what appears to be a prospect, he exclaims, "How bursts / The landscape on my sight" (139–40). Lines 140–59 give us a vivid description of what the speaker sees, the whole of which forms "A curious picture!" (159). But suddenly we realize that this literally *is* a picture, not nature but art, and the poem takes off in an unexpected direction that disorients the reader:

> A curious picture, with a master's haste
> Sketched on a strip of pinky-silver skin,
> Peeled from the birchen bark! Divinest maid!
> Yon bark her canvas, and those purple berries
> Her pencil!
>
> (159–63)

It takes a moment for the reader to get the picture and fill in the speaker's leaps of thought. But the remaining lines make the situation clear: this is the work of the girl he loves, with whom he has had some sort of quarrel, and with whom he desires a reunion that would be as intense and intimate as that of the merging waves. In the end, it turns out that the speaker is the lovesick man who has been haunting him, and his lover, the Naiad of the mirror. The fictitious man obviously was created to be a projection of that negative aspect of himself which, as in the case of Jonson's use of grotesque self-images, would free himself from it; but, in the end, the two men come together.

This identification occurs because Coleridge does not have the ability of Jonson or, especially, of Milton to entertain opposites that stay apart; the assimilating power of his mind is too great. Moreover, he is reluctant to relinquish anything, to make the renunciation of one alternative that choice necessitates. He holds on to everything, even the things or ideas he claims he does not want—perhaps at the cost of what he might really want. When at the end of "The Picture" the lover rushes off to return the sketch to the girl, he claims that the work of art is of no real use to him: "Why should I yearn / To keep the relique? 'twill but idly feed / The passion that consumes me" (181–83). He claims to need the real girl, for art is merely a substitute that cannot satisfy his desire. But at the end of the poem he is still in the woods, holding the picture and not the girl. He gains an image for a self-contained, autonomous construct that has, like the mirror itself, perfect unity, but perhaps at the expense of real people who are usually less coherent, even fragmented.

Coleridge idealizes art as a place where dualisms are transcended by being absorbed into a unified and autonomous system. The definition of art as self-contained and self-referential, the counterpart of the concept of the autonomous individual with which it has been closely allied, suits Coleridge's desire to use art as a means of evading reality and social obligations—some very real personal debts he incurred. Financially as well as emotionally, he was always a bit of a baby, dependent on others; unlike Milton, who was supported by his father, Coleridge saw himself as a kind of orphan constantly seeking adoption, searching for father figures who would take him home and care for him, making it possible for him to devote himself to reading and writing. In the last years of his life, James Gillman filled the role, while also attempting to play mother by regulating Coleridge's opium intake. To Gillman, Coleridge recalled an adolescent experience of reading in which, "My whole being was, with eyes closed to every object of present sense, to crumple myself up in a sunny corner, and read, read, read; fancy myself on Robinson Crusoe's island, finding a mountain of plumb-cake, and eating a room for myself, and then eating it into the shapes of tables and chairs—hunger and fancy!"[95] In this wonderful recollection, to read means to eat the world, as "hunger and fancy" appear as analogous methods of containing reality. For Coleridge, this is a vague memory of his own paradise lost, a time when he had everything inside himself.

With Romanticism, the earthly paradise of romance, always potentially a "garden of poesie," is internalized, becoming the "paradise within" that is the bower of the imagination, a mental landscape where inner and outer

realms appear to meet.[96] Like all *loci amoeni* in foreign territory, this one
may be suspected of being a trap, as a place for the refreshment of poetic
vision turns into a prison impeding the poet's return to the real world of
social and moral responsibility. In "This Lime-Tree Bower, My Prison,"
for example, the poet is kept from going out with his friends by an accident
(though not an insignificant one—Sarah Coleridge spilt boiling water on
his foot). But this captivity frees his mind, which expands to create a sur-
rogate space, a bower of the imagination that threatens to replace the real
one. To keep this from happening, he constantly recalls his friend Charles
Lamb. When rested in too long, the paradise of the imagination might
turn into a gothic landscape, as the relation between man and nature, subject and object, inner and outer, turns into that of eater and eaten, and the
most basic concept of relation, the child at the mother's breast, becomes
suffocating circularity: the uroboros preying upon itself.

Coleridge's poetry reveals a deep ambivalence toward his own theories
and ideals, which seems to keep him from carrying them through lest they
prove too all-consuming. In his version of Milton's "Nativity Ode," the
"Religious Musings," written ostensibly on Christmas Eve, 1794, there is
a tension between an emphasis upon the incarnation—the reconciliation
of man with God that provides the model for the incarnation of meaning
in symbolic figures—and a proleptic movement toward the apocalypse—
the absolute identification of God and man that involves the end of figuration altogether. This is quite different from Milton's characteristic tendency to get to the point and pass over the humiliation of Christ, especially
his death, in order to focus on the triumph of the Son. For Coleridge, the
death takes disturbing precedent: "Lovely was the death / Of Him whose
life was Love!" (28-29). Coleridge keeps leaping to premature visions of
the ultimate total identity of man and God, the end of all alienation, when
he, as Bloom nicely describes it, "whoops"[97] about the time when:

> by exclusive consciousness of God
> All self-annihilated it shall make
> God its Identity: God all in all!
> We and our Father one!
>
> (42–45)

Coleridge keeps looking forward to the apocalypse, when the weakness he
identifies with himself will be annihilated by being turned into the omnipotent God. In fact, the actual incarnation is oddly absent from this nativity
ode, forgotten in the fervor for even closer relations.[98] As I mentioned
earlier, the main impediment to Coleridge's conversion to Trinitarian
Christianity was, as it was for Augustine, the doctrine of the incarnation.
While Coleridge's concept of the symbol is based on the Christian formulation of the incarnation, his own abstract way of thinking seems to find a

more comfortable form of expression in personifications.[99] Even in this poem on the incarnation, there are few human figures and an abundance of personified abstractions. History itself is described not as a sequence of human figures among whom Christ appears—figures that are, according to typology, both real and significant—but as a series of personified vices and virtues, or abstract and indefinite figures like the "vacant Shepherd" (198) and the apostrophied "poor Wretch" (278) and "aged Women" (287). The only individualized human figures are the saints of the millennium: Milton, Newton, Priestley, and Hartley. But they too have been oddly abstracted in order to form an idiosyncratic community that overlooks both chronology and compatibility; while this is a choir Coleridge can dream of joining, it would seem unlikely that anyone else would fit into such a group.

Caught up in enthusiasm for his own abstract reflections, the poet has difficulty bringing himself down to earth:

> Till then
> I discipline my young and novice thought
> In ministries of heart-stirring song,
> And aye on Meditation's heaven-ward wing
> Soaring aloft I breathe the empyreal air
> Of Love, omnific, omnipresent Love.
>
> (410–15)

The movement here imitates, in a greatly diluted form, Milton's retreat from the apocalypse in the "Nativity Ode," in which he represents his poem as being stopped when "But wisest Fate says no" (149). Milton creates the appearance of intervention by an external force, a power different from and above himself, which guarantees the order and meaning not only of his poem but of history itself. Coleridge often attempts to use external figures to pull himself out of potentially solipsistic reveries: characters such as Charles in "This Lime-Tree Bower, My Prison," Sarah in "The Eolian Harp" (whom he gets to say "no" for him to the idea of pantheism, which he cannot reject totally on his own), his son in "The Nightingale," Sara Hutchinson in "Dejection," even the infamous man from Porlock—all form a pattern of figures represented as outside of himself that he can turn to when his thoughts become too self-consuming. But the debated question of the existence of the man from Porlock indicates the ultimate vulnerability of the figure of the outsider as a source of stability: even the outside is seen from inside the poet's mind, where extremes tend to meet. Coleridge lacks Milton's strength to pull himself back from a premature apocalypse through the creation of even an adequate *fiction* of difference or otherness. Whereas Milton curtails himself, like the Son, to gain greater power, Coleridge cannot limit or restrain himself. He comes down to earth only for a brief moment, and then is off again on a flight of fancy, propelled by "Love, omnific, omnipresent Love."

As W. S. Gilbert suggested, at the point where extremes meet the sublime may turn into the ridiculous; McFarland notes how the Romantic "largeness of aspiration and expansion of range are willy-nilly accompanied by an uncertainty of taste and blurring of poetic forms."[100] In Gilbert's *Patience*, the word *transcendental* is parodied as the transcendental term that means everything—and therefore nothing. In his desire to take everything in, Coleridge becomes often unintelligible or even just plain silly. So Byron commented on his "Explaining metaphysics to the nation— / I wish he would explain his explanations" (*Don Juan*, "Dedication," 15–16). Byron also lamented that "Coleridge might have been anything: as it is he is a thing 'that dreams are made of,' " a complaint echoed by Hazlitt, who believed that "Mr. C., with great talents, has, by an ambition to be everything, become nothing."[101] To be everything is to be nothing, as Romantic Prometheanism, the age's version of satanic insatiability, becomes the self-dissipation of Comus.[102]

Byron's description of Coleridge by means of a quotation from Shakespeare (a thing "that dreams are made of," *Tempest* 4.1.157) is rather intriguing. For Coleridge, as I mentioned earlier, the difference between Milton and Shakespeare is one of methods of identification, as Milton introjects others into himself, while Shakespeare projects himself into others. But both processes require a stable sense of a difference between inside and outside, which therefore need identification. Coleridge's attempt at Miltonic introjection leads to self-projection, an abstraction of his identity and meaning, because his sense of the difference between inside and outside is confused. Perhaps one could say simply that, like Robinson Crusoe, he has weak ego boundaries and is infantile and oral. But Coleridge's self-defenses are more complex and interesting than those of Crusoe, as is also the way in which he attempts to make the strange familiar by denying differences. As he cannot bear the loss that is involved in either personal or poetic development, nor the possibility of guilt that is generated by the admission of aggression toward one's sources, he represents relations as benign and symbiotic. But the prolongation of a childlike suspension of identity is, for him as it is in the gothic, threatening. By refusing to "grow up," to accept loss, his own potential aggressivity (evident in his poetic thefts), and subsequent guilt, he tries to revoke individual identity in favor of an ideal of corporate identity that has its roots not only in the oral phase but in earlier formulations of relationships. But in a time which demands that individuals be autonomous, and that authors control the meaning and boundaries of their textual private property, such an ideal appears to be a fallacious regression to a Golden Age that is both infantile and cannibalistic. Coleridge's fantasy is of a "Self, that no alien knows" ("Religious Musings," 154), a self for which there is no other, who is as generously open as Terence, whom Burton quotes at the beginning of his third book: "Homo sum, humani à me nihil alienum puto" ("I am a man, I think nothing human alien from me," *Anatomy* 3.7). The appropriate image for such a man in the modern world turns out to be a combination of Comus and the Narcissus who dissolved through excessive self-knowledge, as Coleridge's fable of identity and transcendence takes the shape of the self-annihilating circle of the serpent swallowing up itself.

MELVILLE

The *Pequod* first appears to Ishmael as "A cannibal of a craft, tricking herself forth in the chased bones of her enemies," decked out with the teeth of sperm whales, and "A noble craft, but somehow a most melancholy!"[103] Like the vessel, Melville's *Moby-Dick* is a crafty cannibal of a work, which flaunts the different forms and authors it has greedily incorporated. Encyclopedias, philosophical and theological treatises, travelogues, whaling manuals, and sea stories are absorbed with as much gusto as the literary works of Dante, Rabelais, Shakespeare, Milton, Burton, and Browne, in order to create this "romance-anatomy" that combines the narrative structure of the quest with the encyclopedic scope of the anatomy form.[104]

His reading of Renaissance authors may have suggested to Melville this method, which appears as a kind of imitatio or Burtonesque collation of material. Melville's use of sources is, like Burton's, more eclectic and omniverous than that of the typical imitator. His sources often seem chosen for the simple reason that he has read them: as in the case of Coleridge, whatever gets into his mind gets into his text. Yet the work produced by this internalization is obviously very different from any of Coleridge, though it also attempts a reconciliation of differences into a single whole. *Moby-Dick* is a kind of a democratic work that has room for all kinds of literature brought together in a literary version of the American ideal of *e pluribus unum*. As it incorporates and revises so many of the genres, themes, and motifs that I have been discussing, and furthermore explicitly identifies its own dream of community and communion with cannibalism, it seems a fitting work with which to end this section of my anatomy.

Sharon Cameron has recently shown how the text dramatizes problems of identity, representing a fantasy of the transcendence of a bodily defined self by means of a complete physical identification with others.[105] I would like to look further at the way this fantasy is represented, and at its relation to Melville's attempt to create a *textual* body that identifies many different voices. In his *Anatomy*, Burton attempted to synthesize all previous thought under the name "Melancholy," which became for him the transcendental term covering and containing all meaning. As "Melancholy" subsumed Erasmus's "Folly," so "Moby-Dick" subsumes "melancholy," which Ishmael not only associates with the *Pequod* but turns into his own motive for going whaling. His quest begins as a remedy for spleen (23); it ends in the mad hunt for the great white whale. Like the melancholy which is the source of both pleasure and pain, Moby-Dick is potentially divine and demonic, a primary word that identifies antithetical meanings. But Melville further outdoes Burton by choosing for his title a more literal kind of anatomy in which to ground his enterprise. Like Rabelais's *Gargantua* and *Pantagruel*, Melville's title refers to a grotesque body. As modern individuals can only meet through bodily encounters, he thoughtfully provides them with a real anatomy in which they can come together. But his transcendental term may indeed seem to swallow everything when it is imagined as the monumental body and gaping mouth of Moby-Dick, an enormous abyss of no return which, unlike the mouth of Pantagruel, contains things by completely consuming them.

As Cameron's argument implies, Ahab's quest is ultimately similar to that of Coleridge, as he longs for a restoration of wholeness through total identification with others. But whereas Coleridge attempts this through a denial of individual identity, Ahab inversely attempts it through the expansion and intensification of his own, since he imagines himself as the one man who can include multitudes. His attempt to contain all others turns him into not Christ, who identifies by incarnating individuals, but into Dante's Lucifer, who subsumes by consuming. In the episode of "The Doubloon," interpretation becomes a means of absorbing all meaning to himself, as he sees that all signs "are Ahab" (551). This reading is dramatized in the last days of the quest, when the crew becomes "one man, not thirty" (700), and "all the individualities of the crew, this man's valor, that man's fear, guilt and guiltiness, all varieties were welded into oneness" (701). The democratic principle of social representation is subverted as the body of men turns into the single body of Ahab. As in the *Inferno*, microcosm and macrocosm, the head and its members, collapse when the body politic Hobbes described as a Leviathan becomes indistinguishable from its leader, Ahab who, furthermore, by the principle you are what you eat, ultimately becomes the Leviathan, Moby-Dick.

In *Moby-Dick*, as in the gothic, the relation between victor and victim, pursuer and pursued, is both rigidly defined and endlessly reversible, as it involves simultaneous aggression and identification. For Ahab, the whale is a rival source and end of meaning, and a figure for the unity and wholeness he desires.[106] The beast's body is one white blank, with no convenient and comforting boundary lines. On the one hand, this extreme physical unity, which is not the reconciliation of differences but their absence altogether, connects the whale with the squid, on which he is rumored to feed, and which appears as a ghostly mass of chaos incarnate: "No perceptible face or front did it have; no conceivable token of either sensation or instinct; but undulated there on the billows, an unearthly, formless, chance-like apparition of life" (366). On the other hand, this unity reminds Ishmael of the transcendental oneness of God, for, gazing at the whale's brow, "you feel the Deity and the dread powers more forcibly than in beholding any other object in living nature. For you see no one point precisely; not one distinct feature is revealed; no nose, eyes, ears, or mouth; no face; he has none, proper; nothing but that one broad firmament of a forehead, pleated with riddles; dumbly lowering with the doom of boats, and ships, and men" (447–48). One individual in the sense of indivisible whole, he appears as an inscrutable primal word in whom antithetical senses are spatially conflated. His "pyramidal silence" is read as proof of a genius too profound to be communicated (448–49), and Ishmael observes, "what has the whale to say? Seldom have I known any profound being that had anything to say to this world, unless forced to stammer out something by way of getting a living" (478)—an identification of art with material motives that debunks it, subverting the ideals of writers like Ben Jonson. But the voicelessness of a dying whale also provokes both pity and terror, for "the fear of this vast dumb brute of the sea was chained up and enchanted in him; he had no voice, save that choking respiration through his spiracle, and this made the sight of him unspeakably pitiable; while still in his amazing bulk, portcullis jaw, and omnipotent tail, there was enough to appal the stoutest man who so pitied" (457). The horror of silence is that one can never know for certain what lies behind it and what it means: whether it indicates the transcendence of language or is the sign of an empty blank object that simply has nothing to say.

Similarly, in "The Whiteness of the Whale," white is terrifying in its ability to represent simultaneously the total absence and presence of color. The indifference of the whale, which is implicitly identified with and differentiated from the kinds of coolness manifested by Queequeg, Stubb, Ahab, the Carpenter, and occasionally Ishmael himself, becomes also frightening in its ambiguity, for it appears as an attribute of both super- and sub-human natures: a quality equally of a transcendent deity and of an unfeeling blank object world. Like gigantic man-mountains, such as Polyphemos and Atlas, the monster is an ambivalent figure that points toward opposing meanings but also threatens to collapse them within its enormous anatomy. As an external and alien source of significance whose very difference, like that of the cannibals of the New World, makes it terrible, Moby-Dick seems to incarnate the concept of otherness so completely as to necessitate a dualistic universe in which self and other are locked in endless conflict. At the same time, however, and again like the cannibals, the monster threatens any structure based upon binary oppositions; and it ultimately subsumes the ego that opposes it.

It is precisely the whale's ability to incorporate antitheses that drives Ahab mad. His quest for identity, like that of Satan, involves the rejection of the suspense of ambiguity in favor of a definitive interpretation. According to him: "All visible objects, man, are but as pasteboard masks. But in each event—in the living act, the undoubted deed—there, some unknown but still reasoning thing puts forth the mouldings of its features from behind the unreasoning mask. If man will strike, strike through the mask! How can the prisoner reach outside except by thrusting through the wall? To me, the white whale is that wall, shoved near to me. Sometimes I think there's naught beyond. But 'tis enough" (220–21). Trapped in a world created by uncertain signs, Ahab can find release only in interpretation that has been literalized into an act of aggression. The potential violence in the hermeneutic model of the rending of the veil, the stripping of an outside appearance from an inside reality (which Rabelais had indicated with his model of the dog with the bone), here emerges, as, to attain the unmediated vision he desires and "get at" the truth, Ahab must literally pin it down with his harpoon.

In the end, however, the sign that subsumes all significance also consumes Ahab, as he is swallowed up by the sea, and perhaps by the monster as well. Hunter and hunted switch roles and then become one when Ahab falls into Moby-Dick's "open-doored marble tomb" (691). For Melville, as for Milton, to resolve ambiguity is suicidal and tragic, and to discover identity is to lose it, to be eaten by another. Melville's ocean is the locus for the dissolution of identity, or rather, his version of the world of the *Metamorphoses*, in which identification turns into cannibalism, and water is the type for all influences that threaten individual autonomy. The primal sea is that archetypal parent who devours its children, as, not satisfied with the destruction of men, it turns upon its own kind, "a fiend to his own offspring; worse than the Persian host who murdered his own guests; sparing not the creatures which itself hath spawned" (363). Ishmael reflects upon the enduring world of the flood: "Consider, once more, the universal cannibalism of the sea; all whose creatures prey upon each other, carrying on eternal war since the world began" (364).

But the ship springs a leak, and the cannibalistic world seeps into and influences this vessel—which is, as I implied in opening, analogous to the text itself, and to which Ahab also compares his own body (603–4). The notion of autonomy and bodily wholeness is undermined by external forces that seep in. Melville keeps returning to images of physical consumption and food, partially as a means of asserting the material base of his text, but also to emphasize the human dependence on external nourishment that makes us open, and therefore vulnerable. Images of eating recur constantly throughout the text; like the *Odyssey*, this is an "eating poem." We pass from the eels wriggling down Ishmael's throat in the chapter dedicated to "Chowder," to the slithering dumplings of "The Decanter," in which a literal and minutely catalogued feast becomes also food for thought, as Ishmael, "devoted three days to the studious digesting of all this beef, beer, and bread, during which many profound thoughts were incidentally suggested to me, capable of a transcendental and Platonic application" (570). The text keeps grounding itself and its subject in the body until, however, relations begin to become defined as purely material and ultimately cannibalistic, in which the other is regarded as food. At the center of the labyrinthine cannibal craft, the minotaur Ahab presides over silent meals conducted like terrible communions. In the meantime, on the upper decks the sailors become indistinguishable from the sharks who gaze up at their human battles and banquets, for, "were you to turn the whole affair upside down, it would still be pretty much the same thing, that is to say, a shocking sharkish business enough for all parties" (385). And in retrospect, the frantic Ishmael sees cannibalism flooding the entire world, as he begins to sound like Ovid's Pythagoras: "Go to the meatmarket of a Saturday night and see the crowds of live bipeds staring up at the long rows of dead quadrupeds. Does not that sight take a tooth out of the cannibal's jaw? Cannibals? Who is not a cannibal?" (393).

Cannibalism becomes the image for the self who desires a total identification with others, achieved by swallowing them and reducing them to itself, either literally or through interpretation. Ahab's Prometheanism, his insatiability, turns into a form of narcissism, as he is driven to solipsism by the ultimate impenetrability of an external and other world that denies the complete physical union he desires.[107] His expansion becomes inverted as contraction, the reduction of everything to the self, which is finally the repudiation of anything other than the self. Walking dualism that he is, as he stumps along on flesh and wood, life and death (310), he insists on his essential integrity and inviolability—"even with a broken bone, old Ahab is untouched. . . . Nor white whale, nor man, nor fiend, can so much as graze old Ahab in his proper and inaccessible being" (705)—and dreams of being freed from all "that mortal inter-debtedness" by being reduced to the "one small, compendious vertebra" (601). He rejects external nourishment to feed only upon himself, appearing to Ishmael like a hibernating grizzly bear: "in his inclement, howling old age, Ahab's soul, shut up in the carved trunk of his body, there fed upon the sullen paw of its gloom!" (206).[108] In the sea-world, ultimate narcissism is the grotesque self-cannibalism of the dying sharks who form perfect uroboroi as they "viciously snapped, not only at each other's disembowelments, but like flexible bows, bent round, and bit their own; till those entrails seemed swallowed over and over again by the same mouth, to be oppositely voided by the gaping wound" (395).

However, the text does offer other possible models for relations as alter-

216 · Chapter 5

natives to Ahab's cannibalistic fable of identity through the presentation of a series of couples that recall the partnerships of the *Inferno*. The dialogues between Bildad and Peleg, the Captain of the *Samuel Enderby* and Bunker, Stubb and Fleece, Ahab and Pip, provide different paradigms for human exchange and communion, not all of which are infernal. One of the most pleasant of these is the relation between Bunker and his captain, which involves a playful bantering of words. The constantly emphasized ability of language to deceive and mean more than the speaker intends here permits the Captain's teasing revision of Bunker's lines, which becomes a sign of their mutual understanding and affection. But elsewhere wordplay can obscure communication. Stubb not only confuses poor Fleece, but also double-crosses both the French Captain and the translator—his partner in crime, with whom he is supposed to have an understanding. In conversation with others, Ahab, in particular, invests his partner's words with a meaning the speaker cannot grasp and responds to him in a different language, usually the foreign tongue of Shakespearean tragedy. The ability of words to mean more than was intended is one source of poetic fertility and power, but Ahab tries to appropriate that power to himself and use it as a weapon against others in his attempt to circumscribe meaning as his own private property.

The major alternative to narcissism in the text is represented in the friendship between Ishmael and Queequeg, Christian and cannibal, which, in the almost totally masculine universe of the text, is represented as a comic nuptial. But it is a metaphorical marriage that is consummated only verbally when they retire to bed for "some little chat," as "there is no place like bed for confidential disclosures between friends" (85). This, along with his generally free and easy boudoir behavior, illustrates the change Queequeg effects in the misanthropic Ishmael, who had at first maintained, "I don't know how it is, but people like to be private when they are sleeping" (41). The relationship with Queequeg softens Ishmael, opening up his voice and creating in him a desire for communication that transforms the melancholy and taciturn loner who begins abruptly, "Call me Ishmael," into the loquacious rambler who hardly ever shuts up.

The two men are closely connected by several of the many lines that bind the story together in imagistic unity. They appear as the complementary weavers, necessity and chance, who operate the mat-making machine which Ishmael interprets as the "Loom of Time" that spins his fate (288). As an alien—and a real live cannibal at that—Queequeg is Ishmael's "other," representing to him the unforeseen elements that constantly and uncontrollably intersect with and penetrate the destiny he weaves for himself. The constant movement of the line, the sense of an incessant and rhythmical interaction between self and other, necessity and chance, prevents the relation from becoming a rigid bond of total identity. Still, this reciprocal line is in its own way as real as the literal line that ties Ishmael to Queequeg as he descends into the body of the beast. Ishmael imagines that "an elongated Siamese ligature united us. Queequeg was my own inseparable twin brother; nor could I any way get rid of the dangerous liabilities which the hempen bond entailed" (416). He characteristically meditates upon this particular and very real position to extrapolate a higher meaning: "So strongly and metaphysically did I conceive my situation then, that while earnestly watching his motions, I seemed distinctly to perceive my own individuality was now merged in a joint stock company of two; that my free will had received a mortal wound; and that another's mistake or misfortune might plunge innocent me into unmerited disaster or death" (416). His own situation then expands into a type for the interdependence of all mankind, as "I saw that this situation of mine was the precise situation of every mortal that breathes; only in most cases, he, one way or another, has this Siamese connection with a plurality of other mortals" (416).

Ishmael and Queequeg's relation expands to include both marriage and Siamese fraternity, and to represent a penetration of the self that is potentially a mortal wounding: the ideal of friendship, though here the meeting of opposites rather than Montaigne's kindred spirits, is becoming overburdened and the connections almost incestuously overinvolved, and so from this point on the friendship is not developed further, although its continuation is understood. Queequeg is too alien to be assimilated and identified with Ishmael, even by means of an ideal such as that of Montaigne. His foreignness is never domesticated, and his resolute difference keeps their relation from becoming too intimate—or cannibalistic. Intense and overly complicated connections are in the end nooses, as Ishmael suggests when he notes, "All men live enveloped in whale-lines. All are born with halters round their necks" (372). For one man to be bound and identified too closely with another could prove suffocating and silence all voice and communication.

At the end of the book, Ishmael and Queequeg are divorced by death rather than romantically united by it, as Dante's famous couple is. It is Ahab and his silent partner, Fedallah, who in death are not divided, but share one end in the fulfillment of the prophecy that bound their fates together. At the fulfillment of his quest, moreover, Ahab's whale-line literally turns into a noose that strangles him as it ties him rigidly to the beast he has hunted. He becomes bound in complete identity to his shadow and the whale because he refused to accept less complete connections with others. As his self-expansion turns into reduction, he curses all reliance upon real others that undermines his illusion of autonomy. He is the fulfillment of Ben Jonson's ideal image of the self as an essential, internal, and impenetrable being that is freed from dependence on all external properties; appropriately for a sailor, he draws upon the imagery of *Robinson Crusoe* and sees every man is an island. As a result, Ahab sets himself up as an insular, centered ego surrounded by an alien watery circumference to which it is related only by antagonistic identification. On the last day of the chase, his head becomes the isolated center of a circle described by Moby-Dick. In the end, center and circumference are identified, restoring Jonson's ideal image for the individual in a truly gothic way, when Ahab's rapacious ego is swallowed up.

It is Ishmael, *"floating on the margin"* (724) of the destruction, who gradually comes to a *"vital centre,"* Queequeg's coffin, which proves to be his lifeline. Ishmael creates a new version of Jonson's ideal of the self as a centered circumference, as he fluctuates, sometimes wildly, between the two extremes. He often asserts his self-grounding on his own "insular Tahiti" (364), claiming that "amid the tornadoed Atlantic of my being, do I myself still for ever centrally disport in mute calm" (499). He advises his readers to imitate the well-insulated whale, securely wrapped in his blubber: "Do thou, too, live in this world without being of it" (401)—a comically parodic reference to the medieval concept of man as *alienus*, exile in this world, who while inside it remains somehow outside or, in the stoic version particularly, above it. Yet Ishmael is aware of the difficulty simply of stoically preserving an untouched ego. Pip, who falls overboard and becomes the center of waters whose "ringed horizon began to expand around him miserably" (530), undergoes a sea-change that leaves him not melancholy but totally mad. But he is only an extreme example of the individual's inability, like that of the leaking ship, to keep external influences out.

Moreover, Ishmael's own tendency is actually toward self-dissolution. The sea fascinates the hypothetical man on the masthead, who, like Coleridge's lovesick youth, is a projection of the narrator himself, and of his tendency to become one with what he sees through self-annihilation, as "lulled into such an opium-like listlessness of vacant, unconscious reverie is this absent-minded youth by the blending cadence of waves with thoughts, that at last he loses his identity, takes the mystic ocean at his feet for the visible image of that deep, blue, bottomless soul, pervading mankind and nature . . ." (214). The dream of transcendence makes one lose one's balance until, "move your foot or hand an inch; slip your hold at all; and your identity comes back in horror. Over Descartian vortices you hover. . . . Heed it well, ye Pantheists!" (214–15). Remembering the presence of the body is a means of restraining the flights of fancy of the mind into the pantheistic dissolution of differences; here the Cartesian separation of the two has a redeeming effect.

Ishmael has his own visions of being united with all men in a single body by "that democratic dignity which, on all hands, radiates without end from God; Himself! The great God absolute! The centre and circumference of all democracy! His own omnipresence, our divine equality!" (160)—restoring, for a moment at least, the image of the centered circumference to its original owner. With the other members of the crew, he is absorbed into Ahab's infernal version of this vision, becoming submerged for several chapters in the mob that acts as one man. His individual voice is silenced after the experience on the masthead (chapter 35) and resurfaces only when the subject is "Moby-Dick" (chapter 41), as he admits his intense identification with Ahab's quest but begins to separate himself from it. He replaces Ahab's desire to pin the whale down with a harpoon with his own attempt to represent it as scientifically and factually as possible. A later vision of a united community takes a more nonsensical form. In "A Squeeze of the Hand," Ishmael ecstatically foresees an eternity consisting of angelic sperm squeezers, and even cries out for the realization of this heaven on earth: "let us all squeeze ourselves into each other; let us squeeze ourselves universally into the very milk and sperm of kindness" (533). The crazily comic and naughty wordplay (the closest the text can come to releasing erotic energy) makes such a vision, in contrast to the serious and tragic perspective of Ahab, fertilely fanciful.

Moreover, this ludicrous representation of community serves as an antidote to the terrors of dissolution. The madness of Pip becomes the controlled insanity of Ishmael that steers a course between two extremes: complete loss of self in the cannibalistic sea and total insularity. While Ishmael warns us to cling to our own insular Tahitis, "God keep thee! Push not off from that isle, thou canst never return!" (364), the completely isolated ego becomes a barren Encantada, the insular mind of Ahab that feeds upon itself.

Ishmael maintains a balance between these two extremes by means of an expansion and contraction quite different from that of Ahab. From Burton, Melville takes a narrative form that is not a straight and narrow line but rather a crazy flux between opposites. The whale is a large subject to cover, providing "a most congenial theme whereon to enlarge, amplify, and generally expatiate" (579). Ishmael is intent upon "spinning him out to the uttermost coil of his bowels" (579) as best he can, but to do justice to his monstrous subject he must inflate himself:

> Unconsciously my chirography expands into placard capitals. Give me a condor's quill! Give me Vesuvius' crater for an inkstand! Friends, hold my arms! For in the mere act of penning my thoughts of this Leviathan, they weary me, and make me faint with their outreaching comprehensiveness of sweep, as if to include the whole circle of the sciences, and all the generations of whales, and men, and mastodons, past, present, and to come, with all the revolving panoramas of empire on earth, and throughout the whole universe, not excluding its suburbs.

Such, and so magnifying, is the virtue of a large and liberal theme! We expand to its bulk (580).

The phrase "not excluding its suburbs" replaces Burton's "Hoo!" as a means of bringing the soaring imagination down to earth. Comic expansion becomes its own means of deflation and so subverts Ishmael's authority. His claims to credibility become increasingly ludicrous as they become more elaborate, as, for example, when he proudly presents us with the precise measurements of the whale, "copied verbatim from my right arm, where I had them tatooed; as in my wild wanderings at that period, there was no other secure way of preserving such valuable statistics. But as I was crowded for space, and wished the other parts of my body to remain a blank page for a poem I was then composing—at least, what untatooed parts might remain—I did not trouble myself with the odd inches; nor indeed, should inches at all enter into a congenial admeasurement of the whale" (576). Such crazy details, triumphantly presented as absolute proof of the truth of his claims, suggest that Ishmael may be mad, or at best a dubious authority.

Ishmael presents his own body, however, as a part of his characteristic attempt to ground meaning in fact. The whale's body is captured by being represented—literally carved like the tatoos that also mark the cannibals' bodies—on Ishmael's physical anatomy, which is thus turned into a text. As Cameron has shown, Ishmael keeps returning to images of a corporeal self: of matter, such as food, and to scientific facts. As his own tendency is to be carried away, like the man on the mast, by flights of fancy, he constantly reaches out toward the concrete facts that stubbornly insist upon the existence of an external world beyond the circumference of the self. In his interpretation of reality, he asserts the primacy of the letter.

Like Ahab, Ishmael believes that the physical world is meaningful, for, "some certain significance lurks in all things, else all things are little worth, and the round world itself but an empty cipher, except to sell by the cartload, as they do hills about Boston, to fill up some morass in the Milky Way" (549). But the alternative to a world imagined as a white blank that is both completely full and completely empty—the Coleridgean "O" of both the God who is alpha and omega and also of the abyss—is one filled with a "certain significance," as meaning is tempered by Ishmael's constant lapses into nonsense. Unlike Ahab, Ishmael accepts the uncertainty of interpretation. Looking at the picture at the Spouter Inn, the "boggy, soggy, squitchy picture truly, enough to drive a nervous man distracted," he finds "a sort of indefinite, half-attained, unimaginable sublimity about it that fairly froze you to it, till you involuntarily took an oath with yourself to find out what that marvellous painting meant" (36). But he himself never definitively does; his own opinion that it probably represents a whale is undermined by his tendency to see all reality as very like a whale.[109]

While Ishmael sees whales everywhere, he recognizes that his quest to poetically capture and represent the monster is futile. The whale's anatomy is sung, celebrated, scientifically studied, and anatomized, but it remains ultimately elusive and indescribable. This is not because of its insubstantiality but rather its excessive bodily reality, which makes it more food for thought than can be digested by a single imagination. As Ishmael points out in his discussion of "The Whale as Dish," "the whale would by all hands be considered a noble dish, were there not so much of him; but when you come to sit down before a meat-pie nearly one hundred feet long, it takes away your appetite" (391). The whale represents the material and bodily reality that resists total assimilation into either the mind or the text and is therefore ultimately unrepresentable: "the great Leviathan is that one creature in the world which must remain unpainted to the last. . . . So there is no earthly way of finding out precisely what the whale really looks like. And the only mode in which you can derive even a tolerable idea of his living contour, is by going a whaling yourself; but by so doing, you run no small risk of being eternally stove and sunk by him. Wherefore, it seems to me you had best not be too fastidious in your curiosity touching this Leviathan" (352). The quest for the Leviathan cannot be satisfied by substitutes; unfortunately, however, its fulfillment may involve the annihilation of the questor.

Such is the fate of Ahab, whose quest ends with a resounding conclusion. Ishmael's story, however, is satisfied with more provisional closure and containment. *Moby-Dick* for him is never finished, for it must be retold constantly and reinterpreted by both readers and the narrator himself, who knows that he is questing after something that can never be fully captured in words. For this reason he explains: "I promise nothing complete; because any human thing supposed to be complete, must for that very reason infallibly be faulty . . . it is a ponderous task; no ordinary letter-sorter in the Post-office is equal to it. To grope down into the bottom of the sea after them; to have one's hands among the unspeakable foundations, ribs, and very pelvis of the world; this is a fearful thing" (181–82). Perfection and completion of any human endeavor is an illusory goal; Ishmael's task is less ambitious yet still dangerous, as it involves a probing into the origins of things, a return to a source, which might not only be cannibalistic but, as the bodily imagery here suggests, incestuous. But Ishmael never reaches such a point; even at the very center of the whale herd, witnessing "young Leviathan amours in the deep" (498), he remains an outsider, peering in from the circumference of the circle to a mysterious center he cannot fully apprehend.

At the same time, however, when Ishmael dreams of rest from the weariness of questing and storytelling, it takes the form of a return home to an originating point and the restoration of original identity sought by Odysseus. He wonders: "Where lies the final harbor, whence we unmoor no more? In what rapt ether sails the world, of which the weariest will never weary? Where is the foundling's father hidden? Our souls are like those orphans whose unwedded mothers die in bearing them: the secret of our paternity lies in their grave, and we must there to learn it" (624). We end when we find out where we started from. But for Melville as well as Milton, the discovery of identity can be destructive. To know one's father may be to discover, like Oedipus, that one has become him. Like Milton's Satan, Ahab wants to be an autonomous, self-generated figure, "self-begot, self-rais'd / By our own quickening power" (*Paradise Lost* 5.860–61).[110] He is the revolutionary son who sets himself up against the father only to become ultimately indistinguishable from him, because he accepts and so consolidates the roles and definitions of power of past authorities even as he appears to challenge them. By directly defying this ambiguous power, which he sees incarnated in the large form of Moby-Dick, Ahab only perpetuates it in the vicious circle of binary oppositions.

However, Ishmael, who lays no claim to authoritative interpretation or original identity, takes on the role not of a father but of a son. Acknowledging his debts to others, he allows himself to be adopted by a number of literary ancestors (as well as his whaling predecessors) and finally by the mother figure of the *Rachel*, who offers an alternative to the father sought by Ahab. The orphan and outsider who is willingly subservient to figures of naval and literary authority, who never sets himself up in opposition to Ahab as Ahab sets himself against the whale, suggests an alternative authorial position that avoids rivalry with past creators and offers a different interpretation of identity.

Ishmael's position recalls the strategy of subordination of Milton's Son—a strategy which, however, resulted in the ultimate consolidation of Milton's power and authority in literary tradition. Melville uses a similar tactic with extremely different results, as a way of breaking from Miltonic traditions of poetry and identity. Ishmael's deference to other authorities and to time itself permits a loquacious self-expansion that does not directly get him to a point but, by deferral, creates a space large enough to accommodate a variety of potentially conflicting voices. By avoiding a rigid interpretation of his own tale, he accepts the provisional nature of words and symbols, and admits that signs can potentially contain both divine and demonic meanings. The whale's tail reminds him of "majestic Satan thrusting forth his tormented colossal claw from the flame Baltic of Hell. But in gazing at such scenes, it is all in what mood you are in; if in the Dantean, the devils will occur to you; if in that of Isaiah, the archangels" (485). Such instability of meaning might suggest that all signs are "mere sounds, full of Leviathanism, but signifying nothing" (195). According to Ishmael, Leviathanism is language that lacks an identifiable external referent: it is the empty names of fictitious whales which, like the vacant tombstones of Father Mapple's church—signs which cannot, as they claim, contain real bodies, for they have been lost at sea—are deceptive representations. Ishmael's own desire to base his narrative in concrete facts and material evidence, to control the spirit by asserting the strength of the letter, is part of an attempt to give his story real substance and so keep it from becoming mere Leviathanism.

But the facts are not always as well grounded as Ishmael imagines, as Melville continues to undermine his narrator's credibility by sneaking in a false fact or source. He plays with Rabelaisian enthusiasm on the fact that, in a literary universe made of words, fact and fiction are difficult to differentiate. And, for all its bulk and claims to be grounded in unassailable fact, the book *Moby-Dick* obviously can never contain the real presence of the whale to whom the name refers. As in *Paradiso* 33, where Dante offers a text, the volume that contains the universe, as an alternative to the body of Lucifer who incorporates by consumption, so in *Moby-Dick*, the textual body and that of its ostensible source, the whale's monstrous body, are ultimately differentiated. The name "Moby-Dick" is itself a Leviathanism, for it does not really correspond directly to any visible object in the real world. However, the relation between the two bodies suggests a concept of indirect referentiality, one that is not rigidly definitive and thereby reductive, that recalls the link between Ishmael and Queequeg. The symbol is tied to a source of meaning from which it yet remains distinct; as the referent is an all-consuming whale, this is probably just as well.

In *Moby-Dick*, any return to a source, either of meaning or of the self, is represented as disastrous, a premature apocalypse that is annihilation. In order to avoid incest and cannibalism, the text, like Milton's Son, defers the revelation of its meaning, which is equivalent to that of its identity.[111] For Ishmael there is no final prospect from which "the secret part of the tragedy" (322) can be seen in an apocalyptic revelation of all meaning. With its proliferation of voices and stories, *Moby-Dick* seems to prevent the possibility of a return to a single source. The number of sources complicates the book's genealogy until it becomes like the crazy family tree of whaling that wreaks havoc upon history, syncretizing times and places in the tradition of the Renaissance mythologists who believed, anticipating Coleridge, that all religious systems could be collated. Aware of the ludicrous impossibility of tracing sources (which the gothic represents as a more sinister failure), Melville uses a Rabelaisian method of simultaneously establishing and parodying a convoluted lineage that twists and turns to relate the oriental Vishnu, Greek Perseus, and Christian Saint George. In the process, he manages to invert the usual relation between the literal and the figurative, as the actual enterprise—which the author himself embarked on, and thus on which in some sense the text is based—becomes grounded in a mythological past in which it was founded by fictitious figures.

Melville's own fantasy, which is defined against Ahab's but recalls that of Burton, is to create an anatomy that assimilates all sources in a way that makes impossible the idea of a single originating source. In *Pierre*, published in 1852, a year after *Moby-Dick*, the son's attempt to redeem his dead father leads only to incest and suicide. That text takes as its epigraph the metamorphosis of the thieves in *Inferno* 25.46–78, which itself recalls that of Ovid's Hermaphroditus, which I think Dante "stole" to suggest one possible result of the appropriation and identification of poetic figures. Pierre's kinship system collapses in stages, as his relations become increasingly confused. His mother is his sister, his sister is his lover, and his lover tells him, "thou art my mother and my brothers and all the world, and all heaven, and all the universe to me—thou *art* my Pierre."[112] The name "Pierre" is the incestuous version of the cannibalistic sign "Moby-Dick," for it dissolves the differences between relations. Like *Moby-Dick*, *Pierre* attempts to incorporate different forms and voices. But whereas *Moby-Dick*, whose anatomical model is a grotesque body indeed, is ultimately an encyclopedic, sprawling work whose own form or genre is hard to pin down, *Pierre* attempts a different creation *e pluribus unum*, in which the many are reduced to the individual human body of Pierre. The attempt at a more complete synthesis and sublimation of differences only ends in chaos: the novel never seems quite sure of what it wants to be and finally becomes, like the hermaphrodite, "not double now / Nor only one!" (111).

Whereas *Moby-Dick* represents the suspension of identity, *Pierre* traces its later tragic discovery through the revelation of origins. The attempt to redeem and recreate the father—who, as many critics have noticed, is ultimately Milton's antithesis, Shakespeare—fails as a strategy for writing.[113] But *Moby-Dick* presents the problem differently, as in the earlier work it is Melville's aim not to redeem the father but slyly to eliminate him altogether. His method here deviates crucially from that of Milton, a fact which may reflect their very different relations to their real fathers. Milton's father supported him financially until he was in his early thirties; when Melville was twelve, his father went mad and died—thus completely eliminating himself—so that the boy was forced to take his place in the family and, finally, to go to sea to make money. Whereas Milton found freedom by claiming he could choose his own father, Melville imagines liberation as occurring when one chooses not to have a father at all. Both Ishmael and the whale are represented as fatherless, and the last word of the text is "orphan." The ideal text Melville imagines is a completely autonomous verbal structure cut off from its origins, as he writes, "Would that all excellent books were foundlings, without father or mother, that so it might be, we could glorify them, without including their ostensible authors!"[114]

Such a text could not insist, however, like Ahab or Satan, on its own fallacious originality, but could instead use a number of sources to prevent a single one from turning into too formidable a father. The vulnerability of the orphan emphasized by the gothic to Melville appears as a source of power. While Ahab's egotism ends in reduction, Melville's dependence upon others leads to self-expansion: his narrative, like Burton's, grows by incorporating the host of writers he invites into his story. Unlike Coleridge's work, his text is not passively open, for the assimilation and recreation of internalized material is carefully controlled. By revising previous works, reinterpreting them in ways often quite outrageously beyond their creator's original intentions, Ishmael seems subtly to turn them into prefigurations and types of his own tale. Indirectly, he appears to accomplish what Ahab cannot do: by absorbing the past he gains control over it.

However, Melville deliberately chooses a narrator who is susceptible to outside influences and who often appears to lose control over both himself and his tale. Ishmael dramatizes the continuing fragility of the boundaries between self and other, or a text and its sources, those aliens against which the individual defines itself but which it has taken into and so identified with itself. The boundary of the mind is, furthermore, less definite than that of the body, and though a textual body has physical substance, its material is not confined within its borders but may enter into other textual bodies, as well as minds. In nineteenth-century America, Melville longs for a democratic equality and communion among fatherless brothers who mutually partake not of the flesh but of the word "Moby-Dick," a dream that has its obvious analogues in earlier formulations of communion. What makes Melville different from both Milton and Burton is that he democratically wants to imagine the possibility of maintaining differences between equal brothers without the fiction of a God, a Father, or a transcendent figure beyond the text, such as the author himself, to guarantee those differences.

For Melville, furthermore, spirit and flesh are not completely polarized, as the textual and monstrous bodies are nominally identified by the one name. In that other "eating poem," *The Odyssey*, with which I began (approximately twenty-five hundred years ago), Odysseus's quest turns out to be potentially identifiable with the bodily appetite that is incarnated in the cannibal Polyphemos, even though that bodily appetite threatens to subsume it. Ahab's dream of wholeness may be a projection of the demonic underside of Melville's fantasy, but both quests end in the body of Moby-Dick. In the end, Melville's own ideal can never be completely free from the bodily counterparts that it is bound to throughout the text and that are, ultimately, incest and cannibalism. But it can never be totally identified with them either, and with that lack of total identity it is satisfied.

CONCLUSION

In Which Everything Is Included and Nothing Concluded

> But if ye bite and devour one another, take heed
> that ye be not consumed one of another.
> —Galatians 5:15

> The history of the world, my sweet, . . .
> Is who gets eaten and who gets to eat, . . .
> How comforting for just once to know, . . .
> That those above will serve those down below.
> —Stephen Sondheim, *Sweeney Todd,*
> *The Demon Barber of Fleet Street*

> Eating people is wrong.[1]
> —Flanders and Swann, *The Reluctant Cannibal*

LIKE THE Modern Hiawatha's mittens, oppositions seem infinitely reversible as long as the assumptions upon which they are based remain unquestioned. Undoubtedly the contrast between inside and outside is a useful and necessary one for the negotiation of everyday life in the body; the inability to distinguish between the two is one of the terrors of the gothic and a sign of paranoia. But these are also relative and relational terms, determined by position, not essence. It appears to me, however, that the awareness of a difference between inside and outside easily generates a desire to bridge that gap by getting the outside in, making the alien familiar, the uncanny canny—and therefore ultimately eliminating difference altogether. But, as Aristotle observed, what is outside society is ambiguous, being both potentially super- and sub-human—God, any authoritative transcendental term whose separation is seen as a guarantee of meaning, or an alien whose existence threatens meaning. As a result, the very project of bridging dualisms is viewed with ambivalence, as the loss of externality is potentially the loss of the possibility of significance.

To a certain extent, the story I have been telling, which extends from Homer to here, is one of increasing internalization, a movement toward a world in which everything is imagined as being "inside." This has certainly been the dream underlying the hope of the scientific mastery of nature, as well as various forms of imperialism; it has also been the nightmare underneath the gothic, which acknowledges the more infernal side of incorporation. In order to work toward a conclusion that will bring us into this century and qualify this oversimplified scheme, I would like to look briefly at two modern thinkers whose works I have been drawing on since my introduction, and whom I now would like to discuss as representatives of the modern privileging of "insideness": Sigmund Freud and Northrop Frye. As I began my discussion of texts with the *Odyssey*, the paradigm for all quest-romances, it seems fitting that I should move out of it by looking at two authors, influential for our approaches to literary texts, both of whom incorporate the pattern of romance and its orality into their theories. With Freud, quest-romance is internalized as the story of individual sexual development, a journey, like that of Odysseus, both forward and backward, in which, however, the two directions are no longer reconcilable. For Frye, romance is "the structural core of all fiction,"[2] which he describes in oral terms as an autonomous hunger, an appetite that "is never satisfied with its various incarnations," and so "will turn up again, as hungry as ever, looking for new hopes and desires to feed on."[3] Freud's quest looks back to the perfect identification of self and other in the oral phase, while Frye reads romance as attempting to recapture a lost Golden Age that he associates with childhood innocence, even the "pre-genital period of youth,"[4] for, "The perennially childlike quality of romance is marked by its extraordinarily persistent nostalgia, its search for some kind of imaginative golden age in time or space."[5] Both see internalization as playing a crucial role in the formation of unity and autonomy—of the individual, for Freud, and of both individual and verbal structures, for Frye—and so they offer two models for the process of turning the outside inside, and its consequences.

Freud

Freud's universe is like Ovid's, in which every action is significant. The mind is explicitly imagined as a text, and Freud compares repression to "the omission of words or passages" that causes "the corruption of a text."[6] All action not only reveals some meaning which is behind or underneath it, but is also (as was not the case in Ovid's world) readable with the aid of psychoanalysis. But significance is still a sign of guilt, for as one critic notes, to say that all gestures have meaning is to mean that "they are guilty. . . . Everything has a meaning: the man who forgets something means something by it; the man who makes a mistake in writing is expressing his most secret thoughts; if he arrives at an appointment too early, there is some reason for it; if he arrives too late, that, too, has its deeper meaning."[7] As in the gothic world of Coleridge's Mariner, it is our insignificant actions that give us away by externalizing a deep meaning we are trying to conceal even from ourselves.

As he tries to reveal this inner buried meaning, the psychoanalyst becomes the descendant of the humanist who struggled to restore the corrupt text, and analysis itself becomes a new version of the necromantic metaphor of the revival of buried and dead desires. However, in mental life, as in the gothic, nothing ever really dies, but rather goes underground into the subconscious where it haunts us unless it is once more brought to the surface. The analyst raises Hell, as Freud's quoting of *Aeneid* 7.312 as the motto of *The Interpretation of Dreams* suggests.[8] The lines, "Flectere si nequeo superos, Acheronte movebo" ("if I cannot bend the Higher Powers, I will move the Infernal Regions"), are actually spoken by the wrathful Juno; the analyst is not, as one might expect, Aeneas who descends into Hell to discover secrets about his own identity (as Giamatti suggested the humanist did also in his revival of the text), but rather a supernatural being who has the power to call up and control subterranean psychic forces. He provides a personal apocalypse of our innermost selves, which are buried deep inside us and are inaccessible without his grace. Those who cannot remember the past are condemned to repeat it: it is only when it is resurrected and remembered that the patient can possess a whole, fully integrated ego.[9]

Freud's basic concept of the analytic situation is therefore essentially dualistic, consisting of the strictly separated terms of patient (usually female) and doctor (usually male), the latter playing the role of a transcendent deity who guarantees meaning and the identity of his follower. Yet his "outsideness" is made problematic by the fact that he is in fact involved in a relation and is potentially even susceptible to the countertransference, a threat that Freud, however, can only briefly entertain.[10] Furthermore, like the humanist who assumes the existence of a definitive text that can be recuperated, Freud appears to believe that there is such a thing as a stable and coherent ego that the analyst can restore to integrity. Much psychoanalysis since Freud has imagined differently both the role of the analyst, who is seen as part of a relation rather than an omniscient outsider, and the possible goal of analysis, but has still found in Freud's theories the possibility for these different models.[11] Although Freud clings to the idea of a unified and integral identity, his notion of the subconscious makes the concept questionable. He claims that "Normally there is nothing of which we are more certain than the feeling of our self, of our own ego. This ego appears to us as something autonomous and unitary, marked off distinctly from everything else."[12] But, according to his theory of the formation of identity, one's inner center is an alien, for the self is built out of lost objects of desire that have been introjected as a means of accepting their loss.

In Freud's view, oral incorporation is the basic model for psychic processes, such as introjection, internalization, and incorporation—terms not, however, clearly distinguished in his work—that involve the mental assimilation of external objects which, lost as possessions, become internalized and identified with the self.[13] When one can't *have* one's cake, one has to *eat* it in order to *be* it. As a result, the ego is formed largely by a kind of mental imitatio that has its base in physical digestion. So Freud speaks of the identification with others by which we fashion ourselves as "the assimilation of one ego to another one, as a result of which the first ego behaves like the second in certain respects, imitates it and in a sense takes it up into itself. Identification has been not unsuitably compared with the oral, cannibalistic incorporation of the other person."[14] He notes that the impulse behind this process bears a strong resemblance to the desire for the incorporation of the other's power that has been traditionally associated with cannibalism:

> An interesting parallel to the replacement of object-choice by identification is to be found in the belief of primitive peoples, and in the prohibitions based upon it, that the attributes of animals which are incorporated as nourishment persist as part of the character of those who eat them. As is well known, this belief is one of the roots of cannibalism and its effects have continued through the series of usages of the totem meal down to Holy Communion.[15]

Internalization appears to involve both identification and the assertion of power, as the self absorbs the other's energy in its own interest. Incorporation, further, is involved in the ego's division of the outside world into two opposed poles, in which "good" becomes equated with what is "edible" and "bad" with what is poisonous, as stated in the passage I quoted in my introduction: "Expressed in the language of the oldest, that is, of the oral, instinctual impulses, the alternative runs thus: 'I should like to eat that, or I should like to spit it out'; or, carried a stage further: 'I should like to take this into me and keep that out of me.' That is to say: it is to be either *inside* me or *outside* me."[16]

However, while eating here ideally implies the possibility of choice and control, other forms of internalization threaten the difference between inside and outside: in particular, the internalization of external authority that creates the superego. Freud's superego is both a residue of object-choices and a reaction formula against them, and it therefore places the ego in an uncomfortable double bind, for it simultaneously commands and prohibits identification with authority figures.[17] As in the case of the consumed father of *Totem and Taboo*, what has been internalized is not the power of authority but its force of prohibition. The ego is placed in the power of an alien within, whose internalization makes it easier for it to monitor the ego's thoughts, so that, as Bloom notes, "each of us is her or his own worst enemy."[18]

While Freud describes relations as based upon an oral model, the oral phase is only the first stage in his internalized quest-romance of sexual development, in which a hero (the young ego) struggles to attain his goal (genital sexuality) against a host of temptations (perversions and the desire to prolong early stages of development). With Freud, the quest is now inside us, mapped onto our bodily functions, which become separated into stages, a kind of sexual career that has to be developed in proper order.[19] Because in human beings the achievement of the final aim is postponed with the deferral of sexual maturity in the latency period, the danger of becoming sidetracked increases, and "Every step along this long path of development can become a point of fixation,"[20] if "at any point in the preparatory sexual processes fore-pleasure turns out to be too great and the element of tension too small. The motive for proceeding further with the sexual process then disappears, the whole path is cut short, and the preparatory act in question takes the place of the normal sexual aim."[21] These first phases are means that threaten to become ends in themselves, Freud's version of Circe's island or Coleridge's bower, the pleasant but foreign places, which, if lingered in too long, will prevent the hero from finishing his quest by discovering his "normal"—that is, genital—sexual identity, a discovery that, according to Freud, occurs during the oedipal crisis.

The oral phase is therefore only the first stage in Freud's sexual odyssey. For him, it, like the Golden Age, is originally a state of total identification between self and other, where also the appetites are not yet differentiated: "sexual activity has not yet been separated from the ingestion of food; nor are opposite currents within the activity differentiated. The *object* of both activities is the same; the sexual *aim* consists in the *incorporation* of the object—the prototype of a process which, in the form of identification, is later to play such an important psychological part."[22] In his later works, Freud will follow Abraham in dividing that stage into a preambivalent phase and an oral-sadistic phase.[23] As I mentioned in my introduction, Freud claims that the baby originally has no need to incorporate anything, for it is aware of nothing outside of itself. The discovery that the mother's breast is actually other and separate is the beginning of the sadistic cannibal stage, during which the infant tries to recover and assimilate to itself what has suddenly taken on a threatening life of its own. The oral stage is therefore both a state of primal identity and wholeness, and the point at which the dualism between the self and other, defined basically as eater and eaten, is discovered, introducing both desire and hostility toward the desired object.

As Freud came to realize, moreover, no past experience of satisfaction is ever relinquished by the ego. Sexual development is not a linear passage from one phase to another, but rather an incremental movement, "so that part of the earlier organization always persists side by side with the later, and that even in normal development the transformation is never complete, the final structure often containing vestiges of earlier libidinal fixations."[24] Though the goal of sexual development is genital sexuality, the model for satisfaction is in fact a remnant of the first phase that has been carried along through the later stages. For Freud, the baby at the breast provides a model for the satisfaction of all desire: "No one who has seen a baby sinking back satiated from the breast and falling asleep with flushed cheeks and a blissful smile can escape the reflection that this picture persists as a prototype of the expression of sexual satisfaction in later life."[25] As adults we sense that our present relation to the world around us is merely "a shrunken residue of a much more inclusive—indeed all-embracing—feeling which corresponded to a more intimate bond between the ego and the world about it,"[26] and which we strive to recapture. Sexual development is Freud's version of the fall from communion, as "originally the ego includes everything, later it separates off an external world from itself."[27] To be aware of individual identity is to be aware of a loss of a greater corporate, even grotesque, identity, the symbiosis with the mother, a loss that the individual never fully accepts. As a result, the end of the quest is once more a return to its beginning, as "There are thus good reasons why a child sucking at his mother's breast has become the prototype of every relation of love. The finding of an object is in fact a refinding of it."[28]

However, the tension between the aims of the two phases creates a situation in which the quest can never be fulfilled. The oral phase provides a model for complete identification that genital sexuality, with its less absolute form of incorporation, cannot achieve. As the quest moves forward, it still looks backward, and end and beginning can never be completely united. Furthermore, Freud's own commitment to the ideal of genital sexuality and the importance of the father makes his attitude to orality ultimately ambivalent. Orality remains on the margin of his theories, a place of origin and a metaphor for psychic processes that he does not fully explore. His center of attention is the oedipal crisis, described as a form of sublimation that leads to the establishment of separate individual identity through the detachment from the mother and turning to the father. Orality, though the model for the formation of identity, becomes implicitly identified with regression to an earlier stage of development that threatens both individual identity, with its normal genital sexuality, and civilization itself.

In Freud's description of the instincts, however, men appear generally to strive backward rather than forward, for "*an instinct is an urge inherent in organic life to restore an earlier state of things* which the living entity has been obliged to abandon under the pressure of external disturbing forces."[29] Change comes from *outside*; on its own, life would not develop, but would strive to repeat the past and finally return to its original state of being, as Odysseus struggled to return home. Essentially, therefore, "*the aim of all life is death*,"[30] the perfect peace and harmony that is the absence of all external excitation and stimulation. It is only because the direct path backward is obstructed by resistances that the instincts allow us to move forward, "though with no prospect of bringing the process to a conclusion or of being able to reach the goal."[31]

The death instinct, *Thanatos*, attempts to restore the original state of inertia that is nonbeing; when Freud comes to describe the conservative element in its antithesis, *Eros*, the erotic drive, he turns to the story of the *Symposium*.[32] Later, he will claim that the force of Eros "strives to make the ego and the loved object one, to abolish all spatial barriers between them."[33] Therefore: "At the height of being in love the boundary between ego and object threatens to melt away. Against all the evidence of his senses, a man who is in love declares that 'I' and 'you' are one, and is prepared to behave as if it were a fact."[34] Erotic desire aims for the complete identification of self and other associated with the oral phase. But a similar sensation and loss of identity is experienced in certain phobias and in religious mania, and sexual intercourse exposes the illusion, for in it bodies are not completely and permanently incorporated as one, and "something in the nature of the function itself . . . denies us full satisfaction and urges us along other paths."[35]

If sex cannot satisfy by recreating the symbiotic union between mother and child, human beings must still find some satisfaction on earth. The result of sexual frustration is the sublimation of erotic desire into culture, which owes its existence to our eternal dissatisfaction. Freudian sublimation involves the transformation of sex into art, and yet the ultimate opposition of the two: "For what motive would induce man to put his sexual energy to other uses if by any disposal of it he could obtain fully satisfying pleasure. . . . It seems, therefore, that the irreconcilable antagonism between the demands of the two instincts—the sexual and the egoistic—have made man capable of ever greater achievements."[36] Although sexual energy is channeled into art, Freud, like Ben Jonson, sees the latter as ultimately detached from and opposed to its material base. For this reason Bloom compares Freud's sublimation to metaphor, in which "Poetry is the outside term, and sexuality the inside one"[37] and which, like all metaphors for Bloom, creates a situation represented by "hopeless dualistic images of inside as opposed to outside."[38] What we desire is the inside part of the trope, the real thing signified; what we get is the outside, the figure, as an unsatisfactory substitute that we never fully accept.

However, as psychoanalysis involves the tracing of the mind to the body and the identification of mental and corporeal instincts, the division between the two antitheses seems less than absolute, as analogy is complicated by contiguity. The implication of Freud's final vision of incremental sexual development is that the oral phase is not succeeded by the oedipal phase, but rather the latter is added to the former. Oedipal rivalry is itself oral cannibalism, as the story of *Totem and Taboo* makes clear. The representative of authority and separateness, the Father, is an outside alien who must be brought inside and his power appropriated, lest it retaliate from within.

But this internalization of the Father is analogous to the internalization of the analyst himself, the transcendent deity whose externality is the only guarantee of meaning. The fact that the analyst remains *outside* the treatment assures for Freud the possibility of restoring a stable, coherent ego to the patient, for the separated authority is also the model for the external stimulus that keeps the organism from destroying itself. For Freud, unlike Klein and other of his followers, identification is not only regressive but ultimately murderous of both identity and meaning, as it dissolves the inside/outside boundaries that are necessary for the restoration of the unified self. Reparation, even sublimation, through internalization is therefore just cleverly disguised repetition, just as in Christian communion "The very deed in which the son offered the greatest atonement to the father brought him at the same time attainment of his wishes *against* the father. He himself became God, beside, or more correctly, in place of, the father. A son-religion displaced the father-religion."[39] Communion is really cannibalism, as it is "a fresh elimination of the father, a repetition of the guilty deed."[40] For Freud, unlike Tork and Abraham, there can be no real difference between internalization, metaphor, and incorporation, antimetaphor. From this perspective, the deference of Milton's Son is merely the most subversive and clever kind of cannibalism of all, in which the Son identifies with the will of his Father in order to subsume it finally to his own.

Freudian sublimation, therefore, cannot free mental processes from their bodily bases, but only disguise them and make them more palatable. As Van den Berg notes, Freud's quest for meaning remains bound to a past to which it looks back as a point of origin, a source that can explain a present situation.[41] His story, like that of the *Metamorphoses*, is one of a continuing fall, in which meaning and events are overdetermined by an original sin: the eating of the Father, who is both alien and authority. The consequence of that fall is the end of any principle of transcendence or psychoanalytical redemption that could achieve closure, as the past repeats itself in a gigantic quest-romance that is ultimately, as Freud discovered analysis to be, interminable.

Frye

For Northrop Frye, internalization is the means of asserting human freedom through the sublimation of nature into art. Frye's ideal appears as a reassertion of Renaissance humanism revised through the odd combination of Blake and Oscar Wilde.[42] While appropriating the topos of the world as text, he turns the relation between nature and art, which in the Renaissance was more commonly defined as that between object and its mirror reflection, into one between form and content, outside and inside, and ultimately eater and eaten, for: "Literature does not reflect life, but it doesn't escape or withdraw from life either: it swallows it. And the imagination won't stop until it's swallowed everything. No matter what direction we start off in, the signposts of literature always keep pointing the same way, to a world where nothing is outside the human imagination."[43] The chief aim of Frye's imagination is to "swallow" whatever is nonhuman—and which he therefore assumes to be formless—in order to make it human and comprehensible by giving it an anatomy, either physical or textual, as in the case of Frye's own *Anatomy*. The imagination desires an apocalyptic revelation of "a world of total metaphor, in which everything is potentially identical with everything else, as though it were all inside a single infinite body."[44] For Frye, metaphor, which, as Bloom's reading of Freudian sublimation reminds us, often appears as the trope of dualism and the suspicious separation of inside and outside, becomes the means for the transcendence of dualisms. It unites different works so that all literature can be imagined as a single all-inclusive anatomy, made up of various works that "interpenetrate" to create an autonomous literary universe.

Frye's model for this autonomous verbal structure of literature is the Bible, which he reads as "a gigantic myth, a narrative extending over the whole of time from creation to apocalypse, unified by a body of recurring imagery that 'freezes' into a single metaphor cluster, the metaphors all being identified with the body of the Messiah, the man who is all men, the totality of *logoi* who is one Logos, the grain of sand that is the world."[45] For Frye, the textual body of the Bible itself is analogous to the physical body of Christ, the one unique individual who is also a corporate body in whom all human beings meet in the transcendence of racial, class, and sexual differences: "There is neither Jew nor Greek, there is neither bond nor free, there is neither male nor female: for ye are all one in Christ Jesus" (Galatians 3:28).[46] The anatomies of the Bible and of Christ provide Frye with models for identity in which individuality appears to be transcended through metaphorical relations.

Frye is aware of the problem of the heterogeneity of the Bible and the question of its authorship but is relatively unconcerned with such problems. What is important for him is the fact that the Bible has been read and been influential as a unity. This is not the unity of authorship that is produced with the foregrounding of the individual author, in which coherence and meaning are guaranteed through the existence of a single controlling mind outside of the text, for the idea of the author has no place in Frye's reading of the Bible. Instead he believes that "It is futile to try to distinguish what is 'original' in the Bible, the authentic voices of its great prophetic and poetic geniuses, from the later accretions and corruptions sometimes alleged to surround them. The editors are too much for us: they have pulverized the Bible until almost all sense of individuality has been stamped out of it."[47] The unity of the Bible lies in its internal structure, created by metaphors. In fact, metaphor as the central means of Frye's fable of identity is derived largely from its role as the controlling mode of biblical thought. From the Bible, Frye derives also the binary oppositions of apocalyptic and demonic imagery that he applies to the secular scriptures. The former represents the world we desire and construct; the latter, the world we see and experience. Each of these worlds can be imagined also as a single body: the body of Christ of which all men are members, and the body of Lucifer that incarnates the tyranny of the natural world surrounding and oppressing man. Furthermore, each of these anatomies is defined by a method of incorporation and identification. The apocalyptic union of all men is represented in sexual imagery as "the 'one flesh' metaphor of two bodies made into the same body by love,"[48] and in vital terms as communion, the apocalyptic absorption of the flesh and blood of a God-man, which is the most simple and vivid image for the process of civilization, "where man attempts to surround nature and put it inside his (social) body."[49] More generally, it is represented through metaphor itself, which for Frye is the most radical means of identification. The demonic versions of these metaphors are hermaphroditism, incest, and cannibalism, which for Frye act as kinds of "antimetaphors."

As the Bible provides Frye with the paradigm for the body of literature in which different works form a coherent and unified system organized internally through metaphor, so the role of the critic is like that of the pulverizing biblical editor: the homogenization of authorial voices. Although Frye seems to prefer the Bible's "artificial" creation myth, in which the universe is created by an external artist with an Aristotelian sense of structure, to earlier "natural" creation myths that suggest the organic birth and development of a world without beginning or end,[50] his own vision of literature assumes the existence of an autonomous structure organized from within itself with little need for human aid. All literature, not merely romance, exists somehow independently of its various incarnations, a reality that precedes its appearances. It "shapes itself, and is not shaped externally,"[51] forming "a total body of vision that poets as a whole are entrusted with, a total body tending to incorporate itself into a single encyclopaedic form."[52] While for Frye, who here seems to adhere to the classical identification of *mater* with matter, nature is always the mother of a poem, the poet is not the father but merely a midwife, who is "responsible for delivering it in as uninjured a state as possible, and if the poem is alive, it is equally anxious to be rid of him, and screams to be cut loose from all the navel-strings and feeding-tubes of his ego."[53] The real father is a kind of secularized Holy Ghost: "the true father or shaping spirit of the poem is the form of the poem itself, and this form is the manifestation of the universal spirit of poetry."[54] Like Melville, Frye wants to eliminate an identifiable father, any principle of authority or source that can be located outside the literary system. The poem becomes an ideal orphan related only to the siblings who are other poems by the fact that all speak with the voice of Frye's divine ventriloquist, who is literature itself.

Like Coleridge's description of truth as a divine ventriloquist, Frye's elimination of the individual ego, which he dismisses from imaginative creation as an interfering nuisance, prevents the quarrels among poets that originate in egotism and ensures the continuity of tradition and the stability of the literary system. Unlike that of Bloom, Frye's vision of poetic influence is basically benign. One poet does not really influence a later one, for both are seen as existing simultaneously within a single tradition, defined spatially as an anatomy, of conventions and genres. The synchronic body of literature is big enough to accommodate all authors at once, so that writers do not have to push each other out in order to make room for themselves, to eat or be eaten, as they do in Bloom's less happy and diachronic family romance of literary relations. Although Frye does admit a degree of personal confrontation in literature—revealed in metaphors "suggesting a kind of poetic incarnation" that takes literature "through a process of absorption followed by misunderstanding, that is, establishing a new context"[55]—this assimilation and reincarnation is undergone in the service of the continuity of a tradition in which nothing is ever lost or relinquished. For Frye, as for Freud, the past is carried forward into the present; for Frye, however, the two can harmoniously cohabit. Like Burton's, his vision is incremental, absorbing everything, discarding nothing, and working against time in order to bring all art together in a body that offers a simultaneous presence and plenitude, a literary apocalypse that may be accessible at any time.

While art absorbs everything, as in Jonson's masque it, too, must finally be internalized. The devaluation of the poets' individuality leads to a focus on the reader or critic and on literature as an internal experience that emphasizes consumption over production. According to Frye, "the strength and power do not stop with the work out there, but pass into us," for, "the poem is also a power of speech to be possessed in his own way by the reader, and some death and rebirth process has to be gone through before the poem revives within him, as something now uniquely his, though still also itself."[56] Like Burton, Frye argues that one can possess the past without consuming it or affecting its substance.

In contrast to Freud, therefore, Frye formulates a quest-romance whose goal is total identification, the incorporation of everything within a single anatomy, that is foreshadowed by his own *Anatomy*. He attempts to describe a world totally inside the imagination: "it is how the world looks after the ego has collapsed. The 'outside' world disappears, but it does not disappear into the 'inside': that kind of metaphor has been left far behind."[57] Yet metaphor, the trope dependent on a difference between inside and outside, seems less qualified to be a means of transcending this dualism than of perpetuating it. For Frye, the crucial difference between the apocalyptic body of Christ, the one man who represents us all, and that of Lucifer, the Leviathan, or any totalitarian dictator who claims to represent the members of his political body, is that in the first case the metaphor can be reversed: "from a metaphor of integration into a wholly decentralized one, in which the total body is complete within each individual. The individual acquires the internal authority of the unity of the Logos, and it is this unity that makes him an individual."[58] Inside and outside can trade places; although the dualism is not actually transcended, the poles are prevented from being completely set and determined by the construction of a reversible relation. In the body of Lucifer, however, inside and outside are rigidly, and therefore antagonistically, opposed.

But Frye's own divisions seem less flexible than his ideal, as his own focus remains on an inside finally separated from what is outside. The difference between Christ and Lucifer is also that between what Frye, following Blake, refers to as "The Real Man, the Imagination" and the natural man or Selfhood, which "must be annihilated before the true Self can appear."[59] Frye's division of these inner and outer selves, connected also with his Kantian aesthetics, recalls Ben Jonson and his detachment of art from the material motives and the body even as he tries to formulate it in terms of an anatomy.

As his imagery suggests, Frye's imagination is essentially oral, and like Freud's infant it works dialectically, "separating what is wanted from what is not wanted."[60] He connects the construction of apocalyptic and demonic poles with Christianity's "dialectical habit of mind that divides the world into those with us and those against us"[61]—a method of differentiation no more sophisticated than that of Freud's infant, who defines good and evil according to what can and cannot be assimilated to the self. In his critique of Frye, Frederic Jameson traces the black/white figuration of romance to the completely relative terms of self and other, and notes that the latter is not feared because he is evil, "rather he is evil *because* he is Other, alien, different, strange, unclean, and unfamiliar."[62] In Frye's description of the opposition between art and nature, art—the mind, imagination and principle of order—is surrounded by an outside nature that is chaotic and formless. The apocalypse of the imagination involves the complete reversal of the world of sense experience, as "nature becomes, not the container, but the thing contained."[63] The inside term must internalize the outside, not only in order to free itself, but in order to free the outside, which through sublimation achieves a human form.

This is the language of modern science, which Frye wishes to appropriate for criticism, and which goes back to the Socratic method of divide and conquer, in which a dualism is isolated as justification for subsuming one term by another.[64] Despite Frye's claim that, for him, "Identity is the opposite of similarity or likeness, and total identity is not uniformity, still less monotony, but a unity of various things,"[65] his own incremental vision seems to strive toward the breakdown of real differences, which are replaced by a single opposition. While this eliminates the conflict among individual authors that Bloom puts back into literary relations and other modern biblical scholars expose in the Bible, it does so through a rather suspicious form of sublimation. Frye's theory is based on the paternalistic assumption that what is outside needs subsuming, that the natural order is really disorderly and formless, rather than offering a possible alternative order to that of the mind.[66] What appeals to him about the anatomy form is its self-containment: it is the ideal autonomous verbal structure that denies the existence of anything outside. But this means that Frye's hungry imagination is not only saturnine but also a bit of an imperialist: it swallows and appropriates what is outside of itself by a form of colonial discourse, a strategy that identifies criticism not only with melancholy but also with cannibalism.

On the Way Out

I have ended with Freud and Frye partly as a means of showing how the opposition between inside and outside is structured, not only into texts, but also into some of the methods with which we approach these texts. To try to unravel the relationship between inside and outside involves as dizzying reversals as those of Hiawatha's mittens, and is no doubt as futile. My aim is really only to try to point out that there is a relationship operating behind (inside? a metaphor in sheep's clothing?) a number of our basic assumptions about experience and ourselves, and to explore how dualisms depend on a promise of a false transcendence or sublimation, the end of all opposition, which is in fact achieved through the cannibalistic subsumption of one term by the other.

As I have been arguing, images of incorporation or internalization that hold out the hope of transcendence are similar to promises to restore the Golden Age. In England, since Sidney at least, this has been a common expectation of the role of art, as to defamiliarize the familiar has been identified most frequently with its idealization: the tidying up of all the messiness of life. Descriptions of the Golden Age, like those of the New World, are primarily negative: it was a time of no work, no private property, no laws, no clothes, a time different from the present (regardless of when that present is). It can only be imagined through negatives because, finally, the unfamiliar can only be grasped through the familiar, the other by means of the self, just as the mind can only be imagined through analogies with the body. All language is potentially colonial discourse, as in order to make ourselves understood by others we constantly have to make the strange familiar, the uncanny canny. The danger occurs when these analogies are forced to tell a fable of *total* identity, when differences are first pushed into complete antitheses that then meet by being collapsed into total identification.

The opposition between inside and outside is one of the most basic examples of a human desire to impose dualistic structures on experience—to make Miltonic choices and parcel out confusing liminal states into either/or antitheses. Such oppositions seem essential to a biped being, but what this one dramatizes is the tendency of such structures to collapse into monistic identity. This particular antithesis, associated with the aesthetic ideal of taste, offers an illusion of choice, the belief that one can make clear-cut distinctions and control substances while subsuming them to oneself. The black-and-white division that is seen as the essence of taste—the view that things are *either* inside me *or* outside me—presumes a line between self and other as clear-cut as bodily boundaries would seem to suggest. However, not only does actual eating undermine this concept, but the perception of the body as a rigidly defined unit is itself not immutable. For Homer, the body was an aggregate of members whose coherence was not required and was therefore not imagined, and, since Freud, psychoanalysts such as Klein and Lacan have argued that the child's first experience is one of fragmentation, and that the sense of a separate self appears later—for Lacan it is based on the illusion of the mirror stage. To a modern adult, however, the return to a stage before individuation usually appears to involve the loss of a sense of unity that has been achieved with difficulty through individual or cultural development; it therefore belongs to the gothic, in which earlier states come back to haunt us in terrifying forms. So, for example, the Homeric experience of disunified being reappears in a short story by Clive

Barker, "The Body Politic," in which hands rebel against the heads they fed.[67]

The very fact that the body can be symbolic, viewed as a microcosm representing society and the world, indicates that it is caught up in a complicated web of relations in which it is both inside and outside. Boundaries do exist to create differences between persons, but they are less substantial and less easily defined than we, following Descartes, like to imagine. As Terry Eagleton speculates, "Perhaps what is outside is also somehow inside, what is alien also intimate—so that man needs to police the absolute frontier between the two realms as vigilantly as he does just because it may always be transgressed, has always been transgressed already, and is much less absolute than it appears."[68] Translated into a twentieth-century context, Paracelsus's description of the identity between inside and outside, microcosm and macrocosm, with which I prefaced my introduction, seems a source of terror that creates a desire for constant vigilance and control. Psychoanalysis has brought to light what the metaphors for imitatio and the concept of self-fashioning always assumed—namely, that, as Joan Riviere writes, "There is no such thing as a single human being, pure and simple, unmixed with other human beings. . . . other persons are in fact . . . parts of ourselves. . . . We are members of one another."[69] The question is—why does it seem so scary, "as though anything inside one which is not 'oneself' pure and simple is and must be dangerous—or pathological."[70]

One result of the different critiques of binary oppositions with which I began has been a number of recent attempts at "reconstructing individualism," through studies of the various factors that have been involved in the construction of the termini designating the modern autonomous individual and his counterpart, the autonomous verbal structure. Much of this effort has come from Marxist writers attempting to expose the strategies of market relations that underlie our assumptions, and from feminists, who see the classical definition of autonomy and its accompanying myth of a return to origins as fantasies of the male individual that are produced by gender divisions.[71] With these various attempts, it seems, as Stephen Greenblatt puts it, "as if our property rights to ourselves had been called into question."[72] The location of individuality and personal identity in possession and ownership, the division of the world into the categories *meum* and *tuum*, and the definition of the self as a form of private property are, however, culturally conditioned. For the feminist Hélène Cixous, the very idea of property and the proper (whose opposite is not only the improper but also the metaphorical) is itself a patriarchal fiction, connected to a fear of expropriation and denial of loss that leads to an oedipal quest for origins in which women do not participate, and which they in fact can subvert.[73]

These different explorations and attempts to imagine an alternative individualism and model for relations suggest that the imposition of coherence, unity, and autonomy on both the self and the world through a preliminary formation of dualistic relations that ultimately can be neatly resolved is becoming acknowledged as an inadequate means of dealing with experience. This is obvious, too, in the world of literary systems, where a tendency of criticism until recently has been to "make sense" in a way that meant, as Rabelais foresaw, plugging up all the textual gaps and holes. It is not just the melancholy mind, nor even the critical one, that wants to idealize and smooth over differences. As Derrida has shown, it is the tendency of the Western tradition, steeped in metaphysics, "to make the end coincide with the means, create an *enclosure*, make the definition coincide with the defined, the 'father' with the 'son'; within the logic of identity to balance the equation, close the circle."[74] This is a desire to tell a story of loss followed by an anticipated total recovery, a narrative uroboros that circles back to its beginning, in which all lost objects are recuperated and incorporated through a *coincidentia oppositorum*. But the best image for this succession and continuity that is potentially sheer tautology might be Ovid's phoenix, the father who is his own son and heir. The focus on continuity may be a perpetuation of the Augustan emphasis on inheritance, the preservation of property and the past without change. Behind it, too, seems to be the belief that the present can be explained by the past, an effect by a cause, and a text by its author and source—which tends to end up meaning that the present is bound to the past. These notions are all related; as Edward Said notes, "the unity, or integrity, of the text is maintained by a series of genealogical connections: author-text, beginning-middle-end, text-meaning, reader-interpretation, and so on. Underneath all these is the imagery of succession, of paternity, of hierarchy."[75]

However, Derrida and others have helped to make us aware of how one of the most essential "properties" of man undermines this myth: language. We cannot use words simply to express some prior, inner subject, because the self is not separate from language. Nor is it identical with it, for language is precisely what cannot be completely appropriated as private property; as Bakhtin writes:

> language . . . lies on the border between oneself and the other. The word in language is half someone else's. It becomes "one's own" only when the speaker populates it with his intention, his own accent, when he appropriates the word, adapting it to his own semantic and expressive intention. . . . And not all words for just anyone submit easily to this appropriation, to this seizure and transformation into private property: many words stubbornly resist, others remain alien, sound foreign in the mouth of the one who appropriated them and who now speaks them; they cannot be assimilated into his context and fall out of it; it is as if they put themselves into quotation marks against the will of the speaker. Lan-

guage is not a neutral medium that passes freely and easily into the private property of the speaker's intentions; it is populated—overpopulated—with the intentions of others. Expropriating it, forcing it to submit to one's own inner intentions and accents, is a difficult and complicated process.[76]

For Derrida, it is writing, traditionally opposed to speech as a debased and secondary form of communication, that is especially transgressive in its breaking down of the boundaries between inside and outside. Although "writing, the letter, the sensible inscription, has always been considered by Western tradition as the body and matter external to the spirit, to breath, to speech, and to the logos. And the problem of soul and body is no doubt derived from the problem of writing from which it seems—conversely—to borrow its metaphors," like all oppositions between inside and outside the relation is more contorted, as "the meaning of the outside was always present within the inside, imprisoned outside the outside, and vice versa."[77] What Derrida is interested in is precisely not the setting up of termini between the two, but rather an investigation of the margins that separate and identify them, and the notions of limits and self-containment: "we are less interested in breaking through certain limits, with or without cause, than in putting in doubt the right to posit such limits in the first place. In a word, we do not believe that there exists, in all rigor, a Platonic text, closed upon itself, complete with its inside and outside. Not that one must then consider that it is leaking on all sides and can be drowned confusedly in the undifferentiated generality of its element."[78] The opposition between a tightly sealed text or individual and a leaky, even shipwrecked, one fallaciously suggests that the boundaries between inside and outside can only be either rigid and absolute or nonexistent. The fact that for Derrida there is no definitive *outside* to a text[79] means that we have to redefine what the termini are, first of all by rethinking classical notions of referentiality in which what is inside the text refers to something outside, whether reality or the author's mind. Representation, both literary and political, can itself be a myth of fall and return in which a signifier leads back to a transcendental signified; in place of such myths, Derrida offers the processes of *différance*, dissemination, supplementation, by which he attempts to avoid the simple sublimation and subsumption of differences.

I would like to end by circling back to my beginning, not to create a perfect enclosure, but in order to refer indirectly at last to works that, while central to my thought, remain outside of my anatomy—the things I cannot incorporate, but that seem to me to offer the beginnings of a way out. I have said that although Freud's oral phase of identification plays an important role as a model for psychic formation, in his writings it is generally marginalized, turned into a mere metaphor, in favor of a focus on the oedipal crisis of separation which he sees as determining individual identity.

In my analyses of different texts, I have referred frequently to the works of Melanie Klein who, revising Freud, pushed the crucial point of identity formation back into the oral phase. During the writing of this book, I became increasingly interested in Klein's studies, which gave me a context within which to work·out my own ideas on orality and, particularly, to explore the significance of the fact that the first relation is that between eater and eaten. Klein's work has been less influential than Freud's, partly because it is secondary, and partly perhaps because her focus on the significance of the mother rather than of that of the father seems less acceptable to a male-dominated tradition. But her work is becoming increasingly important, especially in relation to feminist revisions of Freud. I was only half joking when I said in my preface that I want to do for cannibalism what Freud did for incest; moreover, I am not alone.[80] Recently, there has been an increase in interest in the oral stage (which feminist revisions of Freud especially, following Klein, shift from periphery to center), in cannibalism itself, in female body images, and in the relation between women and food—a cluster of ideas, all of which are related (though, one hopes, not necessarily incestuously).[81] Women are traditionally associated with food; as Caroline Walker Bynum has noted, one obvious reason for this is that that is how we, both men and women, first encounter them, a fact that also makes it easy to identify women with production and men with consumption.

The interest in the oral phase of development has resulted in increased attention to the role the mother plays in the infant's maturation, which has coincided with other studies on the perception of women in different cultures. Women occupy a marginal place in society, occupying the boundary between nature and culture; like Derrida's writing, they unsettle the line between inside and outside.[82] According to Cixous, woman "crosses limits: she is neither outside nor in, whereas the masculine world would try to 'bring the outside in if possible.' "[83] Both Cixous and Julia Kristeva identify the "masculine" with the setting up of binary oppositions, which the "feminine" subverts by failing to settle into either/or categories. Whereas the male, as the model for the modern individual, is seen as representing unity, the second sex that, as Irigary describes it, is in many ways "not one," is associated with duality and therefore duplicity.[84] The female body is seen as transgressive, a naturally grotesque body that is always exceeding itself, blurring the distinctions between itself and the world outside, breaking down property lines by its fluidity, and so suggesting the simultaneous construction and dissolution of identity.[85] The female appears as a confusing collapsing of opposites, and therefore a highly ambivalent primal figure uniting antithetical senses. In order to reaffirm the distinctions they seem to threaten, women are usually commonly parceled out into the antithetical stereotypes of virgin and whore.[86] The misogyny underlying the Western tradition depends on a sexist version of colonial discourse and is connected with a view of women as outsiders, aliens within society who must be controlled, as they are duplicitous (a characteristic also applied to wily, untrustworthy foreigners). The female body is a subversive *mons veneris* that must be turned into a *hortus conclusus*, a piece of nature to be ordered and fenced in so that what should be private property is not held in common. Furthermore, as the basic function of binary oppositions is to be reductive, the sexual difference between male and female easily aligns itself with man/nature, mind/matter, and so easily allies itself with theological and philosophical discourse. So, whereas man is treated in terms of substance, woman is seen as property (providing philosophical grounds for defining women as possessions), belonging to the world of appearances. This set of identifications makes women analogous to metaphor, the trope that polarizes appearance and reality, and to rhetoric, ambiguity, and all language that is somehow excessive and potentially deceitful.[87] After all, women not only wear makeup but also talk too much.

As recent studies such as those of Dorothy Dinnerstein, Nancy Chodorow, and Jessica Benjamin have shown, the fact that women "mother"—that is, raise children—produces a deep ambivalance toward women on the part of both sexes. The development of the modern introverted family structure has also meant that the first relationship and object of desire becomes overdetermined, because the mother appears as an all-powerful goddess, both encouraging and threatening the infant's emerging identity. The mother's body is the paradise that is lost when the infant begins to realize its own separate identity. As the traditional association of the female body with the hortus conclusus suggests, women become stereotyped for men as Paradises Lost out of which, however, and in direct antithesis to which, male identity is formed.

But obviously the relationship to this ideal lost world is different for women. Recent studies of the development of the sexes, which correct Freud's (not to mention Aristotle's) assumption that the male identity is the norm from which the female deviates (a premise scandalously false at a biological level), describe women in terms of continuity with the mother, and men in terms of discontinuity.[88] While male sexual identity is achieved through the discovery of sexual difference and the need to turn from the mother to the absent father who represents separation, female development and discovery of sexual identity involves a continuing identification with the first love object because both are female. As a result of this, women tend to develop a less rigid sense of ego boundaries than men, and a more fluid sense of the relation between the self and the world outside.

The result of this asymmetry of development is the production of the sexual binary opposition, the couple, so alienated and different from one another that they can only meet, and then incorporate, when one subsumes the other. So Cixous sees the basic opposition as "a couple posed in op- position, in tension, in conflict . . . a couple engaged in a kind of war in which death is always at work," which reveals the truth that although bi- nary oppositions are seen to produce meaning, "while meaning is being constituted, it only gets constituted in a movement in which one of the terms of the couple is destroyed in favor of the other."[89] Furthermore, as autonomy and relatedness, separation and dependence, become totally op- posed and identified with rigid sexual stereotypes, the former becomes imagined as an absolute alienation that is ultimately self-alienation, and the latter as regression, a return to a Golden Age that involves, for the male, the loss of sexual identity. So, for Coleridge, the only imaginable alterna- tive to solipsism is self-dissipation—and ultimately the extremes meet.

The traditional association of women with narcissism, as well as their identification with a paradise or hortus conclusus, a closed and self-con- tained space from which the male is excluded through the discovery of his separate sexual identity, suggests a further ambivalence built into the con- cept of autonomy. Autonomy is desirable for a self who wants, as Augus- tine believed we all want, to contain and know everything without in turn being known or contained: to be only a subject and never an object, to eat without being eaten. For such a self, autonomy in the other appears as infernal, similar to the narcissistic self-sufficiency that for both Augustine and Dante parodies the God who, for them (as later for Descartes), is the one truly self-contained being.[90] When defined through opposition, the category of the other has to be denied autonomy lest it turn into a cannibal, and so it must be represented as secondary, dependent—and ultimately food.

Like other perceived oppositions, that between man and women can slide into the basic and rigid terms of eater and eaten, which make reci- procity or communion impossible. For writers like Cixous and Kristeva, the subversion of the male/female opposition, which reduces and confines sexuality to a single dualism, is in fact the deconstruction of the traditional Western concept of identity. The present identification of men with sepa- ration and women with relation is a product of social conditions, in the Western tradition given new weight and authority since the Renaissance, and neither of the two poles is in itself adequate. For one thing, neither total detachment nor total relation is possible. But neither are the illusions of either pole pleasant, as total detachment would involve the consolida- tion of all differences as absolute laws of separation leaving the self totally isolated, while total relation would be the dissolution of all differences, which simply washes away any notion of a self. In either case, the very notion of a "self" becomes meaningless through either lack of or too much relation. At their most extreme points, both antitheses are cannibalistic, as, like all binary oppositions, they collapse into each other.

For Cixous, the mean between sexual opposition is an ideal bisexuality, which she claims is different from the emblem of the hermaphrodite and defines as "being 'neither out nor in,' being beyond the outside/inside opposition," and "the possibility of extending into the other, of being in such a relation with the other that I move into the other without destroying the other."[91] Here, however, she sounds rather like Northrop Frye, obscurely promising an end to dualisms. Toril Moi notes her fondness, similar to that of Frye, for fairy tales and myths that describe "a universe where all difference, struggle and discord can in the end be satisfactorily resolved."[92] For Moi, this suggests a desire for plenitude and an inability to accept loss that lead Cixous to fantasize a return to Lacan's Imaginary, a seductive and sirenlike realm which, like Freud's oral phase and Frye's romance, "seems to promise an entire spectrum of fulfilments: identity, integrity, harmony, tranquillity, maturity, selfhood."[93] And, as Stephen Greenblatt has shown, "empathy," the identification with the other, which is allied to the Odyssean talent for improvisation and the "ability to insert oneself into the consciousness of another," can be used as a weapon against the other as well, a draining of its difference.[94] All ideals of identification border on colonial discourse, in which the inside/outside opposition is not escaped but covertly reversed.

Evelyn Fox Keller argues for a different vision of the mean between extremes, claiming first that: "Autonomy too sharply defined, reality too rigidly defined, cannot encompass the emotional and creative experiences that give life its fullest and richest depth. Autonomy must be conceived of more dynamically and reality more flexibly if they are to allow for the ebb and flow of love and play."[95] Criticizing the modern privileging of scientific detachment and objectivity, Keller urges "a more realistic, more mature, and more humble relation to the world in which the boundaries between subject and object are acknowledged to be never quite rigid and in which knowledge of any sort is never quite total."[96] When autonomy is insisted upon and rigidly defined, it is easy to feel frightened of what is outside, of what we don't know but which might know us. But even if one can't contain everything, one can know something and, moreover, be known and contained by others without necessarily being consumed by them. Our boundary lines might be strengthened rather than weakened through the acceptance of the fact that, as well as setting us apart, they let ourselves out and let others in, and that this interchange is not necessarily a horror story.

But what Keller sees as an ideal of dynamic autonomy, a kind of provisional self-definition that combines both identification and separation, requires a delicate balance indeed, in which the desire to control, through knowledge and other means, what is outside the self is itself controlled. While food can be an image for exchanges, it is also a symbol of choice, and the division of experience into either/or experiences. Studies of eating disorders in women, as well as Bynum and Bell's work on medieval female saints (not to mention any observation of an average infant), have made it clear that choosing what one takes in or excludes can be a strategy for control and domination, both of self and others, and at times even a form of sadism. What and how we eat can be used to assert identity and to manipulate others—or both. As Sade's cannibal host, Minski, demonstrates, the enlightened rational being that asserts its autonomy claims to have total power over others that enables him or her to treat the other as food.

The desire to move beyond a view of experience structured around binary oppositions could be seen, therefore, as a refusal to judge the world in terms of eater and eaten. In this more flexible version of reality, not everything can be known and explained, subsumed by the human mind. But this does not mean now, as it did for Augustine and Dante, that a transcendental term guaranteeing human identity and meaning waits *outside* this world as a place for man to return to. One can't go home again for the simple reason that one *is* at home—or as much at home as one is likely to get in a world where alienation is the norm for most people. Reconstructing individualism involves a reconsideration of all systems through which we perceive reality and of our myths about our own autonomy and self-sufficiency. Art might be used not to restore the Golden Age through the resolution of conflict but rather to help us perceive our own world, estranged because overly familiar, through the exposure, not the elimination, of conflict.[97] Rather than caulking up the leaky holes of the vessels that are our physical and textual bodies, art and interpretation may simply enable us to recognize where they are.

A return to an earlier state of existence, a Golden Age of symbiosis, is not regressive because of its identification with the mother's uncannily ambivalent womb/tomb, but because, like the gothic, it involves a confusion of inside and outside which marks ignorance of differences that actually exist rather than the conscious acceptance of them. Attention paid to differences, both in the movement away from the classical structuralist definition of difference as antithesis and in the introduction of studies of peripheral, previously heretical, groups outside the orthodox canon—women, gnosticism, and other "deviant" beliefs and cultures—seems the beginning of a way out. Studies of these marginal groups reveal rather than gloss over the gaps and inconsistencies in Western tradition and destroy the illusion of an unbroken cultural inheritance, a myth of succession that serves to identify father and son, past and present, cause and effect. In relation to the gothic, I suggested that it is the concealment—even idealization—of sources and traditions that produces a world of terror. Perhaps interpretation can at least help us begin to sort out *how* things get inside us in order to free us from pasts we cannot fully remember. What seems to be needed is not a more simplified construct for organizing reality, another transcendental term or master molecule theory that can swallow all the others, but rather more complicated ones, which could cross disciplinary boundaries while acknowledging their existence. To pretend that there are no termini at all is to remain in Lacan's Imaginary or Freud's oral stage of total symbiotic merging: the difficulty is recognizing their existence without turning them into not only laws but even gods. After almost two thousand years, we are still searching for an exit from the closed system of a world very much like that of the *Metamorphoses*—the encylopedic text written during the construction of Western tradition—where the laws regulating exchanges are all the more rigid when they are not known, and where human beings are too easily reduced to food. While most of us would agree with Ovid's Pythagoras that eating people is wrong, like Ovid, we are still not quite sure how to avoid it.

Notes

INTRODUCTION
METAPHORS AND INCORPORATION

1. This first citation is an example of the endnote as a method of incorporation, as it attempts to include all the texts it therefore is able to exclude. These include the works of Claude Lévi-Strauss, Jacques Derrida, Michel Foucault, Roland Barthes; of feminists such as Hélène Cixous, Julia Kristeva, Sherry Ortner, Nancy Chodorow, Evelyn Fox Keller; of Marxists such as Raymond Williams, Mikhail Bakhtin, Terry Eagleton, Peter Stallybrass and Allon White, which will be referred to and so partially incorporated in the notes.

2. See Jacques Derrida, *Dissemination*, trans. Barbara Johnson (Chicago: University of Chicago Press, 1981), 103. Derrida has conducted the broadest critique of the logic of antitheses, which he also sees as involving an oppressive union: "in a classical philosophical opposition we are not dealing with the peaceful coexistence of a *vis-à-vis*, but rather with a violent hierarchy"; *Positions*, trans. Alan Bass (Chicago: University of Chicago Press, 1981), 41.

3. On the apparent authority and solidity of this opposition, see Gaston Bachelard, *The Poetics of Space*, trans. Maria Jolas (Boston: Beacon Press, 1964), 211–31.

4. See Leonard Barkan, *Nature's Work of Art: The Human Body as Image of the World* (New Haven and London: Yale University Press, 1975), for a discussion of literary uses of the body as an image for *discordia concors*, the coherence of diversity in a single organization. My argument has been influenced by anthropological studies of bodily symbolism, and in particular its relation to the construction of boundaries. See especially the works of Mary Douglas: *Implicit Meanings: Essays in Anthropology* (1975; reprint, London: Routledge and Kegan Paul, 1978); *Purity and Danger: An Analysis of the Concepts of Pollution and Taboo* (1966; reprint, London: Routledge and Kegan Paul, 1984); *Natural Symbols: Explorations in Cosmology* (New York: Pantheon Books, 1982).

5. Sigmund Freud, "Negation," in *General Psychoanalytical Theory*, ed. Philip Rieff (New York: Macmillan, 1963), 214–15.

6. "Of Cannibals," in *The Complete Essays of Montaigne*, trans. Donald M. Frame (Stanford, Calif.: Stanford University Press, 1976), 152. All further quotations will be taken from this edition.

7. Max Horkheimer and Theodor W. Adorno, *Dialectic of Enlightenment*, trans. John Cumming (New York: Continuum Publishing Corporation, 1982), 150, 16. See also Hayden White, "The Forms of Wildness," in *The Wild Man Within: An Image in Western Thought from the Renaissance to Romanticism*, ed. Edward Dudley and Maximillian E. Novak (Pittsburgh: University of Pittsburgh Press, 1972), 3–38, who discusses the identification of what is different from or alien to a society with the concepts of madness, heresy, and especially wildness. On the different uses of the image of the body in political theories describing the shape of society and

the relations of its members, see David George Hale, *The Body Politic: A Political Metaphor in Renaissance English Literature* (Mouton, The Hague, Paris: Mouton and Co., 1971).

8. See Melanie Klein, "On the Theory of Anxiety and Guilt," in *Envy and Gratitude and Other Works 1946–1963* (New York: Dell Publishing Co., 1977), 25–42, esp. 30. For discussions of the rhetoric of conquest and "colonial discourse," see: Edward W. Said, *Orientalism* (New York: Vintage Books, 1978); Tzvetan Todorov, *The Conquest of America*, trans. Richard Howard (New York: Harper and Row, 1984); and Peter Hulme, *Colonial Encounters: Europe and the Native Caribbean 1492–1797* (London and New York: Methuen, 1986).

9. The frequency of the charge of cannibalism has caused one anthropologist to argue that the charge itself is simply a strategy never founded on actual events; see W. Arens, *The Man-Eating Myth: Anthropology and Anthropophagy* (New York: Oxford University Press, 1979). For a response to Arens, see Peggy Reeves Sanday, *Divine Hunger: Cannibalism as a Cultural Construct* (Cambridge: Cambridge University Press, 1986), 9–10.

10. Cf. also Derrida, *Dissemination*, 101: "The immortality and perfection of a human being would consist in its having no relation at all with any outside."

11. See the *Oxford English Dictionary*, 5:179. In its rare forms, *incorporation* can mean "to furnish with a body," and "to copulate"; the more usual significances are: "to combine or unite into one body or uniform substance"; "to put into or include in the body or substance something else; to put one thing in or into another so as to form one body or integral whole"; "to take in or include as part or parts of itself (especially of literary material)"; and "to combine or form into a society or organization; *especially* to constitute as a legal constitution." Three basic forms of exchange are therefore possible: the first might be called generally "incarnation," as it involves the investment of something previously formless with a body; the second is a kind of "consubstantiation," in which two bodies join to form a new whole; while the third could be considered as either "sublimation" or "cannibalism"—two related activities, as we'll see—as it involves the subsumption of one body by another. The bodies involved in these various interactions can be personal, textual, or corporate.

12. See Mary Douglas, "Deciphering a Meal," in *Implicit Meanings*, 249–75, for a reading of the structures of various eating taboos, including both the dietary prohibitions in the Old Testament and the contemporary distinction between meals and snacks. The most elaborate analysis of the structure of food symbolism in different cultures appears in the works of Lévi-Strauss; see especially: *Structural Anthropology*, trans. Monique Layton (New York: Basic Books, 1963); *The Raw and the Cooked: Introduction to a Science of Mythology*, vol. 1, trans. John and Noreen Weightman (New York: Harper and Row, 1969); *The Origin of Table Manners: Introduction to a Science of Mythology III* (London: Harper and Row, 1978). See also Jack Goody, *Cooking, Cuisine and Class: A Study in Comparative Sociology* (Cambridge: Cambridge University Press, 1982).

13. Mikhail Bakhtin, *Rabelais and His World*, trans. Hélène Iswolosky (Cambridge, Mass.: MIT Press, 1968), 281.

14. An anthropological interpretation of the relation between eating and inter-

course is offered by Lévi-Strauss who, noting the French pun, claims that "they both effect a conjunction by complementarity" (*The Savage Mind* [Chicago: University of Chicago Press, 1972], 106): it seems to me that in both cases this complementarity is very vulnerable. For discussions that combine psychoanalytical and anthropological approaches to the subject of sex and cannibalism, see the essays in the deliciously titled *Destins du cannibalisme*, ed. J.-B. Pontalis (*Nouvelle Revue de Psychoanalyse*, no. 6 [Fall 1972]). A study of the relation between copulation and cannibalism in literature and the representation of the unmentionable has been made by C. J. Rawson; see "Cannibalism and Fiction: Reflections on Narrative Form and 'Extreme Situations,' " parts 1 and 2, *Genre* 10 (Winter 1977): 667–711, and *Genre* 11 (Spring 1978): 227–313.

15. See, for example, Caroline Walker Bynum, *Holy Feast and Holy Fast: The Religious Significance of Food to Medieval Women* (Berkeley and Los Angeles: University of California Press, 1987), 37.

16. Theodor Reik, *Myth and Guilt: The Crime and Punishment of Mankind* (New York: Universal Library, 1957), 174.

17. Thomas Aquinas, *Summa Theologica*, 3 vols., trans. Fathers of the English Dominican Province (New York: 1947–48), 1.2.27.1; 2.

18. See below, Conclusion.

19. *Ovid's Metamorphoses Englished, Mythologized and Represented in Figures by George Sandys*, ed. Karl K. Hulley and Stanley T. Vandersall (Lincoln: University of Nebraska Press, 1970), 207.

20. Voltaire, *Philosophical Dictionary*, trans. Peter Gay (New York: Harcourt, Brace and World, 1962), 86.

21. See Hayden White, *The Wild Man Within*, 19. On the use of language as a tool in conquest: see Todorov, *Conquest of America*, 76–77 and 190–91; Stephen Greenblatt, "Learning to Curse: Aspects of Linguistic Colonialism in the Sixteenth Century," in *First Images of America: The Impact of the New World on the Old*, ed. Fredi Chiapelli (Berkeley: University of California Press, 1976), 2:561–80.

22. In *Ben Jonson: The Complete Masques*, ed. Stephen Orgel (New Haven and London: Yale University Press, 1969), 411.

23. On the relation of the two meanings of *sapere*, "to taste of, smack of, savour of, have the flavour of" and "to have taste, have discernment, be sensible, be discreet, be wise, discern," see Richard Broxton Onions, *The Origins of European Thought About the Body, the Mind, the Soul, the World, Time, and Fate* (Cambridge: Cambridge University Press, 1988), 61–65. For a brief discussion of the development of the concept in English from physical tasting to aesthetic taste, see Raymond Williams, *Keywords: A Vocabulary of Culture and Society* (rev. ed., New York: Oxford University Press, 1983), 313–15.

24. See Jacques Lacan, "The Signification of the Phallus," in *Ecrits: A Selection*, trans. Alan Sheridan (New York and London: W. W. Norton and Company, 1977), 281–91.

25. Walter Ong, *The Presence of the Word: Some Prolegomena for Cultural and Religious History* (Minneapolis: University of Minnesota Press, 1967), 5.

26. Versions of this widespread myth appear in the teachings of Pythagoras, Mani, and their descendants, and in the Kaballists' figure of Adam Kadmon.

27. Northrop Frye, *Fearful Symmetry: A Study of William Blake* (Princeton: Princeton University Press, 1947), 288.

28. On the neoplatonic use of the image of the hermaphrodite as a symbol for an ideal union between lovers that transcends sexual opposition and the boundaries of individual bodies, see A. R. Cirillo, "The Fair Hermaphrodite: Love-Union in the Poetry of Donne and Spenser," *Studies in English Literature* 1, no. 9 (Winter 1969): 81–95. In alchemy, the hermaphrodite, or *Rebis*, was the figure for the materialization of spirits, a kind of chemical incarnation that is the complement of the sublimation or refinement of matter; see Edgar Wind, *Pagan Mysteries in the Renaissance* (New York: W. W. Norton and Co., 1958), 211–17.

29. *Timaeus* 42c; *Plato: The Collected Dialogues*, ed. Edith Hamilton and Huntington Cairns (reprint, Princeton: Princeton University Press, 1982), 1171.

30. Wind, 135, n. 22. The reference is to Plotinus, *Enneads* V.i. 7.

31. On the two traditions of the Golden Age, see W.K.C. Guthrie, *In the Beginning* (London: Methuen, 1957), 95–96. On the relationship among nostalgia, melancholy, and cannibalism, see below, chapter 4.

32. Patricia Parker, "Anagogic Metaphor: Breaking Down the Wall of Partition," in *Centre and Labyrinth: Essays in Honour of Northrop Frye*, ed. Eleanor Cook et al. (Toronto: University of Toronto Press, 1983), 44.

33. For further discussions of different treatments of the trope, see the essays in Sheldon Sacks, *On Metaphor* (Chicago and London: University of Chicago Press, 1979). For metaphor and the relation between rhetorical control and social control, see also Patricia Parker, *Literary Fat Ladies: Rhetoric, Gender, Property* (New York: Methuen, 1987), 36–53, 97–125.

34. According to Coleridge, these antithetical aims formed the two poles around which the *Lyrical Ballads* were structured; see below, chapter 5.

35. See Terry Eagleton, *Marxism and Literary Criticism* (Berkeley and Los Angeles: University of California Press, 1976), 64–66.

36. Northrop Frye, *Anatomy of Criticism: Four Essays* (Princeton: Princeton University Press, 1957), 136.

37. Jacques Derrida, *Margins of Philosophy*, trans. Alan Bass (Chicago: University of Chicago Press, 1982), 270.

38. Eater and eaten seem also to be behind the binarisms of victor and victim, imitator and model, which are René Girard's revisions of Freud's primal relation; see especially *Violence and the Sacred*, trans. Patrick Gregory (Baltimore and London: Johns Hopkins University Press, 1977).

39. Francis Bacon, *The Advancement of Learning*, ed. G. W. Kitchin (London: J. M. Dent & Sons, 1973), 31.

40. Augustine, *Confessions*, 2 vols. (1912; reprint, Cambridge, Mass.: Harvard University Press, 1977), 7.10; 147. All further quotations will be taken from this edition and will be cited by book and chapter. Page numbers are those of the translation of R. S. Pine-Coffin (Harmondsworth: Penguin Books, 1961).

41. See Sigmund Freud, "The Antithetical Sense of Primal Words" and "The Uncanny," in *On Creativity and the Unconscious*, ed. Benjamin Nelson (New York: Harper Colophon Books, 1958), 55–62 and 122–61.

42. M. I. Finley, *The World of Odysseus* (1954; reprint, Harmondsworth: Penguin Books, 1979), 100.

43. See J. Hillis Miller, "The Critic as Host," in *Deconstruction and Criticism*, ed. Harold Bloom et al. (New York: Seabury Press, 1979), 217–53. I find the figures of the guest and host more useful images for relation than Michel Serres's parasite; see his *The Parasite*, trans. Lawrence R. Schehr (Baltimore and London: Johns Hopkins University Press, 1982). For Serres, exchanges can go only one way and relations are fixed: a sender always sends and a receiver always receives. There can be no real reciprocity, as one cannot exchange words for food: "Solid and wind" (97) are not equivalent. The advantage of the figure of the parasite for Serres is that it upholds differences, disrupts continuity, harmony, homogeneity (126–27). The advantage of the host for me is that, as Serres himself notes (16), it is a model that hides who's who and obscures rather than rigidly defines identity. As a result, it makes possible exchanges between unidentical but complementary substances such as words and food.

44. On classical hearth celebrations, see Numa Denis Fustel de Coulanges *The Ancient City: A Study on the Religion, Laws, and Institutions of Greece and Rome* (Baltimore and London: Johns Hopkins University Press, 1980), 17–48.

45. Miller, "The Critic as Host," 225.

46. See Abraham and Torok, "Introjecter-Incorporer: Deuil ou Melancholie," in *Destins du cannibalisme*, 111–21, esp. 117.

47. Derrida, *Margins*, 76. See also his *Positions*, 43–44, and 96, where he notes that the logic of Hegelian dialectic involves in particular a self-estrangement, or defamiliarization, which is nonthreatening, as a return is guaranteed as a third stage. In Ben Jonson we shall be seeing a similar attempt at a controlled self-projection; see below, chapter 3.

48. See Sanday, *Divine Hunger*, 95–101. For Montaigne, it is precisely the fact that cannibalism is a symbolic act that makes the cannibals appear more civilized than modern men, whose tortures have no meaning; see below, chapter 4.

49. Peter Stallybrass and Allon White, *The Politics and Poetics of Transgression* (Ithaca, N.Y.: Cornell University Press, 1986), 197.

CHAPTER I
CLASSICAL INCREMENTAL VISIONS

1. *The Country and the City* (New York: Oxford University Press, 1973), esp. 9–12. Williams eloquently demonstrates how these two poles, which like nature and culture are similar to outside and inside, have been used as ways of organizing experience that have in fact kept us from confronting experience.

2. Ibid., 297.

3. For a deconstruction of the longing for and attempt to locate a natural unfallen order, see Derrida's reading of Lévi-Strauss and Rousseau, in *Of Grammatology*, trans. Gayatri Chakravorty Spivak (Baltimore and London: Johns Hopkins University Press, 1974), 95–268.

4. Terry Eagleton, *Marxism and Literary Criticism*, 27.

5. Ernst Cassirer, *An Essay on Man: An Introduction to a Philosophy of Human Culture* (New Haven and London: Yale University Press, 1944), 81. Although

here Cassirer is not speaking of the Greek world in particular, his description has been applied to it and provides a useful beginning for a discussion of Ovid.

6. See, for example: Finley, *The World of Odysseus*; R. G. Collingwood, *The Idea of Nature* (London: Oxford University Press, 1945), 3–4, 29–92; George Perrigo Conger, *Theories of Macrocosms and Microcosms in the History of Philosophy* (New York: Columbia University Press, 1922).

7. See Bruno Snell, *The Discovery of the Mind in Greek Philosophy and Literature*, trans. T. G. Rosenmeyer (New York: Dover Publications, 1953), 17–19.

8. See Snell, 5–6, and Finley, 25.

9. See Snell, 44. Coleridge, who was obsessed with questions of personal identity and subjectivity, cites Homer as the example of a poet who lacks all subjectivity; see *Table Talk*, May 12, 1830 (London: George Bell and Sons, 1884), 74–75.

10. Eric A. Havelock, *Preface to Plato* (Cambridge, Mass., and London: Belknap Press, 1963), 198–201 esp.

11. See Finley, 74–107, and also his *Economy and Society in Ancient Greece* (Harmondsworth: Penguin Books, 1981). On the relation between eating and talking in a medieval oral culture, see Dom Jean Leclercq, *The Love of Learning and the Desire for God*, trans. Catherine Misrahi (New York: Fordham University Press, 1961), 89–90.

12. See Finley, *The World of Odysseus*, 64–73, and *Economy and Society*, 233–45. For discussions of the concept of the gift as a model for transaction, see Marcel Mauss's classic, *The Gift*, trans. Ian Cunnison (New York and London: W. W. Norton and Co., 1967), and Lewis Hyde, *The Gift: Imagination and the Erotic Life of Property* (New York: Vintage Books, 1979).

13. See Finley, *The World of Odysseus*, 98–101, and Horkheimer and Adorno, *Dialectic of Enlightenment*, 49.

14. See Snell, 165, who discusses reasons for the Greek abhorrence of lying.

15. All quotations are taken from *The Odyssey of Homer*, trans. Richard Lattimore (New York: Harper and Row, 1965).

16. On the theme of identity and disguise, see Pietro Pucci, *Odysseus Polutropos: Intertextual Readings in the "Odyssey" and the "Iliad"* (Ithaca and London: Cornell University Press, 1987), 76–97 esp.

17. Harold Bloom, "First and Last Romantics," in *The Ringers in the Tower: Studies in Romantic Tradition* (Chicago: University of Chicago Press, 1971), 3.

18. As Terry Eagleton notes, this is also the pattern that Freud reduces to the game of *fort-da*; see *Literary Theory: An Introduction* (Minneapolis: University of Minnesota Press, 1983), 185–86. Derrida reads Freud's scene as itself a very controlled staging of the mastery and recovery of loss; see "Coming into One's Own," in *Psychoanalysis and the Question of the Text*, ed. Geoffrey Hartman (Baltimore and London: Johns Hopkins University Press, 1978), 114–48.

19. Henry Fielding, *Tom Jones* (Clinton, Mass.: Airmont Publishing Co., 1967), 372.

20. On the strictness of the guest-host bond, see Finley, *The World of Odysseus*, 100.

21. See, for example, *The Odyssey*, 1.160 and 250–51, and 13.396.

22. See Finley, *World of Odysseus*, 60, who relates the terror of exile to the construction of society on the model of the *oikoi*, or household.

23. Aristotle, *Politics* 1.2 (1253a), trans. Thomas Alan Sinclair (Harmondsworth: Penguin Books, 1962), 28–29.

24. As Snell notes, Homer's bodily model for knowing is seeing: "The eye, it appears, serves as Homer's model for the absorption of experiences" (18). The analogy between eating and seeing is emphasized by the blinding of Polyphemos.

25. On the role of the belly, *gaster*, in the poem, see also Pucci, *Odysseus Polutropos*, 157–87.

26. See also Pucci, 191–208. The association of the belly with fraud will reappear in Dante, who also draws upon the Pauline tradition, in which Christ and the belly are set up as antithetical sources of motivation identified with true and false discourse; see Romans 16:17–19, and Philippians 3:18–21, and below, chapter 3.

27. Polyphemos is too big to be eaten, but his punishment is also a form of poetic justice in which the analogy between eye and mouth is played upon. When the visual hole is filled by the stick that substitutes for the body of Odysseus destined for the oral cavity, Polyphemos is not fed but blinded. Freud identifies the fear of being blinded with the fear of castration; as images for the loss of identity, both might be compared to the fear of being consumed.

28. On the theme of return, see also Pucci, 127–54.

29. See Hugo Rahner, "Odysseus at the Mask," in *Greek Myths and Christian Mystery* (London: Burns and Oates, 1963), 89ff., and John Freccero, "The Prologue Scene," in *Dante: The Poetics of Conversion*, ed. Rachel Jacoff (Cambridge, Mass.: Harvard University Press, 1986), 15–24.

30. See below, chapter 2. See also Tzvetan Todorov, *The Poetics of Prose*, trans. Richard Howard (Ithaca, N.Y.: Cornell University Press 1977), 61–63, who interprets the lengthy procrastination of Odysseus's return as an indication of his real desire to draw out his own narrative: to have words, lies, figures that are aliens, rather than the truth, or proper literal meaning, associated with home. In fact, both Dante's and Todorov's comments are anticipated by Athene in *Odyssey* 13.330–36.

31. See Horkheimer and Adorno *Dialectic of Enlightenment*, 43–80. For a reading of Odysseus as the prototype for a specifically masculine concept of identity, see Catherine Keller, *From a Broken Web: Separation, Sexism, and Self* (Boston: Beacon Press, 1986), 7–11 and passim.

32. Todorov, *The Conquest of America*, 80–88. See also Stephen Greenblatt, "Improvisation and Power," in *Literature and Society*, ed. Edward W. Said (Baltimore and London: Johns Hopkins University Press, 1980), 57–99.

33. On the relation of speech and writing and the values attached to them, see Derrida, especially *Of Grammatology*, 35 and passim.

34. Horkheimer and Adorno, 61.

35. See ibid., 31.

36. The most common of these words come from *biotos*, which means both life and the means of living.

37. For the projection of Freud's description of the individual sexual development onto the history of class development, see the essays in Ernest Borneman, *The Psychoanalysis of Money* (New York: Urizen Books, 1973).

38. See Hesiod, *Works and Days*, trans. Apostolos N. Athanassakis (Baltimore and London: Johns Hopkins University Press, 1983), which, with its insistence on biographical detail, is seen as part of the first upsurge of the individualism that began with the rise of lyric poetry and culminated in Socrates.

39. Plato, *Symposium* 215a; Hamilton, *Plato: The Collected Dialogues*, 566.

40. See Havelock, *Preface to Plato*, 203 and 223.

41. For a critique of the Platonic model for knowledge, see Evelyn Fox Keller, *Reflections on Gender and Science* (New Haven and London: Yale University Press, 1985), 18–32 esp. As Derrida has suggested, the relation between Socrates and Plato is itself a dualism, in which Plato appears as the external expression, or writing, and Socrates as the internal uncorrupted source and meaning, as voice; see, for example, *Dissemination*. In *The Post Card: From Socrates to Freud and Beyond*, trans. Alan Bass (Chicago and London: University of Chicago Press, 1987), the inversion of this relation opens up for Derrida the possibility of a countertradition.

42. See Leo C. Curran, "Transformation and Anti-Augustanism in Ovid's *Metamorphoses*," *Arethusa* 5 (1972): 75–77. Through Philip Slater and R. D. Laing, Curran reads metamorphosis as the representation of false defenses against the loss of identity.

43. See Marcel Mauss, "A Category of the Human Mind: The Notion of Person; the Notion of Self," trans. W. D. Halls, in *The Category of the Person: Anthropology, Philosophy, History*, ed. Michael Carrithers et al. (Cambridge: Cambridge University Press, 1985), 1–25, 17 esp. One of the crucial places for the translation of Roman notions of the persona into modern thought is in Hobbes's *Leviathan*, ed. C. B. Macpherson (Harmondsworth: Penguin Books, 1968), 217–22.

44. See *Laws* 8.843b; Hamilton, 1407. According to Plato, all standards of hospitality depend upon the respect for the other's territory: it is significant that Odysseus is a thief. See also de Coulanges, *The Ancient City*, 53–64, who sees property as an extension of the enclosure around the hearth that is sacred to each family's private "interior" Penates. The right to private property may therefore be related to ancient ancestor worship and the desire to perpetuate the past.

45. Ovid, *Fasti* (Cambridge, Mass: Harvard University Press, 1976), 2.7. 657–60. The translation, by Sir James Frazer, is from this edition (105). On the function of termini in Roman life, see de Coulanges, 60–63.

46. See J. A. Crook, *Law and Life in Rome, 90 B.C.–A.D. 212* (Ithaca, N.Y.: Cornell University Press, 1967), 139, and Barry Nicholas, *An Introduction to Roman Law* (Oxford: Clarendon Press, 1962), 98–157, 153–57 esp.

47. See Nicholas, 65–69, and Crook, 107–10, who notes that this meant (in theory if not always in practice) keeping children in an extremely extended childhood ended only by the death of the father.

48. Ovid, *Metamorphoses*, 2 vols., trans. Frank Justus Miller, 3d ed., rev. G. P. Goold (Cambridge, Mass.: Harvard University Press, 1977), 1:1.7–9. Unless otherwise noted, all further quotations and translations will be taken from this edition.

49. See, for example, 7.12.822, and 6.382, and especially 15.104. Richard Lanham argues that, for Ovid, the writer is the only possible authority, but even his identity as the *homo rhetoricus* whom Lanham contrasts with Plato's *homo seriosus* seems vulnerable, as it is based on the shaky ground of language; see *The Motives of*

Eloquence: Literary Rhetoric in the Renaissance (New Haven and London: Yale University Press, 1976), 6, 48–64. For Lanham, Plato and Ovid constitute the two poles around which Western thinking on the nature of the individual has revolved: the individual as either "a central self, an irreducible identity" (1), or the individual as "fundamentally a role player" (4), a "social self" (6), a polarity that I would redefine as the vision of an individual constituted prior to expression (or language) and relation, and that of an individual constructed through expression (language) and relation. Lanham's desire to rewrite the relationship between these two poles as a "symbiotic relationship of the two theories of knowledge, theories of style, ways to construct reality" (34) is a rhetorical counterpart to other contemporary projects to establish an adequate relation between oppositions, although I am suggesting that symbiosis is a problematic model.

50. In *The Gods Made Flesh: Metamorphosis and the Pursuit of Paganism* (New Haven and London: Yale University Press, 1986), Leonard Barkan notes that Lycaon's crime confuses sacrifice with cannibalism, which suggests that Zeus is anxious about being his father's son; furthermore, as well as being the god of gifts, in the form of Zeus Lycaeus, he was associated with human sacrifice (see 26–27 and 296, n. 10).

51. Ovid has changed his sources in order first to emphasize Actaeon's innocence in contrast to Pentheus's deliberate sacrilege, and then to question the very concept of innocence; for a list of sources, see Brooks Otis, *Ovid as an Epic Poet* (1966; reprint, London and New York: Cambridge University Press, 1975), 133–35 and 396.

52. See also Barkan, *The Gods Made Flesh*, 45–48, who sees the two stories as dramatizing problems of self-awareness.

53. Ovid, *The Art of Love and Other Poems*, trans. J. H. Mozley (Cambridge, Mass.: Harvard University Press, 1979). See G. Karl Galinsky, *Ovid's "Metamorphoses": An Introduction to the Basic Aspects* (Berkeley and Los Angeles: University of California Press, 1975), 4. Whereas earlier critics felt the poem lacked coherence, recent ones, such as Galinsky and Otis, find in it an underlying unity. See Otis, 79, 83–89, for his attempt to make sense of the interlacing of stories by schematizing motifs, an attempt, however, which may say more about Otis's conception of the unity of a poem than Ovid's.

54. *Tutus* can also mean "watchful" and "on guard" (qualities which Niobe, in her overconfidence, lacks), suggesting that safety is achieved only through constant vigilance.

55. Claude Lévi-Strauss, *The Naked Man*, trans. John and Doreen Weightman (London: Jonathan Cape and Harper and Row, 1981), 141. See also René Girard, *Violence and the Sacred*, in which cannibalism and incest are identified when subsumed under Girard's transcendental term of imitative desire or violence.

56. See Barkan, *The Gods Made Flesh*, 245, who sees this theme as the source of the tale's attraction for Shakespeare. As Matthew Rowlinson also pointed out to me, the tale traces the replacement of speech by writing.

57. For demonic images of the tongue as a weapon that separates rather than unites, see Frye, *Fearful Symmetry*, 282. The tongue as a source of division plays a

role in medieval representations of Envy, who was traditionally depicted as self-cannibalistic; see below, note 61.

58. See Nicholas, *Introduction to Roman Law*, 80–90, Crook, *Law and Life in Rome*, 103, and Simone de Beauvoir, *The Second Sex*, trans. H. M. Parshley (New York: Bantam Books, 1952), 85–86. Married three times, Ovid would have experienced some of the advantages of the new practices that made it easier to sever connections more neatly, but he also seems aware that they could create further complications.

59. See Barkan, *The Gods Made Flesh*, 48, 51, 61–62, 64, 70, and 91, for further discussion of this kind of rhetoric in Ovid, which Barkan notes is the verbal equivalent of incest. It also certainly could be considered as cannibalistic language, in which meaning is produced to be consumed. For Dante it is the language of suicide, as Ovid's lines are echoed by Pier delle Vigne, who claims that his wounded spirit "ingiusto fece me contra me giusto" ("made me unjust against my just self"—*Inferno* 13.72). For a discussion of Dante's episode that is also suggestive for reading Ovid's rhetorical strategy here, see Leo Spitzer, "Speech and Language in *Inferno* XIII," in *Dante: Twentieth Century Views*, ed. John Freccero (Englewood Cliffs, N. J.: Prentice-Hall, 1965), 78–101.

60. See Otis, *Ovid as an Epic Poet*, 65–70, for a discussion of Ovid's significant changes of his source material in this story in order to construct a little allegory, similar to that of Spenser's Malbecco, of the all-consuming power of appetite.

61. Envy, the belief that another is gaining at one's own expense, is traditionally represented as self-cannibalistic, since the envious person enacts upon himself the impoverishment that the other's plenty makes him feel; see, for example, Spenser's *Faerie Queene* 5.13.31ff. On Envy and its relation to Melancholy, see further below, chapter 4.

62. As Otis points out (239), the simile is also an allusion to both Homer and Virgil.

63. See, for example, Galinsky, *Ovid's "Metamorphoses,"* 14–25, 185–91 and 210–61, as well as Otis, 19.

64. See Galinsky, 220.

65. The last books have proved the test for interpretations of Ovid's attitude toward his time and Augustus; see Curran, "Transformation and Anti-Augustanism," Charles Little, "The Non-Augustanism of Ovid's *Metamorphoses*," *Mnemosyne* 25 (1972): 389–401, and Charles Segal, "Myth and Philosophy in the *Metamorphoses*: Ovid's Augustanism and the Augustan Conclusion of Book XV," *American Journal of Philology* 15, no. 3 (1967): 257–92. Segal reads Pythagoras's speech as simply satiric; I appreciate the humor but find it pretty black.

66. For Pythagorean and Orphic beliefs, see G. S. Kirk and J. E. Raven, *The Pre-Socratic Philosophers* (Cambridge: Cambridge University Press, 1957), and E. R. Dodds, *The Greeks and the Irrational* (Berkeley: University of California Press, 1957).

67. Harold Skulsky, *Metamorphosis: The Mind in Exile* (Cambridge and London: Harvard University Press, 1981), 28.

68. See, for example, *Res Gestae* 8.5, in which Augustus writes: "By new laws passed on my proposal I brought back many exemplary practices of our ancestors that were perishing in our time and I myself have handed on to posterity for imitation exemplary practices in many fields," quoted from Gordon Williams, *Techniques and Ideas in the "Aeneid"* (New Haven and London: Yale University Press, 1982), 238.

69. "Although the parent is dead, the state of ownership continues" (de Coulanges, *The Ancient City*, 65). See also Crook, *Law and Life in Rome*, 118–22, and Nicholas, *Introduction to Roman Law*, 237–38. This separation of substance and property in succession (which endows property with immortality) anticipates the notion of the modern corporation and of "the King's two bodies"—the natural, which perishes, and the legal, which survives as the heir; see Nicholas, 238, and Ernst H. Kantorowicz, *The King's Two Bodies: A Study in Medieval Political Theology* (Princeton: Princeton University Press, 1957).

70. Petronius, *The Satyricon and the Fragments*, trans. J. P. Sullivan (1965; reprint, Harmondsworth: Penguin Books, 1976), 162–63. This kind of logic is also behind readings of real "endo-cannibalism" (eating of one's kin) as an economic means of keeping substances in the family; see Sanday, *Divine Hunger*, 7.

71. While Pythagoreanism stopped at vegetarianism, other Orphic strands carried both eating and sexual taboos to an extreme in attempts to prevent any possible transgression. As Hans Jonas notes in relation to the Manichees' peculiar beliefs about ingestion, "Turned into a principle of practice, this conception engenders an extreme quietism which strives to reduce activity as such to what is absolutely necessary" (*The Gnostic Religion*, 232)– which is, unfortunately, not very much. Margaret Atwood's *The Edible Woman* (New York: Warner Books, 1969) shows, from a modern woman's perspective, one consequence of seeing food as more than mere matter with which we feed our egos.

72. Northrop Frye, *Spiritus Mundi: Essays on Literature, Myth and Society* (Bloomington and London: Indiana University Press, 1976), 122.

73. On the significance of the ideal of *pietas*, loyalty to the past, in Roman thought, see Williams, *Techniques and Ideas in the "Aeneid,"* 54–56, 143, 214, and 238. On the concept of *auctoritas* as the augmentation and thus preservation of an original founding moment, see Hannah Arendt, "What Is Authority?" in *Between Past and Future: Eight Exercises in Political Thought* (1961; reprint, Harmondsworth: Penguin Books, 1980), 91–141.

74. Otis, *Ovid as an Epic Poet*, 19.

75. So, too, as contrast to Frye's vision of the perpetuation of authority, see Hannah Arendt's description of metamorphosis as an image of its breakdown: "Its loss is tantamount to the loss of groundwork of the world, which indeed since then has begun to shift, to change and transform itself with an ever-increasing rapidity from one shape into another, as though we were living and struggling with a Protean universe where everything at any moment can become almost anything else" ("What Is Authority?" 95).

76. See Galinsky, *Ovid's "Metamorphoses,"* 24.

77. See, for example, Segal, 289–92.

78. In Barthes, *Image/Music/Text*, trans. Stephen Heath (New York: Hill and Wang, 1977), 142–47.

CHAPTER II
THE WORD AND FLESH

1. In *The City of God*, 12.13–14, Augustine attacks pagan myths of eternal return and endless metempsychosis, arguing that the incarnation and resurrection of Christ promise an ultimate end to history, which will also be a unique return to an original beginning. For the differences between classical and Christian concepts of circular versus linear time, see John Freccero, "Dante's Ulysses: From Epic to Novel," in *Dante: The Poetics of Conversion*, 136–51, and Northrop Frye, *The Great Code: The Bible and Literature* (New York and London: Harcourt Brace Jovanovich, 1982), 71–86.

2. William James, *The Varieties of Religious Experience*, ed. Martin E. Marty (Harmondsworth: Penguin Books, 1982), 170.

3. Ibid., 171–72.

4. Ibid., 189.

5. See also Geoffrey Galt Harpham, *The Ascetic Imperative in Culture and Criticism* (Chicago and London: University of Chicago Press, 1987), 94, who notes the tension in James's description between the radical effects of conversion and its vague and weak cause.

6. Cf. ibid., 97.

7. For a discussion of Augustine's paradigmatic role as individual, see John Freccero, "Autobiography and Narrative," in *Reconstructing Individualism: Autonomy, Individuality, and the Self in Western Thought*, ed. Thomas C. Heller, Morton Sosna, and David E. Wellbery (Stanford, Calif.: Stanford University Press, 1986), 16–29.

8. Ibid., 28.

9. Kenneth Burke, *The Rhetoric of Religion: Studies in Logology* (Berkeley and Los Angeles: University of California Press, 1961), 160–63.

10. Harpham, *The Ascetic Imperative*, 101.

11. See also Burke, 217, who notes the appropriateness of having an oral—and therefore infantile—image for "original" sin.

12. For the religion of the Manichees, see Hans Jonas, *The Gnostic Religion* (Boston: Beacon Press, 1958), 206–37, and Peter Brown, *Augustine of Hippo* (Berkeley and Los Angeles: University of California Press, 1969), 46–60.

13. Claude Rawson, "Cannibalism and Fiction," part 2, 249. As I will argue further in chapter 3, the strategy of projecting grotesque materiality onto other religions and then dwelling on it obsessively appears especially during the Reformation; on the Protestant "excremental vision," see also Norman O. Brown, *Life Against Death: The Psychoanalytical Meaning of History* (1968; reprint, Bungay, Suffolk: Sphere Books, 1970).

14. *In Iohannis Evangelium*, tractatus xxvi (*Corpus Christianorum: Series Latina*, [hereafter *CCL*], 36.268; translation mine).

15. See, for example, Harpham, 95–96. Sin itself is a perverse imitation of God, as "perverse te imitantur omnes, qui longe se a te faciunt et extollunt se adversum

te" ("All who desert you and set themselves up against you merely copy you in a perverse way"; 2.6; 50). The early books are interested in perverse forms of imitation that lead to the dissipation rather than the construction of identity; on the relation between imitation and eating, see below, chapter 3.

16. On the identification of words and food in an oral culture, see Dom Jean Leclercq, *The Love of Learning and the Desire for God*, 90.

17. On the elimination of Patricius from the text, see also Harpham, 107–8.

18. On the elevation of writing in the later books and *On the Trinity*, see Harpham, 111.

19. See, for example, Derrida, *Of Grammatology*, 35.

20. In *CCL*, 32:13. The translation is from D. W. Robertson, Jr., *On the Christian Doctrine* (Indianapolis: Bobbs-Merrill, 1958), 14.

21. Augustine's sin at this particular point is lust, described through images of water and mist which suggest the dissipation of identity by sin that leads to the creation of the self as a "regio egestatis" ("barren waste," 2.10; 53), as physical virility is identified with sterility. The narrator Augustine, however, claims that his sexual appetite was a misplaced hunger for God; cf. 3.1.

22. Burke, *The Rhetoric of Religion*, 162–63.

23. Ibid., 129–33.

24. Freccero, "Autobiography and Narrative," 19.

25. Freud, "The Dissection of the Psychical Personality," in *New Introductory Lectures on Psychoanalysis*, trans. James Strachey (New York and London: W. W. Norton, 1965), 71. The German reads, "Wo Es war, soll Ich werden."

26. Freccero, 26–27.

27. P. Brown, *Augustine of Hippo*, 325; on Pelagius's response, see 177.

28. As Brown shows, Augustine was not alone in this; according to him, the deity at Carthage was "an all-absorbing, maternal figure, to whom even Christian parents wisely dedicated their children" (33), and, further, "In a land which, to judge from Monica, had a fair share of formidable mothers, the *Catholica*, the Catholic Church was The Mother: 'One Mother, prolific with offspring: of her are we born, by her milk are we nourished, by her spirit we are made alive' " (212). See also P. Brown, *Augustine of Hippo*, 28–34, for a discussion of Augustine's relations with his mother, and Harpham, *The Ascetic Imperative*, 109–11, who sees the narrative working toward a sublimation of Monica into the Church. For later continuations of the association of Christ with maternal imagery, see Caroline Walker Bynum, *Jesus as Mother: Studies in the Spirituality of the High Middle Ages* (Berkeley: University of California Press, 1982).

29. Brown, *Augustine of Hippo*, 252. For Luther, who uses Augustine frequently as a model, preaching is in fact a kind of giving milk, a suckling of the congregation with words; see Erik Erikson, *Young Man Luther: A Study in Psychoanalysis and History* (New York and London: W. W. Norton, 1958), 198.

30. See also Harpham, 109.

31. On the emphasis on fertility in the last books, see also Harpham, 131–34.

32. See *In Iohannis Evangelium*, tractatus xxiv, *CCL* 36.246.

33. For studies of typology, see: Jean Daniélou, *From Shadows to Reality: Studies in the Biblical Typology of the Fathers*, trans. Dom Wustan Hibberd (London: Burns

and Oates, 1960); Northrop Frye, *The Great Code: The Bible and Literature*, 78–138; and Erich Auerbach, "Figura," reprinted in *Scenes from the Drama of European Literature*, trans. Ralph Manheim (Minneapolis: University of Minnesota Press, 1984), 11–76.

34. Epistle 13.7; quoted from *Dante Alighieri: Tutte le opere*, ed. Luigi Blasucci (Florence: Sansoni, 1981), 343; all translations from this edition are mine.

35. *Diversus* has in fact a wide range of meanings: from the root *verto*, "to turn," it has the sense of turned against, opposite, conflicting, contrary; but it also means simply remote, different, apart, and, even, individually. One of its antitheses is *converto*, "to turn back."

36. See, for example: John Freccero, "The Firm Foot on a Journey without a Guide," in *Dante: The Poetics of Conversion*, 29–54; and Robert Durling, " 'Io son venuto': Seneca, Plato, and the Microcosm," *Dante Studies*, 93 (1975): 95–129, "Farinata and the Body of Christ," *Stanford Italian Review* 2 (1981): 5–35, and, especially, "Deceit and Digestion in the Belly of Hell," in *Allegory and Representation: Selected Papers from the English Institute, 1979–80*, ed. Stephen Greenblatt (Baltimore and London: Johns Hopkins University Press, 1981), 61–93.

37. See, for example, Freccero, "The Prologue Scene," and Giuseppe Mazzotta, *Dante: Poet of the Desert* (Princeton: Princeton University Press, 1979), 82.

38. Erich Auerbach, *Dante: Poet of the Secular World*, trans. Ralph Manheim (Chicago and London: University of Chicago Press, 1929), 75.

39. On the image of "pan de li angeli" in the *Convivio* and its relation to the representation of food in the *Commedia*, see Daniel J. Ransom, "Panis Angelorum: A Palinode in the Paradiso," *Dante Studies* 95 (1977): 81–94; Freccero, "Casella's Song: *Purgatorio* II, 112," in *Dante: The Poetics of Conversion*, 186–94; R. A. Shoaf, "Dante's *columbi* and the figuralism of Hope in the *Divine Comedy*," *Dante Studies* 93 (1975): 27–59.

40. *Convivio* 2.1, quoted from Blasucci, 123.

41. For relevant studies of the problems of the *Convivio* and its relation to the *Commedia*, see Ulrich Leo, "The Unfinished *Convivio* and Dante's Rereading of the *Aeneid*," in *Sehen und Wirklichkeit bei Dante. Analecta Romanica* 4 (1957): 71–104; as well as the works by Ransom and Freccero cited above. For related discussions of Dante's retrospect on his philosophical phase, see Mazzotta, *Dante*, 281–82, and Joseph Mazzeo, *Medieval Cultural Tradition in Dante's "Commedia"* (Westport, Conn.: Greenwood Press, 1977), 183–85.

42. Text and translations for the *Commedia* are taken from *The Divine Comedy*, trans. with a commentary by Charles S. Singleton, 6 vols. (Princeton: Princeton University Press, 1970).

43. See Durling, "Deceit and Digestion," 64, and passim.

44. See Freccero, "Bestial Sign and Bread of Angels (*Inferno* 32–34)," *Yale Italian Studies* 1, no. 1 (Winter 1979), 53–66. The evasiveness of Ugolino's last line, which has caused critics, including Singleton, to stoutly deny the possibility that the father ate the son (the end which makes the most thematic sense, as Freccero brilliantly shows), could be cited as one further example of the poetics of fraud that hide an unbearable truth. Dante's presentation of Ugolino's story also provides an

example of the relation between cannibalism and narrative reticence discussed by Rawson in "Cannibalism and Fiction."

45. Freccero, "Infernal Irony: The Gates of Hell," *Modern Language Notes* 99, no. 4 (September 1984): 777–78.

46. See Singleton, *Inferno: Commentary*, 98. Like Augustine, Francesca's crucial experience involves the identification of herself with a text she is reading; see T. K. Swing, *The Fragile Leaves of the Sibyl* (Westminster, Md.: Newman Press, 1962), 299, who notes also the verbal echo of the conversion scene in the *Confessions*. While the results of the two experiences seem dramatically opposed—Augustine finds God, Francesca goes to Hell—the antithesis may be a vulnerable one, and Francesca, who will be followed by both Madame Bovary and Dorian Gray, reveals one very sinister side of any dream of turning, or sublimating, life into art.

47. For Dante's use of metamorphosis here and its relation to the continuation of pagan tradition within a Christian context, see Barkan, *The Gods Made Flesh*, 137–70. I agree with Robert Hollander that, although the reading of Ovid in the *Convivio* is neoplatonic, there is no need to insist on Dante's reliance upon the allegorists for a knowledge of Ovid, especially as it appears to me that Dante's use of Ovid in the *Inferno* goes directly against that tradition; see *Allegory in Dante's "Commedia"* (Princeton: Princeton University Press, 1969), 210–14.

48. Thomas Aquinas, *Summa* 2,2.66.6; quoted from Skulsky, *Metamorphosis*, 118.

49. See Skulsky, 116–18, and Lawrence Baldassaro, "Metamorphosis as Punishment and Redemption in *Inferno* xxiv," *Dante Studies* 99 (1981): 89–111.

50. See, for example, Richard Terdiman, "Problematical Virtuosity: Dante's Depiction of the Thieves (*Inferno* xxiv–xxv)," *Dante Studies* 91 (1973): 27–45, and Peter S. Hawkins, "Virtuosity and Virtue: Poetic Self-Reflection in the *Commedia*," *Dante Studies* 98 (1980): 1–18, as well as Skulsky, 127–28.

51. Baldassaro, 97–98.

52. Skulsky, 127.

53. See also Barkan, *The Gods Made Flesh*, 165–66, who notes how early commentators read these three metamorphoses as representing the three forms of change that were possible. What I am arguing is that the difference between these forms is, like all infernal distinctions, tenuous.

54. Singleton, *Inferno: Commentary*, 389.

55. Mazzotta, *Dante*, 95.

56. See especially Freccero, "The Prologue Scene" and "Dante's Ulysses," for Ulysses as a palinode to Dante's earlier self.

57. Freccero, "The Prologue Scene," 20.

58. See Ransom; Freccero, "Casella's Song"; and Shoaf, "Dante's *colombi*."

59. The mirror plays an important role throughout the *Commedia*; for some reflections on Dante's use of the image, see Kevin Brownlee, "Dante and Narcissus (*Purg.* xxx. 76–99)," *Dante Studies* 96 (1978): 201–6, and R. A. Shoaf, *Dante, Chaucer, and the Currency of the Word: Money, Images, and Reference in Late Medieval Poetry* (Norman, Okla.: Pilgrim Books, 1983).

60. On this opposition, see Mark Musa, *The Advent at the Gates: Dante's "Comedy"* (Bloomington and London: Indiana University Press, 1974), 111–28, and

Teodolinda Barolini, *Dante's Poetics: Textuality and Truth in the "Comedy"* (Princeton: Princeton University Press, 1984), 40–52.

61. See Shoaf, "Dante's *colombi*," who traces the image of the dove from *Inferno* 5, through the revision of the *Convivio* in *Purgatorio* 2, to this passage.

62. See Barolini, 85–97.

63. See ibid.

64. Durling, "Deceit," 83–84; for a further discussion of the relation between inspiration and eating in the *Purgatorio*, see Richard Adams, "Inspiration and Gluttony: The Moral Content of Dante's Poetics of the 'Sweet New Style,' " *Modern Language Notes* 91, no. 1 (January 1976): 30–59.

65. Durling, "Deceit," 84. For further comments on the substitution of procreation for excretion, see chapter 3.

66. On the thickening of language in the *Paradiso*, see Shoaf, *Dante, Chaucer and the Currency of the Word*, 68.

67. See Jacob Burckhardt, *The Civilization of the Renaissance in Italy*, 2 vols. (New York: Harper and Row, 1958), 1:143.

68. Leo Spitzer, "Notes on the Poetic and the Empirical 'I' in Medieval Authors," *Traditio* 4 (1946): 414–22.

69. Ibid., 416.

70. "Renaissance" is itself a loose and inaccurate term that gives an illusory coherence to a chaotic variety of styles and times. I use it in its traditional sense partly for convenience and partly for its thematic appropriateness for my argument later. Recently, the discovery of the individual, seen as central in defining the Renaissance, has been pushed back to earlier times; see, for example, Colin Morris, *The Discovery of the Individual 1050–1200* (Toronto: University of Toronto Press, 1972), and Bynum, *Jesus as Mother*, 82–109. Bynum disagrees with Morris, arguing that although the Middle Ages saw a discovery of a "self," it was not an "individual" in the modern sense because the self was still defined through groups. According to Bynum, however, it was the Fourth Lateran Council of 1215 (fifty years before Dante's birth), to which I shall soon return, that heralded the end of the medieval balance between self and group (109).

71. See Gerhart B. Ladner, "*Homo Viator*: Medieval Ideas of Alienation and Order," *Speculum* 17, no. 2 (April 1967): 233–59. The *Commedia*, like the *Metamorphoses*, was written in exile, and, as Mazzotta observes, for Dante exile was "the very condition of the text, its most profound metaphor" (145).

72. The fact that Dante acknowledges his debt to his source and then sends him back to Limbo (where Ovid is as well) suggests an ambivalence that may be based less on religious differences than on poetic rivalry—though the two might be considered indistinguishable.

73. See *Inferno* 2.93, *Paradiso* 10.87 and 15.28–30.

Chapter III
THE REFORMATION OF THE HOST

1. This very general summary, which is intended only to indicate the central issues and so ignores the significant differences among the Protestant positions, is based on the accounts given in: Dom Gregory Dix, *The Shape of the Liturgy* (Lon-

don: Dacre Press, 1945); R. Kevin Seasoltz, ed., *Living Bread, Saving Cup: Readings in the Eucharist* (Collegeville, Minn.: The Liturgical Press, 1982); Malcolm Ross, *Poetry and Dogma: The Transformation of Eucharistic Symbols in Seventeenth-Century English Poetry* (New Brunswick, N.J.: Rutgers University Press, 1954); Jaroslav Pelikan, *The Christian Tradition*, vol. 4: *Reformation of Church and Dogma (1300–1700)* (Chicago and London: University of Chicago Press, 1984); and the *Catholic Dictionary*, ed. Donald Attwater, (New York: Macmillan, 1961), articles on the Mass and Eucharist.

2. Quoted from Dix, 256. *Repraesentio* means primarily to make present, display, show, manifest. Tertullian uses the word at times to refer to the physical body of Christ. A secondary meaning, important for Christianity with its vocabulary of talents and debts, and also for the related analogy between language and money, is to pay down, pay in cash or ready money.

3. For the identification of the body of Christ with individual bodies who together create the corporate body of the Church, see 1 Corinthians 12:12–31. See also Hale, *The Body Politic*, 28–32.

4. See also Peter Hulme, *Colonial Encounters*, 85, who sees the Fourth Lateran Council as the start of one wave of charges of cannibalism against foreigners. As mentioned earlier, Caroline Walker Bynum also sees this council as marking the beginning of the end of the delicate balance between individual and society achieved in the Middle Ages; see Bynum, *Jesus as Mother*, 109.

5. See, further, Pelikan, 193.

6. In *Holy Feast, Holy Fast*, Bynum shows how women's revolt against the authority of the medieval Church especially often took the form of an appropriation of the Eucharist.

7. The following summary is based on Kantorowicz, *The King's Two Bodies*, esp. 193–232; see also Hale, *The Body Politic*, 32–47.

8. See Bynum, *Holy Feast*, 53–56.

9. John Donne, *Sermon 72*, quoted from Ross, 167.

10. *The Babylonian Captivity of the Church*, in Martin Luther, *Three Treatises* (Philadelphia: Muhlenberg Press, 1960), 133.

11. *In Iohannis Evangelium*, tractatus cxxiv, 11–12, in *CCL*, 36:254 (my translation).

12. Thomas Turke, "The Holy Eucharist and the Papish Breaden God," 1625; quoted from Ross, *Poetry and Dogma*, 77. As well as accusing the Catholic Church of turning communion into cannibalism, some of the reformers claimed that it reduced it to that other physical form of incorporation, sexual intercourse. So William Fulke, in "The Cavills of N. Sander . . . about the Supper" (1581), makes the Catholic Sander say: "Moreover I have often said: Our *coniunction with Christ in this Sacrament, is like the carnall copulation betwene the wife and husband*, where twaine are in one flesh, yet tary not alwaies corporally ioyned togither." To which the good Protestant Fulke indignantly replies, "You haue often made a *shamelesse, beastly and filthy comparison betwene so high a mystery, and so grosse and carnall copulation*." (Quoted from D. Douglas Waters, *Duessa as Theological Satire* [Columbia, S.C.: University of Missouri Press, 1970], 64.)

13. See further chapter 4 below.

14. *On Christian Doctrine*, 1.28, in *The Complete Prose Works of John Milton*, ed. William Alfred et al. (New Haven and London: Yale University Press, 1973), 6.553–54.

15. Ibid., 555.

16. Ibid.

17. Ibid., 556.

18. Ibid., 560.

19. On Rabelais's incarnational model for figuration and eucharistic model for interpretation, see David Quint, *Origin and Originality in Renaissance Literature: Versions of the Source* (New Haven and London: Yale University Press, 1983), 167–206, and Dennis Costa, *Irenic Apocalypse: Some Uses of Apocalyptic in Dante, Petrarch and Rabelais* (Los Angeles: Anna Libra and Co., 1981), 107–38. For Rabelais's relation to medieval traditions of feasting in general, see Bakhtin, *Rabelais and His World*, 278–302.

20. Rabelais, *Gargantua*, prologue, 45; Cohen, 39. All quotations of Rabelais will be taken from the following editions: *La Vie très horrificque du grand Gargantua* (Paris: Garnier-Flammarion, 1968); *Pantagruel: Roy des Dipsodes* (Paris: Garnier-Flammarion, 1969); *Le Tiers Livre des faicts et dicts heroïques du bon Pantagruel* (Paris: Garnier-Flammarion, 1970); *Le Quart Livre des faicts et dicts heroïques du bon Pantagruel* (Paris: Garnier-Flammarion, 1971); and *Le Cinquieme Livre* (Paris: Editions Gallimard et Librairie Générale Française, 1969). These will be cited by book, chapter, and page, followed by the page number of the translations. These are from *Gargantua and Pantagruel*, trans. J. M. Cohen (Harmondsworth: Penguin Books, 1955).

21. Bynum, *Holy Feast*, 64–65.

22. This plays on the paradox used by Dante as well as other Christian writers, in which God is the food that increases appetite with eating.

23. Quint, *Origin and Originality*, 201.

24. See Margaret Mann Phillips, *Erasmus On His Times: A Shortened Version of "The Adages of Erasmus"* (Cambridge: Cambridge University Press, 1967), 77–97.

25. Ibid., 82.

26. Ibid., 81.

27. Ibid., 85.

28. Ibid., 91.

29. Ibid., 93.

30. On the limitations of both Rabelais's and Bakhtin's assumed reading community, and particularly its exclusion of women, see Wayne C. Booth, "Freedom of Interpretation: Bakhtin and the Challenge of Feminist Criticism," in *The Politics of Interpretation*, ed. W.J.T. Mitchell (Chicago and London: University of Chicago Press, 1983), 51–82.

31. See *Dictionnaire de la Langue Française du Siezième Siècle* (Paris: Librairie Ancienne Honoré Champion, 1932), 10:59–60.

32. Bakhtin, 325. See also Erich Auerbach, "The World in Pantagruel's Mouth," in *Mimesis: The Representation of Reality in Western Literature*, trans. Willard R. Trask (Princeton: Princeton University Press, 1953), 262–84.

33. See Bakhtin, 325–26, and M. A. Screech, *Rabelais* (London: Duckworth, 1979), 35–39, for discussions of the tradition from which Rabelais was drawing.

34. Terence Cave, *The Cornucopian Text: Problems of Writing in the French Renaissance* (Oxford: At the Clarendon Press, 1979), 187, 189. For Cave's interpretation of the darker implications of the figures of the Danaïdes and Tantalus, see 171–72.

35. See Joan Kelly, "Early Feminist Theory and the *Querelle des Femmes*," in *Women, History, and Theory* (Chicago and London: University of Chicago Press, 1984), 65–109.

36. See Screech, 72–73.

37. See Barkan, *Nature's Work of Art*, 73, and Hale, *The Body Politic*, 11–47. Durling ("Deceit and Digestion," 70–71) speculates on the significance of John of Salisbury's version of this tale, in which wealth is seen as the food of the body politic, for Dante. Cusanus's may be most significant for Rabelais's representation of lawyers as cannibalistic. Livy's is important for *Coriolanus*; for two recent suggestive studies of the role of the belly and eating in Shakespeare's play, see: Janet Adelman, " 'Anger's My Meat': Feeding, Dependency, and Aggression in Coriolanus," in *Representing Shakespeare: New Psychoanalytic Essays*, ed. Murray M. Schwartz and Coppélia Kahn (Baltimore and London: Johns Hopkins University Press, 1980), 129–49; and Stanley Cavell, " 'Who does the wolf love?': *Coriolanus* and the interpretation of politics," in *Shakespeare and the Question of Theory*, ed. Patricia Parker and Geoffrey Hartman (New York and London: Methuen, 1985), 245–72.

38. According to Epicurus, the belly, *gaster*, was "the beginning and root of all good"; see Pucci, *Odysseus Polutropos*, 157–64, and Onians, *The Origins of European Thought*, 88. Onians also notes (485–90) the traditional association of food with genius: wine, especially, was seen as going to the head, and a well-fed belly could "break forth," as in Job 32:18ff. and Ezekiel 3:3–4—a tradition Rabelais alludes to in his chapter 58.

39. See Screech, 439–48, esp. 441.

40. As the episodes with which I am primarily concerned appear to me to be closely connected to the earlier books, I am treating them as Rabelais's work. For a discussion of the problems of style and quality, see Thomas M. Greene, *Rabelais: A Study in Comic Courage* (Englewood Cliffs, N.J.: Prentice-Hall, 1970), 100–102.

41. See especially Plato, *Laws* 937e–938c; Hamilton, *Plato: The Collected Dialogues*, 1487–88.

42. See also, for example, Goya's *Los Caprichos* 21, a drawing similar in concept to Rabelais, in which the lawyers are represented as monstrous (and male) cats, tearing the wings off their (female) clients

43. Lévi-Strauss, *Tristes Tropiques*, trans. John and Doreen Weightman (New York: Atheneum, 1978), 387–89.

44. On the image of the source, see Quint.

45. Frere Jean may, of course, be close to a Rabelaisian theory of poetic inspiration, in which food feeds the genius. There is a long materialist tradition, however, of reducing inspiration to indigestion, according to which, for example, Plotinus's mystical experiences were really a form of dyspepsia. So, too, Pertelote tells

Chaunticleer that "Swevenes engenren of replecciouns" (Chaucer, "Nun's Priest's Tale," 2923); Scrooge accuses Marley's ghost of being a bit of undigested beef or an overdone potato, as "there's more of gravy than the grave in you"; Bram Stoker claimed to have written *Dracula* after an attack of indigestion; while Milton may have believed his blindness—and thus indirectly his insight—to have been caused by indigestion. Even from the most materialistic perspective, however, in which all anxiety of influence is mere indigestion, the realization that one's center cannot be controlled at will and that foreign matter (even if only a bit of potato) invited in can attack its host from within, is rather unsettling.

46. On the difference between these two hermeneutics, see Thomas M. Greene, *The Light in Troy: Imitation and Discovery in Renaissance Poetry* (New Haven and London: Yale University Press, 1982), 92–95, and 237, for a discussion of their use in *Gargantua*. According to Greene, the older model, the image of the stripping of the veil, "presupposed a fullness of knowledge awaiting the successful interpreter" and identified past with present, while the newer, temporal one of a gradual unearthing and revival "withheld a single all-divulging key" and preserved the distance between the two times (94). For the relation of this image of unearthing to the notion of a "Renaissance," see below, chapter 5.

47. Bruno's work, *La cena de le ceneri*, copies Rabelais's in other aspects as well, notably in its use of catalogues and certain images. One crucial difference, however, can be seen in the authors' self-presentation, which could be used to uphold a schematic distinction between the medieval monk and the Renaissance man, but which certainly reflects very different self-images. Bruno appears as the Nolan who has a solution for every problem, religious or astronomical; he takes himself very seriously and pretends to a greater originality than was his (and which Rabelais would never have bothered to claim). Rabelais, on the other hand, inflates his ego only to be deflated; he subverts his own claims to authority and originality, both of which would set him in an inhospitable relation to other writers—and lay him open to charges of heresy.

48. All quotations of the poems and *Discoveries* are taken from *Ben Jonson: The Complete Poems*, ed. George Parfitt (New Haven and London: Yale University Press, 1975). The texts of the masques are from *The Complete Masques*, ed. Stephen Orgel (New Haven and London: Yale University Press, 1969), and the plays are from *Ben Jonson: Three Comedies*, ed. Michael Jamieson (Harmondsworth: Penguin, 1966).

49. See, for example, Robert M. Adams, "On the Bulk of Ben," in *Ben Jonson's Plays and Masques*, ed. Robert M. Adams (New York and London: W. W. Norton and Co., 1979), 482–99, and Wilson, noted below.

50. Reprinted in *Ben Jonson: A Collection of Critical Essays*, ed. Jonas A. Barish (Englewood Cliffs, N.J.: Prentice-Hall, 1963), 60–74.

51. E. Pearlman, "Ben Jonson: An Anatomy," *English Literary Renaissance* 9 (1979): 364–94.

52. Ibid., 386.

53. See Charles Nicholl, *The Chemicall Theatre* (London, Boston, and Henley: Routledge and Kegan Paul, 1980), 29.

54. On the Renaissance formation of the proper relation between art and na-

ture, which has its most famous expression in English in Sidney's *Apology*, see Northrop Frye, "Nature and Homer," in *Fables of Identity: Studies in Poetic Mythology* (New York and London: Harcourt Brace Jovanovich, 1963), 39–51.

55. See Georges Poulet, *The Metamorphosis of the Circle*, (Baltimore: Johns Hopkins Press, 1966), xi–xxv. On the shifting use of this image in the seventeenth century, see Marjorie Hope Nicholson, *The Breaking of the Circle: Studies in the Effect of the "New Science" on Seventeenth Century Poetry* (rev. ed., New York: Columbia University Press, 1960), 47–48 esp.

56. See Peter Stallybrass and Allon White, *The Poetics of Transgression*, 78. I found their discussion of Jonson's separation of "higher" theater from "lower" marketplace very helpful in formulating my own argument.

57. See, for example, Thomas M. Greene, "Ben Jonson and the Centred Self," *Studies in English Literature* 10 (1970): 325–48; Richard S. Peterson, *Imitation and Praise in the Poems of Ben Jonson* (New Haven and London: Yale University Press, 1980), 26–38, and Jonas A. Barish, "Jonson and the Loathèd Stage," in *A Celebration of Ben Jonson*, ed. William Blissett, Julian Patrick, and R. W. Van Fossen (Toronto and Buffalo: University of Toronto Press, 1973), 27–53.

58. Greene, "Ben Jonson and the Centred Self," 342.

59. On the Renaissance ideal of self-fashioning, see: Thomas M. Greene, "The Flexibility of the Self in Renaissance Literature," in *The Disciplines of Criticism*, ed. Peter Demetz, Thomas M. Greene, and Lowry Nelson, Jr. (New Haven and London: Yale University Press, 1968), 241–64; and Stephen Greenblatt, *Renaissance Self-Fashioning from More to Shakespeare* (Chicago: University of Chicago Press, 1980). For Derrida, a similar self-projection that is made possible by a belief in an ultimate return to a proper identity is the basis of Hegelian dialectics; see *Positions*, 96.

60. Wilson, "Morose Ben Jonson," 62.

61. John Palmer, *Ben Jonson* (Port Washington, N.Y.: Kennikat Press, 1934), 129.

62. For Jonson's use of the tradition, see Peterson and Terrance Dunford, "Consumption of the World: Reading, Eating, and Imitation in *Every Man Out of His Humour*," *English Literary Renaissance* 14 (1984): 131–47. For further discussions of the significance of the different images for imitatio, see Terence Cave, *The Cornucopian Text*, 35–77; Thomas M. Greene, *The Light in Troy*, 28–103; G. W. Pigman III, "Versions of Imitation in the Renaissance," *Renaissance Quarterly* 33 (1980): 1–33.

63. Quoted from *The Complete Poetry of John Donne*, ed. John T. Shawcross (Garden City, N.Y.: Doubleday Anchor Books, 1967).

64. This, again, is characteristic of satire, dependent upon a complete discrepancy between inside and outside, which suggests that what is hidden under the sublime may be merely excrement. So both Bruno in *La cena* and Jonson in "On the Famous Voyage" transform the epic descent into the bowels of Hell into a descent into the refuse from human bowels. In the *Cinquième Livre*, 32, Rabelais also plays upon the scatalogical potential of mellification (a variation of the digestive metaphor for imitatio) and the process by which an unsavoury image is replaced with a more tasteful one is reversed as the travelers are fed: "ung plain plat

de merde couvert d'estrongs fleuris: c'estoit ung plat plain de miel blanc, couvert d'une guimple de soye cramoisine" ("a plate of shit covered with strange flowers: that is to say, a dish of white honey, covered with a piece of cloth of bright silk," 323; translation mine).

65. According to Freud, children identify ingestion and birth as part of a single process. The switch has the obvious advantage of idealizing the process of digestion. Jonson himself, however, sees another possiblity for a relation between bodily hunger and sexual appetite, in "On Gut":

> Gut eats all day, and lechers all the night,
> So all his meat he tasteth over, twice:
> And, striving so to double his delight,
> He makes himself a thoroughfare of vice.
> Thus, in his belly, can he change a sin,
> Lust it comes out, that gluttony went it.

(Epigram 118)

The two are identified not by sublimation but by regurgitation. See Pearlman, 385–86, for a discussion of this poem in relation to the negative aspects of Jonson's lack of differentiation between bodily impulses.

66. The dangerous proximity of imitatio to theft was seen by du Bellay; see Margaret W. Ferguson, *Trials of Desire: Renaissance Defenses of Poetry* (New Haven and London: Yale University Press, 1983), 18–53.

67. Cave, *The Cornucopian Text*, 64–65.

68. See Greene, *The Light in Troy*, 264–93, esp. 278–86.

69. Ibid., 284, 285. For a relevant and revealing reading of the invitation poems that also discusses the relation between different kinds eating and imitation in the light of Jonson's famous bulk, see Joseph Lowenstein, "The Jonsonian Corpulence, or The Poet as Mouthpiece," *English Literary History* 53, no. 3 (Fall 1986): 491–518.

70. Stanley Fish, "Authors-Readers: Jonson's Community of the Same," *Representations* 7 (1984): 26–58.

71. See Pearlman, 384, and Raymond Williams, *The Country and the City*, 27–34.

72. Fish, 57.

73. On the dangers imitatio represents to Jonson, see Dunford.

74. See Don. K. Hendrick, "Cooking for the Anthropophagai: Jonson and His Audience," *Studies in English Literature* 17 (Spring 1977): 233–45.

75. Pearlman, 388.

76. In Orgel, *The Complete Masques*, 411.

77. See Barish.

78. On the union of neoplatonic idealism and Jacobean ideology in masques, see Stephen Orgel, *The Illusion of Power: Political Theatre in the English Renaissance* (Berkeley and Los Angeles: University of California Press, 1975).

79. Stephen Greenblatt, *Renaissance Self-Fashioning*, 9.

80. Stephen Orgel, *The Jonsonian Masque* (New York: Columbia University Press, 1967), 5.

81. Angus Fletcher, *The Transcendental Masque: An Essay on Milton's "Comus"* (Ithaca and London: Cornell University Press, 1971), 34.

82. See Orgel, *The Jonsonian Masque*, 70–72, for a description of the first performance and its reception, and also Leah Sinanglou Marcus, "The Occasion of Ben Jonson's *Pleasure Reconciled to Virtue*," *Studies in English Literature* 19 (Spring 1979): 271–93.

83. See Richard Peterson, "The Iconography of Jonson's *Pleasure Reconciled to Virtue*," *The Journal of Medieval and Renaissance Studies* 5, no. 1 (Spring 1975): 123–53.

84. Ibid., 151.

85. Fletcher, 109.

86. Walter Ong, *The Presence of the Word*, 117–18. In *Epicoene, or The Silent Woman*, Morose, who wants his ears "banqueted with pleasant and witty conferences" (2.5.47), treats words as objects and sound as a form of physical invasion, through a confusion of the senses that is the parody of the ideal of synesthesia and also indicates the dangers of identifying different appetites. For Jonson, as for Rabelais, the ears and mouth are analogous as means of taking things in. But the need to absorb sounds tempers the need to consume food, which is why both writers find it frightening that the belly has no ears. By stopping up his ears and blocking off the aural hole through which the external world can figuratively enter the self, Morose opens wider the oral cavity, turning himself into a voracious, greedy mouth that hungers after gold and recognizes what is outside of itself only as food.

87. On the sublimity of hearing in the Western tradition and particularly in Hegel, see Derrida, *Margins*, ix–xxix, 69–108, especially 92. For Jonson, however, like Augustine, it is the printed word that is more sublime, as more lasting than the spoken.

88. Jonas Barish, "Jonson and the Loathèd Stage," 37. See also Dunford, 133, for Jonson's tendency to distinguish between written and performed plays. According to Joseph Lowenstein, Jonson's abstraction of his works' essence from their material accidents is a way of establishing authorial property rights over his texts, so that Jonson, caught between patronage and market systems, is an important precursor of the modern notion of the author; see "The Script in the Marketplace," *Representations* 12 (1985): 26–58.

89. Barish, "Jonson and the Loathèd Stage," 37.

90. Peterson, "The Iconography," 127–29.

91. See Orgel, *Jonsonian Masque*, 153–59, who gives Orazio Busino's account of the masque, and Peterson, "The Iconography," 142–45.

92. Greenblatt, *Renaissance Self-Fashioning*, 2–3, notes how the concept of the *imitatio Christi* influenced the idea of self-fashioning.

93. Peterson, *Imitation and Praise*, 112–57. Peterson, unlike Wilson and Adams, reads the poet's physical rotundity as part of his self-positioning in this tradition and an emblem of inner wholeness. The OED connects the Old English and Old German words for the body, positing an earlier identification in the Greek and medieval Latin words for "cask." The traditional use of the vessel as a figure for personal and textual identity may be behind Rabelais's choice of the word *calfreter* for interpretation.

94. Ibid., 131–34.

95. Peterson, "The Iconography," 147.

96. For a discussion of the conflicting associations of Hercules in the context of *Faerie Queene* 5, see Jane Aptekar, *Icons of Justice: Iconography and Thematic Imagery in Book Five of "The Faerie Queene"* (New York and London: Columbia University Press, 1979), 154–99.

97. In *Imitation and Praise*, 43, Peterson cites Aeneas as a prototype for Jonson's heroes who are steadfast in their travels.

98. See Wind, *Pagan Mysteries*, 226–30, and Geoffrey Hartman, "Evening Star and Evening Land," in *The Fate of Reading and Other Essays* (Chicago and London: University of Chicago Press, 1975), 147–78.

99. See, for example, *The Vision of Delight* where the spectators who desire to become "all . . . eyes" (210) are struck dumb with admiration; and *News from the New World Discovered in the Sun*, where the king is represented as a blinding light that can only be seen by being read.

100. As Orgel notes (180–81), the word *ground* (255), has associations with architecture and painting, but the musical significance seems to take priority and even subsume the others; Orgel notes the increase of music in the verse of this section.

101. See Marcus, 291, who also discusses the significance of feasting as a political issue at the time, and James's attempt to present himself as a mediator between courtly feast and puritan famine.

102. James Boswell, *The Life of Samuel Johnson LLD*, 2 vols. (New York and London: J. M. Dent and Sons, 1906), 2:16 and 1:290. According to Boswell also, at table the famous conversationalist minded nothing but his belly: no words came out of his mouth until he had finished shoveling food in.

103. See Lowenstein, "The Script in the Marketplace," and Pearlman, 383–84, who discusses Jonson's elimination of production in order to identify himself with the rich and powerful consumers.

104. For discussions of Milton's mortalism, see: W. B. Hunter, "Milton's Power of Matter," *Journal of the History of Ideas* 13 (1952): 551–62, and "Milton's Materialistic Life Principle," *Journal of English and Germanic Philology* 45 (1946): 68–76; George Williamson, "Milton and the Mortalist Heresy," *Studies in Philology* 32 (1935): 553–79; and Christopher Hill, *Milton and the English Revolution* (New York: Viking Press, 1977), 317–33. For discussions of Milton's religious beliefs, see the essays in W. B. Hunter, C. A. Patrides, J. H. Adamson, *Bright Essence: Studies in Milton's Theology* (Salt Lake City: University of Utah Press, 1973).

105. Unless noted, all quotations of Milton's works are taken from *John Milton: Complete Poems and Major Prose*, ed. Merritt Y. Hughes (Indianapolis: Odyssey Press, 1957).

106. On Milton's use of financial metaphors and their relation both to his father's business and to the Christian concept of debt (implicit also in the secondary meaning of *repraesentio*, as "to pay"), see William Kerrigan, *The Sacred Complex: On the Psychogenesis of "Paradise Lost"* (Cambridge and London: Harvard University Press, 1983), 44–45, and John Guillory, "The Father's House: *Samson Agonistes* in Its Historical Moment," *Re-Membering Milton: Essays on the Text and*

Traditions, ed. Mary Nyquist and Margaret W. Ferguson (New York and London: Methuen, 1987), 148–76. Milton's relation to his father looks back to a late medieval tradition in which it was common for a merchant to dedicate his son to God as a way of redeeming the father's mercenary pursuits and subliming his material origins; such an ideal of an intellectual or artistic child produced by the labor of his parents as a means of justifying that labor is still common today.

107. See Georgia B. Christopher, *Milton and the Science of the Saints* (Princeton: Princeton University Press, 1982), 121, and R. A. Shoaf, *Milton, Poet of Duality* (New Haven: Yale University Press, 1985), 102–3. Calvin, in particular, focused on the figure of metonymy; see Pelikan, *The Christian Tradition*, 4:194.

108. Shoaf, 103.

109. See Patricia Parker, *Inescapable Romance: Studies in the Poetics of a Mode* (Princeton: Princeton University Press, 1979), 114–58. See also Jim Swan, "Difference and Silence: John Milton and the Question of Gender," in *The (M)other Tongue: Essays in Feminist Psychoanalytic Interpretation*, ed. Shirley Nelson Garner, Claire Kahane, and Madelon Sprengnether (Ithaca and London: Cornell University Press, 1985), 164.

110. Hartman, "Adam on the Grass with Balsamum," in *Beyond Formalism: Literary Essays, 1958–70* (New Haven and London: Yale University Press, 1978), 131. See also Lieb, *The Dialectics of Creation: Patterns of Birth and Regeneration in Paradise Lost* (Amherst: University of Massachusetts Press, 1970). On Milton's use of food imagery and its relation to forms of psychic internalization, see Kerrigan, *The Sacred Complex*, 193–262.

111. Hartman, 131.

112. On the significance of Milton's "or," see Leslie Brisman, *Milton's Poetry of Choice and Its Romantic Heirs* (Ithaca, N.Y.: Cornell University Press, 1973).

113. See also Parker, 132 and 137, who describes the fall as an "attempt to hasten the ascent, to circumvent the process of education by degrees" by means of a shortcut that results in the "Satanic reduction of meaning, the premature collapse of words and things."

114. See Lieb, 22–30, for a discussion of the different kinds of holes in *Paradise Lost*. The devils in general confuse holes out of which one is born with abysses of no return. So, in Book 2.147–49, Belial speaks of being swallowed by "the wide womb of uncreated night," identifying "womb" not only with "tomb" but also specifically with the jaws of death, and so conflating creation with the annihilation of identity. Infernal attitudes toward wombs, from Mammon and Satan who ransack the womb of nature to build first Pandemonium and then artillery, to Death and the hell-hounds who violently attempt to return to their mother's womb, suggest an ambivalence toward origins, from which the devils attempt to detach themselves, yet with which they still identify through infernal creation and procreation. But this fear of being swallowed up by one's source before one has a chance to detach oneself from it appears also in Milton's early poems about premature death, where wombs turn into tombs; see, for example, "An Epitaph on the Marchioness of Windsor" and "On the Death of a Fair Infant Dying of a Cough."

115. See Frank Kermode, *Shakespeare, Spenser, Donne: Renaissance Essays* (London: Routledge and Kegan Paul, 1971), 84–115, for a discussion of this counter-

Symposium (usually hosted by Ovid, as representing the materialist alternative to the Platonic ideal) in relation to the banquet scene of *Paradise Regained*, Christ's first temptation, which recalls this one of Eve.

116. This tradition inverts the more obvious relation between man and woman, in which the first is drawn from the body of the latter. One effect of this inversion is to reinforce an identification of men with wholeness and autonomy—the values associated with the individual—and women with dependency and relation; see below, Conclusion. Milton follows this tradition but then inverts it, in turn, as it is Adam who first realizes his need for others, and Eve who, in different ways, is associated with autonomy. His representation of Eve's self-sufficiency as in some sense narcissistic suggests the anxiety on which the first inversion is based. For Adam, Eve's body is already potentially a paradise lost from which he is excluded (8.546–59), just as for the male infant the mother's body, with which it was first in total identity but against which it must later define itself, represents an identification that it both desires but must guard against for fear of regressing and losing its newly won sexual identity. With the new codification of sexual roles in the seventeenth century, the appropriation of a male part by a female (represented as comic in Shakespeare) appears to be more threatening; in *Samson Agonistes*, Dalila's crime is her attempt to play Samson's part of national hero, thus breaking down sexual stereotypes. On the relation of the drama to the development of modern gender divisions, see John Guillory, "Dalila's House: *Samson Agonistes* and the Sexual Division of Labour," in *Rewriting the Renaissance: The Discourses of Sexual Difference in Early Modern Europe*, ed. Margaret W. Ferguson, Maureen Quilligan, and Nancy J. Vickers (Chicago and London: University of Chicago Press, 1986), 106–22.

117. For discussions of the theological background behind and the issues involved in this interpretation, see the essays by Hunter, Adamson, and Patrides in *Bright Essence*, 29–77. For a study of the importance of the concept of sonship in Milton (which connects him with Pelagius rather than Augustine), see Hugh MacCallum, *Milton and the Sons of God: The Divine Image in Milton's Epic Poetry* (Toronto: University of Toronto Press, 1986).

118. See also Irene Samuel, "The Dialogue in Heaven: A Reconsideration of *Paradise Lost* III, 1–417," *Publication of the Modern Language Association* 72 (1957): 601–11. Samuel contrasts the scene with the dialogue in Hell and argues that the Father wants the Son to speak independently—unlike Satan, who prompts Beelzebub—and that this show of independence causes the Father's response and the elevation of the Son. It's hard to say what the Father wants, but certainly it is greatly to Milton's advantage to present it that way.

119. The unorthodox earning of equality by merit was noted by Stella Perce Revard in "The Dramatic Function of the Son in *Paradise Lost*: A Commentary on Milton's 'Trinitarianism,' " *Journal of English and Germanic Philology* 66 (1967): 45–58. This shift enables Milton again to create a model of a son who repays his father with, even more than the father's money, his own "talents."

120. See *The Works of John Milton*, ed. James Holly Hanford and Waldo Hilary Dunn (New York: Columbia University Press, 1933), 15:275. Milton is actually

quoting Luke 2:52 and John 21:17, and so is speaking ostensibly with a higher authority.

121. Hunter, *Bright Essence*, 126, notes how the humiliation of the Son can, paradoxically, be identified with his exaltation and interprets the War in Heaven as Milton's revision of the passion, which characteristically substitutes triumph for degradation. Christopher, *Milton and the Science of the Saints*, 130–31, points out further that, as Calvin refers to the cross as a triumphal chariot, Milton may be replacing the ascent of the cross with the ascent of the chariot of paternal deity, in which, too, the Son acts as the Father. It is typical of Milton to steer clear of the incarnation and focus on the Son's projected exaltation; even in the "Nativity Ode," the presence of Christ on earth seems obscured by an impulse to get to the apocalypse (prevented only by the device of the intervention of Fate in line 149), while the attempt to represent the humiliation of "The Passion" breaks down completely.

122. The image of the poet as vessel in Milton's works appears first in "Lycidas," in which Lycidas, the projection of Milton's own fears of premature disaster, drowns in a leaky vessel built under ominous influences. The gloomy epigraph from Petronius that appeared on the title page of the volume in which "Lycidas" was printed, "Si recte calculam ponas, ubique naufragium est" ("If you reckon rightly, there is shipwreck everywhere"), suggests the topicality of the image.

123. Swan, "Difference and Silence," 168. On the role of binary oppositions in the poem, see also Shoaf, *Milton: Poet of Duality*, 169–89 esp.

124. Cf. Augustine, for whom sight presented a constant source of temptation, as the visual images never stop although sounds do (*Confessions* 10.34; 239); for later writers, hearing offers a greater temptation, as it is a form of perception that cannot be stopped: the danger lies in us, not in objects outside ourselves.

125. Quoted from *The Romantics on Milton*, ed. Joseph Anthony Wittreich (Cleveland: The Press of Case Western Reserve University, 1970), 369, 381.

126. Samuel Johnson, *Lives of the English Poets* (London: Oxford University Press, 1977), 1:122.

127. See Kerrigan, *The Sacred Complex*, 202.

128. See also Evelyn Fox Keller, *Reflections on Gender and Science*, 56–65, and Lillian S. Robinson, "Woman under Capitalism: The Renaissance Lady," in *Sex, Class and Culture* (New York and London: Methuen, 1978), 150–77. For the relation of these divisions to *Comus*, see Richard Halpern, "Puritanism and Maenadism in *A Mask*," in *Rewriting the Renaissance*, 88–105.

129. See Wittreich, 166, 229.

130. On the different voices and kinds of influences in the masque, see John Guillory, *Poetic Authority: Spenser, Milton and Literary History* (New York: Columbia University Press, 1983), 68–93. A useful catalogue of sources can be found also in *A Variorum Commentary on the Poems of John Milton*, vol. 2, pt. 3, ed. A.S.P. Woodhouse and Douglas Bush (New York: Columbia University Press, 1972), 755–84.

131. See Wittreich, 194. Keats incorporates this distinction in his articulation of the difference between his own negative capability and Wordsworth's egotistical sublime.

132. Ibid.

133. John Dryden, *Essays*, 2 vols., ed. W. P. Ker (reprint, New York: Russell and Russell, 1961), 2:247.

134. Christopher Ricks, *Milton's Grand Style* (Oxford: Oxford University Press, 1963), 111. Milton's subsumption of Shakespeare may be most cleverly worked out in the companion poems "L'Allegro" and "Il Penseroso," where Shakespeare seems to be clearly identified with the allegro poet of negative capability and nature, and Milton with the penseroso poet of defined subjectivity and art. Even as he defines himself against Shakespeare, Milton sets up a relation that allows him to contain his precursor by an analogy with the sublimation of nature by art, or a refinement of "old experience" into "something like Prophetic strain" (173–74).

135. Harold Bloom, *The Anxiety of Influence: A Theory of Poetry* (Oxford: Oxford University Press, 1973), 27. For further corrections of Bloom's description of Jonson, see Dunford, "Consumption of the World," 144.

136. See Bloom, *Anxiety of Influence*, 20–23, 27, 32, and *A Map of Misreading* (Oxford: Oxford University Press, 1975), 125–59.

137. See James Nohrnberg, "Paradise Regained by One Greater Man," in *Centre and Labyrinth*, 83–114. Kerrigan, *The Sacred Complex*, 132, also notes the ambiguity of quotation in *The Christian Doctrine*, in which Milton's apparent sacrifice of his own words enables him to speak as God.

138. See also Swan, "Difference and Silence," 164–68.

139. Bloom, *Anxiety of Influence*, 39.

140. Ibid., 148.

141. Ibid., 151.

142. On the trope of *metalepsis* or "transumption," see Harold Bloom, *The Breaking of the Vessels* (Chicago and London: University of Chicago Press, 1982), 73–107, and John Hollander, *The Figure of Echo: A Mode of Allusion in Milton and After* (Berkeley: University of California Press, 1981), 113–49.

143. See Kerrigan, 82–85, who notes that for Freud these two answers are the same.

144. See, for example, *The Reason of Church Government*, Hughes, 665–71; *An Apology for Smectymnuus*, Hughes, 690–95; *The Second Defense of the People of England*, Hughes, 828–32.

145. *Apology for Smectymnuus*, Hughes, 694.

CHAPTER IV
UNDER THE SIGN OF SATURN

1. See T. S. Eliot, "The Metaphysical Poets," in *Selected Essays* (London: Faber, 1964), 241–50; Marjorie Hope Nicholson, *The Breaking of the Circle*; Michel Foucault, *The Order of Things: An Archaeology of the Human Sciences* (New York: Random House, 1970); Timothy J. Reiss, *The Discourse of Modernism* (Ithaca and London: Cornell University Press, 1982); and Bloom, *The Anxiety of Influence*. In *Holy Feast*, 31–69, Bynum describes the change as one in attitudes toward eating. Perhaps all of the above can be read into Milton, whose narrative structure, for example, begins as a circle, and only after the Fall takes a linear form.

2. For Ruskin's view of the Renaissance, see especially *Modern Painters*, 3.8, and *The Stones of Venice*, 2.6 and 3.3, in *The Works of Ruskin*, ed. E. T. Cook and

A. Wedderburn (London: George Allen, 1904), 5:130–48, 10:180–269, and 11:135–95. Like Bakhtin, a fellow admirer of the grotesque, Ruskin denounces the Renaissance for its quest for perfection, which they both find ultimately deadening. On the role of the opposition between individual and society, see Burckhardt, *The Civilization of the Renaissance*, 143–44; Raymond Williams, *The Long Revolution* (1965; reprint, Harmondsworth: Penguin Books, 1984), 89–119; and Christopher Hill, *Society and Puritanism in Pre-Revolutionary England* (Harmondsworth: Penguin Books, 1964), 467–84. In "The Cartesian Masculinization of Thought" (in *Sex and Scientific Inquiry*, ed. Sandra Harding and Jean F. O'Barr [Chicago and London: University of Chicago Press, 1987], 247–64), Susan Bordo discusses the Renaissance as a protracted birth trauma involving the separation of the male individual from unity with a female natural world. However, this birth is imagined as a rebirth, in which individuals asserted control and mastery by claiming to choose their own terms of revival—as Milton chose his own fathers—and thus symbolically to become the father of themselves. While, according to Freud, this is what all men want, and to Bloom, what all post-Miltonic poets want, it is also, of course, the position of Oedipus; Bordo notes that this attempt to gain control in order to compensate for the loss of an organic world (or, in psychoanalytic terms, for the loss of the mother's breast) also marks the beginning of oedipal conflict. I shall be returning to the Renaissance as a rebirth as well as fall in chapter 5.

3. Bakhtin, *Rabelais and His World*, 18.

4. Ibid., 23.

5. Ibid., 29. As I mentioned earlier, I am using the term "Renaissance" in its traditional, if vague, sense, in which it is used to impose the coherence and unity of a revived classical ideal on an actually incoherent and disjointed body of times and countries.

6. Ibid., 29.

7. Ibid., 320.

8. Ibid. See also Barkan, *Nature's Work of Art*, and Hale, *The Body Politic*, for different studies of the particularly Renaissance uses of the body as an image for the coherence of diversity and resolution of differences.

9. Bakhtin, 321–22. For further examination of the changes in representation of the body occurring during the seventeenth century, see Stallybrass and White, *The Poetics of Transgression*, and Francis Barker, *The Tremulous Private Body: Essays on Subjection* (London and New York: Methuen, 1984).

10. Bakhtin, 320. See also Foucault's studies of the Renaissance construction of the norm or proper and the complementary policing of different forms of excess: *The History of Sexuality*, vol. 1, trans. Robert Hurley (New York: Vintage Books, 1980); *Discipline and Punish: The Birth of the Prison*, trans. Alan Sheridan (New York: Vintage Books, 1979); *Madness and Civilization: A History of Insanity in the Age of Reason*, trans. Richard Howard (New York: Vintage Books, 1973); and "Body/Power," in *Power/Knowledge: Selected Interviews and Other Writings 1972–1977*, ed. Colin Gordon (New York: Pantheon Books, 1980), 55–62.

11. Swan, "Difference and Silence," 158.

12. See the *OED* for listings under "individual," which is derived from the Latin

individuus. Swan, 158–60, discusses the redefinition of the word in relation to the codification of modern sexual identity; Raymond Williams, *The Long Revolution*, 90–95, discusses the shift in terms of the changing relations between individual bodies and political ones; see also his *Keywords*, 161–65. Much of my discussion has been influenced also by the essays included in *Reconstructing Individualism*. As I suggested in chapter 2, locating precisely the emergence of the individual is more complicated than Burckhardt believed; according to Alan Macfarlane, capitalism and individualism were present in English society well before the seventeenth century; see *The Origins of English Individualism: The Family, Property and Social Transaction* (Oxford: Basil Blackwell, 1978). I am persuaded by Macfarlane's argument but believe that they only emerged with the Restoration as the dominant and normative forms of experience.

13. See Williams, *The Long Revolution*, 90–95, and Hale, *The Body Politic*, who traces the replacement of an organic model for society by a contractual one.

14. For some suggestions on the relation of discussions of the three persons of the Trinity to the development of the concept of the person, see Mauss, "A Category of the Human Mind," 19–20.

15. See René Descartes, "Sixth Meditation," in *Discourse on Method and the Meditations*, trans. F. E. Sutcliffe (Harmondsworth: Penguin Books, 1968), 164.

16. On the development of this attitude toward nature and its wider significance, particularly for the construction of modern gender roles, see Keller, *Reflections on Gender and Science*, 62–65 esp.; Carolyn Merchant, *The Death of Nature: Women, Ecology and the Scientific Revolution* (San Francisco: Harper and Row, 1980); and Bordo, "The Cartesian Masculinization of Thought."

17. On the different models of knowledge, see Ernst Cassirer, *The Individual and the Cosmos in Renaissance Philosophy*, trans. Mario Domandi (Philadelphia: University of Pennsylvania Press, 1963), 123–91, and Catherine Belsey, *The Subject of Tragedy: Identity and Difference in Renaissance Drama* (London and New York: Methuen, 1985), 55–92. In terms of a psychoanalytical reading of history, the older model of knowing, like feudalism, corresponds again to the oral phase, and the later, like capitalism, to the anal phase.

18. I am grateful to John Hollander for pointing out to me the striking similarity between the two passages.

19. For a summary of Aristotle's discussions of substance and later philosophical arguments, see the entry under "Substance and Attributes," in *The Encyclopedia of Philosophy* (New York and London: Collier Macmillan, 1967), 8:36–40. For Dante, property and essence are identifiable, while Stephen Greenblatt notes the close relation between identity and property in Shakespeare, claiming that "I think property may be closer to the wellsprings of the Shakespearean conception of identity than we imagine"; "Psychoanalysis and Renaissance Culture," in *Literary Theory/Renaissance Texts*, ed. Patricia Parker and David Quint (Baltimore and London: Johns Hopkins University Press, 1986), 220.

20. See Gilbert Ryle, *The Concept of Mind* (New York: Harper and Row, 1949).

21. Macfarlane, *The Origins of English Individualism*, 5.

22. On the ambiguous meanings of property for Locke, see Macpherson, noted below, and James Tully, *A Discourse on Property: John Locke and His Adversaries*

(Cambridge and London: Cambridge University Press, 1980). As Locke uses the word to mean both an abstract right and also nature that one has appropriated by labor, the two seem to be potentially conflated, so that all rights are commodities one is able to alienate.

23. C. B. Macpherson, *The Political Theory of Possessive Individualism: Hobbes to Locke* (Oxford: Oxford University Press, 1962), 3.

24. Ibid., 264.

25. For a discussion of some of the premises behind the concept of the authorial right to possess poetic property, see Foucault, "What Is an Author?" in *Textual Strategies: Perspectives in Post-Structuralist Criticism*, ed. Josué V. Harari (Ithaca, N.Y.: Cornell University Press, 1979), 141–60. On the development of authorial property rights as an extension of Locke's theories, see Mark Rose, "The Author as Proprietor: Donaldson vs. Becket and the Genealogy of Modern Authorship," *Representations* 23 (Summer 1988): 51–85. A number of writers have seen *Aereopagitica* as an anticipation of the concept of authorial control; see, for example, Abbe Blum, "The Author's Authority: *Aereopagitica* and the Labour of Licensing," in *Re-Membering Milton*, 74–96.

26. On the radical religious ideas released during the revolution and suppressed by the subsequent events, see Christopher Hill, *The World Turned Upside Down: Radical Ideas During the English Revolution* (Harmondsworth: Penguin Books, 1975).

27. See Lawrence Stone, *The Family, Sex and Marriage in England 1500–1800* (abridged ed., Harmondsworth: Penguin Books, 1979), 169–72, and Norbert Elias, *The History of Manners: The Civilizing Process*, Vol. I, trans. Edmund Jephcott (New York: Pantheon Books, 1978). The introduction of eating utensils alone symbolized a changing relation to food. Not only did the fork (which became common in aristocratic households during the sixteenth century) make eating more proper and genteel, but it created a rigid distinction between eater and eaten. The fork thus separated the self both from the lower classes (who ate with their fingers) and also from material substances, which were now encountered only at the other end of a sharp, metallic, weaponlike utensil. As the reformers indicated, not only *what* you eat, but *how* you eat is a means of asserting identity.

28. Macpherson, *Political Theory of Possessive Individualism*, 271.

29. On the significance of enclosure as an image and its role in the fantasy of a lost pastoral ideal, see Williams, *The Country and the City*, 96–107 and 136–39. It would seem appropriate that men dressed as women, whose bodies are naturally grotesque and transgressive, played a large part in the riots objecting to the confinement of land by enclosure; see Natalie Zemon Davis, "Women on Top," in *Society and Culture in Early Modern France* (Stanford: Stanford University Press, 1965), 148–49, and Mary Russo, "Female Grotesques: Carnival and Theory," in *Feminist Studies/Critical Studies*, ed. Theresa de Laurentis (Bloomington: Indiana University Press, 1986), 216–17.

30. See also Keller, *Reflections on Gender and Science*, 62–65.

31. On the ambivalent status of things outside of market relations in capitalist society, see Raymond Williams, *The Long Revolution*, 133–37.

32. Bloom, *Anxiety of Influence*, 27.

33. On the construction of art as refuge from the work world, see Eagleton, *Literary Theory*, 19–22, and Williams, *Culture and Society, 1780–1950* (1961; reprint, Harmondsworth: Penguin Books, 1965), 48–64.

34. See Jean Hagstrum, *Sex and Sensibility: Ideal and Erotic Love from Milton to Mozart* (Chicago and London: University of Chicago Press, 1980), and Stone, *Family, Sex and Marriage*, 149–253 esp. Stone's description of the replacement of the open lineage family, a wider social unit not cut off from other social relations, by the modern nuclear family turned in upon itself (and thus conducive to the intense oedipal relations not previously possible) suggests another way of seeing the transition from medieval to modern as a kind of fall.

35. On the new differences in education and socialization, and general segregation between the sexes, see Stone, 181–253.

36. For Mill's comment and other more cynical observations on the ideal of the family and marriage as paradise on earth, see Stone, 222. On the development of the new ideology of femininity as a means of subsuming women within the couple, see Jane Spenser, *The Rise of the Woman Novelist: From Aphra Behn to Jane Austen* (Oxford: Basil Blackwell, 1986), 11–22 esp. The new understanding and reading of the anatomical differences between the sexes, which began with the rise of the new science and complicated the old Aristotelian version that a woman was simply a deficient man—one whose sexual organs were inverted inside rather than emerging outside—played a significant part in the later inscription of gender differences; see, for example, the essays in Catherine Gallagher and Thomas Laqueur, eds., *The Making of the Modern Body: Sexuality and Society in the Nineteenth Century* (Berkeley and Los Angeles: University of California Press, 1987).

37. See Barry Weller, "The Rhetoric of Friendship in Montaigne's *Essais*," *New Literary History* 9 (1978): 503–23.

38. Quoted from Thomas Roche, *The Kindly Flame: A Study of the Third and Fourth Books of Spenser's "Faerie Queene"* (Princeton: Princeton University Press, 1964), 135, n. 46. Spenser's book of friendship involves a mixing of identities that at its best is the "infusion sweete" (4.2.34) of Chaucer into the poem, and at worst a "traduction"in which the figures become as interchangeable as the souls in Hell.

39. Montaigne, "Of Friendship," *Essays*, 1.28; Frame, *The Complete Essays of Montaigne*, 139.

40. "Of Friendship," in *Francis Bacon: A Selection of His Works*, ed. Sidney Warhaft (Toronto: MacMillan, 1965), 113.

41. Ibid., 115.

42. See Hulme, *Colonial Encounters*, 16–17, 78–87 esp.

43. On the construction and manipulation of deviant practices for the production of a cultural norm, see also the essays in *Cannibals, Witches, and Divorce: Estranging the Renaissance*, ed. Marjorie Garber (Baltimore and London: Johns Hopkins University Press, 1987). Greenblatt also notes how the strategies of self-fashioning can be adapted to those of imperialism and the conquest of the cultural alien in the name of national authority; see his *Renaissance Self-Fashioning*, 157–92.

44. See Hulme, 157–58.

45. On Crusoe as exemplar of radical individualism, see Ian Watt, *The Rise of the Novel* (Berkeley and Los Angeles: University of California Press, 1957), 60–92.

Other discussions I have benefited from are those of Hulme, 175–222, E. Pearlman, "Robinson Crusoe and the Cannibals," *Mosaic* 10 (1976): 39–55, Thomas M. Kavanagh, "Unravelling Robinson: The Divided Self in Defoe's *Robinson Crusoe*," *Texas Studies in Literature and Language* 20 (1978): 416–32, and Homer O. Brown, "The Displaced Self in the Novels of Daniel Defoe," *English Literary History* 38 (1971): 562–90. Brown, who notes similarities between Crusoe and both Odysseus and Augustine, points out how "Otherness for a Defoe character is generic, anonymous" (567). With the polarization of the individual and society, the opposite of being an individual and having an identity can only be imagined as being part of a group with which one is totally merged and identified. The "mob," increasingly denounced in the seventeenth century, is seen as subsuming individual identity as voraciously as any cannibal culture. On the reduction of the other to an unindividuated member of the masses, see also Williams, *The Long Revolution*, 129–31.

46. Pearlman, 54–55.

47. On the cannibal joke, see Hulme, 82–83.

48. See A. W. Brian Simpson, *Cannibalism and the Common Law* (Chicago: University of Chicago Press, 1984).

49. Piers Paul Read, *Alive: The Story of the Andes Survivors* (New York and London: Avon Books, 1975).

50. Reports in *The Times* (London), December 30, 1972, and *The New York Times*, January 1, 1973.

51. See Sanday, *Divine Hunger*, 95–101. As I mentioned in my introduction, it is for this reason that Sanday compares cannibalism to alchemical sublimation. For Montaigne, it is precisely the symbolic quality of cannibalism, the fact that it has a meaning that both victor and victim share, that makes it less horrifying than some of the senseless atrocities of his own country.

52. See Hulme, 188–89, for a comparison of Crusoe and Descartes as prototypes of the isolated and insular "self-made" man.

53. In Stephen King, *Skeleton Crew* (New York: G. P. Putnam's Sons, 1985), 361–78.

54. See "A Study of Envy and Gratitude," in *The Selected Melanie Klein*, ed. Juliet Mitchell (New York: The Free Press, 1986), 211–29.

55. Ibid., 215.

56. See Robert Burton, *The Anatomy of Melancholy*, 3 vols. (London: G. Bell and Sons, 1926–27), 1:305–11. All further quotations of Burton will be taken from this edition.

57. See Tztevan Todorov, "L'Etre et L'Autre: Montaigne," *Yale French Studies* 64 (1983): 113–44. As Todorov notes, arguing within the opposition between cannibal and civilized man, Montaigne is able only to invert the poles, not to subvert them.

58. See "Of Husbanding Your Will," in which Montaigne explains that, although the mind must be provided with material, "it should feed only on itself" (Frame, 771). See also Todorov, 131–32.

59. Frame, 142.

60. See Weller, "Rhetoric of Friendship," and François Rigolot, "Montaigne's Purloined Letters," *Yale French Studies* 64 (1983): 145–66.

61. Quoted from Weller, 516.

62. On the development of the anatomy as a literary form, see Devon L. Hodges, *Renaissance Fictions of Anatomy* (Amherst: University of Massachussets Press, 1985).

63. Ibid., 17.

64. See Freud,"Mourning and Melancholia," in *General Psychological Theory*, ed. Philip Rieff (New York: Macmillan, 1963), 164–79, and Klein, "A Contribution to the Psychogenesis of Manic-Depressive States," in *The Selected Melanie Klein*, 115–45, and "Mourning and Its Relation to Manic-Depressive States," 146–74. For both, melancholy originates in a narcissistic relationship, but while for Freud it is caused by a failure of detachment, Klein explains it in terms of a failure to form healthy and secure attachments with a real other. For Klein, also, melancholy, like envy, is oral in origin, having its paradigm in the loss of the breast during weaning. See also Sanday, *Divine Hunger*, 146, who sees cannibalism as a means of working through melancholy.

65. A number of critics have commented upon the appropriateness of Burton's choice. See Joan Webber, *The Eloquent "I": Style and Self in Seventeenth-Century Prose* (Madison, Milwaukee, and London: University of Wisconsin Press, 1968), 82, who points out an analogy between Democritus's theory of creation through atoms and Burton's creation through the collation of fragments. Ruth Fox, *The Tangled Chain: The Structure of Disorder in the Anatomy of Melancholy* (Berkeley, Los Angeles, London: University of California Press, 1976), 224–26, discusses the way in which the persona serves as a means of simultaneous identification and differentiation between the two men that is part of Burton's general purpose and method. For further relevant suggestions about the use of the persona in early novels as a means of authorial revelation and concealment, see Homer Brown, "The Displaced Self."

66. Among the wide body of studies on melancholy, see Erwin Panofsky, *The Life and Art of Albrecht Dürer* (Princeton: Princeton University Press, 1955), 156–71; Lawrence Babb, *The Elizabethan Malady* (East Lansing: Michigan State University Press, 1951); Walter Benjamin, *The Origin of German Tragic Drama*, trans. John Osborne (London: New Left Books, 1977), 148–58; and Rudolph and Margot Wittkower, *Born under Saturn: The Character and Conduct of Artists* (New York and London: W. W. Norton and Co., 1963). As Hodges notes (120), the disease also known as "la maladie anglaise" was often traced to the influence of England's maritime climate, "which could make the mind lose its firmness"—ironically, insularity leads to self-dissipation—and to excessive political liberty and freedom of choice, which were suspected of having a similar effect.

67. See Bloom, *Anxiety of Influence*, 7.

68. *De vita libri tres* 2.15.

69. For Derrida's discussion of the function of the *pharmakon*, which represents binary oppositions between which one cannot choose or ambiguity that cannot be resolved, see his *Dissemination*, 65–171.

70. Whereas Burton's earlier critics focused upon the scientific ordering of the

anatomy and analyzed it in terms of an ultimate coherence, recent ones have shifted their attention from this ostensible stable center in order to concentrate on the peripheral material, the digressions, which undermine such order—a shift that obviously reflects significant changes in assumptions about texts. See, for example, Fox, *Tangled Chain*, as well as Stanley Fish, *Self-Consuming Artifacts: The Experience of Seventeenth Century Literature* (Berkeley: University of California Press, 1972), 303–52.

71. It is common for Burton's critics to comment on the intimate relation, perhaps the indistinguishability, between his life and text; see, for example, Joan Webber, who says, "*The Anatomy* was Burton's life. It might even be said that the book is a prototype for the transformation of man into art" (80).

72. See also Hodges, *Renaissance Fictions*, 118.

73. See Ernst Robert Curtius, *European Literature and the Latin Middle Ages*, trans. Willard R. Trask (Princeton: Princeton University Press, 1973), 83–85, for a discussion of the tradition of assuming an authorial position of deference, subordination, and sometimes inadequacy.

74. In 3.7, for example, Burton first quotes Catullus, then names him directly, then goes on to quote other unnamed authors (who an editor will reveal as being Mantuan, Terence, Martial, and Ovid) under the heading of "he," which not only seems to merge them into one but to refer back to Catullus. Such confusions of sources cause Fish to claim that "Meaningless are the concepts of authorship and attribution, for when all are infected with the same disease, all speak with the same, that is one, voice" (331). See also Hodges, 115–16, on some of the peculiarities of Burton's method of quotation.

75. There is one figure who Burton admits does stand out amid this mess of undifferentiated madmen: "*Nemo; nam Nemo omnibus horis sapit, Nemo nascitur sine vitiis, Crimine Nemo caret . . . Nemo bonus, Nemo sapiens, Nemo est omni parti beatus &c* and therefore *Nicholas Nemo*, or Monsieur *No-body* shall go free" (1.134). The embodiment of "No-one" is a favorite feature of the Saturnalia, a figure representing the liberation from and indeed inversion of normal experience; see Bakhtin, *Rabelais and His World*, 413–15. Perhaps the character is related indirectly to the persona of Nobody assumed by Odysseus to escape consumption by Polyphemos. In Burton it provides an inadequate solution to the fluctuation of extremes, only offering a mirror image of its antithesis, Democritus Jr., who is on the verge of becoming everyone.

76. Fish, *Self-Consuming Artifacts*, 329.

77. Burton's prose style might be compared with Balzac's description of Montaigne's: "His discourse isn't a whole body—it's a body in bits, cut off members, and although the parts are close together they stay separate. Not only are there no nerves to join them; there are no cords or knots of flesh to hold them together: for the Author is the enemy of all sorts of liaisons, whether of Nature or of Art" (quoted from Morris W. Croll, "The Baroque Style in Prose," in Stanley Fish, ed., *Seventeenth-Century Prose: Modern Essays in Criticism* [New York: Oxford University Press, 1971], 36; translation mine). In contrast, however, Burton is, typically, both a dismemberer and a joiner.

78. On collation, see A. Bartlett Giamatti, "Hippolytus among the Exiles," in

Exile and Change in Renaissance Literature (New Haven and London: Yale University Press, 1984), 12–32.

79. Ibid., 18.

80. Ibid., 32.

81. For Burton's interest in proverbs, see Fox, *Tangled Chain*, 110 and 268. Whereas Burton subsumes proverbs into his errant narrative, Erasmus presents each proverb separately as a static verbal emblem before which the reader moves, as the author opens it up like a Silenus, moving from comments upon its source, history, and uses, to a discussion of his own time and enterprise. For both writers proverbs are, as Kenneth Burke describes them, "equipment for living," but the interpretive skills necessary for survival in the seventeenth century are very different from and perhaps more complex than those used in the sixteenth.

82. Margaret Mann Phillips, *The "Adages" of Erasmus* (Cambridge: Cambridge University Press, 1964), 8. All quotations from the *Adages* used here are from this edition.

83. Money is a constant concern for Burton, as a disturber of both social and personal peace. Melancholy men are terrified of poverty (as Freud will also claim), as it causes public impotence: wealth for Burton, as for Volpone, has transformative powers; see, for example, 1.399–412. Lack of money is one of reasons scholars are melancholy. But those who have it are possessed by their possessions and eaten up with avarice; see 1.329 and 2.167–68, 175. As always with Burton, there can be no choice between opposites, as they are essentially identical.

84. Fish, 308.

85. Rosalie Colie, *Paradoxica Epidemica* (Princeton: Princeton University Press, 1966), 453, 458.

86. Fox, 36.

87. Thomas Browne, *Religio Medici* (New York: J. M. Dent and Sons, 1965), 42.

88. For a summary of Burton's revisions, see Fox, 6–7. The only substantial deletion was that of the farewell to the reader, in which Burton had originally revealed his true identity. As I mentioned, this change had the effect of incorporating the author himself more fully into his own text.

89. See Fish, 339–43, for a discussion of Burton's attitude toward suicide. At the end of vol. 1, he treats it as a temptation by the certainty of despair to end the constant restlessness of melancholy, to resolve ambiguity, like Milton's Satan, through self-destruction. According to Anthony Wood, in order to fulfill his own calculation of the date of his death—thus claiming control over his own ending—Burton committed suicide; see Wood, *Athenae Oxonienses* (London, 1691), 534–35.

CHAPTER V
THE REFORMED DEFORMED

1. See, for example, Greene, *The Light in Troy*, 90, who claims that "Petrarch took more or less alone the step an archaic society must take to reach maturity: he recognized the *possibility of a cultural alternative.*"

2. Ibid., 92.

3. See Harold Bloom, "First and Last Romantics," in *The Ringers in the Tower*, 4.

4. On the relation of the Revolution to the gothic, see Ronald Paulson, *Representations of Revolution (1789–1829)* (New Haven and London: Yale University Press, 1983), who discusses the question: "How does a writer or artist represent something he believes to be unprecedented—hitherto unknown and unexperienced?" (1), using the traditional conventions and material he has inherited.

5. See Melanie Klein and Joan Riviere, *Love, Hate, and Reparation* (New York: W. W. Norton and Co., 1964), 57–119, and "A Contribution to the Psychogenesis of Manic Depressive States," and "Mourning and Its Relation to Manic Depressive States," in *The Selected Melanie Klein*, 115–45, and 146–74. In practice, however, it seems, unfortunately, more common for most of us simply to repeat the worst parts of our earliest relations.

6. See Klein, "Mourning," 164.

7. Pierre Fédida, "Le Cannibale Mélancolique," in *Destins du cannibalisme*, 125.

8. Leo Bersani, *A Future for Astyanax: Character and Desire in Literature* (New York: Columbia University Press, 1984), 287.

9. See D. H. Lawrence, *Studies in Classic American Literature* (reprint, Harmondsworth: Penguin Books, 1977), 70–88. Valuing individual identity highly, Lawrence is equally contemptuous of Whitman's work, which he sees as achieving also "Post-mortem effects" (170) by a process of identification that is easily parodied as meaningless drivel: "I am everything and everything is me and so we're all One in One Identity, like the Mundane Egg, which has been addled quite a while" (173).

10. Torok and Baraham, "Introjecter-Incorporer," 116

11. Stephen Greenblatt argues further that psychoanalysis is "the fulfillment and effacement of specifically Renaissance insights: psychoanalysis is, in more than one sense, the end of the Renaissance"; see "Psychoanalysis and Renaissance Culture," 210.

12. Freud will read demoniacal possession as a form of obsession; see "A Neurosis of Demoniacal Possession in the Seventeenth Century," in *On Creativity and the Unconscious*, 264–300. For Freud, psychoanalysis is the truth that was hidden underneath all the older mythologies, which, once projected, must now be re-introjected, for "owing to the projection outwards of internal perceptions, primitive men arrived at a picture of the external world which we, with our intensified conscious perception, have now to translate back into psychology" (*Totem and Taboo*, 64).

13. Norman H. Holland and Leona F. Sherman, "Gothic Possibilities," *New Literary History* 8 (1976–77): 283. For further discussions of the gothic, see: David Punter, *The Literature of Terror* (London: Longmans, 1980); William Patrick Day, *In the Circles of Fear and Desire: A Study of Gothic Fantasy* (Chicago: University of Chicago Press, 1985); Eve Kosofsky Sedgwick, *The Coherence of Gothic Conventions* (New York and London: Methuen, 1980); and Claire Kahane, "The Gothic Mirror," in *The (M)other Tongue*, 334–51.

14. For one discussion of this theme in English literature, see Margaret Gent,

" 'To Flinch from Modern Varnish': The Appeal of the Past to the Victorian Imagination," *Victorian Poetry* (New York and London: Edward Arnold, 1972), 11–35.

15. There is a certain caginess in Browning's justification for appropriation on the ground that the object had never been owned before, an argument that sounds similar to the explorers' rationalization of the takeover of Indian territory; see above, chapter 4.

16. See Bram Stoker, *Dracula* (New York: Bantam Books, 1981), 298. A Protestant who grew up in Catholic Ireland, Stoker was obviously both fascinated and repelled by all acts of bodily incorporation, which he found difficult to imagine except through their projection into their most lurid forms.

17. See Michael McKeon, *The Origins of the English Novel, 1600–1740* (Baltimore and London: Johns Hopkins University Press, 1987).

18. Jay Macpherson, *The Spirit of Solitude: Conventions and Continuities in Late Romance* (New Haven and London: Yale University Press, 1982), 54.

19. See, for example, Samuel Taylor Coleridge, *Biographia Literaria*, ed. James Engell and W. Jackson Bate, 2 vols. (Princeton: Princeton University Press, 1983), 1:164.

20. See Macpherson, *The Spirit of Solitude*, 233. On the Godwins' "family romance," see Paulson, *Representations of Revolution*, 239–47; Sandra M. Gilbert and Susan Gubar, *The Madwoman in the Attic: The Woman Writer and the Nineteenth-Century Literary Imagination* (New Haven and London: Yale University Press, 1979), 187–247; and the essays in *The Endurance of "Frankenstein": Essays on Mary Shelley's Novel*, ed. George Levine and U. C. Knoepflmacher (Berkeley, Los Angeles, London: University of California Press, 1979), 77–202 esp.

21. Charles Brockden Brown, *Wieland, or The Transformation. Together with the Memoirs of Carwin the Biloquist. A Fragment* (New York and London: Harcourt Brace Jovanovich, 1926), 1. All further references are to this edition.

22. See also Girard's theories of triangular or imitative desire for the relationship between identification and antagonism in exchanges between rivals: especially *Deceit, Desire and the Novel: Self and Other in Literary Structure*, trans. Yvonne Freccero (Baltimore and London: Johns Hopkins University Press, 1965).

23. Quoted from Macpherson, *Spirit of Solitude*, 227.

24. An earlier unfinished manuscript, however, provides the text with a gloomier ending. Caleb, refusing to relinquish his belief in his own innocence and integrity, sinks into madness, cursing Falkland, in a passage very clearly modeled on Clarissa's ramblings after her rape.

25. William Godwin, *Caleb Williams* (Oxford: Oxford University Press, 1982), 326 .

26. Percy Bysshe Shelley was the first critic to point out the similarity between the endings of *Frankenstein* and *Caleb Williams*; see Macpherson, 227. Percy Shelley's own confrontation with Milton takes place in *Prometheus Unbound* and is resolved through a method similar to that of *Caleb*, as the antagonism between Prometheus and Jupiter is broken when the son revokes his curse. While in *Caleb* this leads to an ambiguous conclusion, for Shelley it causes a complete apocalypse of the imagination through the tremendous power of sympathy, praised in his *Defense*

of Poetry as the alternative to reason, which for Shelley is not choosing but the "calculating faculty." Prometheus, who began as Milton's Satan, is redeemed, and, as a result, not only does Jupiter, Milton's God, simply dissolve, but the incarnation is completely avoided: the second son of God, who according to Shelley would actually consolidate the power of the Father (as Milton himself effectively did), never appears.

27. See, for example, Derrida, *Of Grammatology*, 27–65. This emphasis upon voice is connected to the idealization of hearing as the most intimate and innocent way of knowing—an idealization that Milton inherited from Jonson and complicated; see above, chapter 3.

28. This, which again sounds similar to Girard's concept of imitative desire, is a frequent premise behind Brown's works. In *Edgar Huntley*, for example, the hero "catches" sleepwalking from another.

29. The existence of angelic and demonic forces is debated throughout the book, and even the skeptical Pleyel is convinced when sensory evidence is produced (although that evidence proves ultimately wrong). Clara still believes in the external source of voices while no longer believing in divine agency. In *Caleb Williams*, a theory of social conditioning provides a transitional stage between allegory and psychology, as Caleb's sense of personal injustice develops into one of social responsibility. The hierarchical cosmology has been turned—through a step anticipated by Milton, whose devils are definitely upper-class, despite their revolutionary zeal—into a social structure dominated by aristocrats who torment their inferiors. The enemy is still external and in a superior position, but it is now human. Individual identity is not fashioned by demonic influence but social environment. So Mr. Collins tells Caleb, "I consider you as a machine: you are not constituted, I am afraid, to be greatly useful to your fellow men; but you did not make yourself; you are just what circumstances inevitably compelled you to be" (310).

30. It is, however, difficult to distinguish Clara's stylistic flaws from Brown's. He wrote extremely quickly and often seems uncertain as to his own intentions, most obviously in the case of the *Memoirs*, which becomes embroiled in more plot complications than he could ultimately resolve. His use of the conventional diction of the time often seems out of place and unable to accommodate the diverse elements he almost chaotically incorporates into his fictions—elements of the supernatural, western adventures, scenes of the Revolution, and so on—which themselves often do not mix but instead suggest his own deep impressionability.

31. Falkland himself, however, is both Bluebeard and Milton's Lady. Having from youth "imbibed the love of chivalry and romance" (10) from literary influences, his ruling passion becomes honor, and he "would have purchased the character of a true, gallant and undaunted hero, at the expense of worlds" (103). Honor for him is what chastity was for Milton, but he attempts to maintain, even *purchase*, the *appearance* of an intact and integral self despite his knowledge of his own guilt. This, significantly, he traces not to the act of murder but to the fact that his victim, Tyrrel, touched and so contaminated him. Clara, too, is concerned with hiding her passions and preserving an appearance of being completely untouched. The maintaining of this facade, necessary by the standards of social as well as literary conventions, is what partially causes her misunderstanding with Pleyel.

32. On the changing perception of the ideal of "self-fashioning," see Greene, "The Flexibility of the Self in Renaissance Literature." Rawson ("Cannibalism and Literature 1," 682–84 esp.) discusses the nineteenth-century protean author as vampire. Perhaps one of the most striking examples of the kind of self-fashioning possible for the enlightened isolated individual motivated purely by self-interest can be seen in the figure of one Lady who has turned into Comus: Sade's Juliette. Her sister, Justine, persists in playing the role of the Lady, totally oblivious to actual changes in the world, and her insistence upon innocence invites exploitation. To be innocent is to be open, and Sade suggests some very ingenious methods of filling up holes. Juliette, however, turns her openness into a source of power, as she sucks experience into herself. Her most obvious counterpart is the cannibal host Minski, a demonic man-mountain who eats absolutely everything, especially his guests. According to him, to be rational is to reject hospitality and justice, and to observe no law except that of self-interest, as subject/object positions are absolute and nonreciprocal. Rules are only a matter of convention or personal taste, and there is therefore no reason not to indulge one's own tastes, no matter how disgusting they may seem to others. As Sade points out, this behavior cannot be denounced for being "unnatural": any rational mind can see that Nature herself is a cannibal who demands the realization of all possibilities and that satisfaction of all desires.

33. On the role of the Protestant notion of election and vocation in *Samson Agonistes*, see John Guillory, "The Father's House." As well as playing on *Paradise Lost*, *Wieland* is a gothic version of *Samson* and also *Comus*, all curiously intertwined. This, however, may testify merely to the consistency and unity of Milton's work.

34. As not much was known about this heresy before the twentieth century, it is unlikely that Brown knew more about the Albigensians than the fact that they were a secret mystery cult with a dualistic mythology which was persecuted during the Middle Ages. Maturin's last novel, *The Albigenses* (1824), represents the sect primarily as the victim of the oppressive medieval Church. Stone (*The Family, Sex and Marriage*, 309) notes, however, that from the sixteenth century on, it had been associated with homosexuality and social deviancy. Certainly Wieland Sr.'s conversion to a Manichean faith, which inverts Augustine's spiritual progress, leaves him open to the influence of not one but two powerful sources. We now know also that the central heresies of the sect were its denial of the incarnation and of the mass, which it replaced with a spiritual supper—heresies which are not unlike certain spiritualizing tendencies of Protestantism itself. In *Wieland*'s case, the internalization of religious worship has a grotesquely literal conclusion. On the Albigensians, see R. I. Moore, *The Origins of European Dissent* (1977; reprint, Oxford: Basil Blackwell, 1985), 177–82, and 218–24 esp.

35. This weird end recalls the fate of the belly-god in Jonson's masque, whose self-transcendence is revealed to be really an explosion which occurs when the vessel that cannot express what it has assimilated bursts. A similar idea appears in the most famous literary scene of spontaneous combustion, that of Krook in Dicken's *Bleak House*. Krook's store is stuffed with the things he has amassed and hoards, as "Everything seemed to be bought, and nothing to be sold there" ([New York: Dodd,

Mead and Company, 1951], 47). From the beginning Krook seems a potentially combustible character, whose breath issues "in visible smoke from his mouth, as if he were on fire within." As Krook himself explains, his refusal to part with any of his possessions makes him the perfect embodiment of that perfect embodiment of excellence (according to W. S. Gilbert): the Law. For Dickens, as I mentioned earlier, the law is cannibalistic (Mr. Vholes is described as both cannibal and vampire), a futile opposition between indistinguishable opposites (Jarndyce vs. Jarndyce), whose only imaginable end is not transcendence but "the same death eternally— inborn, inbred, engendered in the corrupted humours of the vicious body itself, and that only—Spontaneous Combustion, and none other of all the deaths that can be died" (428). It requires a grotesque apocalypse, imagined as quite literally a big bang, to put an end to the self-perpetuating and uncreative rhetoric of the law; although Christ claimed to fulfill rather than abolish it, for Dickens there is little redeemable or redeeming in a legal system that has become dangerously self-contained and predatory.

36. On the arguments for and against using Cicero as a single model, see Greene, *The Light in Troy*, 181–89, and G. W. Pigman III, "Imitation and the Renaissance Sense of the Past: The Reception of Erasmus' *Ciceronianus*," *The Journal of Medieval and Renaissance Studies* 9 (1972): 155–77.

37. Bakhtin, *Rabelais and His World*, 466.

38. Quoted from Christopher Hill, *Milton and the English Revolution*, 308.

39. On the way in which the Protestant attempt to align the will with God could lead to the appropriation of the power to act as God, see Max Weber, *The Protestant Ethic and the Spirit of Capitalism*, trans. Talcott Parsons (New York: Charles Scribner's Sons, 1958), 113–14.

40. On the gothic's undermining of textual private property and all notions of the "proper," see Patricia Parker, *Literary Fat Ladies*, 172–77.

41. See Samuel Taylor Coleridge, *Biographia Literaria*, vol. 2, chap. 14, 7–8, in which Coleridge outlines the antithetical aims of two authors of the *Lyrical Ballads*.

42. On this neoplatonic doctrine, see Ernst Cassirer, *The Individual and the Cosmos in Renaissance Philosophy*, 7–45, and 123–91, and Wind, *Pagan Mysteries*, 105–12, 191–238. A general discussion of the connections between Romanticism and neoplatonism can be found in M. H. Abrams, *Natural Supernaturalism: Tradition and Revolution in Romantic Literature* (New York: W. W. Norton and Co., 1971), 141–324, especially 141–54. In *Romanticism and the Forms of Ruin: Wordsworth, Coleridge and the Modalities of Fragmentation* (Princeton: Princeton University Press, 1981), 289–341, Thomas McFarland notes some of the Romantic reworkings of writers like Bruno, Cusanus, Paracelsus, and Boehme; in *Coleridge and the Pantheist Tradition* (Oxford: At the Clarendon Press, 1969), 35–36, he points out Coleridge's very early reading of these authors, which preceded that of their German descendants, and their enduring influence upon him. The most complete treatment of Coleridge's use of the concept of the *coincidentia oppositorum* can be found in Alice D. Snyder, *The Critical Principle of the Reconciliation of Opposites as Employed by Coleridge* (Ann Arbor, Mich.: Ann Arbor Press, 1918).

43. Samuel Taylor Coleridge, *The Friend*, ed. Barbara E. Rooke (Princeton: Princeton University Press, 1969), 1:110.

44. *The Notebooks of Samuel Taylor Coleridge*, ed. Kathleen Coburn (Princeton: Princeton University Press, 1957), vol. 1: 1725.16.376–77.

45. Coleridge, "On Poesy or Art," quoted from *Inquiring Spirit: A New Presentation of Coleridge from his Published and Unpublished Prose Writings*, ed. Kathleen Coburn (Toronto: University of Toronto Press, 1979), 209.

46. "On Poesy or Art," quoted from Earl R. Wasserman, "The English Romantics: The Grounds of Knowledge," in *Romanticism: Points of View*, ed. Robert F. Gleckner and Gerald E. Enscoe (Detroit, Mich.: Wayne State University Press, 1975), 339.

47. McFarland, *Romanticism*, 27. See also Serres, *The Parasite*, 248–49, where he notes the relations among a cluster of Greek words and their figurative meanings. From *sumballein*, to reunite, we derive the word symbol; from *diaballein*, to separate, we get the word diabolical, providing another example of an assumption that duality and division are essentially evil.

48. Coleridge, *The Statesman's Manual*, 29.

49. Ibid., 30.

50. Ibid., 31. This description is set, however, in hortatory subjunctives, which urge men to seek such satisfaction while implying that they do not.

51. Quoted, in turn, from Harold Bloom, *Figures of Capable Imagination* (New York: Seabury Press, 1976), 15.

52. Paul de Man, "The Rhetoric of Temporality," in *Interpretation: Theory and Practice*, ed. Charles S. Singleton (Baltimore: Johns Hopkins University Press, 1969), 173–209.

53. See McFarland, *Romanticism*, 3–55 esp.

54. *Collected Letters of Samuel Taylor Coleridge*, ed. Earl Leslie Griggs (Oxford: At the Clarendon Press, 1956–71), 2:1102. All further citations from the letters will be from this edition.

55. Ibid., 2:959.

56. Ibid., 2:976.

57. *Notebooks*, 2:2091.

58. See M. H. Abrams, "The Correspondent Breeze: A Romantic Metaphor," in *The Correspondent Breeze: Essays on English Romanticism* (New York and London: W. W. Norton and Co., 1984), 25–43.

59. *Collected Letters*, 3:490.

60. For an account of the physical and mental effects of Coleridge's drug addiction, see Molly Lefebure, *Samuel Taylor Coleridge: A Bondage of Opium* (New York: Stein and Day, 1975). Even if addicts are somehow preconditioned inherently to habituation, drug addiction is an extremely literal example of the infiltration of a bodily system by an alien and tyrannical power.

61. Quoted from Coburn, ed., *Inquiring Spirit*, 194.

62. See McFarland, *Coleridge and the Pantheist Tradition*, 1–52.

63. See, again Coleridge, *Biographia Literaria*, 1:164 and note.

64. Bloom, *Figures of Capable Imagination*, 15.

65. See M. H. Abrams, *The Mirror and the Lamp: Romantic Theory and the Crit-*

ical Tradition (Oxford: Oxford University Press, 1953), 169. Coleridge's famous description of the primary and secondary imaginations, the forces of dissolution and reunion, are framed with quotations from Milton and John Davies that equate assimilation with sublimation; see Coleridge, *Biographia Literaria* 12 and 13. For Coleridge, the concept of sublimation, which he takes partially from Schiller's *aufhebung*, is associated with the reconciliation of opposites.

66. Klein, "Mourning and Manic-Depressive States," 154.

67. See McFarland, *Coleridge and the Pantheist Tradition*, 107–90, and 147 esp., for a detailed reading of Coleridge's relations to the material he assimilates.

68. *Notebooks*, 2:2372.

69. McFarland, *Romanticism*, 127–28, n. 111.

70. Kathleen Coburn, "Reflections in a Coleridge Mirror: Some Images in His Poems," in *From Sensibility to Romanticism: Essays Presented to Frederick A. Pottle*, ed. Frederick W. Hilles and Harold Bloom (New York: Oxford University Press, 1965), 415–37. For further discussion of the role of the mother's breast in Coleridge from a specifically Kleinian perspective, see Margery Durham, in "The Mother Tongue: *Christabel* and the Language of Love," in *The (M)other Tongue*, 169–93, and Dorothy Dinnerstein, *The Mermaid and the Minotaur: Sexual Arrangements and Human Malaise* (New York: Harper and Row, 1977), 95–105.

71. Coburn, 432.

72. See Jacques Lacan "The Mirror Stage as Formative of the Function of the I," in *Ecrits: A Selection*, trans. Alan Sheridan (New York and London: W. W. Norton and Co., 1977), 1–7.

73. See, for example, *Notebook* 52, quoted in Coburn, ed., *Inquiring Spirit*, 261.

74. John Beer, *Coleridge the Visionary* (London: Chatto and Windus, 1959), 69–71, 96, 112–23, 127–28, 184–98 esp. Beer notes also the recurrent image of the suffocating snakes that appears in such poems as "Christabel" and "Dejection"; furthermore, Coleridge frequently used images of serpents to describe the effects opium had upon him. As in Milton, the snake is an image of demonic possession—here, especially by Milton. Keats found the scene of Satan's incarnation in the serpent suffocating. In *The Glory of Hera: Greek Mythology and the Greek Family* (Boston: Beacon Press, 1971), 75–122, Philip E. Slater reads the snake as a symbol for what he calls the "oral-narcissistic dilemma," which "originates in a failure to negotiate successfully from the infantile state of total narcissism to one involving an awareness of the separate existence of others" (88). For Slater, as for Klein, orality is fraught with ambivalence: the infant's terror that the mother will devour it is intensified (if not caused completely by) its own desire to swallow her, which creates a potentially irresolvable conflict between a desire to merge with her totally and a desire to be free and autonomous.

75. Quoted from Beer, 69.

76. Ibid., 127.

77. Quoted from Abrams, *Natural Supernaturalism*, 162.

78. See, for example, Erich Neumann, *The Great Mother* (Princeton: Princeton University Press, 1955), 18.

79. *Collected Letters*, 4:545.

80. Ibid., 1:28.

81. This kind of confusion of authorial identity is typical of the *Biographia*. In the middle of chapter 13, on the imagination, Coleridge claims to have just received a letter that has made him decide to change the direction of the rest of the section and put off his original intent. The letter, of course, was written by Coleridge himself. This kind of tactic, when combined also with the plagiarisms, makes it extremely difficult to tell who is speaking at any given moment and whether voices are coming from inside or outside the text.

82. It is no coincidence that the rise of nonsense literature, with Gilbert, Lear, and Lewis Carroll, and the consolidation of the gothic as a form, with writers such as Stoker and Lefanu, both occurred in the late nineteenth century. Both genres are essentially parodic, parasites on the periphery of the literary canon, and at least potentially subversive of normal ways of defining identity and meaning; the works of Lear and Carroll show the familiar becoming often disturbingly unfamiliar.

83. All quotations are taken from W. S. Gilbert, *The Bab Ballads*, ed. James Ellis (Cambridge, Mass.: The Belknap Press, 1970).

84. Gilbert is extremely fond of emphasizing the comic side of the *lex talionis*, which he reduces to the law of the Mikado, whose "object all sublime" is "to make the punishment fit the crime."

85. *Collected Letters*, 2:864. The classic reading of the poem as the representation of a "sacramental universe" is that of Robert Penn Warren, "A Poem of Pure Imagination: An Experiment in Reading," excerpted in *Twentieth Century Interpretations of "The Ancient Mariner,"* ed. James D. Boulger (Englewood Cliffs, N.J.: Prentice-Hall, 1969), 21–47.

86. On Coleridge's religious development and its relation to his poetry, see McFarland, *Coleridge and the Pantheist Tradition*, 176–255. Coleridge's development is largely formulated in religious terms—a formulation more common of medieval than modern man, for whom religion is, ideally, separate from literature or politics. Coleridge's attempt to identify religion, philosophy, and literature, which the *Magnum Opus* was designed to do, again suggests a longing for an imaginary time of wholeness and unified experience that preceded a fall into division and alienation.

87. Quoted from McFarland, *Coleridge and the Pantheist Tradition*, 68.

88. Ibid., 87.

89. All quotations from Coleridge's poetry are taken from *Poetical Works*, ed. Ernest Hartley Coleridge (Oxford: Oxford University Press, 1969).

90. See also Harold Bloom, *The Visionary Company: A Reading of Romantic Poetry*, rev. ed. (Ithaca and London: Cornell University Press, 1971), 211–12.

91. On the theme of nature as a blank page, see Harold Bloom, *The Breaking of the Vessels* (Chicago and London: University of Chicago Press, 1982), 75–95, who sees Coleridge as one of the poets "of the universal blank, the void of decreation" (84).

92. *Table Talk*, 87 (May 31, 1830).

93. *Collected Letters*, 2:781.

94. On the lack of opposites within the unconscious and dreams, see Sigmund Freud, "The Unconscious," in *General Psychological Theory* (New York: Macmillan, 1963), 116–50, 134–35 esp., and his *The Interpretation of Dreams*, trans. James

Strachey (New York: Avon Books, 1965), 351–53. Freud's id also has no awareness of negatives; see Freud *New Introductory Lectures on Psychoanalysis*, trans. Strachey (New York: W. W. Norton and Co., 1965), 65–66.

95. Quoted from Lefebure, *Samuel Taylor Coleridge*, 78.

96. See Bloom, "The Internalization of Quest Romance," and Patricia Parker,
"The Progress of Phaedria's Bower: Spenser to Coleridge," *English Literary History*
40 (1973): 372–97.

97. Bloom, *Figures of Capable Imagination*, 7.

98. This, however, is something Coleridge's poem shares with Milton's. Milton,
too, seems overeager to get to the apocalypse, where the Son with whom he identifies will be, not humble as he is in the incarnation, but all-powerful. Coleridge's
interest in rushing to this point also seems to be part of a fantasy of achieving
power, as it is the perfect fulfillment of his desire to overcome his own weakness by
absorbing the strength of others. However, while Milton sees man as ultimately
becoming God through the process of Christ becoming man, his emptying himself
in *askesis*, for Coleridge, the process does not appear as advantageously reciprocal,
and his achievement of identity with God requires total self-annihilation.

99. See Stephen Knapp, *Personification and the Sublime: Milton to Coleridge*
(Cambridge and London: Harvard University Press, 1985), 7–50. Angus Fletcher
interprets Coleridge's typical use of personification as a method of overcoming anxiety about transitions; see " 'Positive Negation': Threshold, Sequence, and Personification in Coleridge," in *New Perspectives on Coleridge and Wordsworth: English Institute Essays*, ed. Geoffrey Hartman (New York: Columbia University Press,
1972), 133–64. Fletcher focuses upon the figures in "Limbo"; to me, these abstractions seem connected with a fear of getting stuck in endless transitions, a perpetual
kind of limbo in which movement leads nowhere. Such futile restlessness, which
recalls the wanderings of the Mariner, seems related to the failure of any definitive
incarnation to take place (suggested by the replacement of symbol by allegory) that
paradoxically occurs because the universe appears to be excessively symbolic. The
world of the "Ancient Mariner" is like that of Ovid, in which meaning is too completely incarnated. The revelation of significance is therefore the simultaneous discovery of guilt, which in turn leads to a fear of all action and ultimate paralysis
through the inability to imagine any final release or way of moving outside the
closed system of signification.

100. McFarland, *Romanticism*, 229.

101. Quoted from ibid., 345.

102. See also ibid., 228–36.

103. Herman Melville, *Moby-Dick, or The Whale*, ed. Charles Feidelson, Jr. (Indianapolis: Bobbs Merrill, 1964), 105–6. All further quotations are from this edition.

104. Frye uses the term "romance-anatomy" to describe the genre of *Moby-Dick*
in his *Anatomy*, 313. On Melville's voracious and omniverous reading, see Fiedel-
son, xvii; for his assimilation of Renaissance works especially, see F. O. Matthiessen, *American Renaissance* (London: Oxford University Press, 1941), 119–32,
412–51 and passim.

105. Sharon Cameron, *The Corporeal Self: Allegories of the Body in Melville and*

Hawthorne (Baltimore and London: Johns Hopkins University Press, 1981). According to Cameron (6), Melville's concerns reflect particularly American ways of defining identity in terms of the body.

106. As such, the whale is for Melville what the breast was for Coleridge and will be for Klein's infant—an external source of satisfaction and meaning that it wants to incorporate for itself—and has been read as a symbol of the pre-oedipal mother; see Edmund Bergler, "A Note on Herman Melville," *American Imago* 2 (Winter 1954): 385–97. In the almost totally masculine world of the novel, the whale plays the role of the female body, the sexual other whose perceived autonomy and wholeness appears threatening, as it not only frustrates the male desire to contain it, even by representation, but also reveals it own power to contain and consume.

107. See Thomas Woodson, "Ahab's Greatness: Prometheus as Narcissus," in *Moby-Dick as Doubloon*, ed. Herschel Parker and Harrison Hayford (New York: W. W. Norton and Co., 1970), 340–56.

108. The image recalls Ugolino who, shut up in the Tower of Famine, "ambo le mani per lo dolor mi morsi" ("bit both hands for grief," *Inferno* 33.57; my translation). Like Ugolino, Ahab tries to pin down signs and identity to a definitive meaning, and so substitutes cannibalism for the less extreme forms of communion that are offered him. Ahab also seems to play on Dante's counselor of fraud, Ulysses; in *Pierre*, it is the metamorphoses of the thieves that interests him as an image for the dissolution of identity.

109. Here Melville's model is both Burton, who reduces everything to melancholy, and the Browne of "The Garden of Cyrus," a truly eccentric narrator who sees quincunxes everywhere. In this essay, Browne attempts to find a balance between the mind and nature, despite the fact that the natural tendency of the depicted mind is to impose its own obsessed order on nature. Yet the obviousness of this obsession keeps us from taking it seriously and in the end makes the whole thing playful, so that the ordering process never becomes totally confining. While the essay is ultimately a celebration of the fertility not of nature but of the creating mind acting upon the natural world, the conclusion, in particular, suggests that there are some things in nature which cannot be subsumed.

110. See W. H. Auden, *The Enchafèd Flood, or The Romantic Iconography of the Sea* (1950; reprint, Charlottesville: University of Virginia Press, 1950), 136, for the fantasy of self-begetting in *Moby-Dick*.

111. So, as Cameron argues, the theme of identity in fact subsumes the theme of interpretation, on which most previous critics have focused; see 19 and passim.

112. Herman Melville, *Pierre, or The Ambiguities* (New York: Signet Classics, 1964), 351. All further quotations are from this edition.

113. On the importance of Shakespeare for Melville generally, see Matthiessen, *American Renaissance*, 412–35, 449–51; for some suggestions about the use of Lear in *Moby-Dick*, see Cameron, *Corporeal Self*, 72–74. Whereas Milton appears as Bloom's demon of continuity, Shakespeare at times seems to offer the hope of discontinuity; it is Shakespeare's voice, also, that in *Wieland* Carwin uses to wake Clara, thus preventing her dangerous dreams (which recall the dreams in *Paradise Lost*) from coming true.

114. Melville, "Hawthorne and His Mosses," in *The Portable Melville*, ed. Jay Leyda (Harmondsworth: Penguin Books, 1952), 400.

CONCLUSION
IN WHICH EVERYTHING IS INCLUDED AND NOTHING CONCLUDED

1. Also used by Malcolm Bradbury as a title for a novel about academic life: *Eating People Is Wrong* (Harmondsworth: Penguin Books, 1959).

2. Frye, *The Secular Scripture*, 15.

3. Frye, *Anatomy*, 186.

4. Frye, *Secular Scripture*, 53. For further parallels between Frye's romance and Freud's oral phase, see Frederic Jameson, *The Political Unconscious: Narrative as a Socially Symbolic Act* (Ithaca, N.Y.: Cornell University Press, 1981), 142.

5. Frye, *Anatomy*, 186.

6. Sigmund Freud, "Analysis Terminable and Interminable," in *Therapy and Technique* (New York: Macmillan Publishing Co., 1963), 254. On the analogy between the psyche and the text in Freud, see Derrida, "Freud and the Scene of Writing," in *Writing and Difference*, trans. Alan Bass (Chicago: University of Chicago Press, 1978), 196–231.

7. J. H. Van den Berg, *The Changing Nature of Man: Introduction to a Historical Psychology*, trans. H. F. Croes (New York: W. W. Norton and Co., 1961), 120.

8. See Freud, *The Interpretation of Dreams*, title page and 647.

9. See, for example, "Recollection, Repetition and Working Through," in *Therapy and Technique*, 157–66.

10. On different theories of the countertransference, see the article in J. Laplanche and J.-B. Pontalis, *The Language of Psycho-Analysis*, trans. Donald Nicholson-Smith (New York and London: W. W. Norton and Co., 1973), 92–93.

11. For an intersubjective model of the analytic situation, see Nancy Julia Chodorow, "Towards a Relational Individualism: the Mediation of Self Through Psychoanalysis," in *Reconstructing Individualism*, 197–207.

12. Sigmund Freud, *Civilization and its Discontents*, trans. James Strachey (New York: W. W. Norton and Co., 1961), 12–13.

13. On the different readings of these various processes, see Laplanche and Pontalis, 211–12, 226–27, and 229–31.

14. Freud, "The Dissection of the Psychical Personality," in *New Introductory Lectures on Psychoanalysis*, trans. James Strachey (New York: W. W. Norton and Co., 1965), 56.

15. Sigmund Freud, *The Ego and the Id*, trans. Joan Riviere (New York: W. W. Norton and Co., 1960), 19, n. 2.

16. Freud, "Negation," in *General Psychological Theory*, 214–15.

17. See, for example, Freud, *The Ego and the Id*, 24.

18. Bloom, *The Breaking of the Vessels*, 65.

19. While Freud sees this as an essential human condition, this rigid monitoring of sexual development has only been possible in England since the seventeenth century and the rise of modern child-rearing practices, such as weaning and toilet training. As Lawrence Stone has shown, before then oral and anal stages could not be differentiated; moreover, owing to the less intensely bonded structure of the

premodern family, there could in fact be no real distinct oedipal crisis; see *The Family, Sex and Marriage*, 113–26, and 254–99 esp. As an early writer on the regulation of a child's development and toilet training, John Locke may have helped formulate our notions of modern sexual identity as well as those of personal identity. For the effects of Freud's lack of a historical perspective on modern psychology, see also Van den Berg, *The Changing Nature of Man*.

20. Sigmund Freud, *Three Essays on Sexuality*, trans. James Strachey (New York: Basic Books, 1962), 101.

21. Ibid., 77.

22. Ibid., 64.

23. See, for example, Freud, "Anxiety and Instinctual Life," in *New Introductory Lectures*, 88.

24. Freud, "Analysis Terminable and Interminable," in *Therapy and Technique*, 247. This growing discovery may be connected to Freud's realization that all analysis is ultimately interminable: the quest for a fully integrated and coherent ego cannot be fulfilled, for all desires of all phases insist upon being included and satisfied.

25. Freud, *Three Essays*, 48.

26. Freud, *Civilization and Its Discontents*, 15.

27. Ibid.

28. Freud, *Three Essays*, 88.

29. Sigmund Freud, *Beyond the Pleasure Principle*, trans. James Strachey (New York: W. W. Norton and Co., 1961), 30.

30. Ibid., 32

31. Ibid., 36.

32. Ibid., 51–52. In *Civilization and Its Discontents*, 52–54, n. 3, he suggests, further, that all humans are originally bisexual.

33. Sigmund Freud, *Inhibitions, Symptoms and Anxiety*, trans. Alex Strachey (New York: W. W. Norton and Co., 1959), 48.

34. Freud, *Civilization and Its Discontents*, 13.

35. Ibid., 52.

36. Freud, "The Most Prevalent Form of Degradation in Erotic Life," in *On Creativity and the Unconscious*, 186.

37. Bloom, *A Map of Misreading*, 101.

38. Ibid., 100.

39. Freud, *Totem and Taboo*, 154.

40. Ibid., 155.

41. Van den Berg, 176.

42. For Frye's discussion of the humanist ideal of art as man's second nature, see the *Anatomy*, 93–94, and "Nature and Homer," in *Fables of Identity: Studies in Poetic Mythology* (New York and London: Harcourt Brace Jovanovich, 1963), 39–51. Blake was, of course, the subject of Frye's first book, and has had a continuing influence on his work. Frye is one of the few modern writers to acknowledge the importance of Wilde for contemporary criticism. For Frye, Wilde's most significant contribution, which in fact marked the beginning of modern theory, was in claim-

ing that life has no shape and literature does, so that the former imitates the latter; see Frye, *The Secular Scripture*, 45–46, and *Spiritus Mundi*, 57.

43. Northrop Frye, *The Educated Imagination* (Toronto: The Hunter Rose Company, 1963), 33.

44. Frye, *Anatomy*, 136.

45. Frye, *The Great Code*, 224.

46. See also 1 Corinthians 12:12–31, where Christ is described as a body politic in which the different members are united, as long as they keep to their places.

47. Frye, *Great Code*, 203.

48. Frye, *Anatomy*, 143.

49. Ibid., 143; see also his *Fearful Symmetry*, 281. Frye's version of the primal man who embodies the world is derived largely from his reading of Blake.

50. On these two myths, see Frye, *Secular Scripture*, 181–84.

51. Frye, *Anatomy*, 97.

52. Ibid., 55.

53. Ibid., 98.

54. Ibid.

55. Frye, *Secular Scripture*, 162–63.

56. Frye, *Spiritus Mundi*, 119.

57. Frye, *Secular Scripture*, 187.

58. Frye, *Great Code*, 100. Similarly, Frye's insistence upon the priority of the social group to the individual (which is the social counterpart of the priority of the literary system to individual works) is balanced by his description of the way in which the individual in turn incarnates his society; see, for example, *Anatomy*, 96–97.

59. Frye, *Fearful Symmetry*, 59; see also 348–51. This distinction is the same as that between what Frye calls the imaginative and the imaginary; see "The Imaginative and the Imaginary," in *Fables of Identity*, 151–67.

60. Frye, "The Imaginative and the Imaginary," in *Fables of Identity*, 152.

61. Frye, *Great Code*, 114.

62. Jameson, *The Political Unconscious*, 115.

63. Frye, *Anatomy*, 119.

64. See also Evelyn Fox Keller's critique of scientific discourse and its "master molecule theories" (*Reflections on Gender and Science*, 170), which attempt to explain by containing the universe.

65. Frye, *Anatomy*, 125.

66. For a discussion of some of the implications of the art and nature opposition that raises many questions about Frye's assumptions, see Sherry B. Ortner, "Is Female to Male as Nature Is to Culture?" in *Woman, Culture and Society*, ed. Michelle Zimbalist Rosaldo and Louise Lamphere (Stanford, Calif.: Stanford University Press, 1974), 67–87. Frye's preference for an "artificial" creation by a masculine God rather than a "natural" birth from a maternal deity, and his implicit association of the female with nature and matter, a sign of his Platonic idealism, suggests some of the areas where his assumptions could be further closely scrutinized.

67. Clive Barker, *The Inhuman Condition* (New York: Pocket Books, 1985), 65–117. The story is a clever response to King's "Survivor Type," extending the

theme of the alienation of the mind from the body: in Barker's version, hands, the tools which King's doctor uses to detach parts of himself, are so detached from human consciousness that they break away altogether.

68. Terry Eagleton, *Literary Theory*, 133.

69. Joan Riviere, "The Unconscious Phantasy of an Inner World Reflected in Examples from Literature," quoted from Nancy Julia Chodorow, "Towards a Relational Individualism," 202–3.

70. Riviere, quoted from Chodorow, 203.

71. The recent literature analyzing the production of textual and sexual identity has been copious; I can only name the works that have been most useful for me: the works of Foucault and Eagleton already cited; Pierre Machery, *A Theory of Literary Production*, trans. Geoffrey Wall (London and New York: Routledge and Kegan Paul, 1978); Dorothy Dinnerstein, *The Mermaid and the Minotaur*; Nancy Chodorow, *The Reproduction of Mothering: Psychoanalysis and the Sociology of Gender* (Berkeley and Los Angeles: University of California Press, 1978); Evelyn Fox Keller, *Reflections on Gender and Science*; Catherine Keller, *From a Broken Web*; Carol Gilligan, *In a Different Voice: Psychological Theory and Women's Development* (Cambridge, Mass.: Harvard University Press, 1982); Catherine Belsey, *The Subject of Tragedy*; the essays by Gilligan and Chodorow in *Reconstructing Individualism*; Jessica Benjamin, *The Bonds of Love: Psychoanalysis, Feminism, and the Problem of Domination* (New York: Pantheon Books, 1988).

72. Stephen Greenblatt, "Fiction and Friction," in *Reconstructing Individualism*, 33.

73. See "The Laugh of the Medusa," trans. Keith Cohen and Paula Cohen, *Signs* 1, no. 4 (1976): 875–93, and "Castration or Decapitation?" trans. Annette Kuhn, *Signs* 7, no. 1 (1981): 41–55.

74. Gayatri Chakravorty Spivak, "Translator's Preface," *Of Grammatology*, xx.

75. Edward Said, *Beginnings: Intention and Method* (Baltimore and London: Johns Hopkins University Press, 1975), 162. On the patriarchal nature of classical Aristotelian narrative structure, the pattern of beginning-middle-end that Coleridge turns into a uroboros, see Toril Moi, *Sexual/Textual Politics* (London and New York: Methuen, 1985), 68.

76. Mikhail Bakhtin, *The Dialogic Imagination: Four Essays*, trans. Caryl Emerson and Michael Holquist (Austin: University of Texas Press, 1981), 293–94.

77. Derrida, *Of Grammatology*, 35; on the convolutions of the terms *inside* and *outside*, see also *Positions*, 67. As I have been suggesting in relation to Augustine in particular, the relations between writing and speech, and their complementary senses, seeing (in the form of reading) and hearing, are at times quite complicated.

78. Derrida, *Dissemination*, 130.

79. Derrida, *Of Grammatology*, 158.

80. According to René Girard, who subsumes both incest and cannibalism in his transcendental term *sacrificial violence*, "We are perhaps more distracted by incest than by cannibalism, but only because cannibalism has not yet found its Freud and been promoted to the status of a major contemporary myth" (*Violence and the Sacred*, 276–77). I am not, however, presenting myself as this new Freud, though I do hope to do my bit for putting cannibalism up there in the top ten. If people are

going to worry about unexpressed desires to sleep with their mother, they could examine the impulse to eat her as well.

81. For discussions that focus on the importance of the oral phase and the infant's relation to the mother, see Chodorow, Dinnerstein, and Benjamin; on cannibalism, Sanday and Arens; on female body images, see Susan Rubin Suleiman, ed., *The Female Body in Western Culture: Contemporary Perspectives* (Cambridge, Mass.: Harvard University Press, 1986), Helena Michie, *The Flesh Made Word: Female Figures and Women's Bodies* (New York: Oxford University Press, 1987); on women and food, see especially Bynum, *Holy Feast*, and Rudolph M. Bell, *Holy Anorexia* (Chicago and London: Chicago University Press, 1985). On all of the above subjects, see Rosalind Coward's delicious *Female Desires: How They Are Sought, Bought and Packaged* (New York: Grove Press, 1985). In literary criticism, this interest is reflected in the supplementation of traditional discussions of texts in terms of oedipal conflict with writing on oral imagery and the role of the mother: see, for example, Claire Kahane, "The Gothic Mirror," and Coppélia Kahn, "The Absent Mother in *King Lear*," in *Rewriting the Renaissance*, 33–49.

82. On the relation between women and writing, see Jacques Derrida, *Spurs*, trans. Barbara Harlow (Chicago and London: University of Chicago Press, 1978).

83. Cixous, "Castration or Decapitation?" 54. For discussions of the theories of Cixous and Kristeva, see Moi, 102–26 and 150–73, and Ann Rosalind Jones, "Inscribing Femininity: French Theories of the Feminine," in *Making a Difference: Feminist Literary Criticism*, ed. Gayle Greene and Coppélia Kahn (London and New York: Methuen, 1985), 80–112.

84. See Luce Irigary, *This Sex Which Is Not One*, trans. Catherine Porter (Ithaca, N.Y.: Cornell University Press, 1985).

85. For the female body as a type for Bakhtin's grotesque body, see Patricia Parker, *Literary Fat Ladies*; Peter Stallybrass, "Patriarchal Territories: The Body Enclosed," in *Rewriting the Renaissance*, 123–42; and Mary Russo, "Female Grotesques: Carnival and Theory," in *Feminist Studies/Critical Studies*, 213–29.

86. On the split of female images as a result of women's ambiguous and liminal position in cultures, see Ortner, "Is Female to Male as Nature Is to Culture?"

87. On these different identifications, see R. Howard Bloch, "Medieval Misogyny," *Representations* 20 (Fall 1987): 1–24. On the relation between the control of language and the control of women, see Parker, *Literary Fat Ladies*, 26–35 esp.

88. See especially Chodorow, Dinnerstein, and Gilligan. Bynum, *Holy Feast*, 24–28, sees a similar difference in terms of descriptions of medieval religious experiences, which men represent as conversion and a definitive break with the past, while women describe them as a more gradual development growing out of an earlier life. As I argued earlier, in the case of Augustine, the break and discontinuity is far from clear: that conversion, which occurred much earlier than those studied by Bynum, seems to include elements of both her models.

89. Cixous, "Castration or Decapitation?," 44–45. On the construction of the sadomasochistic couple, see Benjamin, *The Bonds of Love*.

90. On Freud's fear of female narcissism especially, see Sarah Kofman, *The Enigma of Woman: Woman in Freud's Writings*, trans. Catherine Porter (Ithaca and London: Cornell University Press, 1985).

91. Cixous, "Castration or Decapitation?" 55n.

92. Moi, *Sexual/Textual Politics*, 116.

93. Malcolm Bowie, "Jacques Lacan," in *Structuralism and Since: From Lévi-Strauss to Derrida*, ed. John Sturrock (Oxford: Oxford University Press, 1979), 151.

94. Greenblatt, "Improvisation and Power," in *Literature and Society*, ed. Edward Said (Baltimore and London: Johns Hopkins University Press, 1980), 60.

95. Keller, *Reflections on Gender and Science*, 82.

96. Ibid., 148–49.

97. See especially Machery, *A Theory of Literary Production*.

Index